The Role of Science for Conservation

The book aims at describing to a broad audience 50 years of research of the Charles Darwin Foundation as part of the worldwide efforts in conservation science. A model case is presented showing how interdisciplinary work across a broad range of scientific disciplines (evolutionary science, taxonomy, botany, terrestrial and marine ecology, ecological restoration, fisheries science, oceanography, and social and economic science) has contributed to the conservation and sustainable development of the Galápagos archipelago and to the advancement of science. The book describes the state-of-the-art knowledge on the Galápagos socio-ecosystem, presents modern modeling tools for the integration of information from diverse science disciplines, and highlights contrasting viewpoints with regard to future scenarios for reconciling conservation with the socio-economic development of the archipelago. The book is innovative in its multidisciplinary focus on conservation and in presenting up-to-date tools for scenario modeling.

The book is structured into the following four parts: the evolutionary context; biodiversity assessment and monitoring of change; a systemic approach – modeling and restoration; and reconciliation of conservation with socio-economic development. Each part is comprised of several individual chapters and ends with a summary that highlights the main findings and conclusions.

The book integrates the knowledge and reflections of 30 scientists, of which many have dedicated a substantial part of their professional life to the Galápagos archipelago, to the conservation of its biodiversity, and to the sustainable management of its resources. The book can be considered a milestone on the way to the successful conservation and sustainable development of this unique world heritage site.

Matthias Wolff is Director of Marine and Coastal Sciences at the Charles Darwin Foundation, Puerto Ayora, Ecuador.

Mark Gardener is Director of Terrestrial Science at the Charles Darwin Foundation, Puerto Ayora, Ecuador.

Routledge explorations in environmental economics
Edited by Nick Hanley
University of Stirling, UK

1 **Greenhouse Economics**
Value and ethics
Clive L. Spash

2 **Oil Wealth and the Fate of Tropical Rainforests**
Sven Wunder

3 **The Economics of Climate Change**
Edited by Anthony D. Owen and Nick Hanley

4 **Alternatives for Environmental Valuation**
Edited by Michael Getzner, Clive Spash and Sigrid Stagl

5 **Environmental Sustainability**
A consumption approach
Raghbendra Jha and K.V. Bhanu Murthy

6 **Cost-Effective Control of Urban Smog**
The significance of the Chicago Cap-and-Trade approach
Richard F. Kosobud, Houston H. Stokes, Carol D. Tallarico and Brian L. Scott

7 **Ecological Economics and Industrial Ecology**
Jakub Kronenberg

8 **Environmental Economics, Experimental Methods**
Edited by Todd L. Cherry, Stephan Kroll and Jason F. Shogren

9 **Game Theory and Policy Making in Natural Resources and the Environment**
Edited by Ariel Dinar, José Albiac and Joaquín Sánchez-Soriano

10 **Arctic Oil and Gas**
Sustainability at risk?
Edited by Aslaug Mikkelsen and Oluf Langhelle

11 **Agrobiodiversity Conservation and Economic Development**
Edited by Andreas Kontoleon, Unai Pascual and Melinda Smale

12 **Renewable Energy from Forest Resources in the United States**
Edited by Barry D. Solomon and Valeria A. Luzadis

13 **Modeling Environment-Improving Technological Innovations under Uncertainty**
Alexander A. Golub and Anil Markandya

14 **Economic Analysis of Land Use in Global Climate Change Policy**
Thomas Hertel, Steven Rose and Richard Tol

15 **Waste and Environmental Policy**
Massimiliano Mazzanti and Anna Montini

16 **Avoided Deforestation**
Prospects for mitigating climate Change
Edited by Stefanie Engel and Charles Palmer

17 **The Use of Economic Valuation in Environmental Policy**
Phoebe Koundouri

18 **Benefits of Environmental Policy**
Klaus Dieter John and Dirk T.G. Rübbelke

19 **Biotechnology and Agricultural Development**
Robert Tripp

20 **Economic Growth and Environmental Regulation**
Tim Swanson and Tun Lin

21 **Environmental Amenities and Regional Economic Development**
Todd L. Cherry and Dan Rickman

22 **New Perspectives on Agri-Environmental Policies**
Stephen J. Goetz and Floor Brouwer

23 **The Cooperation Challenge of Economics and the Protection of Water Supplies**
A case study of the New York City Watershed Collaboration
Joan Hoffman

24 **The Taxation of Petroleum and Minerals: Principles, Problems and Practice**
Philip Daniel, Michael Keen and Charles McPherson

25 **Environmental Efficiency, Innovation and Economic Performances**
Massimiliano Mazzanti and Anna Montini

26 **Participation in Environmental Organizations**
Benno Torgler, Maria A. Garcia-Valiñas and Alison Macintyre

27 **Valuation of Regulating Services of Ecosystems**
Pushpam Kumar and Michael D. Wood

28 **Environmental Policies for Air Pollution and Climate Change in New Europe**
Caterina De Lucia

29 **Optimal Control of Age-Structured Populations in Economy, Demography, and the Environment**
Raouf Boucekkine, Natali Hritonenko and Yuri Yatsenko

30 **Sustainable Energy**
Edited by Klaus D. John and Dirk Rübbelke

31 **Preference Data for Environmental Valuation**
Combining revealed and stated approaches
John Whitehead, Tim Haab and Ju-Chin Huang

32 **Ecosystem Services and Global Trade of Natural Resources**
Ecology, economics and policies
Edited by Thomas Koellner

33 **Permit Trading in Different Applications**
Edited by Bernd Hansjürgens, Ralf Antes and Marianne Strunz

34 **The Role of Science for Conservation**
Edited by Matthias Wolff and Mark Gardener

The Role of Science for Conservation

Edited by Matthias Wolff and Mark Gardener

Routledge
Taylor & Francis Group
LONDON AND NEW YORK

First published 2012
by Routledge
2 Park Square, Milton Park, Abingdon, Oxfordshire OX14 4RN

Simultaneously published in the USA and Canada
by Routledge
711 Third Avenue, New York, NY 10017

First issued in paperback 2016

Routledge is an imprint of the Taylor & Francis Group, an Informa business

British Library Cataloguing in Publication Data
A catalogue record for this book is available from the British Library

Library of Congress Cataloging in Publication Data
A catalog record has been requested for this book

ISBN: 978-1-138-24386-6 (pbk)
ISBN: 978-0-415-68071-4 (hbk)

Typeset in Times New Roman
by Wearset Ltd, Boldon, Tyne and Wear

Contents

Figures

Tables

Contributors

Rachel Atkinson is affiliated with the Charles Darwin Foundation, Galapagos (Ecuador) and focuses her research on ecological restoration, invasive species management, threatened plant conservation, building capacity for long term solutions to conservation and other related issues.

Stuart Banks is affiliated with the Charles Darwin Foundation, Galapagos (Ecuador) and focuses his research on oceanography, marine ecology, marine managed area design and related topics.

Marjan van den Belt is affiliated with Ecological Economics Research New Zealand (EERNZ), Massey University Palmerston North (New Zealand) and focuses her research on participatory approaches, system dynamics, scenario planning/envisioning, ecosystem services based valuation and management, integrated assessments, adaptive capacity and resilience.

Frank Bungartz is affiliated with the Charles Darwin Foundation, Galapagos (Ecuador) and focuses his research on biodiversity science and species inventories, taxonomy, vegetation science, lichenology.

Rodrigo Bustamante is affiliated with CSIRO Marine and Atmospheric Research, Ecosciences Precinct. Brisbane (Australia) and focuses his research on marine ecology, conservation biology, biodiversity and ecosystem modelling, management strategy evaluation, spatial management, ecosystem-based management, climate and ocean change impacts and adaptation strategies modelling.

Victor Carrion is affiliated with the Galapagos National Park Service (Ecuador) and focuses his research on restoration of island ecosystems and species eradications.

Robert Costanza is affiliated with the Institute for Sustainable Solutions, Portland State University, Portland OR (USA) and focuses his research on transdisciplinary integration, ecological economics, landscape ecology, ecological modeling, energy and material flow analysis, environmental policy, social traps, incentive structures and institutions.

Sharon L. Deem is affiliated with the Saint Louis Zoo, Saint Louis, Missouri (USA) and focuses her research on veterinary medicine and epidemiology – spread of diseases between humans, domestic animals and wildlife and the impact of environmental changes and human contact on the health and conservation of wild species.

William H. Durham is affiliated with Stanford University, Stanford, California (USA) and focuses his research on evolution, gene-culture coevolution, Darwin, Galapagos, Costa Rica, conservation, environmental anthropology.

Irenäus Eibl-Eibesfeldt is affiliated with the Film Archive for Human Ethology of the Max-Planck-Society in Andechs (Germany) and focuses his research on human behavior, its phylogenetic roots and adaptations to cultural change (see Urban Ethology).

Mark Gardener is affiliated with the Charles Darwin Foundation (Ecuador) and focuses his research on invasive species, ecological restoration and fire ecology.

James P. Gibbs is affiliated with the Department of Environmental and Forest Biology, State University of New York College of Environmental Science and Forestry, Syracuse, New York (USA) and focusses his research on conservation biology and ecological monitoring.

Christophe Grenier is affiliated with the Institute de Géographie de l'Université de Nantes (France) and focuses his research on geography of conservation and globalization with emphasis on tropical coastal and island systems (Galápagos, Easter Island, Costa Rica, Madagascar).

Grant Harper is affiliated with the Tasmanian Parks and Wildlife Service (Australia) and focuses his research on invasive species management, ecology of introduced predator species, island restoration ecology and bird ecology.

Henri Herrera is affiliated with the Charles Darwin Foundation (Ecuador) and focuses his research on Galápagos ant taxonomy, invasive ants and other introduced species of insects.

Patricia Jaramillo is affiliated with the Charles Darwin Foundation (Ecuador) and focuses her research on botany, biodiversity and restorations of ecosystems with emphasis on the genetic diversity for the conservation of the threatened Galapagos endemic species.

Matthew J. James is affiliated with the Department of Geology, Sonoma State University, Rohnert Park, California 94928 (USA) and focuses his research on history of 1905-06 Galápagos expediton, Galápagos marine invertebrate paleontology, Galápagos conservation, as well as the life and work of Charles Darwin.

Gustavo Jiménez-Uzcátegui is affiliated with the Charles Darwin Foundation (Ecuador) and focuses his research on disease monitoring, vertebrate taxonomy and population dynamics.

Annika Krutwa is affiliated with the Leibniz Center for Tropical Marine Ecology (ZMT), Bremen (Germany) and focuses her research on subtidal community ecology, marine biodiversity, resource management and marine mammals.

Bryan Milstead is affiliated with the US Environmental Protection Agency, Narragansett, Rhode Island (USA) and focuses his research on natural resource management, monitoring, population analysis, knowledge management, and aesthetics.

Patricia G. Parker is affiliated with the Department of Biology, University of Missouri–St. Louis (UMSL) and Saint Louis Zoo, both in Saint Louis, Missouri (USA) and focuses her research on phylogeography of birds and their pathogens, behavioral ecology, population genetics and evolutionary ecology.

Cesar Peñaherrera-Palma is affiliated with the Charles Darwin Foundation (Ecuador) and focuses his research on sharks and pelagic fish species abundance and dynamics in the Eastern Tropical Pacific, marine environmental variability and its influence on biological and ecological life aspects of pelagic fishery resources, as well as ultrasonic and satellite telemetry.

Diego Ruiz is affiliated with the Leibniz Center for tropical marine ecology (ZMT), Bremen (Germany) and focuses his research on trophic modeling, marine biogeography of the South East Pacific ecosystem and marine monitoring.

Franz Smith is affiliated with the Climate Adaptation Flagship CSIRO Marine and Atmospheric Research, Brisbane, Queensland (Australia) and focuses his research on biodiversity, macroecology, bio-physical coupling, ecosystem modeling and systematic conservation planning.

Nathalia Tirado is affiliated with the Charles Darwin Foundation (Ecuador) and focuses her research on marine ecology, zooplankton ecology and taxonomy, as well as geographic information systems.

Carlos A. Valle is affiliated with the Universidad San Francisco de Quito (GAIAS) (Ecuador) and focuses his research on evolutionary behavioral ecology, community and population ecology and biological conservation, phylogeography of birds and their pathogens, behavioral ecology, population genetics and evolutionary ecology.

Mariana Vera is affiliated with the Charles Darwin Foundation (Ecuador) and focuses her research on marine ecology, sessile fauna with emphasis on corals, scientific diving, fisheries and conservation.

Noah K. Whiteman is affiliated with the Department of Ecology and Evolutionary Biology, University of Arizona (USA) and focuses his research on molecular, ecological and the evolutionary basis of host–parasite interactions.

Matthias Wolff is affiliated with the Leibniz Center for Tropical marine Ecology (ZMT) (Germany) and focuses his research on resource assessment, trophic modeling, marine ecology, as well as interdisciplinary and ecosystem-based approaches to resource management.

Frauke Ziemmeck is affiliated with the Charles Darwin Foundation (Ecuador) and focuses her research on vegetation ecology and phytosociology.

Part I

The evolutionary context

1 What Darwin found convincing in Galápagos

William H. Durham

Introduction

The Darwin Bicentennial in 2009 prompted a number of useful reassessments of how far we have come since 1809 in the study of evolution; but it also prompted insightful new work on the topics of where and how Darwin's evolutionary thinking began – that is, on the origin of *The Origin*. What exactly was it during the Beagle voyage and its aftermath that stirred the young Darwin to challenge the fixity of species? The question is particularly interesting in Darwin's case because, in Kuhnian terms, the build-up of scientific challenges ("anomalies") to the prevailing paradigm of special creation – that is, that fixed and immutable species were supernaturally created at some time in the past – were neither numerous nor widely recognized among scholars. It was not a case of growing general discontent with the old paradigm. How then did Darwin assemble enough convincing challenges to the old paradigm – a paradigm he was actually well-trained to sustain – to eventually provoke the paradigm shift of the Darwinian Revolution?

In this chapter, I review anomalies to the special creation paradigm that Darwin quite literally collected on the Beagle voyage, and especially in Galápagos. This is not a general review of Darwin's evidence from the Beagle voyage (for which see Keynes 2003; Eldredge 2005; van Wyhe 2008), nor is it a reassessment of the value to Darwin of all his many observations in Galápagos (as admirably achieved, for example, by Grant and Estes 2009). Rather, I will focus on a few specific anomalies to the old paradigm that led Darwin to evolution and on the role of Darwin's Galápagos experience in that piece of history. I offer two main arguments. First, I argue that Galápagos did not present Darwin with totally new kinds of anomalies to the dominant paradigm, but rather that the archipelago solidified or made clear a growing short list of anomalies that Darwin had picked up earlier in the Beagle voyage. Second, I argue that it was the Galápagos mockingbirds (Darwin's "mocking-thrushes") that were most influential to Darwin, far more than the finches that bear his name, because they shored up his thinking on two key anomalies. As I will argue, the mockingbirds provided unambiguous evidence to question the fixity of species and, in its place, to consider the possibility of "transmutation", as evolutionary change in organisms was called at the time. When later identified as distinct species by John Gould, the mockingbirds convinced Darwin that organisms are indeed subject to evolutionary modification. Although Darwin saw many fine examples of adaptation in Galápagos, including what came to be known as the adaptive radiation of the finches, they were not of great interest until later, when Darwin hit upon the idea of natural selection. Then, suddenly, adaptations in Galápagos and elsewhere became pertinent and exciting. We might say that Galápagos played a key role in leading Darwin to evolution, but not in helping him identify natural selection

Lessons from the voyage, before Galápagos

Darwin was fortunate to have had 3.7 years of adventure and exploration (27 December 1831 to 15 September 1835) before the Beagle arrived in Galápagos, because experiences along the way prepared him in several key respects to appreciate the biota of Galápagos and make the most of his short five weeks there. First, in the course of these pre-Galápagos years, Darwin became a practiced Lyellian geologist. With guidance from the first two volumes of Lyell's *Principles of Geology* (1830), Darwin interpreted the landscapes he saw – first in the Cape Verde Islands, and later in South America – as the product of gradual natural forces, including the elevation and subsidence of land masses, acting over long periods of time. He made appropriate and, for the time, highly accurate inferences about the uplifted coastal terraces of Patagonia, for example, and clearly came to appreciate the depth of time it took gradual natural forces to shape the landscapes he was studying. Darwin became convinced of "the wonderful superiority of Lyell's manner of treating geology, compared with that of any other author" (Darwin, in Barlow 1958:77).

Darwin's second key lesson before Galápagos came from fossils he collected in South America, especially those from the area around Bahia Blanca, Argentina, collected in September and October 1832. Darwin found there a number of fossils that were to become very influential in his thinking – both a diverse collection of mollusk species, many of which were identical, he noted, to living mollusks along the coast, and a number of large vertebrate fossils, including one described in his field notebook as "armadillo" and "Megatherium like armadillo case" (Darwin, in Chancellor and van Wyhe 2009: 53, 57). It is remarkable that Darwin noted, while still in the field, resemblance between fossil bones he excavated and the boney plates of contemporary armadillos.[1] Even so, the fossil armadillo material (now assigned to the taxon, *glyptodon*) might have been easy to dismiss as challenging to the old paradigm, except that it was joined by two additional cases: Darwin also found fossils of an extinct cavy with resemblance to the extant Patagonian cavy, and fossils of an extinct giant ground sloth whose dentition was similar to that of living tree sloths (Brinkman 2010; Eldredge 2009). However, even these pairings of extinct and modern species might not have seemed unusual to the young scientist were it not for one other observation: the persistence of a majority of the mollusk species in the same fossil beds ruled out general catastrophe as the cause of the others' extinction. The implication was that some species survive while others go extinct but are "replaced" by closely allied forms. As Darwin put it a few years after these finds (1839a: 209), "The most important result of this discovery [of fossil megafauna] is the confirmation of the law that existing animals have a close relation in form with extinct species..".[2]

There was one other case of "replacement" of particular influence on the young Darwin, but this was replacement in space, not in time as the fossils had been. It was the case of two species of rheas in South America, ostrich-like birds that live on the open plains of Argentina. At Bahia Blanca, Darwin had seen the large American or "Common" Rhea (*Rhea americana*) and the gauchos told him about a rarer and smaller second species, the Lesser Rhea (*Rhea pennata*, also called "Darwin's Rhea") that was found only south of the Rio Negro in Argentina. However, Darwin did not encounter the Lesser Rhea until January 1834 when the Beagle's artist, Conrad Martens, shot one for dinner. A good start had been made on consuming the carcass when Darwin realized that they were eating precious data. "Fortunately, the head neck, legs, wings, many of the large feathers, and a large part of the skin had been preserved; and from these a very nearly perfect specimen had been put together" (Darwin 1839a: 108–109) back in England, giving Darwin credit for the find. But it was not just a new species; it was a new case of replacement – the Common Rhea north of the Rio Negro was replaced by the Lesser Rhea to the south. Surely it was possible to explain each replacement surprise by arguing that the Creator simply wanted life distributed that way, but the growing list of surprises logically began to raise suspicions.

Darwin's third key lesson from the voyage before Galápagos had to do with what today would be called biogeography. The Beagle voyage revealed interesting, even bewildering, patterns in the geographical distribution of both continental and island species. One such pattern came to light from visiting the Cape Verde Islands, only to be resoundingly confirmed in Galápagos as we shall see below. Although the "volcanic fires of a past age, and the scorching heat of a tropical sun, have in most places rendered the soil unfit for vegetation", making it "an utterly sterile land" (Darwin 1839a: 1–2), the organisms Darwin observed in Cape Verde, although few in number, had a visible similarity to the flora and fauna of the nearby African mainland where ecological conditions could hardly have been more different. By the same token, Darwin later appreciated that the Cape Verde Islands had many environmental features in common with the Galápagos Islands, but with no common organisms between them. Darwin later wrote:

> There is a considerable degree of resemblance in the volcanic nature of the soil, in climate, height, and size of the islands, between the Galapagos and Cape de Verde Archipelagoes: but what an entire and absolute difference in their inhabitants! The inhabitants of the Cape de Verde Islands are related to those of Africa, like those of the Galapagos to America.
>
> (Darwin 1859: 398)

One could again say, by the prevailing paradigm, that the Creator wanted an “affinity” between oceanic islands and neighboring continental areas, but with the multiplication of such anomalies, Darwin eventually began to consider other possible explanations.

When the Beagle visited the Falkland Islands, a second interesting example of biogeographic distribution presented itself in the very tame, and now extinct, wolf-like fox, *Dusicyon australis.* As he wrote in his notes,

> Gauchos & Indians from nearly all parts of [southern] S. America have been here and all say [this fox] is not found on the Continent: an indisputable proof of its individuality as a species. *–It is very curious, thus having a quadruped peculiar to so small a tract of country*.... The sealers say this Fox is not found or any other land quadruped in the other Islands, such as Georgia, Sandwich, Shetland &c &c ... very soon these confident [i.e. tame] animals [will] all be killed: *How little evidence will then remain of what appears to me to be a centre of creation*.... Out of the four specimens of the Foxes on board [the Beagle] ... three are darker and come from the East [Island]: there is a smaller & rusty coloured one which comes from the West Island: [Captain] Lowe states that all from this island are small & of this shade of color.
>
> (Darwin, in Keynes 2000: 209–210, italics added)

The passage shows that Darwin recognized not only that the fox was uniquely found in the Falklands, which initially suggested the islands must be a special “centre of creation” (another notion that came from Lyell), but also that Darwin recognized that the fox was present as two morphologically distinct varieties, one on the East Island and one on the West. Why these unusual patterns of distribution?

Darwin in Galápagos

As the Beagle sailed west toward Galápagos in September 1835, Darwin had therefore seen accumulating evidence for two main Kuhnian anomalies to the dominant paradigm:

1 The “affinity” anomaly: the finding that oceanic islands have biota closely, but selectively, resembling those of neighboring continental areas;
2 The “replacement” anomaly: the finding that similar species may uniquely replace each other in space and time.

The anomalies were both raised prior to Galápagos, but the evidence for them was only partial. Darwin had but one case, from Cape Verde Islands, of the affinity anomaly, and it was neither particularly striking nor convincing by itself. Similarly, although Darwin’s fossils offered several examples of so-called “succession of types” over time, Darwin had only a single example of replacement in space, with the rheas. Another possible example of replacement in space, between the East and West Falklands foxes, appeared to be only a difference between varieties. In short, what was needed, logically, was a confirming set of observations for both anomalies that would cleanly call into question the fixity of species.

What to me is so interesting and provocative about Darwin's short stay in Galápagos is that the biota there provided precisely that set of observations. The archipelago presented enough evidence for both anomalies, in fact, that Darwin was to write just two years later in his personal notebook:

> In July opened first note Book on "transmutation of Species". — Had been greatly struck from about month of previous March on character of S. American fossils — & species on Galapagos Archipelago. — These facts origin (especially latter) of all my views.
>
> (CUL-DAR158.1–76, p. 13)

I argue that the reason Darwin could say "especially latter" and give particular significance to his findings in Galápagos is because they convinced him beyond reasonable doubt of these two principal anomalies.

What was it in the Galápagos that Darwin found so clear and convincing? In a word, I will argue that it was the mockingbirds of the archipelago – the four specimens and three species of the Galápagos genus Mimus (formerly Nesomimus) that Darwin brought back from the archipelago.

Darwin and the Galápagos mockingbirds

Darwin's first mention of the Galápagos mockingbirds or *thenca*, as they are called in Spanish, came from either the first or second island of the four that he visited – it is difficult to know for sure (see discussion in Chancellor and van Wyhe 2009: 418–419). At the time, he penned these words in his Galápagos Notebook:

> The Thenca very tame & curious in these Islds. I certainly recognise [*sic*] S. America in ornithology, would a botanist?
>
> (Darwin, in Chancellor and van Wyhe 2009: 439)

Right away it is clear that Darwin saw the mockingbirds as an unambiguous case of the affinity anomaly, recognizing their close similarity to mockingbirds he had seen along the coast of Chile. Moreover, from his question "would a botanist?" it is evident that Darwin is already at work on the generality of that observation. As his visit to the archipelago progressed, he gained more and more confidence in that affinity, noting that many other bird species resembled their South American counterparts (e.g. doves, flycatchers, and gulls) and the same for lizards and cacti. Later, when Darwin wrote up his Galápagos observations in 1839, after he had been able to confer with expects back home in England, he would emphasize this point:

> … we may infer that, with the exception of a few wanderers, the organic beings found on this archipelago are peculiar to it; and yet that their general form strongly partakes of an American character. It would be impossible for any one [sic] accustomed to the birds of Chile and La Plata to be placed on these islands, and not to feel convinced that he was, as far as the organic world was concerned, on American ground. This similarity in type, between distant islands and continents, while the species are distinct, has scarcely been sufficiently noticed.
>
> (Darwin 1839a: 474)

The passage is noteworthy because Darwin is clearly saying that biotic affinity between oceanic islands and continents, of which Galápagos constitutes but one example, is an unappreciated anomaly to the dominant paradigm. Twenty years later, in *On the Origin of Species*, he would make the same point with even greater force (Darwin 1859: 397–402).

The tameness and curiosity of the mockingbirds is also manifest in this initial passage about mockingbirds from Darwin's Galápagos notebook, harking back to his parallel experience with the Falkland fox and several of its bird species. When Darwin wrote about tameness in the same 1839 report, he noted its anomalous nature and even offered a "sneak preview" of an evolutionary explanation for its emergence:

> I have not met with any account of the *land* birds being so tame, in any other quarter of the world, as at the Galapagos and Falkland Islands … we may, I think, conclude, first, that the wildness of birds with regard to man, is a particular instinct directed against *him,* and not dependent on any general degree of caution arising from other sources of danger; second, that it is not acquired by them in a short time, even when much persecuted; but that in the course of successive generations it becomes hereditary.… We may infer from these facts, what havoc the introduction of any new beast of prey must cause in a country, before the instincts of the aborigines become adapted to the stranger's craft or power.
>
> (Darwin 1839a: 477–478)

All that is missing from this prescient account is explicit reference to the selective preservation of inherited variation in tameness. Today, one cannot help but admire Darwin's additional prescience about the "havoc" caused by newly introduced species in a location – a havoc still underway in Galápagos that has brought the Floreana (Charles) mockingbird close to extinction, (Grant *et al.* 2000), not to mention Galápagos petrels, mangrove finches, and more than 20 species of land plants. In short, the mockingbirds and their tameness offered Darwin striking confirmation of the affinity anomaly – they resemble South American species but are markedly different in Galápagos, including in their tameness.

Turning now to the replacement anomaly, we may note, first, that Darwin shot and preserved only a single specimen of the mockingbirds from each of the first two islands that he visited. On the one hand, this fact confirms beyond doubt that he paid little attention at this time (September 1835) to inter-individual variation among the mockingbirds in any one location, at least among the adults (the chicks are easy to distinguish). Just three years later (October 1838), after reading Malthus and recognizing the culling effect of the "struggle for existence", Darwin would begin to grasp the importance of natural selection acting on such variation. However, during his visit to Galápagos there was no "variation anomaly" for Darwin, as there would be a few years later: one mockingbird specimen from each island was enough. On the other hand, Darwin's single-specimen sampling indicates that the observable differences between mockingbirds of the first two islands were also easy for him to see. It did not take a big collection and elaborate measurements to establish their differences. A few years later, writing in the *Zoology of the Voyage of the HMS Beagle,* Darwin confirmed this fact.

> I fortunately happened to observe that the specimens which I collected in the two first islands we visited, differed from each other, and this made me pay particular attention to their collection.
>
> (Darwin 1839b Part 3 No. 4: p. 63)

It is quite possible that Darwin is being too modest in saying "happened to observe"; the foregoing discussion of replacements suggests that Darwin came to Galápagos on the lookout for more instances of succession in time or space, and this "happens" to be one. Eldredge (2009: 48) is particularly emphatic on this point, suggesting that "the pattern Darwin went to the Galapagos looking for" was "the replacement of closely similar taxa (species or varieties) on different islands".

Darwin went on to collect an additional single mockingbird specimen from each of the two further islands he visited in Galápagos, resulting in specimens from four islands in all: San Cristóbal (then Chatham), Floreana (Charles), Isabela (Albermarle), and Santiago (James). Importantly, three of the specimens were visibly different from one another, while Darwin took the third in the list to be very similar to the first.[3] What is so very interesting is how quickly Darwin realized that these differences were another case of replacement in space. While still in Galápagos, he noted the pattern and also its curious parallel in the famous observation that tortoise carapaces in Galápagos are recognizably different from island to island (and even from volcano to volcano in the case of Isabela Island). In his notebook, Darwin wrote that these mockingbirds, which are

> so closely allied to the Thenca of Chili [*sic*] ([and] Callandra of B. Ayres [*sic*]) [are] *singular from existing as varieties or distinct species in the different Isds.*— I have four specimens from as many Isds.— These will be

> found to be 2 or 3 varieties.— *Each variety is constant in its own Island.*— [note (a)] The Thenca of Albermale Isd is the same as that of Chatham Isd.— [note ends] This is a parallel fact to the one mentioned about the Tortoises. These birds are abundant in all parts: are very tame & inquisitive: habits exactly similar to the Thenca.
>
> (Darwin, in Keynes 2000: 298, emphasis added)

What Darwin found most intriguing was the way that these different forms of the mockingbird "replaced" the mainland species – the thenca of Chile – in Galápagos, and yet also "replaced" one another on different islands. The notes show that Darwin wondered early on if the different forms could be "distinct species" or would be "found to be 2 or 3 varieties". He would seem to have had an inkling that, if truly distinct species, the mockingbird forms could represent island-specific species differences: each "constant in its own Island". Moreover, such an occurrence would raise the possibility of island endemism, in other words of the distinct species of mockingbird – if such they be – having originated, somehow, in Galápagos.

Raise the possibility indeed! How do we know that Darwin took seriously the implications of this mockingbird discovery, and did more than pen the preceding note and just leave it at that? We know in two ways. First, there is striking evidence that the mockingbirds convinced Darwin, once and for all, of the wider significance of the phenomenon of replacement. After the Beagle left Galápagos and headed across the Pacific, Darwin worked on a series of notebooks, including his "Beagle animal notes", recently transcribed and edited by his great grandson, Richard Keynes. In those notes, which were finished by the time of the Beagle's arrival in the Keeling Islands (April 1836), Darwin compiled long lists of candidate replacements, as if to satisfy himself of the concept's generality. There are lists of animals replacing one another between the east and west sides of the Andes, and there are other non-Andes-related replacements as well. The latter begins with a note, "Take all closely allied species …".

> Bizcacha replaced vertically by alpine species many times
> Guanaco [replaced vertically] by vicuna [species]
> Maldonado Cavia (1266) replaced deserts of [Patagonia] by species close (1471 & 1587)
> Tuco-tuco replaced by Tuco tuco of Chile (?) genus?
> Mulita — replaced by Pichiz (mingling)
> Blue fox of Chile replaces common one. —
> Falkland fox replaces ________.
> Galapagos mouse replaces __________.
> Plata Didelphis by Chile species (?)
> Plata otter — Chile otters.
> …
> Thenca. La Plata species & Patagonian & Chile kind.
> La Plata Furnarius replaced by Patagonian kinds.

> Partridges replacing each other on *[illegible]* of Cordillara. C. Bahia Blanca & La Plata.]
> Is there any replacement of sparrows yes
> Any replacement by furnaria yes in islands
>
> (Darwin 1832–36: 45–47)

Replacements, or what Darwin would later call the "law of succession", were clearly very much on his mind. It is but a small, logical step to ask, what causes such replacements and why would they be prominent on the small remote islands of Galápagos? Are they simply more "pet projects" of a supernatural Creator?

The second way we know that Darwin took the mockingbird implications seriously comes from the famous entry in his other notebook, "Ornithological Notes", dated to July 1836 while the Beagle was on its way back to England:

> When I see these Islands in sight of each other, & possessed of but a scanty stock of animals, tenanted by these [mocking] birds, but slightly differing in structure & filling the same place in Nature, I must suspect they are only varieties. The only fact of a similar kind of which I am aware, is the constant asserted difference — between the wolf-like Fox of East & West Falkland Islds. — *If there is the slightest foundation for these remarks the zoology of Archipelagoes — will be well worth examining; for such facts* ["would" inserted] *undermine the stability of Species.*
>
> (Darwin, in Barlow 1963: 262, emphasis added)

Still uncertain about the question of varieties or species as he penned this passage, Darwin used a carat to insert the word "would" after writing the rest of the passage. The words are prophetic: if the mockingbirds truly are different species, then "such facts would undermine the stability of species". In the end, of course, they did just that.

Back in England: are they species?

The Beagle returned to England in early October 1836 and Darwin soon set about the task of getting help with his collections and species identifications. By January of 1837, he had turned over the birds and mammals from the Beagle collection to the Zoological Society of London, where the highly regarded ornithologist John Gould went to work on his bird specimens. On 28 February Gould announced at a Zoological Society meeting that three of Darwin's four Galápagos mockingbird specimens were distinct species, and gave each one a name (the genus was later changed from Gould's designation, "Orpheus" to "Mimus" to honor a precedent). Darwin obviously knew that this was an important claim, and went to see Gould for more discussion of his Galápagos bird collection. In an important piece of science history sleuthing, Sulloway (1982) has dated their meeting to early March 1837, and has even identified the very paper that Darwin used for taking notes on their conversation. Not only did Gould confirm that the mockingbirds represented three distinct species, rather than varieties, but he also reported on the collection in general: "26 true land birds, all new except one: rallus" (the Galápagos rail; Sulloway 1982: 264–265). For Darwin, this must surely have been an exciting conversation, for not only does this make the mockingbirds "island endemics" as we would call them now (i.e. unique species, found only in Galápagos), but it meant the most of the other land birds were also island endemics. Even if Gould were misleading or wrong about one or two mockingbirds, say, there were still more than 20 other cases identified by a leading authority. Among them were nine new Galápagos species of finches that Darwin had more haphazardly collected and labeled: suddenly, as Sulloway's analysis makes clear, Darwin realized that the finch specimens, too, were important. With this much replacement in Galápagos – this much faunal novelty – truly the "stability of species" was undermined, never to be stable again.

Darwin had no choice but to put great credibility in Gould's judgments about what constituted a species difference, even though these were species that Gould had never seen before from habitats Darwin himself barely knew. The two of them had to trust ornithological standards:

> The fact, that islands in sight of each other, should thus possess peculiar species, would be scarcely credible, if it were not supported by some others of an analogous nature, which I have mentioned in my Journal of the Voyage of the Beagle. I may observe, that as some naturalists may be inclined to attribute these differences to local varieties; *that if birds so different as M. trifasciatus, and M. parvulus, can be considered as varieties of one species, then the experience of all the best ornithologists must be given up*, and whole genera must be blended into one species. I cannot myself doubt that M. trifasciatus, and M. parvulus are as distinct species as any that can be named in one restricted genus.
>
> (Darwin 1839b, Part 3 No. 4, pp. 63–64, with genus name changed and emphasis added)

As if to hammer home the point, Darwin's passage concludes:

> The habits of these three species are similar, and they evidently *replace* each other in the natural economy of the different islands; nor can I point out any difference between their habits and those of M. Thenca of Chile.
>
> (ibid. p. 64, emphasis added)

Conclusion

This chapter has proposed a test of a hypothesis about what Charles Darwin found most convincing from his time in the Galápagos Islands during the Beagle voyage. The hypothesis holds that Galápagos data – once confirmed, interpreted and expanded with input from experts back in England – persuaded Darwin of two key anomalies that challenged the dominant paradigm of the special creation of life on

Earth. The "affinity anomaly" concerned the similarity between the biota of oceanic islands and neighboring continental areas. The "replacement anomaly" concerned a pattern in space or in time whereby similar species appear to succeed one another in time or take each other's place in nature. Neither anomaly surfaced anew during Darwin's time in Galápagos – far from it, as we have seen: both anomalies extend back years into the Beagle voyage. These are not the only anomalies that Darwin collected during the Beagle voyage; but my argument has been that they are the important two. What the Galápagos did for Darwin was to give him a set of clear, credible examples – particularly with mockingbirds – of both of these anomalies, calling into question the special creation paradigm, and pointing to the *in situ* transmutation of species, what we would today call "evolution".

As is often the case with Darwin, his own explanations of phenomena have a distinctly autobiographical quality about them. He likes to tell the reader just what he found convincing and why. Although obviously not versed in contemporary Kuhnian terminology, Darwin clearly regarded the anomalies he collected on the Beagle voyage as just that. Consider this noteworthy passage about the replacement anomaly from the autobiography Darwin originally composed as a personal memoir for family:

> During the voyage of the Beagle I had been deeply impressed by discovering in the Pampean formation great fossil animals covered with armour like that on the existing armadillos; secondly, by the manner in which closely allied animals replace one another in proceeding southwards over the Continent; & thirdly, by the South American character of most of the productions of the Galapagos archipelago, & more especially by the manner in which they differ slightly on each island of the group; none of these islands appearing to be very ancient in a geological sense. *It was evident that such facts as these, as well as many others, could be explained on the supposition that species gradually become modified; & the subject haunted me …*
>
> (Darwin, in Barlow 1958: 118–119, emphasis added)

And in his landmark book, *On the Origin of Species*, how does Darwin present his case against the dominant paradigm of special creation? He leads you back to where he once was, in the Galápagos archipelago, with the affinity anomaly in the forefront of his thoughts:

> The most striking and important fact for us in regard to the inhabitants of islands is their affinity to those of their nearest mainland, without actually being the same species. Numerous instances could be given of this fact. I will give only one, that of the Galapagos archipelago.… Here almost every product of land and water bears the unmistakable stamp of the American continent.… The naturalist, looking at the inhabitants of these volcanic islands in the Pacific, distant several hundred miles from the continent, yet feels that he is standing on American land. Why should this be so? Why should the species which are supposed to have been created in the Galapagos archipelago, and

> nowhere else, bear so plain a stamp of affinity to those created in America? … *I believe this grand fact can receive no sort of explanation on the ordinary view of independent creation;* whereas on the view here maintained, it is obvious that the Galapagos Islands would be likely to receive colonists … from America … and that such colonists would be liable to modification;–the principle of inheritance still betraying their original birthplace.
>
> (Darwin 1859: 397–99)

To me it is noteworthy that, in the entire *Origin*, this is the one place where Darwin draws extensively on his own data from Galápagos.

Acknowledgements

I thank John and Patti Zussman for several years of discussion of the life and work of Charles Darwin, Laura Driscoll for research assistance, Niles Eldredge for drawing my attention to Brinkman (2010), and Melissa Brown, the course assistants, and the Human Biology Core at Stanford for suggesting a Kuhnian framework for Darwin's path to the discovery of evolution. I thank several anonymous reviewers for their kind suggestions and support of this project. Like so many Darwin researchers, I freely used and appreciated the website, "The Complete Works of Charles Darwin Online", http://darwin-online.org.uk/. It is cited in the text as "CUL-DAR". Most of all, I thank Robert Hess for providing the perfect writer's cabin in which to prepare this chapter.

Notes

1 Careful sleuthing by Brinkman (2010:8) has shown that Darwin was, in turn, prepped for this discovery by reading during the voyage the account of a Jesuit Priest, Thomas Falkner, who previously described a very large fossil "shell of an animal… [which] seemed in all respects, except size to be the upper part of the shell of the armadillo".

2 Darwin calls it a "confirmation of the law that existing animals have a close relation in form with extinct species" as if the law were previously established independently of his evidence. Brinkman (2010) reviews examples that preceded Darwin, and discusses Lyell's presidential address on the topic to the Geological Society of London in 1837, which included the new examples from the Beagle voyage, but Darwin was still "the first to generalize these facts into his 'law of the succession of types' in 1839" (Brinkman 2010: 373).

3 Phenotypic similarity can be deceptive without careful measurement. Darwin saw "The Thenca of Albermale Isd [as] the same as that of Chatham Isd" (see text) whereas today these are commonly classified as different species (*Mimus parvulus* and *M. melanotis*, respectively), and shown by recent genetic studies not to be close relatives (Arbogast *et al.* 2006).

References

Arbogast, B.S., S.V. Drovetski, R.L. Curry, P.T. Boag, G. Seutin, P.R. Grant, B.R. Grant, and D.J. Anderson. 2006. The origin and diversification of Galapagos mockingbirds. *Evolution* 60(2):370–382.

Barlow, N. (ed.). 1958. *The Autobiography of Charles Darwin, 1809–1882* (Norton & Co: New York, NY).

Barlow, N. (ed.). 1963. Darwin's ornithological notes. *Bulletin of the British Museum (Natural History), Historical Series* 2(7):201–278.

Brinkman, P.D. 2010. Charles Darwin's Beagle Voyage, Fossil Vertebrate Succession, and "The Gradual Birth and Death of Species", *Journal of the History of Biology* 43:363–399.

Chancellor, G. and J. van Wyhe (ed.). 2009. *Charles Darwin's Notebooks from the Voyage of the Beagle* (Cambridge University Press: Cambridge, UK).

Darwin, C.R. 1832–1836. *Beagle animal notes.* CUL-DAR29.1.A1–A49 Transcribed by Richard Keynes.

Darwin, C.R. 1839a. *Narrative of the surveying voyages of His Majesty's Ships Adventure and Beagle between the years 1826 and 1836, describing their examination of the southern shores of South America, and the Beagle's circumnavigation of the globe, Journal and remarks* (Henry Colburn: London, UK).

Darwin, C.R. (ed.). 1839b. Birds Part 3 No. 4 of *The Zoology of the Voyage of H.M.S. Beagle.* by John Gould. Edited and superintended by Charles Darwin (Smith Elder and Co.: London, UK).

Darwin, C.R. 1859. *On the Origin of Species.* Facsimile of the First Edition (1964) (Harvard University Press: Cambridge, MA).

Eldredge, N. 2005. *Darwin: Discovering the Tree of Life.* (Norton & Co: New York, NY).

Eldredge, N. 2009. Experimenting with transmutation: Darwin, the Beagle, and Evolution, *Evolution: Education and Outreach* 2:35–54.

Grant, K.T. and G.B. Estes. 2009. *Darwin in Galapagos: Footsteps to a New World* (Princeton University Press: Princeton, NJ).

Grant, P.R., R.L. Curry, and B.R. Grant, 2000. A remnant population of the Floreana mockingbird on Champion island, Galapagos, *Biological Conservation* 92:285–290.

Keynes, R. 2000. *Charles Darwin's Zoology Notes and Specimen Lists from the H.M.S Beagle* (Cambridge University Press: Cambridge, UK).

Keynes, R. 2003. *Fossils, Finches and Fuegians: Darwin's Adventures and Discoveries on the Beagle* (Oxford University Press: Oxford, UK).

Lyell, C. 1830. *Principles of Geology, being an attempt to explain the former changes of the earth's surface, by reference to causes now in operation* (John Murray: London, UK), Vol. 1–2.

Sulloway, F.J. 1982. Darwin's conversion: The Beagle voyage and its aftermath, *Journal of the History of Biology* 15(3):325–396.

Wyhe, J. van. 2008. *Darwin: The Story of the Man and his Theories of Evolution* (Andre Deutsch: London, UK).

2 Research on evolutionary principles in Galápagos

An overview of the past 50 years

Carlos A. Valle and Patricia G. Parker

Introduction

The classical Darwinian theory maintains that evolution is mainly adaptation by natural selection. Over the 70 years following the publication of *The Origin of Species* in 1859, the Modern Synthesis arose as a fusion between natural selection and Mendelian genetics, and their expansion into population genetics. Two contrasting evolutionary views for adaptive evolution emerged during the development of the Modern Synthesis. Ronald Fisher's (1930) Fundamental Theorem of Natural Selection holds that simple Darwinian mass selection fully explains all adaptive evolution. On the other hand, Sewall Wright (1931, 1932) asserts that selection alone cannot explain adaptive evolution, which requires natural selection acting together with stochastic processes like random genetic drift. Wright's Shifting balance theory of evolution uses the metaphor of an adaptive landscape (Figure 2.1) as a surface representing fitness of a species. On the fitness landscape, each locally adapted population occupies an adaptive peak separated from other peaks by valleys of low fitness (more poorly performing combinations of characteristics in that environment). Natural selection, while promoting an increase in the average fitness of each local population, gets them stuck in a local fitness peak that may be lower than the highest adaptive peak possible for that species. Genetic drift allows each local population to genetically "explore" around its fitness peak. The magnitude of the random shift in mean population fitness from one generation to the next depends upon the size of the population: small populations will take much larger random steps than larger populations. When a shift results in a population approaching the slope of a different adaptive peak, natural selection will pull it toward the new adaptive peak. Thus, drift and selection are more likely to produce a shifting of the population across valleys of low fitness towards a new adaptive peak.

Both remain largely theoretical but their logic and appeal have made them two of the most influential theoretical perspectives in the study of evolution. Furthermore, modern evolutionary biologists agree that evolution consists of both adaptive and non-adaptive (stochastic) components. However, whether evolution is mainly adaptive remains to be answered. We argue that islands offer excellent opportunities to examine this balance.

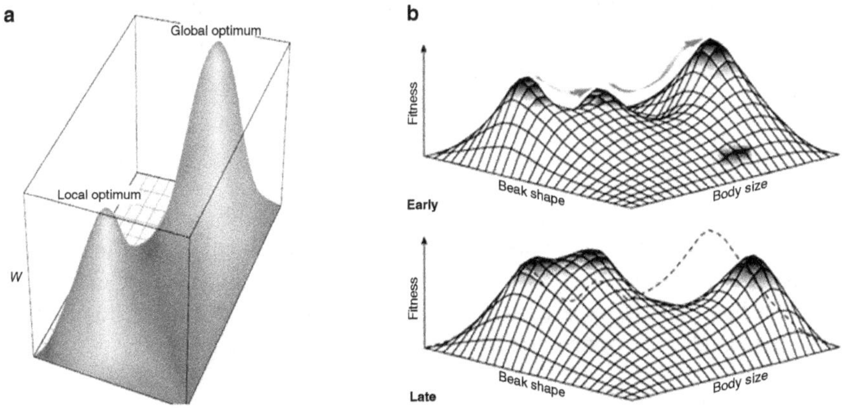

Figure 2.1 (a) Representation of an adaptive landscape with two adaptive peaks. The axes of this surface consist of phenotypic or genotypic continua; thus, each point on the landscape represents a particular combination of characters that are associated with a relative fitness indicated by the height of the surface at that point (source: Orr 2009). (b) Theoretical adaptive landscape for Darwin's finches depicting fitness for different combinations of beak shape and body size (source: Grant and Grant 2002).

Here we present the features that make the Galápagos a unique place for the study of evolution and review a few seminal findings focusing on evolutionary principles. This review is biased towards studies on a few animal species, leaving aside research on plants and other organisms. Tui de Roy's (2009) recent book is the most complete review of research on evolution, ecology and conservation biology in the Galápagos during the last 50 years.

Galápagos, a natural laboratory for testing evolutionary principles

A number of features make Galápagos ideal for testing the fundamental principles of evolutionary theory: its oceanic origin and geology, its geographical location and isolation, the islands' sizes and spatial distribution, its ecological complexity and finally its pristine condition.

True oceanic islands

The Galápagos, like the Azores, Easter Island and Hawaii, were never connected to continental landmasses. The archipelago emerged through volcanic activity at the Galápagos hot spot and the Galápagos ridge (spreading center) (Geist 2009). This means that all lineages found on the islands colonized from an outside source, usually mainland South or Central America. Thus, they established and many eventually evolved into unique insular endemics; some evolved further and diversified into multiple species, while others have shown little or no change. New molecular approaches allow the estimation of colonization dates, examination of rates of change, and evaluation of whether those least-changed lineages are simply more recent arrivals.

Effective isolation

The archipelago's geographic isolation from the mainland (1,000 km from the coast of Ecuador) effectively prevents gene flow between colonizing and parent populations and acts as an ecological filter, thus explaining the archipelago's impoverished biota (compared with mainland Ecuador) and the taxonomic disharmony found in every taxonomic group colonizing the Galápagos.

Opportunity for multiple isolation events

Opportunities for small-scale *in situ* geographic isolation arose gradually within the archipelago as new islands appeared, today numbering around 120 islands, islets and rocks (Snell *et al.* 1996). Thus, colonizing lineages had repeated opportunities for subsequent colonization and further divergence and speciation within the archipelago.

Geological youth

Current geological evidence shows the age of the current Galápagos Islands as no more than 3.0 million years (My) old and about 9.0 Mybp for those that are submerged (Geist 1996). The Galápagos archipelago is ecologically old enough for evolutionary processes to have occurred, but geologically young enough to see evolutionary processes underway; in the words of Grant and Grant (2008), "… it is as though the whole process of speciation is represented in all of its stages from start to finish", referring to Darwin's finches embodying every stage of differentiation (Figure 2.2).

Small size and low ecological complexity

The area of the archipelago (less than 10,000 km^2) is small enough to allow evolutionary biologists to get a fair understanding of its large-scale ecological processes and their evolutionary implications. However, it still is large enough to sustain relatively stable ecological communities involved in natural processes of extinction and colonization. Despite some habitat heterogeneity within and between islands, ecological complexity is low, permitting some unraveling of ecological and evolutionary processes.

Pristine conditions

Even with measurable environmental degradation mostly due to an increased rate of introduction of aggressive exotic organisms (both animals and plants)

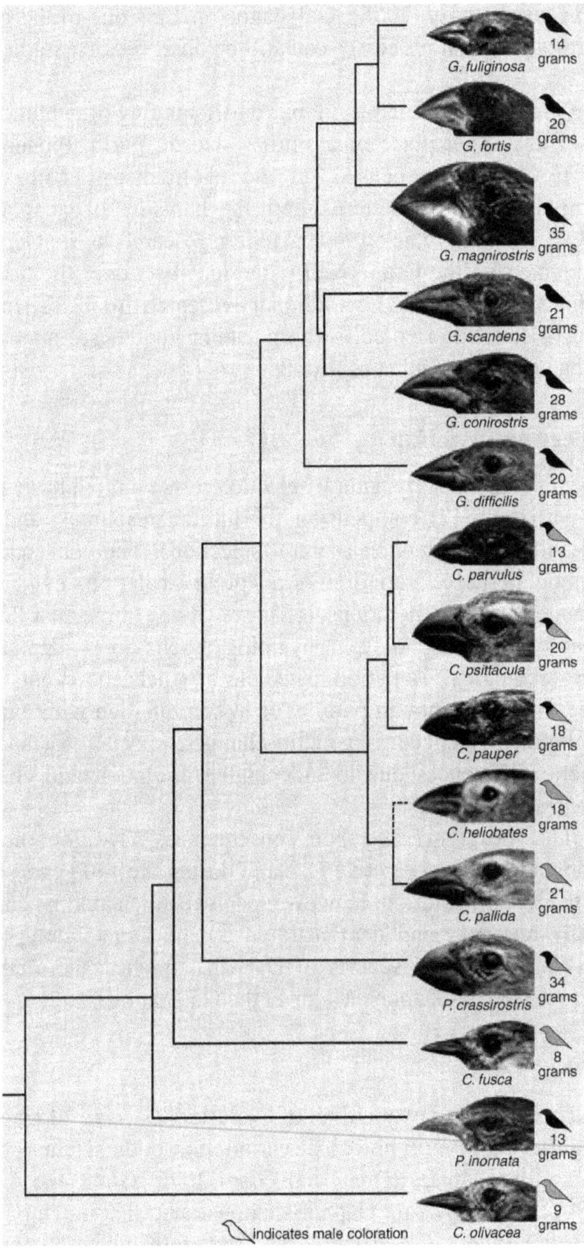

Figure 2.2 Phylogeny of Darwin's finches. Darwin's finches, with exception of the warbler finches, show so much resemblance that even a lay person can correctly infer that they are a group of related species; although their variation in beak structure led even Darwin to hesitate about their common ancestry (source: Freeman and Herron 2004, based on Petren *et al.* 1999).

(Tye and Snell 2002; Causton *et al.* 2006), Galápagos remains one of the most pristine places on Earth, so natural processes can still be observed and studied in a primordial state.

The contribution of Galápagos to increasing our understanding of evolution is unsurpassed by that of any other place of a similar size on Earth. Pioneering research conducted in Galápagos focused on the evolutionary ecology of endemic species, emphasizing the patterns and mechanisms of adaptation (Bowman *et al.* 1983; Perry 1984; Lack 1947). Modern research in the Galápagos, such as that conducted by the Grants and other scientists over the last 50 years, has changed the way we conduct evolutionary research from descriptive patterns to a quantitative science oriented towards testing hypotheses about the evolution of Galápagos organisms and ecosystems.

Testing natural selection in action

The Darwinian Theory of Evolution by natural selection rests on three basic postulates: (1) heritable variation; (2) competition for limited resources; and (3) non-random survival and/or reproduction (natural selection). The consequence of selection acting upon heritable variation is adaptive evolution, evidenced either as genetic change across generations (changes at the molecular level, allele frequencies, karyotype, morphology, physiology, behavior), adaptation, speciation or adaptive (ecological) radiation. The role of stochastic events (i.e. founder effects and genetic drift) may in parallel or in combination with natural selection lead to evolution evidenced as genetic changes, speciation (random accumulation of genetic differences due to independent mutation and chance immigration) and phenotypic radiation.

Although simple, these postulates and their consequences have gone nearly untested in natural populations despite active research during the 150 years since Darwin launched his theory of evolution. However, each postulate and its consequences has been fully observed and demonstrated by the Grants' long-term study focusing mainly on one of 15 species of Darwin's finches, the medium ground finch (*Geospiza fortis*), on Daphne Major in the Galápagos Islands.

Heritable variation

Genetic (heritable) variation is the raw material of evolution. *G. fortis* of Daphne shows remarkably high levels of morphological variation in body size and beak size and shape. Heritability analyses (Boag and Grant 1978; Grant and Grant 2000; Keller *et al.* 2001) of *G. fortis* on Daphne demonstrated that much of that phenotypic variation was heritable (i.e. genetic), and therefore subject to natural selection (Figure 2.3).

Competition

Competition among individuals, the second fundamental ingredient for evolution by natural selection, occurs when resources are limited. Competition for food, both

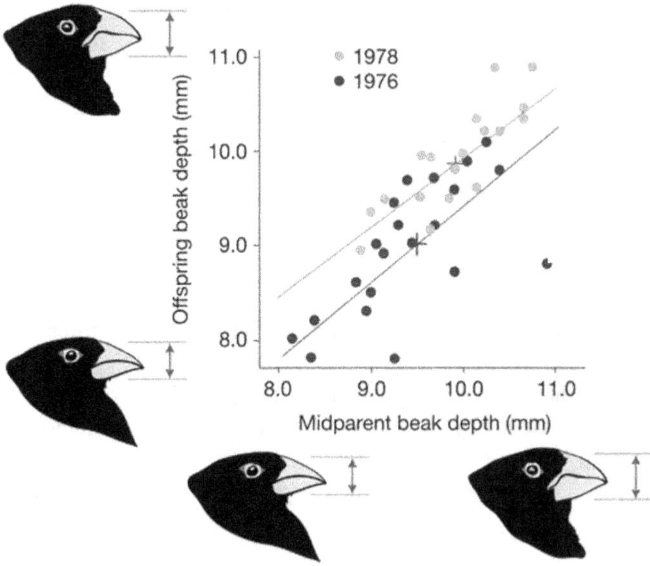

Figure. 2.3 Heritability (in the narrow sense) of morphological traits (beak depth) in two generations of *Geospiza fortis* (1976 and 1978) (source: Freeman and Herron 2004, based on Boag 1983).

intraspecific and interspecific, has been observed on Daphne, especially during recurrent droughts when the finches' food becomes scarce. For instance, during the drought of 1977, Darwin's finches almost depleted their food resources on Daphne and survival strongly favored larger and heavy-beaked individuals. A dramatic shift of *G. fortis* towards a smaller beak size in 2006 is an unquestionable case of ecological character displacement that is attributable to interspecific competition with *G. magnirostris*, the largest of the Darwin finches and a recent colonizer on Daphne. As Grant and Grant (2006, 2008) pointed out, such results suggest a fundamental role for interspecific competition in structuring natural ecological communities and in evolutionary diversification.

Natural selection and evolutionary response to selection

Natural selection is defined simply as non-random variation in survival and/or reproductive success. Such non-randomness can be linked to phenotypic variation among individuals in a population to measure natural selection. The strength of selection on Darwin's finches during the droughts has been measured by selection coefficients, selection differentials, and selection gradients (Figure 2.4). Most selection was found to be directional, although its pattern was complex owing to several factors including oscillating directional selection resulting from shifts in type and abundance of available food resources, which favored large beaks, and occasionally smaller ones, as well as character displacement due to interspecific competition with *G. magnirostris* that led to strong selection against larger size.

Few studies have been able to quantify evolutionary responses in nature. The Grants' study has quantified responses to selection for recurrent events of selection during nearly 40 years of study. In 2006 they recorded the strongest evolutionary response and over time have measured selection and evolutionary responses showing how microevolution proceeds on a short time-scale, something that has not been done with any other species in a natural setting (Figure 2.5).

Adaptation

In a strict sense, an adaptation is any trait or character state that improves the fitness of an individual relative to others in a population. Broadly, however, an adaptation is a trait that suits an organism to its particular ecological niche. Adaptations in morphology, physiology and behavior have been demonstrated for many Galápagos endemic species. Here, however, we refer succinctly to some general findings and the most spectacular examples that call the attention of any Galápagos visitor.

Mockingbirds

The mockingbirds of Galápagos first drew Darwin's attention to geographic variation and began to undermine his belief in the immutability of species. If we could think of a single observation or organism that was the central seed of Darwin's insight and ideas about evolution, that place would be Galápagos and the organism

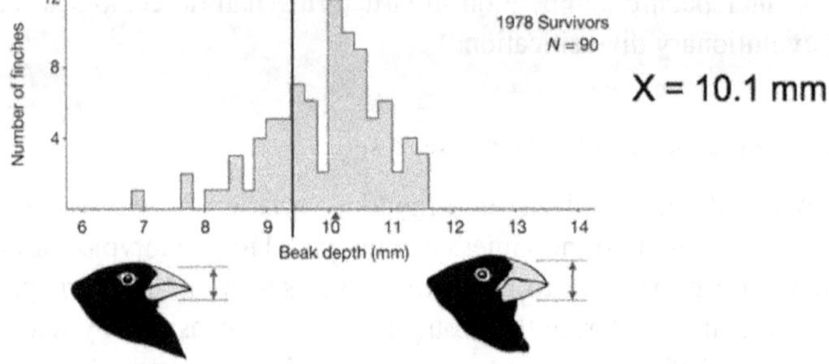

Figure 2.4 A selection episode on *Geospiza fortis* during the drought of 1977. The shift in population means (filled triangles) indicates selection for a larger beak (source: Freeman and Herron 2004).

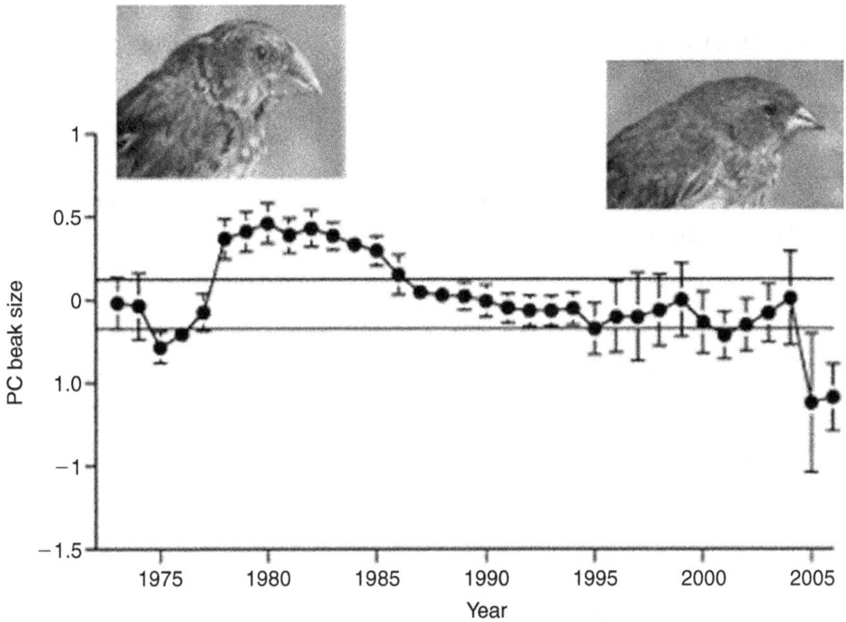

Figure 2.5 Evolutionary response to natural selection in *Geospiza fortis* over more than 30 years of study by the Grants. Dots represent means and vertical lines represent 95% confidence intervals of principal components (PC) values (source: Grant and Grant 2006).

would be the mockingbirds, followed by giant tortoises. Mockingbirds of Galápagos (*Mimus* spp., four currently recognized species) show geographic variation in morphology between islands that has been explained by local adaptation in isolation since all species are allopatric (Abbott and Abbott 1978; Bowman 1983). However, within mockingbird populations the strong dependence of rate of change on island size also suggests a strong role for genetic drift in these isolated populations (Hoeck *et al.* 2010). In addition, there is considerable variation in the degree of sociality across species and islands, attributed to habitat differences (Curry 1989; Curry and Grant 1990). Mockingbirds have responded to harshness of the environment by adjusting their mating system to a cooperative breeding or polygynandrous mating system. This type of "altruistic behavior", seemingly contradicting Darwin's main prediction about selfishness, is today explained in Darwinian terms (Curry 1988) through the inclusive fitness theory first proposed by Hamilton (1964).

Darwin's finches

The beak of the finch in fact epitomizes the classical example of morphological adaptation as first represented by Robert Bowman's (Bowman 1961, 1963, 1983) analogy of different species of Darwin's finch beak with different types of pliers

(Figure 2.6). Darwin's finches continue to surprise us as a remarkable "tool box" for our understanding of how evolution proceeds. Introgressive hybridization is another factor that contributes to beak variation between different species and populations of Darwin's finches (Grant *et al.* 2004). On Daphne, *G. fortis* and *G. scandens* have converged about 20% and 45% in beak shape and body size, respectively. Abzhanov *et al.* (2004, 2006) identified two genetic pathways intervening in the early development of Darwin's finch beaks: bone morphogenetic protein (*Bmp4* gene) regulates depth and width of the beak, while Calmodulin (*CaM* gene) regulates beak length. These two genes provide a mechanistic explanation for the evolution of widely diverse beak sizes and shapes across species from a basic finch beak.

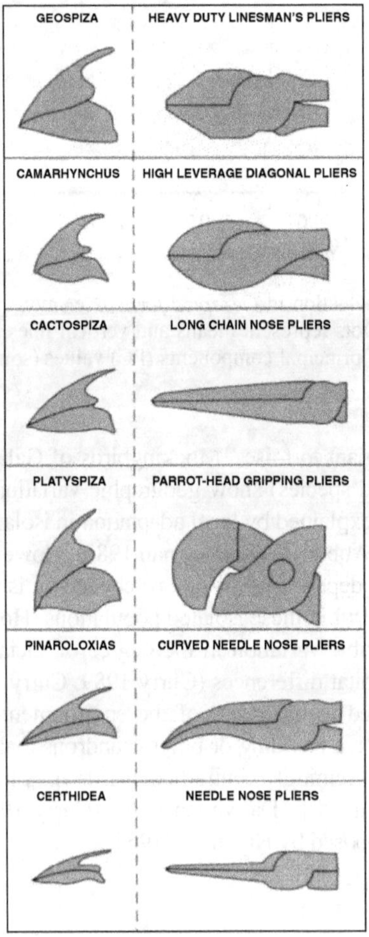

Figure 2.6 Analogy of the different species of Darwin's finch beak with different types of pliers (source: Grant and Grant 2008, based on Grant 1999 and redrawn by T. Grant from Bowman 1963).

Marine iguana

Darwin wrote of a sailor holding a marine iguana (*Amblyrhynchus cristatus*) under water for over an hour, after which the iguana emerged seemingly unharmed (Darwin 1883). Marine iguanas' pre-adaptations for diving (Dawson *et al.* 1977) make them the only marine lizard that feeds primarily on macrophytic algae in the intertidal and subtidal zones. Although most individuals forage at low tide in the intertidal zone or in dives of 10–15 minutes to depths less than five meters, the largest individuals (particularly males) may dive up to depths of 30 m for up to 45 minutes. The most remarkable adaptations for diving include highly efficient salt-excreting glands, osmoregulation capacity, physiological adaptations to tolerate anoxia and behavioral adaptations that allow them to raise their body temperature before diving and to recover temperature after a dive (Morgareidge and White 1969; Turner and Tracy 1983). Marine iguanas have many adaptations besides those related to diving. Martin Wikelski's (Wikelski and Thom 2000) long-term study has found that marine iguanas are able to shrink in size as a physiological response to stress, which enhances survival although the mechanisms are not yet well-understood. As an adaptation to their novel diet, marine iguanas' digestive tracts contain a community of endosymbiotic bacteria able to digest algae.

A strong example of the interaction of selection and drift comes from analyses of the major histocompatibility complex (MHC) of Galápagos birds. This complex of genes presents the first immune defense of organisms against foreign peptides, and it is the variability among alleles across these genes that determine the number and types of pathogens that an individual may resist: more variability within an individual leads to more resistance. The MHC is thought to be under strong selection for variation, with particularly beneficial alleles retained even across species boundaries and variability maintained through balancing selection by exposure to a variety of parasites (Piertney and Oliver 2006). The Galápagos penguin (*Spheniscus mendiculus*) descended from ancestors estimated to have colonized ~4 Mybp (Baker *et al.* 2006) and following that single colonization has undergone population bottlenecks with El Niño events (Valle and Coulter 1987; Vargas *et al.* 2006), reaching low points of only a few hundred individuals. Owing to the stochastic nature of these massive contractions, genetic drift is the strongest explanation for the extremely low allelic diversity found in Galápagos penguin MHC (Bollmer *et al.* 2007), a small fraction of the number found in a much smaller sample of other penguin species. However, the two alleles described by Bollmer *et al.* (2007) show clear signs of selection, both in the excess of nonsynonymous mutations at peptide binding regions of the alleles and in the similarity of these alleles to those in other taxa that have been retained by trans-species selection. Characterization of MHC in Darwin's finches also showed an unusually low polymorphism, characteristic of drift, combined with nonsynonymous mutations and trans-species clustering, suggesting selection favoring particular alleles (Sato *et al.* 2001).

Speciation and evolutionary diversification

Speciation explains the origin of species and specifically refers to the patterns and mechanisms driving the evolution of reproductive isolation between diverging conspecific populations that allow them to coexist as independent evolutionary units. The problem of the origin of species remains a major and central piece of evolutionary theory. Darwin's *The Origin of Species* paradoxically mentions little about how species originate. Despite the existence of a large amount of theoretical work, speciation remains a largely unknown aspect of evolutionary biology, mostly due to the lack of field empirical data to test the adequacy of proposed models.

Why, in Galápagos, have some groups radiated into a large number of species while others have radiated little or not at all? What is the role of time of arrival, ecological opportunities, vagility, sexual selection and other natural history traits? What is the role of ecological interactions such as interspecific competition and predation? Lastly, how much of the observed evolutionary diversification actually represents adaptive radiation (i.e. diversification driven by divergent selection) and how much of it is simple evolutionary radiation resulting from stochastic processes like founder effects and random drift?

General characteristics of the Galápagos evolutionary radiations

The chronology of colonization and diversification of the Galápagos organisms can be inferred by coupling the molecular phylogeny of different lineages with the geological history of the archipelago. The patterns of dispersal, colonization and evolutionary radiation for most of the Galápagos lineages studied so far share a number of features.

Colonization

Molecular studies allow estimates of approximate colonization dates for many Galápagos lineages, examples of which are shown in Table 2.1. This provides a timeline for gauging the speed of subsequent morphological and genetic change. For example, the great morphological (Livezey 1992) and behavioral change (Valle 1994, 2009) in the Galápagos cormorant happened rapidly, evolving from a highly mobile colonizing ancestor to a flightless condition so sedentary that most breeding colonies now show significant genetic differences from all others except their nearest neighbors (Duffie *et al.* 2009). The sedentariness of the Galápagos hawk increased over an even shorter time to the point where each island population is now genetically distinct (Bollmer *et al.* 2006), with significant morphological differences. The eight current island populations of the hawk are small (25–30 individuals for Santa Fé and Pinzón and only a few hundred in the largest populations). The extremely small size of some of the populations and their diverse and flexible diets suggests that genetic drift presents a very strong force driving rapid genetic and

Table 2.1 Colonization estimates and mainland relatives of Galápagos endemics

Taxon	*Common name*	*Mainland relative*	*Colonization estimate*	*Reference*
Arriving to current islands:				
Camarhynchus, *Certhidea*, and *Geospiza* finches	Darwin's finches	*Tiaris* finches	2–3 MYA	Sato *et al.* 2001
Geochelone nigra subspecies	Galápagos giant tortoises	Chaco tortoise *Geochelone chilensis*	2–3 MYA	Caccone *et al.* 1999, 2002
Phalacrocorax harrisi	Galápagos flightless cormorant	Double-crested cormorant *P. auritus*, and Neotropic Cormorants *P. brasilianus*	2 MYA	Kennedy *et al.* 2009
Buteo galapagoensis	Galápagos hawk	Swainson's hawk *B. swainsoni*	<300 KYA	Bollmer *et al.* 2006
Aedes taeniorhynchus	Black salt-water mosquito		~200 KYA	Bataille *et al.* 2009a
Arriving to now-submerged islands:				
Phyllodactilus spp.	Geckos		>9 MYA	Wright 1983
Microlophus spp.	Lava lizards		10 MYA	Wright 1983; Lopez *et al.* 1992; Kirizian *et al.* 2004
Conolophus and *Amblyrhynchus* iguanas	Land and marine iguanas		10 MYA	Wyles and Sarich 1983; Rassmann 1997; Gentile *et al.* 2009
Galapaganus spp.	Flightless Galápagos weevils		10 MYA	Sequeira *et al.* 2000
Galagete spp.	Microlepidopterans		>4 MYA	Schmitz *et al.* 2007

morphological change among hawk populations (Bollmer *et al.* 2003, 2005, 2006), and representing speciation in action. Like the mockingbirds described above, the hawk mating system differs across islands from conventional monogamous pairs on Española to 100% polyandrous breeding groups on most islands, providing rich fodder for evolutionary studies of behavioral variation (Parker 2009).

Phylogenetic patterns can also be used to estimate number of colonizations, and therefore the extent to which diversification of different groups occurred on the islands, indicated by monophyly representing single colonizations (Table 2.2). Some of the most diverse radiations on Galápagos resulted from on-site radiation following single successful colonization events.

Phylogeographic pattern of diversification

The diversification of most Galápagos lineages follows the "progression rule", a linear spatial (geographic)–temporal sequence of progressive colonization within the archipelago from older to younger islands. Thus, older species within a lineage are found on older islands and more recently evolved species on newer islands in a pattern that goes from southeast (older islands) to northwest (younger islands). This pattern fits reptiles (Caccone *et al.* 2002), mockingbirds (Arbogast *et al.* 2006) and bulimulid land snails (Parent and Crespi 2006), although the progression rule fails to explain in Darwin's finches, Galápagos hawks (Bollmer *et al.* 2006), the Galagete *microlepidopterans* (Schmitz *et al.* 2007), and the Galapaganus flightless weevil (Sequeira *et al.* 2000). The lack of linear sequence of colonizations may be explained by the fact that the Galápagos Islands did not originate in a linear sequence but rather as clusters of islands about the same age around the hot spot, while the northern and northeastern islands of the archipelago owe their origin to the Galápagos spreading center (Geist 1996, 2009). Another cause seems related to species vagility (Parent *et al.* 2008): among organisms with high vagility, forward and back colonizations are expected to be frequent. Coupling geological history with the time of arrival of the ancestor of the Galápagos cormorant suggests that the western coast of Santa Cruz may have been its center of colonization (Kennedy *et al.* 2009). Subsequently they colonized Santiago, then Isabela and Fernandina as these newer islands appeared and their original foraging grounds changed and deteriorated around Santa Cruz. Range shifts and range contraction during speciation and diversification seems to have been common among Galápagos organisms. Some evidence comes from Galagetes (Schmitz *et al.* 2007); in addition, the restricted distribution of the Pink land iguana (Conolophus marthae) (Gentile *et al.* 2009) may be a relic of a much wider distribution in the archipelago. Finally, recent colonization by the Galápagos hawk (Bollmer *et al.* 2006) when the islands had more or less their current spatial distribution, shows that subsequent dispersal is likely to take place in any direction resulting in rapid expansion followed by further divergence.

Table 2.2 Inferred monophyletic diversification from single colonizations. Number of colonization events and diversification of some of Galápagos' endemic taxa

Taxon	*Common name*	*Number of colonizations*	*Number of extant Species*	*Reference*
Camarhynchus, Certhidea, and *Geospiza* finches	Darwin's finches	One	14 or 15	Sato *et al.* 2001
Mimus spp.	Mockingbirds	One	4	Arbogast *et al.* 2006
Geochelone nigra	Giant tortoises	One	11 subspecies (+ 4 extinct)	Caccone *et al.* 1999, 2002
Conolophus and *Amblyrhynchus* iguanas	Land and marine iguanas	One	2 genera, 4 species	Wyles and Sarich 1983; Rassmann 1997; Gentile *et al.* 2009
Bulimulus spp.	Bulimulid land snails	One	71 species	Parent andCrespi 2006; Parent *et al.* 2008
Galagete spp.	Microlepidoptera	One	12 species	Schmitz *et al.* 2007
Galapaganus spp.	Galápagos weevils	One	10 species	Sequeria *et al.* 2000
Aegialomys, Nesoryzomis, Megarizomys spp.	Rice rats	~Three	5 (+3 extinct)	Clark 1984; Steadman 2009
Microlophus spp.	Lava lizards	Two		Benavides *et al.* 2007
Philodryas, Alsophis spp.	Snakes	Three	3	Thomas 1997; Grehan 2001
Phyllodactilus	Leaf-toed geckos	Three	6	Wright 1983

Rates of speciation

Molecular phylogenetic analyses revealed that rates of speciation were not constant but varied substantially with periods of rapid and slow speciation. Thus, among Darwin's finches only the four basic types (warbler finch, Cocos finch, sharp-beak and vegetarian finch) evolved 1–2 Mybp, while the five tree finches and six ground finches evolved during the last million years (Grant and Grant 2008). Speciation and diversification of the Darwin's finches may have accelerated as the number of extant islands increased, changes in level of isolation between islands and subsequent changes in altitude, as well as changes in climate (from warmer and wetter to arid) and vegetation, all of which increased habitat heterogeneity (Grant and Grant 2008). That explanation is in part contested (Parent *et al.* 2008) under the argument that there is no firm evidence that the number of islands has increased over time. However, a pattern similar to that envisaged for Darwin's finches has also been inferred for the Galagete (Schmitz *et al.* 2007), which, following colonization and the first divergence within the Galápagos about 3.3 Mybp, underwent a first "mini-radiation" 2.0 Mybp and the beginning of a large radiation took place about 1.8 Mybp, coinciding with the emergence of new islands.

Cryptic speciation

Molecular genetics analyses revealed recurrent cases of cryptic speciation among quite different lineages of Galápagos endemics. These include giant tortoises (two morphologically similar populations but highly differentiated at the genetic level on Santa Cruz; Russello *et al.* 2005), Darwin's finches (two morphologically similar species of warbler finch; Tonnis *et al.* 2005), Galagetes (Schmitz *et al.* 2007) and the Galápagos hawk with genetically differentiated inter-island populations (Bollmer *et al.* 2005, 2006). A final example is a mite recognized as a single species, Myialges caulotoon, found on flightless cormorants and Galápagos hawks. This mite is vectored by hippoboscid flies, and the cormorant and hawk are known to have ectoparasitic hippoboscids of two different genera; thus, genetic analysis of the mite revealed two reciprocally monophyletic lineages (Whiteman *et al.* 2006). Cryptic speciation among Galápagos organisms is undoubtedly much more common than is currently suspected or described, but a determination of the full extent requires further molecular genetics and phylogenetic analyses of most organisms that have not yet been studied.

These examples provide a few illustrations of the pivotal role that Galápagos has played in the development of evolutionary thought. That role continues today in many ongoing studies, and will undoubtedly continue into the future as evolution proceeds under the scrutiny of a new generation of scientists in this iconic archipelago.

Acknowledgements

Our own work in Galápagos has been made possible by the support of the Galápagos National Park and the Charles Darwin Foundation. Our understanding of evolutionary events has benefited from interactions with a large number of colleagues and collaborators, most notably Peter and Rosemary Grant, Tjitte de Vries, Noah K. Whiteman, and Jennifer K. Bollmer. We would like to thank Alexandra Ávila for reading and making suggestion to an early draft of the manuscript.

References

Abbott, I. and L.K. Abbott. 1978. Multivariate study of morphological variation in Galápagos and Ecuadorian mockingbirds, *Condor* 80:302–308.

Abzhanov, A., W.P. Kuo, C. Hartmann, B.R. Grant, P.R. Grant and C.J. Tabin. 2004. Bmp4 and morphological variation of beaks in Darwin's finches, *Science* 305:1462–1465.

Abzhanov, A., M. Protas, P.R. Grant, B.R. Grant, and C.J. Tabin. 2006. The Calmodulin pathway and evolution of elongated beak morphology in Darwin's finches, *Nature* 442:563–567.

Arbogast, B.S., S.V. Drovetski, L.R. Curry, P.T. Boag, G. Seutin, P.R. Grant, B.R. Grant and D.J. Anderson. 2006. The origin and diversification of Galápagos mockingbirds, *Evolution* 60:370–382.

Baker, A.J., S.L. Pereira, O.P. Haddrath and K.A. Edge. 2006. Multiple gene evidence for expansion of extant penguins out of Antarctica due to global cooling, *Proc. R. Soc. Lond. B.* 273:11–17.

Bataille, A., A.A. Cunningham, V. Cedeno, L. Patino, A. Constantinou, L.D. Kramer and S.J. Goodman. 2009. Natural colonization and adaptation of a mosquito species in Galápagos and its implications for disease threats to endemic wildlife, *Proc. Nat. Acad. Sci. USA* 106:10230–10235.

Benavides, E., R. Baum, D. McClellan, and J.W. Sites, Jr. 2007. Molecular phylogenetics of the lizard genus Microlophus (Squamata: Tropiduridae): aligning and retrieving indel signal from nuclear introns, *Syst. Biol.* 56:776–797.

Boag, P.T. and P.R. Grant. 1978. Heritability of external morphology in Darwin's finches, *Nature* 274:793–794.

Bollmer, J.L., R.T. Kimball, N.K. Whiteman, J.H. Sarasola, and P.G. Parker. 2006. Phylogeography of the Galápagos hawk (*Buteo galapagoensis*): a recent arrival to the Galápagos Islands, *Molecular Phylogenetics and Evolution* 39:237–247

Bollmer, J.L., T. Sanchez, M.D. Cannon, D. Sanchez, D. Cannon, J.C. Bednarz, T. de Vries, M.S. Struve and P.G. Parker. 2003. Variation in morphology and mating system among island populations of Galápagos Hawks, *The Condor* 105:428–438.

Bollmer, J.L., F.H. Vargas, P.G. Parker. 2007. Low MHC variation in the endangered Galápagos penguin (Spheniscus mendiculus), *Immunogenetics* 59:593–602.

Bollmer, J.L., N.K. Whiteman, M.D. Cannon, J.C. Bednarz, T. de Vries and P.G. Parker. 2005. Population genetics of the Galápagos Hawk (Buteo galapagoensis): genetic monomorphism within isolated populations, *Auk* 122:1210–1224.

Bowman, R.I. 1961. Morphological differentiation and adaptation in the Galápagos finches, *Univ. Clif. Publ. Zool.* 58:1–326.

Bowman, R.I. 1963. Evolutionary patterns in Darwin's finches, *Occas. Papers Calif. Acad. Sci.* 44:107–140.

Bowman, R.I. 1983. Contributions to science from the Galápagos, in R. Perry (ed.), *Galápagos*, pp. 277–311 (Pergamon Press: Oxford).

Bowman, R.I., M. Berson and A.E. Levinton (ed.). 1983. *Patterns of evolution in Galápagos organisms* (American Association for the Advancement of Science: Pacific Division, San Francisco, CA).

Caccone, A., J.P. Gibbs, V. Ketmaier, E. Suatoni, and J. R. Powell. 1999. Origin and evolutionary relationships of giant Galápagos tortoises, *Proc. Natl. Acad. Sci. USA* 96:13223–13228.

Caccone, A., G. Gentile, J.P. Gibbs, T.H. Fritts, H.L. Snell, J. Betts and J.R. Powell. 2002. Phylogeography and history of giant Galápagos tortoises, *Evolution* 56:2052–2066.

Causton, C.E., S.B. Peck, B.J. Sinclair, L. Roque-Albelo, C.J. Hodgson and B. Landry. 2006. Alien insects: Threats and implications for conservation of the Galápagos Islands, *Annals of the Entomological Society of America* 99:121–143.

Clark, D.A. 1984 Native land mammals, in R. Perry (ed.), *Key environments: Galápagos*, pp. 225–231 (Pergamon Press: Oxford, UK).

Curry, R.L. 1988. Influence of Kinship on Helping Behavior in Galápagos Mockingbirds, *Behavioral Ecology and Sociobiology* 22:141–152.

Curry, R.L. 1989. Geographic Variation in Social Organization of Galápagos mockingbirds: Ecological Correlates of Group Territoriality and Cooperative Breeding, *Behavioral Ecology and Sociobiology* 25:147–160.

Curry, R.L., and P.R. Grant. 1990. Galápagos mockingbirds: territorial cooperative breeding in a climatically variable environment, in P.B. Stacey and W.D. Koenig (ed.) *Cooperative breeding in birds: long-term studies of ecology and behavior*, pp. 290–331 (Cambridge Univ. Press: Cambridge, U.K).

Darwin, C. 1883. *Journal of Researches* (New Edition: Appleton, N.Y).

Dawson, W.R., G.A. Bartholomew and A.F. Bennett. 1977. A Reappraisal of the Aquatic Specializations of the Galápagos Marine Iguana (*Amblyrhynchus cristatus*), *Evolution* 31: 891–897.

Duffie, C.V., T.C. Glenn, F.H. Vargas and P.G. Parker. 2009. Genetic structure within and between island populations of the flightless cormorant (*Phalacrocorax harrisi*), *Molecular Ecology* 18:2103–2111.

Fisher, R.A. 1930. *The genetical theory of natural selection* (Clarendon: Oxford, UK).

Geist, D. 1996. On the emergence and submergence of the Galápagos Islands, *Not. Galápagos* 56:5–9.

Geist, D. 2009. Islands on the move, in T. de Roy (ed.), *Galápagos-preserving Darwin`s legacy*, pp. 130–137 (David Bateman Ltd: New Zealand).

Gentile, G., A. Fabiani, C. Marquez, H.L., Snell, H.M. Snell, W. Tapia and V. Sbordoni. 2009. An overlooked pink species of land iguana in the Galápagos, *PNAS* 106: 507–511.

Grant, P.R. and B.R. Grant. 2000. Quantitative genetic variation in populations of Darwin's finches, in T. A. Mousseau, B. Sinervo and J. Endler (ed.), *Adaptive variation in the wild*, pp. 3–40 (Academic Press: New York, NY).

Grant, P.R., and B.R. Grant. 2006. Evolution of character displacement in Darwin's finches, *Science* 313: 224–226.

Grant, P.R. and B.R. Grant. 2008. *How and why species multiply: the radiation of Darwin's finches* (Princeton University Press: Princeton, NJ).

Grant, P.R., B.R. Grant, J.A. Markert, L.F. Keller and K. Petren. 2004. Convergent evolution of Darwin's finches caused by introgressive hybridization and selection, *Evolution* 58: 1588–1599.

Grehan, J. 2001 Biogeography and evolution of the Galápagos: integration of the biological and geological evidence, *Biol. J. Linn. Soc.* 74:267–287.

Hamilton, W.D. 1964. The genetical evolution of social behavior, I and II, *J. Theor. Biology* 7:1–52.

Hoeck, P.E.A., J.L. Bollmer, P.G. Parker and L.F. Keller. 2010. Differentiation with drift: a spatio-temporal genetic analysis of Galápagos mockingbird populations (*Mimus* spp.), *Phil. Trans. R. Soc. B.* 365:1127–1138.

Keller, L.F., P.R. Grant, B.R. Grant and K. Petren. 2001. Heritability of morphological traits in Darwin's finches: misidentified paternity and maternal effects, *Heredity* 87: 325–336.

Kennedy, M., C.A. Valle and H.G. Spencer. 2009. The phylogenetic position of the Galápagos Cormorant, *Molecular Phylogenetics and Evolution* 53: 94–98.

Kizirian, D., A. Trager, M.A. Donnelly and J.W. Wright. 2004 Evolution of Galápagos Island lava lizards (Iguania: Tropiduridae: Microlophus), *Mol. Phylogenet. Evol.* 32:761–769.

Lack, D. 1947. *Darwin's finches* (Cambridge University Press: Cambridge, UK).

Livezey, B.C. 1992. Flightlessness in the Galápagos cormorant (*Compsohalieus [Nannopterum] harrisi*): heterochroncy, giantism and specialization, *Zoological Journal of the Linnean Society* 105:155–224.

Lopez, T.J., E.D. Hauselman, L.R. Maxson and J.W. Wright. 1992 Preliminary analysis of phylogenetic relationships among Galápagos Island lizards of the genus Tropidurus, *Amphibia-Reptilia* 13:327–339.

Morgareidge, K.R. and F.N. White. 1969. Cutaneous vascular changes during heating and cooling in the Galápagos marine iguana, *Nature* 223:587–591.

Orr, H.A. 2009. Fitness and its role in evolutionary genetics, *Nature Reviews Genetics* 10:531–539.

Parent, C.E. and B.J. Crespi. 2006. Sequential colonization and diversification of Galápagos endemic land snail genus Bulimulus (*Gastropoda, Stylommatophora*), *Evolution* 60: 2311–2328.

Parent, C.E., A. Caccone and K. Petren. 2008. Colonization and diversification of Galápagos terrestrial fauna: a phylogenetic and biogeographical synthesis, *Philosophical Transactions of the Royal Society B* 363:3347–3361.

Perry, R (ed.). 1984. *Galápagos* (Pergamon Press: Oxford, UK).

Parker, P.G. 2009. A most unusual hawk: One mother and several fathers, in de Roy, T (ed.), *Galápagos-preserving Darwin's legacy*, pp. 130–137 (David Bateman Ltd: New Zealand).

Piertney, S.B. and M.K. Oliver. 2006. The evolutionary ecology of the major histocompatibility complex, *Heredity* 96:70–91.

Rassmann, K. 1997. Evolutionary age of the Galapagos iguanas predates the age of the present Galapagos Islands, *Mol. Phylogenet. Evol.* 7:158–172.

Roy, T. de (ed.). 2009. *Galápagos-preserving Darwin's legacy* (David Bateman Ltd: New Zealand).

Russello, M.A., S. Glaberman, J.P. Gibbs, C. Marquez, J.R. Powell and A. Caccone. 2005. A cryptic taxon of Galapagos tortoise in conservation peril, *Biol. Lett.* 1:287–290.

Sato, A., W.E. Mayer, H. Tichy, P.R. Grant, B.R. Grant and J. Klein. 2001. Evolution of MHC Class II B genes in Darwin's finches and their closest relatives: birth of a new gene, *Immunogenetics* 53:792–801.

Schmitz, P., A. Cibois and B. Landry. 2007. Molecular phylogeny and dating of an insular endemic moth radiation inferred from mitochondrial and nuclear genes: the genus Galagete (Lepidoptera: Autostichidae) of the Galapagos Islands, *Mol. Phylogenet. Evol.* 45:180–192.

Sequeira, A.S., A.A. Lanteri, M.A. Scataglini, V.A. Confalonieri and B.D. Farrell. 2000. Are flightless Galapaganus weevils older than the Galapagos Islands they inhabit? *Heredity* 85:20–29.

Snell, H.M., P.A. Stone and H.L. Snell. 1996. A summary of geographic characteristics of the Galápagos Islands, *J. Biogeography* 23:619–624.

Steadman, D.W. 2009. Vertebrate diversity – the long view, in T. de Roy (ed.), *Galápagos – preserving Darwin`s legacy*, pp. 46–52 (David Bateman Ltd: New Zealand).

Thomas, R.A. 1997 Galápagos terrestrial snakes: biogeography and systematics, *Herpetol. Nat. Hist.* 5:19–40.

Tonnis, B., P.R. Grant, B.R. Grant and K. Petren. 2005. Habitat selection and ecological speciation in Galapagos warbler finches (*Certhidea olivacea* and *Certhidea fusca*), *Proc. R. Soc. B* 272:819–826.

Turner, J.S., and C.R. Tracy. 1983. Blood flow to appendages and the control of heat exchange in American Alligators, *Physiological Zoology* 56:195–200.

Tye, A., and H.L. Snell. 2002. Status and threats to the terrestrial biodiversity of the Galápagos, in *A biodiversity vision for the Galápagos Islands* (Charles Darwin Foundation and World Wildlife Fund: Puerto Ayora, Galápagos).

Valle, C.A. 1994. *The ecology and evolution of sequential polyandry in Galápagos cormorants (*Compsohalieus [Nannopterum] harrisi*)*, Ph.D. dissertation (Princeton University, Princeton, USA)

Valle, C.A. 2009. The Flightless Cormorant – the evolution of female rule, in T. de Roy (ed.), *Galápagos-preserving Darwin`s legacy*, pp. 162–169 (David Bateman Ltd: New Zealand).

Valle, C.A., and M.C. Coulter. 1987. Present status of the flightless cormorant, Galápagos penguin, and greater flamingo populations in the Galápagos Islands, Ecuador after the 1982–83 El Niño, *Condor* 89:276–281.

Vargas, F.H., S. Harrison, S. Rea and D.W. Macdonald. 2006. Biological effects of El Niño on the Galápagos penguin, *Biological Conservation* 127:107–114.

Whiteman, N.K., P. Sanchez, J.F. Merkel, H. Klompen and P.G. Parker. 2006. Cryptic host specificity of an avian skin mite (Epidermoptidae) vectored by louse flies (Hippoboscidae) associated with endemic Galápagos bird species, *Journal of Parasitology* 92:1218–1228.

Wikelski, M. and Thom C. (2000). Marine Iguanas Shrink to Survive El Niño, *Nature* 403:37–38.

Wright, J.W. 1983. The evolution and biogeography of the lizards of the Galápagos archipelago: evolutionary genetics of Phyllodactylus and Tropidurus populations in R.I. Bowman, M. Berson and A.E. Leviton (ed.) *Patterns of evolution in Galápagos organisms*, pp. 123–155. (American Association for the Advancement of Science, Pacific Division: San Francisco, CA).

Wright, S. 1931. Evolution in Mendelian populations, *Genetics* 16:97–159.

Wright, S. 1932. The roles of mutation, inbreeding, crossbreeding and selection in evolution, *Proc. 6th Int. Cong. Genet.* 1:356–366.

Wyles, J.S. and V.M. Sarich. 1983. Are the Galápagos iguanas older than the Galápagos? Molecular evolution and colonization models for the archipelago, in R.I. Bowman, M. Berson and A.E. Leviton (ed.) *Patterns of evolution in Galápagos organisms*, pp. 177–185. (American Association for the Advancement of Science, Pacific Division: San Francisco, CA).

3 Evolution of pathogens and parasites on the Galápagos Islands

Patricia G. Parker and Noah K. Whiteman

The history of life on Galápagos has been viewed from the perspective of the islands themselves as ever-changing physical entities (e.g. Geist *et al.* 2002; Munro and Rowland 1996), and from the perspective of the living residents. The highly endemized lineages of birds, mammals, and reptiles have been studied extensively and estimates made for their colonization dates and patterns of diversification, which form the backbone of modern evolutionary studies (see Chapter 2, Valle and Parker). However, the identity, prevalence, impact, and general biology of the parasites and pathogens that inhabit Galápagos species are largely unknown. Here we propose a general framework for considering these organisms that have been ignored, possibly because they are so small. We have begun to appreciate that they, too, are evolving, undergoing adaptive radiations, and invading unoccupied niches. We will leave the applied concerns of surveillance and potential corrective measures for these parasites and pathogens to another chapter (see Chapter 10, Parker and Deem), and explore using them as study species. Going forward, we will use the word "parasite" to refer collectively to viruses, bacteria, and other organisms that live in or on the body of another organism known as the host, from which they draw their nutrition at the expense of the host's fitness.

We have measured the distribution and prevalence of parasites among 26 native and three introduced bird species on 16 islands (Parker *et al.* 2006; Parker 2009b). Across islands, we have documented parasites (1) with long histories with their avian hosts; (2) that have jumped from one host species to another; and (3) that are recent arrivals, some with major impacts. We will discuss each of these categories in turn.

Colonization of parasites with hosts

All biological lineages inhabiting Galápagos are descendants of ancestors that colonized the island system and successfully reproduced. Undoubtedly, there were many unsuccessful colonists. Before human inhabitants complicated the natural life on Galápagos, colonizing parasites arrived exclusively with naturally arriving organisms, such as migratory birds that were blown off course, arthropods caught up in airstreams, or collections of seeds, seedlings, and animals rafting on the ocean's surface from coastal tectonic disturbances. These animals had parasites. If the colonist did not survive, its parasites likely did not survive, unless they jumped to a new host. Even if the colonist did survive, the survival of the parasite depended on the ecosystem or on the colonist, including abiotic features often critical to parasite survival such as seasonal or diurnal patterns in temperature or humidity. Some disease-causing agents may eliminate individuals not healthy enough to survive the colonization. Because of this filtering, far fewer parasites colonize than hosts do, and biological lineages on islands are exposed to fewer parasites than those on continents.

Parasites that successfully establish with the colonizing host lineage may experience environments dramatically different from their ancestral environment. Some may attempt to colonize a new host if necessary, which may allow them to persist until a better alternative appears, or they may adapt to the new host. Thus, the rate at which new host–parasite relationships are formed accelerates on islands, where simplified communities present few options. We will present one detailed example of the co-evolutionary relationships that can result as both host and parasite adapt to their new environments by focusing on the Galápagos hawk (*Buteo galapagoensis*) and the ectoparasite lineages that accompanied its colonization.

The Galápagos hawk (*B. galapagoensis*) (Figure 3.1) is the apex diurnal predator in Galápagos on the islands of Española, Fernandina, Isabela, Marchena, Pinta, Pinzón, Santa Fe, and Santiago. The hawk is endangered because of its small population size and because hawks were extirpated from three large islands (Floreana, Santa Cruz and San Cristobal) by human persecution. The hawk is famous for its unusual mating system, i.e. cooperative polyandry, in which one female and up to eight males cooperate to rear chicks in territories they occupy year-round (de Vries 1975; Parker 2009a). Ecological and population genetic studies on the hawk (de Vries 1975; Faaborg *et al.* 1995; Bollmer *et al.* 2005, 2006) inspired a detailed comparative study on the ecology and evolutionary genetics of the hawk's co-colonizing parasite community.

B. galapagoensis is among the youngest lineages of endemic vertebrates in Galápagos. Molecular phylogenetic evidence (Riesing *et al.* 2003; Bollmer *et al.* 2006) indicated that *B. galapagoensis* is most closely related to *B. swainsoni* (Swainson's hawk) and that the two recently separated from a common ancestor. Using a molecular clock, the split between *B. galapagoensis* and *B. swainsoni* was estimated to have occurred less than 250,000 years ago (Bollmer *et al.* 2006) and, in fact, *B. swainsoni* is paraphyletic with respect to *B. galapagoensis*. Before the advent of modern phylogenetic methods, *B. swainsoni* was deemed unlikely to be the closest relative of *B. galapagoensis* (de Vries 1975). Interestingly, Theresa Clay, a louse systematist, reported the feather louse *Degeeriella regalis* exclusively from the Galápagos and Swainson's hawks (Clay 1958), suggesting a close relationship between these two bird species that was confirmed by DNA sequence data decades later.

When the ancestors of the Galápagos hawk (*B. galapagoensis*) colonized Galápagos, they brought with them a subset of the parasite community living

Figure 3.1 Photograph of a Galápagos hawk on Isla Fernandina in 2004 (source: J. Rabenold).

within the mainland population (Parker *et al.* 2006; Palma 1994). At least five ectoparasite species have been regularly found on the Galápagos hawk, including a fly *Icosta nigra* (Diptera: Hippoboscidae) that feeds on blood; the feather louse *D. regalis* (Ischnocera: Philopteridae) mentioned above (Figure 3.2); the amblyceran louse *Colpocephalum turbinatum* (Amblycera: Menoponidae); an undescribed feather louse in the genus *Craspedorrhynchus*, which is restricted to the head region of the host; and a skin mite *Myialges caulotoon* that uses *I. nigra* as a vector and parasitizes that fly during part of its lifecycle. Each of these species has been reported from *Buteo swainsoni* or other raptors on the mainland, although each now probably represents a cryptic species unique to the Galápagos hawk. We next discuss their natural history, as well as the ecological and evolutionary interactions between the Galápagos hawk and these parasites.

The lice *Colpocephalum turbinatum* and *D. regalis* differ in several natural history traits, including dispersal ability (Marshall 1981). Transmission is primarily vertical between parents and offspring during brooding in *D. regalis*, while

Figure 3.2 Photograph of the louse *Degeeriella regalis*, which parasitizes the Galápagos hawk.

C. turbinatum primarily transmits horizontally, during interactions such as copulation or fighting. However, both species are capable of reproducing on a single host and are relatively permanent parasites. The ecology of the fly *Icosta nigra* is less studied, but it is highly vagile and is found on several falconiform hosts (Maa 1969). All of these parasites are restricted to *B. galapagoensis* in the Galápagos Islands, but host species specificity is generally inversely related to dispersal abilities (Clayton *et al.* 2004). Given the variation across the three parasite species in dispersal, we predicted that *D. regalis* would have the highest degree of population genetic structure, followed by *C. turbinatum* and *I. nigra*. Due to its vertical transmission, we also predicted that only *D. regalis* would track the host's evolutionary history across the archipelago. We used the evolutionary histories of these parasites to create a hypothesis of the host's evolutionary history in the archipelago (Whiteman and Parker 2005; Nieberding and Olivieri 2007).

This system presented a context in which to study host–parasite co-speciation in its earliest stages. Whereas lice and their hosts have served as excellent examples of co-speciation (Hafner *et al.* 1994), there was very little information on whether macroevolutionary patterns, such as co-speciation of parasites and hosts, were recapitulated at the microevolutionary scale. This was a useful system because (1) island populations of the host are genetically and phenotypically differentiating but the overall lineage is young, and (2) a stable parasite community occurs throughout the distribution of the hawk, and variation in life history and population dynamics allows a comparative approach across parasite species.

The patterns

Gene flow of *B. galapagoensis* is restricted by distance between islands and is specifically restricted by water (Bollmer *et al.* 2005, 2006), as *Buteo* species avoid flying over bodies of water. Several Galápagos hawk populations are among the least genetically variable wild bird populations in the world; each small population is nearly fixed for different alleles, including at the most genetically variable neutral markers (minisatellites). Thus, fixation indices between islands approached unity in some cases, indicating fixed differences among monomorphic island populations. Mitochondrial DNA (mtDNA) sequences are typically used for phylogeographic studies and we sequenced >3 kb of mtDNA from all island populations of the Galápagos hawk and from Swainson's hawks. The few genetically variable sites that we found were typically fixed within island populations; either islands had private haplotypes or there were shared haplotypes between islands with no variation within islands. Thus, for both nuclear and mitochondrial genomes, almost no intra-island variation and only slight inter-island variation existed, consistent with the hawk's small population sizes and recent colonization of the islands, and demonstrating the effectiveness of water as a barrier to gene flow for soaring flight requiring thermals or updrafts.

We genotyped one parasite individual of each species from each hawk individual and sampled multiple hawks (at least nine) on each island, usually >20 hawks per island. Using mitochondrial DNA sequence data for four ectoparasite species (*Colpocephalum turbinatum, Craspedorrhynchus* sp., *D. regalis*, and *Icosta nigra*), we found highly structured populations among islands and significant patterns of isolation by distance (Whiteman *et al.* 2006a, 2007, 2009). However, the patterns of gene flow and population history in the parasite tracked those in the host only in *D. regalis*, which has the highest degree of vertical transmission. Modern coalescent methods (Nielsen and Wakeley 2001) allow decoupling of population structure from population history and allow estimates of migration rates and population divergence times. First, we found that the population structure (using the fixation index) between islands of the louse *D. regalis* was positively and significantly related to that of the host as estimated by nuclear markers, even after correcting for geographic distance between islands. Second, we found that population divergence times of the Galápagos hawk and the louse *D. regalis*, based on mtDNA data, were positively and significantly related after correcting for geographic distance between islands (Figure 3.3). This suggests that *D. regalis* moves with hawk genes in contemporary (ecological) time in the form of recent inter-island gene flow, so the colonization histories of the two species are linked. Divergence time between populations and inter-population migration rate of *D. regalis* lice are correlated, but not in a linear way (Figure 3.4). Why is this? Both migration rate and divergence time between populations of hawks and *D. regalis* lice depend on geographic distance; for migration rate the relationship is asymptotic, as the likelihood of successful migration declines with distance. This suggests that there is still some gene flow at relatively short geographic distances between populations that recently split, but that gene flow is negligible for distant populations that split >20,000 years ago.

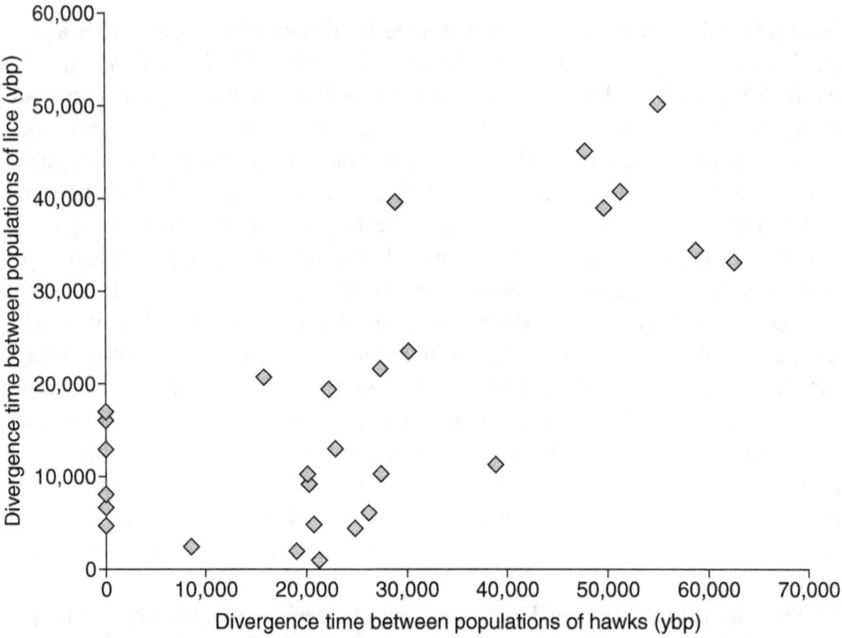

Figure 3.3 Plot of population divergence times for the Galápagos hawk and the louse *Degeeriella regalis*. Data was estimated using the MDIV program. We assumed ten generations/year for the louse and a minimum breeding age of the hawks of three years. We assumed a mtDNA mutation rate of 9×10^{-8} per base pair per generation for both hawks and the lice.

As *D. regalis* individuals move from mother to baby hawk, so lice move from mother to daughter island populations, as new populations of hawks are founded through metapopulation dynamics. This pattern was not found for any of the other parasite species and we speculate that this is due to their higher probability of moving between islands without host genes. We also showed that because *D. regalis* tracked host population structure, its phylogeographic history could be used as a proxy for the host (Whiteman and Parker 2005; Whiteman *et al.* 2007) because there simply was not enough variation in the host's mtDNA dataset to provide information on how four of eight hawk populations were related to one another.

For the two parasites that were not the focus of detailed study we found that while morphological differences between *Craspedorrhynchus* lice on Galápagos and Swainson's hawks were small, they were highly divergent genetically (Whiteman *et al.* 2009). So, while morphological change in parasites is conservative compared to their hosts, neutral genetic change can proceed much more rapidly. Within the Galápagos, our limited sampling showed significant population genetic structure among islands. For the mite *Myialges caulotoon*, we found two cryptic species,

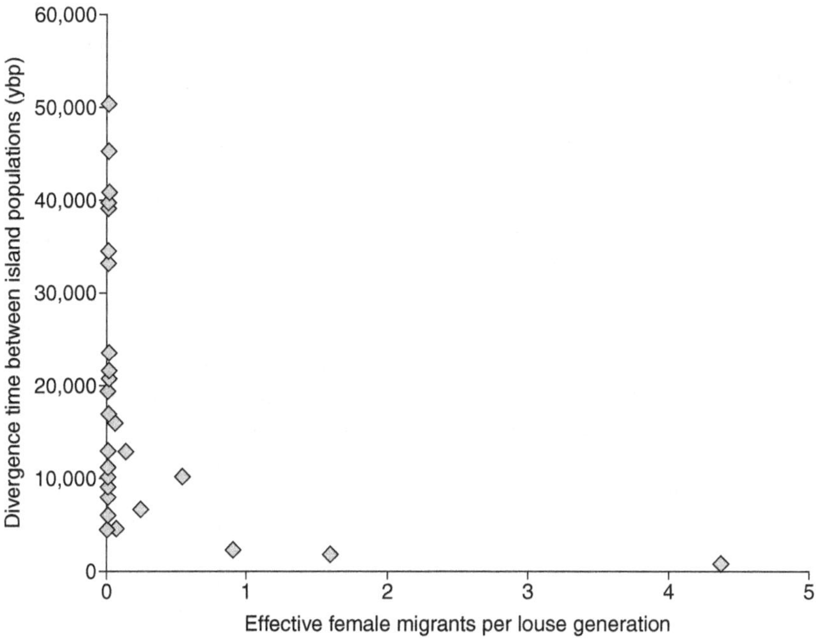

Figure 3.4 Population divergence times versus migration rate of *Degeeriella regalis* lice across eight island populations. Data was estimated using the MDIV program.

one found on the hippoboscid fly species that feeds on flightless cormorants and one found on the hippoboscid species that feeds on hawks. Although hawks and cormorants often occupy the same habitat in the Galápagos, particularly on Fernandina, there is no mitochondrial gene flow between the two mite lineages (Whiteman *et al.* 2006b). In both cases, small morphological changes in parasite lineages mask enormous amounts of neutral genetic divergence.

In summary, the Galápagos hawk and its ectoparasite community provided a rich framework to explore the early stages of host–parasite co-diversification. It showed that ecological and life history traits believed to underlie macroevolutionary patterns, such as co-speciation in hosts and parasites, are important at the microevolutionary scale, providing a link between microevolutionary processes and macroevolutionary patterns. This also underscores the importance of preserving co-evolutionary units in the Galápagos, including native symbionts and parasites, for their own sakes and for what they can tell us about their hosts (Whiteman and Parker 2005).

Host switching

It would normally be difficult to trace the history of the relationship of parasite and host lineages, partly due to variation in host species diversity in time and space. On islands, we predict this to be simplified by the limited number of host species available.

One example of a host switch is the microfilarid nematode infecting the Galápagos penguin (*Spheniscus mendiculus*) and Galápagos flightless cormorant (*Phalacrocorax harrisi*) (Merkel *et al.* 2007); genetics and morphology reveal the same parasite infecting both host species. The geographic ranges of these two Galápagos endemic birds overlap almost completely along the coasts of Isabela and Fernandina, and they are almost certainly bitten by the same hemophagous arthropods. Microfilaria of similar characteristics have been described from a large number of Phalacrocoracidae (cormorants and allies) species throughout the world (e.g. Cleland and Johnston 1911) but none from many studies of wild penguin populations. Thus, we speculate that the cormorant is the primary host, and that the nematode "jumped" to the penguin through shared arthropod vectors. We have surmised, by having found cormorant blood meals in individual mosquitoes, that the vector may be the black salt-marsh mosquito *Aedes taeniorhynchus* found commonly along these same shores (Bastille *et al.* 2009a; Siers *et al.* 2010).

The susceptibility of Galápagos penguins to this parasite may be attributed to its being the only tropical penguin; other penguins may also be susceptible, but live in climates that may not sustain an annual infection cycle. In addition, we expect the Galápagos penguin to be particularly susceptible due to its lack of exposure to pathogens in general (Travis *et al.* 2006) and its extremely reduced major histocompatibility complex (MHC) variability (Bollmer *et al.* 2007). The MHC is responsible for identifying and presenting pathogen peptides on cell surfaces to cytotoxic "killer" T-cells (Hughes and Nei 1993). Therefore, selection favors diversity across loci, making MHC genes the most genetically variable loci. In a single 157 base pair region of one MHC gene, seven penguin species showed between 16 and 23 variable positions per species, while Galápagos penguins showed only three variable positions, indicating a striking lack of polymorphism that likely leaves them unprotected from many pathogens that continental penguins could resist (Bollmer *et al.* 2007).

The geographic spread of this parasite would result from movement of infected birds or vectors from point to point. Significant geographic clustering of *A. taeniorhynchus* genetic groups suggests limited cross-archipelago movements (Bataille *et al.* 2009a), and the cormorants also show profound sedentariness associated with restricted gene flow (Duffie *et al.* 2009). However, the Galápagos penguin shows low genetic structure, suggesting regular large movements among sites (Nims *et al.* 2008). Taken together, this suggests a parasite of cormorants has undertaken a host shift to include penguins, vectored by their shared mosquito pest *A. taeniorhynchus*, and that the new penguin host is responsible for moving the parasite around the archipelago, where it now occurs in sites favoring populations of *A. taeniorhynchus* (Siers *et al.* 2010). However, although this conjecture may nicely describe the transmission dynamic operating today, it cannot explain its history.

The history must be more complex because both avian hosts arrived on the archipelago millions of years before the mosquito. The most recent common ancestor of the Galápagos penguin and its sister species the Humboldt penguin (*S. humboldti*) is estimated to have lived about four million years ago (4 Mybp; Baker *et al.* 2006), making this the estimated colonization date for what is now the Galápagos penguin. Likewise, the most recent common ancestor of the Galápagos flightless cormorant and its sister species the double-crested cormorant (*P. auritus*) is estimated to have lived ~2 Mybp (Kennedy *et al.* 2009). In contrast, the mosquito *A. taeniorhynchus* has an estimated colonization date only 0.2 Mybp (Bataille *et al.* 2009a). If the nematode itself is a long-term resident of Galápagos, there must have been a different vector species (which may still be involved in transmission); alternatively, the parasite is a more recent arrival than *A. taeniorhynchus*, arriving since the establishment of the penguin, the cormorant, and the mosquito, and it was introduced through an additional bird species not yet sampled. Either way, this means we do not yet fully understand the history of this host switch and the conditions under which it occurred. However, the broadening of the host range from cormorants to successful infections in penguins seems clear.

Recent arrivals

Arrivals of exotic organisms have increased explosively over the last five decades with human population expansion (Snell *et al.* 2002). Although parasites have not been part of analyses of Galápagos threats until recent years, it is certain that their arrival has been accelerated by the same pathways by which invasive plants, vertebrates, and arthropods arrived in recent years. Arrivals of parasites that are novel to the archipelago are a grave concern because of the expectation that their impact on immunologically naïve hosts would be more serious than in a host lineage with an evolutionary history involving continual or periodic interactions with the same parasites. We will develop this idea next.

Dove Haemoproteus species

One example that spans the categories of host switching and recent arrivals is the *Haemoproteus* blood parasite species found in the Galápagos doves (Padilla *et al.* 2004; Padilla and Parker 2006). Although considered relatively nonpathogenic, *Haemoproteus* blood parasites infect a broad range of bird species causing fitness-related consequences, such as reduced reproductive potential or lifespan (e.g. Zehtindjiev *et al.* 2008). An index of how well a population is resisting a particular pathogen is the proportion of individuals infected (prevalence), or the proportion of blood cells containing parasites within an infected individual (intensity). Higher values of these indices tend to be associated with recent infections to which the host has limited immune defense.

Rock pigeons (*Columba livia*) were introduced to Galápagos in several pulses during the 1970s (Harmon *et al.* 1987) and were eradicated by 2002.

The only other columbiform bird in Galápagos is the endemic Galápagos dove, *Zenaida galapagoensis*. Padilla and colleagues (2004) found extremely high *Haemoproteus* prevalences (100% on most islands) in Galápagos doves, with intensities as high as 12% (Santiago-Alarcon *et al.* 2008). Genetic analysis shows that the *Haemoproteus* parasites residing in the Galápagos dove populations comprise diverse lineages that are found in other dove species on mainland South America, with no indication of Galápagos-specific differentiation (Santiago-Alarcon *et al.* 2010). This suggests that the multiple introductions of rock pigeons also brought the diverse dove-specific *Haemoproteus* parasites found in South America, and that the eradication of rock pigeons in 2002 occurred after these lineages had already "jumped" into highly susceptible Galápagos doves.

Avipoxvirus

Recent arrivals also include the avipox virus (Figure 3.5; Thiel *et al.* 2005), *Culex quinquefasciatus* (mosquito vector of avian malaria in Hawaii; Whiteman *et al.* 2005) and most recently *Plasmodium* sp. in 2008 (Levin *et al.* 2009), each of which has significantly altered the disease transmission dynamics within the Galápagos biological community.

Avian pox is a mild to severe disease of birds (Figure 3.5) diagnosed in 278 bird species from 70 families in 30 orders worldwide (van Riper and Forrester 2007), caused by a DNA virus of the genus *Avipoxvirus* of the family Poxviridae; 13 strains have been identified (Francki *et al.* 1991; Tripathy 1993) that vary in virulence and host specificity. The most common recognized strains are fowlpox, pigeonpox, and canarypox viruses. We showed that the poxvirus in chickens in Galápagos was identical to that in chickens elsewhere, while the Galápagos passerines were infected with two variants of canarypox virus that differ significantly from fowlpox virus (Thiel *et al.* 2005); similar results were found in Hawaii (Jarvi *et al.* 2008). The genetic stability of avipox viruses is

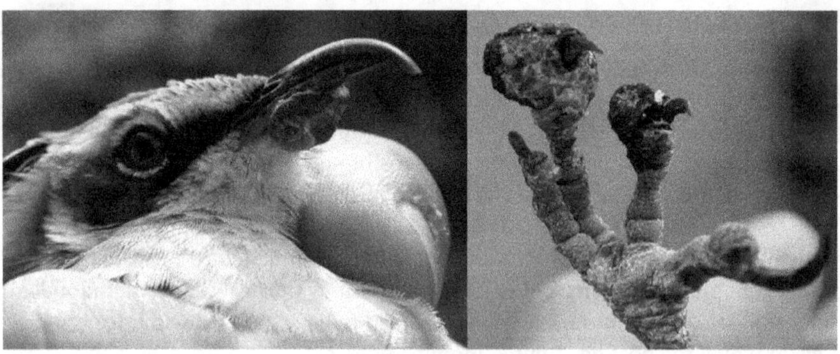

Figure 3.5 Cutaneous lesions on Galápagos mockingbirds (*Mimus parvulus*) caused by the avipoxvirus.

poorly understood, and the potential for recombination of poxviruses among the two canarypox and one fowlpox strains known to occur in Galápagos can continue to generate recombinants of unknown pathogenicity. Again, the immunological naïveté of most host lineages in Galápagos may leave them more susceptible to new combinations than their mainland relatives, presenting an evolutionary blank slate for viral recombinants that may not survive on the mainland due to widespread host resistance.

An important overarching, but untested, hypothesis is that lineage age (time in isolation since colonization) correlates positively with susceptibility to new pathogens. This hypothesis predicts that immune function should decline with time without exposure, predicting that the older (earlier colonizing) lineages will be more vulnerable to new diseases. Only two avian lineages in Galápagos have radiated into multiple species: the finches (colonization 2.7 Mybp; Sato *et al.* 1999, 2001) and the mockingbirds (>2 Mybp; Arbogast *et al.* 2006). These two lineages have the highest prevalences and only known deaths from recently arrived Avipoxvirus (Figures 3.5 and 3.6; Gottdenker *et al.* 2008; Jimenez-Uzcategui *et al.* 2007; Parker *et al.* 2006). While these results are consistent with the predictions of our hypothesis, a test will require comparing disease resistance capability and estimated colonization dates across diverse Galápagos avian lineages. Other colonization estimates for terrestrial Galápagos endemic birds are more recent (<0.25 Mybp for Galápagos hawks, Bollmer *et al.* 2006; ~0.8 Mybp for Galápagos flycatchers, Sari *et al.*, in prep.). Endemic avian lineages and their pathogens for which colonization estimates have been made are shown in Table 3.1. Testing this hypothesis will require many more estimates of this kind, and the development of a standardized measure of impact. Moreover, it will require estimates of colonization times for both hosts and parasites, as hosts that brought their parasites with them have not lacked exposure; we predict greatest impact following extensive periods without exposure (Figure 3.6).

There have been no extinctions of bird species in Galápagos, but island-population-level extinctions have increased 100-fold since the arrival of humans 200 years ago (Steadman 2006). Island populations harbor lower levels of genetic variation than their mainland counterparts (Frankham 1998). One possible cause of extinction of genetically depauperate island populations is that they are more susceptible to new diseases (Dobson and May 1986; O'Brien and Evermann 1988). Our studies of genetic diversity in Galápagos birds have revealed extremely low neutral (microsatellites; Duffie *et al.* 2009; Nims *et al.* 2008) and functional (MHC; Bollmer *et al.* 2007) diversity. However, in this chapter we have tried to take the perspective of the parasite in these interactions, pointing out examples of co-evolution of colonizing parasites with their host lineages; examples of rapid host switching; and opportunities for rapid evolution by recombination made possible by the availability of an array of susceptible hosts representing open niches. There are great opportunities to extend studies of parasites within highly co-evolved communities on islands in comparison to those on continents.

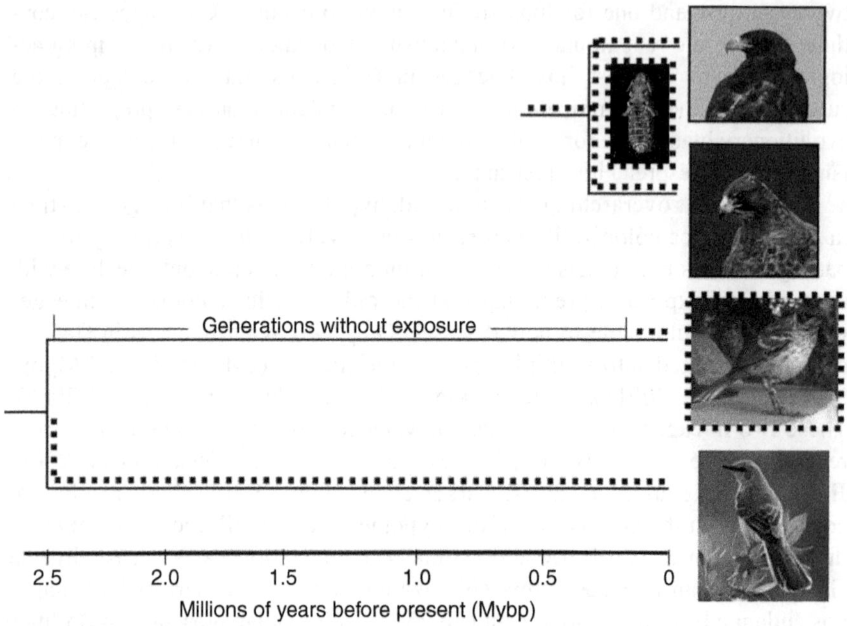

Figure 3.6 Illustration of the hypothesis that time without exposure results in high levels of susceptibility to new pathogens and greater intensity of infection. The lower branches (solid black lines) represent the colonization of the Galápagos >2 Mybp by the ancestral Galápagos mockingbird. The lower lineage remaining on the mainland had continued exposure to the avian poxvirus (dashed line), which "missed the boat" for colonization of Galápagos. The Galápagos mockingbirds on the upper branch were not exposed to this pathogen again until its arrival within the last 120 years and display dramatic infections. The upper branches (solid black) depict the more recent colonization of the archipelago by the hawk that became the Galápagos hawk we know today. Its ectoparasites (dashed lines) came with the colonists and have evolved alongside the hawk (see details in text). The feather louse *Degeeriella regalis* is shown in inset.

Acknowledgments

Our work in Galápagos is facilitated by the Charles Darwin Foundation and permitted by the Galápagos National Park. We particularly appreciate the support of Washington Tapia, Felipe Cruz, and Sonia Cisneros. The University of Missouri–St. Louis and the Saint Louis Zoo have participated in all of this work, a significant part of which was led by Jennifer Bollmer, Diego Santiago-Alarcon, Luis Padilla, and Jane Merkel. Our collaborators in the work on the hawks include Tjitte de Vries and students at Pontificia Católica Universidad del Ecuador, particularly Pablo Sanchez and Paolo Piedrahita, and current UMSL students Jose Luis Rivera and Mari Cruz Jaramillo. On Galápagos, we are frequently joined by Marilyn Cruz in our work on parasites and pathogens, and we

Table 3.1 Galápagos hosts and parasites with estimated colonization dates

Species	*Colonization estimate*	*Reference*
Yellow warbler *Dendroica petechia aureola*	~130 Kybp	Chavez et al., in prep
Galápagos hawk *Buteo galapagoensis*	<250 Kybp	Bollmer *et al.* 2006
Galápagos flycatcher *Myiarchus magnirostris*	~800 Kybp	Sari *et al.*, in prep
Galápagos cormorant *Phalacrocorax harrisi*	2 Mybp	Kennedy *et al.* 2009
Galápagos dove *Zenaida galapagoensis*	2 Mybp	Johnson and Clayton 2000
Galápagos mockingbirds *Mimus* spp.	>2 Mybp	Arbogast *et al.* 2006
Galápagos finches *Geospiza, Camarhynchus, Certhidia* spp.	~2.3 Mybp	Sato *et al.* 1999, 2001; Burns *et al.* 2002
Galápagos penguin *Spheniscus mendiculus*	~4 Mybp	Baker *et al.* 2006
Pathogens or vectors		
Avian malarial blood parasite *Plasmodium* sp.	<20 ybp?	Levin *et al.* 2009
Southern house mosquito *Culex quinquefasciatus*	< 50 ybp	Whiteman *et al.* 2005; Bataille *et al.* 2009b
Avian pox virus Avipoxvirus	<150 ybp	Parker *et al.*, in prep.
Body louse and feather louse of Galápagos hawk *Colpolcephalum turbinatum* *Degeeriella regalis*	~200 Kybp with hawk colonization	Whiteman *et al.* 2007
Black salt-marsh mosquito *Aedes taeniorhynchus*	200 Kybp	Bataille *et al.* 2009a

appreciate having used the facilities under her supervision at the Laboratorio Epidemiologico Patologico y Genetico (LEPG) in Puerto Ayora, as well as the input and collaboration of Virna Cedeno.

References

Arbogast, B.S., S.V. Drovetski, R.L. Curry, P.T. Boag, G. Seutin, P.R. Grant, B.P. Grant and D.J. Anderson. 2006. The origin and diversification of Galapagos mockingbirds, *Evolution* 60:370–382.

Baker, A.J., S.L. Pereira, O.P. Haddrath and K.A. Edge. 2006. Multiple gene evidence for expansion of extant penguins out of Antarctica due to global cooling, *Proc. R. Soc. Lond. B.* 273:11–17.

Bataille, A., A.A. Cunningham, V. Cedeno, L. Patino, A. Constantinou, L.D. Kramer and S.J. Goodman. 2009a. Natural colonization and adaptation of a mosquito species in Galapagos and its implications for disease threats to endemic wildlife, *Proc. Nat. Acad. Sci. USA* 106:10230–10235.

Bataille, A., A.A. Cunningham, V. Cedeno, M. Cruz, G. Eastwood, D.M. Fonseca, C.E. Causton, R. Azuero, J. Loayza, J.D. Cruz Martinez and S.J. Goodman. 2009b. Evidence for regular ongoing introductions of mosquito disease vectors into the Galapagos Islands, *Proceedings of the Royal Society B* 276(1674):3769-3775.

Bollmer, J.L., RT Kimball, N.K. Whiteman, J Sarasola and P.G. Parker. 2006. Phylogeography of the Galápagos Hawk: a recent arrival to the Galápagos Islands, *Molecular Phylogenetics and Evolution* 39:237–247.

Bollmer, J.L., FH Vargas, P.G. Parker. 2007. Low MHC variation in the endangered Galápagos penguin (*Spheniscus mendiculus*). Immunogenetics 59:593–602.

Bollmer, J.L., N.K. Whiteman, M.D. Cannon, J.C. Bednarz, T. de Vries and P.G. Parker. 2005. Population genetics of the Galápagos Hawk (*Buteo galapagoensis*): Genetic monomorphism within isolated populations, *Auk* 122:1210–1224.

Burns, K.J., S.J. Hackett and N.K. Klein. 2002. Phylogenetic relationships and morphological diversity in Darwin's finches and their relatives, *Evolution* 56:1240–1252.

Clay, T. 1958. Revisions of Mallophaga genera: *Degeeriella* from the Falconiformes. *Bulletin of the British Museum of Natural History, Entomology* 7: 121–207.

Clayton D.H., S.E. Bush and K.P.Johnson. 2004. Ecology of congruence: Past meets present. *Systematic Biology* 53: 165–173.

Cleland, J.B. and T.H. Johnston. 1911. The haematozoa of Australian birds II. *J. Roy. Soc. New South Wales* 45:415–444.

Dobson, A.P., R.M. May. 1986. Disease and conservation, in M.E. Soulé (ed.), *Conservation Biology: The Science of Scarcity and Diversity*, pp. 345–365 (Sinauer Associates: Sunderland, MA).

Duffie, C.V., T.C. Glenn, F.H. Vargas and P.G. Parker. 2009. Genetic structure within and between island populations of the flightless cormorant (*Phalacrocorax harrisi*), *Molecular Ecology* 18:2103-2111.

Faaborg, J., P.G. Parker, L. DeLay, T. de Vries, J.C. Bednarz, S. Maria Paz, J. Naranjo and T. Waite. 1995. Confirmation of cooperative polyandry in the Galápagos Hawk (*Buteo galapagoensis*), *Behavioral Ecol. Sociobiol.* 36:83–90.

Fain, A. 1965. A review of the family Epidermoptidae Trouessart parasitic on the skin of birds (Acarina: Sacroptiformes), *Konink VI Acad. Wetensch. Let. Schone Kunst. Belg.* 84 (I-II), 1–176, 1–144.

Francki, R.B., C.M. Fauguet, D.L. Knudson and F. Brown (ed.) 1991. Classification and nomenclature of viruses. Fifth report on the International Committee on the Nomenclature of Viruses, *Archives of Virology*, Supplement 2:94–95 (Springer Verlag: Wien, Austria; New York, NY).

Frankham, R. 1998. Inbreeding and extinction: Island populations, *Conserv. Biol.* 12:665–675.

Geist, D., W.M. White, F. Albarede, K. Harpp, R. Reynolds, J. Blichert-Toft and M.D. Kurz. 2002. Volcanic evolution in the Galapagos: The dissected shield of Volcan Ecuador, *Geochem. Geophys. Geosyst.* 3(10): 1061. doi:10.1029/2002GC000355.

Gottdenker, N.L., T. Walsh, G. Jimenez-Uzcategui, F. Betancourt, M. Cruz, C. Soos, R.E. Miller and P.G. Parker. 2008. Causes of mortality of wild birds submitted to the Charles Darwin Research Station, Santa Cruz, Ecuador from 2002–2004, *J. Wildlife Diseases* 44:1024–1031.

Hafner, M.S., P.D. Sudman, F.X. Villablanca, T.A. Spradling, J.W. Demastes and S.A. Nadler. 1994. Disparate rates of molecular evolution in cospeciating hosts and parasites, *Science* 265:1087–1090.

Harmon, W.H., W.A. Clark, A.C. Hawbecker and M. Stafford. 1987. *Trichomonas gallinae* in Columbiform birds from the Galapagos Islands, *J. Wildlife Diseases* 23:492–494.

Hughes, A.L. and M. Nei. 1993. Evolutionary relationships of the classes of major histocompatibility complex genes, *Immunogenetics* 37:337–346.

Jarvi, S.I., D. Triglia, A. Giannoulis, M. Farias, K. Bianchi and C.T. Atkinson. 2008. Diversity, origins and virulence of Avipoxviruses in Hawaiian forest birds, *Conservation Genetics* 9:339–348.

Jimenez-Uzcategui, G., D.A. Wiedenfeld and P.G. Parker. 2007. Viruela aviar en especies silvestres (Passeriformes) en la isla Santa Cruz, Galapagos, Ecuador, *Brenesia* 67:29–34.

Johnson, K.P. and D.H. Clayton. 2000. A molecular phylogeny of the dove genus Zenaida: Mitochondrial and nuclear DNA sequences, *Condor* 102:864–870.

Kennedy, M., C.A. Valle and H.G. Spencer. 2009. The phylogenetic position of the Galapagos cormorant, *Mol. Phylogenetics Evol.* 53:94–98.

Levin, I.I., D.C. Outlaw, F.H. Vargas, P.G. Parker. 2009. *Plasmodium* blood parasite found in endangered Galapagos penguins (*Spheniscus mendiculus*), *Biological Conservation* 142:3191–3195.

Maa, T.C. 1969. A revised checklist and concise host index of Hippoboscidae (Diptera), *Pacific Insects Monographs* 20:261–299.

Marshall, A.G. 1981. *The Ecology of Ectoparasitic Insects* (Academic Press: London, UK).

Merkel, J., H.I. Jones, N.K. Whiteman, N. Gottdenker, H. Vargas, E.K. Travis, R.E. Miller and P.G. Parker. 2007. Microfilariae in Galápagos penguins (*Spheniscus mendiculus*) and flightless cormorants (*Phalacrocorax harrisi*): genetics, morphology, and prevalence, *J. Parasitology* 93:495–503.

Munro, D.C. and S.K. Rowland. 1996. Caldera morphology in the western Galápagos and implications for volcano eruptive behavior and mechanisms of caldera formation, *J. Volcanol. Geotherm. Res.* 72:85–100.

Nieberding, C. and I. Olivieri. 2007. Parasites: Proxies for host genealogy and ecology? *Trends Ecol. Evol.* 22:156–165.

Nielsen, R. and J. Wakeley. 2001. Distinguishing migration from isolation: A Markov chain Monte Carlo approach, *Genetics* 158: 885–896.

Nims, B., H. Vargas, N. Gottdenker and P.G. Parker. 2008. Low genetic diversity and lack of population structure in the endangered Galápagos penguin (*Spheniscus mendiculus*), *Conservation Genetics* 9:1413–1420.

O'Brien, S.J. and J.F. Evermann. 1988. Interactive influence of infectious disease and genetic diversity in natural populations, *Trends Ecol. Evol.* 3:254–259.

Padilla, L.F. and P.G. Parker. 2006. Monitoring Avian Health in the Galápagos Islands: Current Knowledge, in M. Fowler and R.E. Miller (ed.), *Zoo and Wild Animal Medicine 6: Current Therapy*, pp. 191–199 (Saunders Elsevier: St. Louis, MO).

Padilla, L.R., D. Santiago, J.F. Merkel, R.E. Miller and P.G. Parker. 2004. Survey for *Trichomonas gallinae, Chlamydophila psitacci, Salmonella* spp. and *Haemoproteus* organisms in Columbiformes from the Galápagos Islands, *J. Zoo Wildlife Medicine* 35:60–64.

Palma, R.L. 1994. The identity of *Nirmus obtusus* and other *Quadraceps* species (Phthiraptera: Philopteridae) from Clipperton Island and the Galápagos Islands, J. *Roy. Soc. New Zealand* 24:267–276.

Parker, P.G. 2009a. A most unusual hawk: One mother and several fathers, in T. de Roi (ed.), *Galapagos: Preserving Darwin's Legacy*, pp. 130–137 (Firefly Books: Ontario).

Parker, P.G. 2009b. Parasites and Pathogens: Threats to native birds, in T. de Roi (ed.), *Galapagos: Preserving Darwin's Legacy*, pp. 177–183 (Firefly Books: Ontario).

Parker, P.G., N.K. Whiteman, R.E. Miller. 2006. Perspectives in Ornithology: Conservation Medicine in the Galápagos Islands: Partnerships among Behavioral, Population and Veterinary Scientists. Auk 123: 625–638.

Riesing, M.J., L. Kruckenhauser, A. Gamauf and E. Haring. 2003. Molecular phylogeny of the genus *Buteo* (Aves: Accipitridae) based on mitochondrial marker sequence, Molecular Phylogenetics Evol. 27:328–342.

Riper, C. van, III and D.J. Forrester. 2007. Avian Pox, in N.J. Thomas, D.B. Hunter and C.T. Atkinson (ed.), *Infectious Disease of Wild Birds*, pp. 131–176 (Blackwell Publishing: Oxford, UK).

Santiago-Alarcon, D., D.C. Outlaw, R.E. Ricklefs and P.G. Parker. 2010. Phylogenetic relationships of haemosporidian parasites in New World Columbiformes, with emphasis on the endemic Galapagos dove, *International J. Parasitology* 40:463–470.

Santiago-Alarcon, D., N.K. Whiteman, R.E. Ricklefs, P.G. Parker and G. Valkiunas. 2008. Patterns of parasite abundance and distribution in island populations of Galapagos endemic birds, *J. Parasitology* 94:584–590.

Sato, A., C. O'hUigin, F. Figueroa, P.R. Grant, B.R. Grant, H. Tichy and J. Klein. 1999. Phylogeny of Darwin's finches as revealed by mtDNA sequences, *Proc. Natl. Acad. Sci. USA* 96:5101–5106.

Sato, A., H. Tichy, C. O'hUigin, P.R. Grant., B.R. Grant and J. Klein. 2001. On the origin of Darwin's finches, *Mol. Bol. Evol.* 18:299–311.

Siers, S., J.F. Merkel, A. Bataille, F.H. Vargas and P.G. Parker. 2010. Ecological correlates of microfilarial prevalence in endangered Galapagos birds, *J. Parasitology* 96:259–272.

Snell, H.L., A. Tye, C.E. Causton and R.B. Bensted-Smith. 2002. Current status of and threats to the terrestrial biodiversity of Galapagos, in B. Bensted-Smith (ed.), *A biodiversity vision for the Galapagos Islands*, pp. 30–47 (Charles Darwin Foundation and World Wildlife Fund: Puerto Ayora, Galapagos).

Steadman, D.W. 2006. *Extinction and Biogeography of Tropical Pacific Birds* (University of Chicago Press: Chicago, IL).

Thiel, T., N.K. Whiteman, A. Tirape, M.I. Maquero, V. Cedeno, T. Walsh, G. Jimenez and P.G. Parker. 2005. Characterization of Canarypox-like Viruses Infecting Endemic Birds in the Galápagos Islands, *J. Wildlife Disease* 41:342–353.

Travis, E.K., F.H. Vargas, J. Merkel, N. Gottdenker, R.E. Miller and P.G. Parker. 2006. Hematology, serum chemistry, and serology of the Galápagos Penguin in the Galápagos Islands, Ecuador, *J. Wildlife Diseases* 42:625–632.

Tripathy, D.N. 1993. Avipox viruses, in J.B. McFerran and M.S. McNulty (ed.), *Virus infections of birds*, pp. 5–15 (Elsevier: New York, NY).

Vries, T. de. 1975. The breeding biology of the Galapagos Hawk, *Buteo galapagoensis*, *Le Gerfaut* 65:29–57.

Whiteman, N.K., V.S. Dosanjh, R.L. Palma, J.M. Hull, R.T. Kimball, P. Sánchez, J.H. Sarasola and P.G. Parker. 2009. Molecular and morphological divergence in a pair of closely related birds and their ectoparasites, *J. Parasitology* 95:1372–1382.

Whiteman, N.K., S.J. Goodman, B.J. Sinclair, T. Walsh, A.A. Cunningham, L.D. Kramer and P.G. Parker. 2005. Establishment of the avian disease vector Culex quinquefasciatus Say, 1823 (Diptera: Culicidae) on the Galápagos Islands, *Ecuador. Ibis* 147:844–847.

Whiteman, N.K., R.T. Kimball and P.G. Parker. 2007. Co-phylogeography and comparative population genetics of the Galápagos Hawk and three co-occurring ectoparasite species: Natural history shapes population histories within a parasite community, *Molecular Ecology* 16:4759–4773.

Whiteman, N.K., K.D. Matson, J.L. Bollmer and P.G. Parker. 2006a. Disease ecology in the Galápagos Hawk (Buteo galapagoensis): Host genetic diversity, parasites, and natural antibodies, *Proc. Roy. Soc. London B* 273:797–804.

Whiteman, N.K. and P.G. Parker. 2005. Using parasites to infer host population history: A new rationale for parasite conservation, *Animal Conservation* 8:175-181.

Whiteman, N.K., P. Sanchez, J.F. Merkel, H. Klompen and P.G. Parker. 2006b. Cryptic host specificity of an avian skin mite (Epidermoptidae) vectored by louse flies (Hippoboscidae) associated with endemic Galápagos bird species, *J. Parasitology* 92:1218–1228.

Zehtindjiev, P., M. Ilieva, H. Westerdahl, B. Hansson, G. Valkiūnas and S. Bensch. 2008. Dynamics of parasitemia of malaria parasites in a naturally and experimentally infected migratory songbird, the great reed warbler *Acrocephalus arundinaceus, Experimental Parasitology* 119:99–110.

4 Turning points in evolution

Ethological perspectives on hominization

Irenäus Eibl-Eibesfeldt

Homo sapiens: hit or flop?

Galápagos is known as the "Laboratory of Evolution" and to a great extent our interest in its fauna and flora is motivated by the urge to study the basic laws of evolution in order to understand the processes responsible for our make-up.

Right now most of us would follow Hubert Markl (Markl 1986) who characterized our species as a "Hit of Evolution". Indeed, we populated the world with million societies and developed a technical civilization, which within a century jetted us into the electronic age with telecommunication and space travel. Whether we continue as a hit, however, is questionable and people ponder about our future. We are outbreeding our resources and competition is getting increasingly ruder. Worldwide, we observe the signs of social and environmental degradation. A new generation-bridging survival ethos is needed, which takes into consideration the welfare and happiness of future generations. In order to achieve such a goal, we have to learn more about our endowments and handicaps.

In his book *The Expression of Emotions in Men and Animals* (1872) Charles Darwin presented the results of a cross-cultural study, based on observations as well as on questionnaires he had sent to informants, such as missionaries living amongst natives in different parts of the world. The basic expressions were found to be human universals, and for some of them Darwin described homologous movement patterns in monkeys and apes. In addition, he points at similarities in principle in a great diversity of animals from different taxa including man, revealing basic laws of perception: in aggressive encounters many animals make themselves appear larger and thus stronger, fish by spreading their fins, birds their feathers and man by showing off bearskin hats, feather crowns or other artificial display organs. Darwin also discovered the law of "antithesis", illustrating it with the well-known drawings of a dog displaying anger and fear and of a swan defending his territory (Figures 4.1 and 4.2).

Darwin's work already contains the essentials of the methodology and basic concepts of ethology. One wonders why it took some decades before his contributions were acknowledged in this context.

It certainly had to do with the uprising of a school of psychology known as Behaviorism, which followed the empiristic[1] dogma that all we do and know is

Figure 4.1 A swan defending his territory against an intruder (source: Charles Darwin 1872, Figure 13).

based upon experience. With the discovery of the conditioned reflexes (Pawlow 1927) behaviourists thought to have more or less an element at their disposal to experiment with and to demonstrate by building up networks of conditioned responses, starting at the embryonic stage. Since behaviors were thus considered as responses to stimuli, the term Stimulus-Response-Psychology is often used to characterize Behaviorism.

It took two generations of ethologists, starting with Oskar Heinroth, Konrad Lorenz and Niko Tinbergen (Tinbergen 1951), all building upon fundamental empirical contributions of many others, to correct these one-sided, environmentalist views. It is acknowledged nowadays that phylogenetic adaptations, and thus genes, play a fundamental role in behavioral development, but for a long time the ethological position was attacked by writers who implied that ethologists believed in a sort of simplicistic preformationism. The whole nature–nurture discussion is presented in my two textbooks: *Ethology – the Biology of Behavior* and *Human Ethology* (Eibl-Eibesfeldt 1975; 1989). Since we refer to innate traits in human behavior, I discuss briefly the key term "adaptation".

Figure 4.2a A dog approaching another dog with aggressive intent (source: Charles Darwin 1872, Figure 5).

Figure 4.2b The same dog seeking contact in a submissive posture (source: Charles Darwin 1872, Figure 6).

Key term: adaptation

Adaptedness is a characteristic of all organisms, and any structure that contributes to survival and fitness, as reflected in reproductive success, may be termed an adaptation. Ethologists, in agreement with Karl Popper and Konrad Lorenz, accept critical (hypothetical) realism as their starting point. All organs of an organism, including our brain, the sensory organs and our behaviors, according to this view, represent adaptations to an existing world. They depict facets of an extra-subjective reality, which are relevant for survival. The fins and swimming movements that a fish develops within an egg mirror in this effect fitness-relevant features for the environment, in which the fish will move after hatching. Alternatively, in the phrasing of Popper, they constitute hypotheses about certain characteristics of the external world, in which the fish will find themselves after hatching, hypotheses that are tested by natural selection!

This, in particular, also holds true for our perception, whose function, after all, is to mirror fitness-relevant facets of an outer world. And to those who express their doubts concerning the adequacy of such representations, George Gaylord Simpson used to say "The monkey which had no correct representation of the reality of the branch on which he was about to jump, does not belong to our ancestry" (Simpson 1963). What is more surprising is that these representations of reality in the human being surpass what would be needed for survival on our planet, since they correspond to reality so closely, that we can send spacecraft to distant planets, which then take and send pictures of distant events, such as the volcanic eruptions on the Jupiter moon, Io.

On the other hand, there also are assumptions built into our perception, which, for example, form the basis of visual illusions. Thus, we perceive the moon moving against the clouds, since we hypothesize that objects move in a static environment. This fits into our immediate earthly environment. Here it is important to spot a moving object, be it a predator or prey, as quickly as possible. That we fall prey to an illusion when we look up at the sky does not really matter. In addition, we know that we categorize and thus impose an order onto and into what we perceive. Color perception is a good example. Colors, one could say, are "constructed" as an adaptation to perceive objects, which reflect different wavelengths of the light. Light certainly exists as a continuum of electromagnetic waves from which we perceive wavelengths in the range spanning 450 nm (violet) to approximately 750 nm (red). Using color vision, we can distinguish the red of apples from the green leaves and also use color to send signals to our conspecifics.

Every adaptation requires that the organism did interact at some time with those features or events toward which it proves to be adapted. It is a process of information acquisition, which, in the case of phylogenetic adaptation, took place using the well-known process of selection. The information in this case is stored in the genes, which determine the embryonic and ontogenetic development within a given range of modifiability.[2]

In addition, however, animals and in particular humans learn. In this case, the information is acquired individually through exploratory behavior, in play with others, by mimicking social models or by being taught. In these cases, it is the individual brain that stores the information. In man, the storage of the cumulative cultural knowledge is also assisted by artificial storage organs, such as books. However, even the adaptive modification of behavior occurs within the framework of phylogenetic preparedness.

Learning is biased in many ways. A learning disposition which Konrad Lorenz called imprinting (Lorenz 1935, 1953) is characterized by a sensitive period during which learning takes place. Once learned it is not easily extinguished, since the learning is characterized by the loss of synapses which were not involved in the process (Wallhäuser and Scheich 1987). It's comparable to a photograph: after the film is exposed and developed you cannot expose it again.

Hominization: turning points

Man: the generalist

Evolution as a process of adaptation via natural and sexual selection leads to speciation. We admire the stunning adaptation of many species, however, whose specializations fit so intricate to a narrow ecological niche that its destruction endangers the specialists' future. In contrast to the specialists' narrow evolutionary potential, generalists, such as rats or many passerines, are characterized by a wide evolutionary potential that leads to adaptive radiation in various directions.

Humans belong to the generalists and this is a universal trait. The world population is subdivided into subgroups with specific morphological and physiological characteristics, fitting as "ecotypes" to the special climatic and other challenges of their habitat. Nevertheless, all are generalist – one could say adapted to remain unspecialized – or, better, specialists for cultural adaptation, which includes specializations for different subsistence strategies of populations e.g. as pastoralists and with the professional division of labor that bestowed us with a technical civilization.

Konrad Lorenz (1943) characterized the universality of humans with an imagined athletic competition, whose task consisted in a 100 m sprint, followed by a dive in a pond, retrieving three objects from a depth of 5 m, then swimming 100 m toward the other shore, climbing 5 m up a rope, then walking an additional 10 km. An untrained but healthy adult could perform, but no other mammal could. Some may run, swim or climb faster, but they would fail if challenged in all disciplines. Moreover, if we observe the acrobatic performances of skiers or tennis players we are simply stunned by the brilliant display of sensory–motor interactions in man.

The onset of the process we call hominization started with large tree-climbing primates, who moved by brachiating and climbing. This fostered the development of binocular vision, upright posture and the differentiation of prehensile hands. The larger apes could not move by leaping and climbing like the smaller apes, but had to hold onto branches and move in a semi-upright position, pulling the body forward and upward and at the same time pushing with the hind legs (push and pull climbing – Stemmgreifklettern).

Targeted grasping and stepping, as well as binocular vision developed for estimating distance, were primarily arboreal adaptations, but they served as pre-adaptations for movements on the ground, after the rainforests of Africa shrunk due to climatic change. This type of locomotion freed the hand and promoted the use of tools, such as sticks or stones, for defense. Our thought and perceptual pathways have been significantly influenced by the optic–haptic heritage. We grasp ideas and see connections. Prehensile hands and a keen sense of sight, touch and smell, along with a highly developed and diversified tool culture, enabled man to adapt to the most diverse environmental conditions. Zoologist would label *Homo sapiens* as "euryoek".

Tools, emotionality and language

Chimpanzees make and use tools. Adrian Kortlandt (1965) presented taxodermically stuffed leopards to free-living chimps, which attacked these dummies with heavy sticks. Jane Goodall discovered termite fishing with thin sticks, stems of grass and other lengthy plant material serving as probes. At her invitation, I documented at length termite fishing in the Gombe Reserve (Figure 4.3) (Eibl-Eibesfeldt and Goodall 1986). I was struck by the quietness and patience chimps exhibited in performing this task. This contrasted sharply with the high degree of emotionality that these animals exhibit in most social interactions, with the exception of social grooming. Manipulatory activities such as social grooming and tool use are detached from agonal arousal; thus, when termite fishing, the lack of immediate success does not lead to impatience and loss of temper. I propose that in connection with the development of tool use, the ability to decouple agonal emotions normally aroused by frustrations was selected. Playful exploratory behavior could have served as pre-adaptation since, in the playful fighting in which many carnivores, ungulates and rodents engage, the emotions with which all affective engagements are involved are suppressed and decoupled from the motor patterns of fighting. Playing mammals fight and chase each other, taking turns, without damaging each other. In such situations, free from tension, individuals can practice and acquire techniques of use in later life (Eibl-Eibesfeldt 1950).

Tool use certainly enhances this capacity. With the evolution of handiness in man came the lateralization of the two hemispheres of the brain. The left hemisphere became specialized for controlling the voluntary movements of the right hand, including aimed gripping, throwing and all the refined precision needed for tool construction, artistry, writing and the like. The right hemisphere is predominant for the emotions and their integration up to the highest artistic performances in music, poetry and theatre. The emotions are in fact very old. Our expressions of anger, fear and tender nurturant feelings are very similar to those found in our closest primate relatives. The archaic is often labeled as "primitive" but it forms the basis of our highest feelings.

Figure 4.3 A chimpanzee termite fishing. The probe is already inserted and the free hand serves to catch termites falling off the probe. The female holds material for further probes with her feet (source: I. Eibl-Eibesfeldt, Kigoma Reserve).

The lateralization of the brain permits the control of blood flow to activate one side more than the other and, since both hemispheres are connected, variant modulations can be achieved. Thus, by the activation of the left hemisphere we are able to discuss objectively ("sachlich", as we say in German) otherwise emotionally loaded problems. That's why the left hemisphere is also called the "rational brain".[3]

Language allows us to quarrel and duel with words and the tongue may be as sharp as a dagger – but others can interfere verbally and reconciliation may be achieved. Language allows us, furthermore, to transmit information about objects and skills without the need to show them – and without a lengthy performance. Our cumulative culture is based upon this capacity.

Body language

With our body language, we have a highly differentiated system of communication with some precursors reaching far back into evolutionary history. We mainly express our moods through our facial expressions, as well as through our postures and gestures, and we do this in a generally understandable way that transcends linguistic boundaries. While we speak in different tongues and ethnically distinguish ourselves according to groups of speakers, we communicate with our facial expressions in a "language of the heart" that all human beings understand. Our basic emotions are expressed by people all over the world in the same way. They disclose our subjective moods and at the same time indicate our readiness to act on them.

Smiling expresses a readiness for friendly contact and thus also proves its worth as a placating signal in critical situations. There is no doubt that this expressive movement is an innate phylogenetic adaptation, since children born deaf and blind smile, too, even though they have grown up in darkness and silence without a social model (Figure 4.4). The human face is thought to be the mirror of the soul. Since early childhood we have been adapted to communicate face-to-face. A newborn child is already adapted to this in an extraordinary manner. When it hears its mother's voice, it turns its face toward her – looking for visual contact. Children born blind do this, too, and then later exclusively orient themselves to the source of sound. They also turn their eyes toward their mother, as if able to see her. If no outward damage can be detected, early loss of sight often goes unnoticed (Freedman 1964). Mothers frequently welcome visual contact with their newborns with great joy; they take it to be a sign of personal affection in this context.

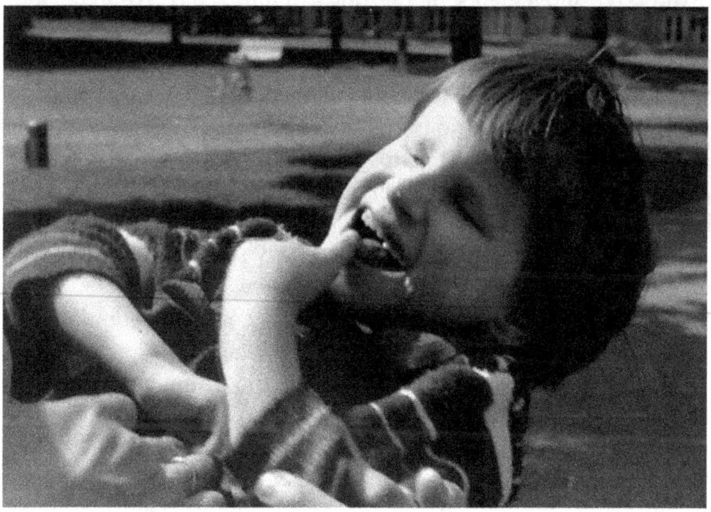

Figure 4.4 Facial expression of a ten-year-old girl born deaf and blind. Still taken from a 16 mm film made by the author.

Facial expressions reliably show a certain readiness for action. If someone puts on an annoyed or even angry face, they are aggressively motivated and we can expect an attack or a confrontation. Every one of us subjectively experiences annoyance or anger in some situations and the assumption that our fellow men feel the same in the same situations has been firmly established. Frequently, a person's mood transmits itself to others via their facial expression. If we see and hear someone crying, it is contagious. When newborns are played tapes of someone crying, they react selectively by joining in the crying. Empathy finds its visible roots here. Joy is also contagious, as are yawning, disgust and fear. Transfers of moods – resonances – of this kind, as well as the expressive facial movements assigned to these feelings, belong to the universals of human behavior.

A few illustrations copied from our film documentation may serve as example. The first shows two approximately one-year-old babies sitting on shoulders opposite each other. Both show embrace intention with a "play face" (a relaxed open mouth display) and wide-open arms (Figure 4.5.). The second is a drawing made by Van Hooff (1971) from a film he had taken illustrating his son playing with a tame chimp. Both show the play face (Figure 4.6), apparently an old shared heritage. Third, I want to show a tender expression showing a Yanomami girl, caressing a baby (Figure 4.7).

Our facial expressions correspond to specific "moods", a word that refers to a certain readiness to act. There are basic expressions indicating fear, anger, disgust, surprise, sadness and so on, which belong to the universals. However, often in this "parliament of motivations" several of the basic expressions are activated to varying degrees and superimpose themselves, which leads to a great variety of expressions. Lorenz (1953) has demonstrated this to be the case for the expressive movements of the dog (Figure 4.8a). Applying the facial action coding system (Ekman and Friesen 1978; Musterle and Rössler 1986; for further references, see Eibl-Eibesfeldt 1989) and following the model of the Lorenz Matrix, Musterle and Rössler created a computer-generated overlap of facial expressions for contact seeking (top to bottom, Figure 4.8b) and contact rejection (top to horizontal). In the cross-cultural comparison it is amazing to see which details are similar. Certainly, social competence is based upon one's ability to read the composite expressions and thereby learning will play a role not yet not thoroughly studied. However, our biases for reading the basic expressions certainly guide us.

The prime importance of the face in interpersonal communication is also indicated by the fact that in humans, as well as in non-human primates, there is a specific brain area designated for discerning faces. In humans, an additional area specializes in recognizing specific faces. If an accident or operation should cause this latter area to fail, the patient is able to perceive faces but can no longer assign them to a specific person. Thus, the ability to visually distinguish has been lost, although the patient can still recognize people by their voices.

(a)

(b)

Figure 4.5 An Eipo baby shows a “play face”. While two Eipo mothers (Irian Jaya) meet each other for a chat, their babies on their shoulders become interested in each other. (a) At the beginning, the little boy facing us looks slightly suspicious. (b) However, when the second baby, with his back toward the camera, began to raise his arms in an intention movement of embrace, the first responds with “play face” and in turn with an intention movement of embrace. The lively expression is universal and its intention not at all difficult to for us interpret. Stills taken from a 16 mm film made in the Western Highlands of New Guinea (Irian Jaya) by the author.

Figure 4.6 A boy playing with a young chimp, which shows the play face. Drawing made from a film made by J.A. van Hooff.

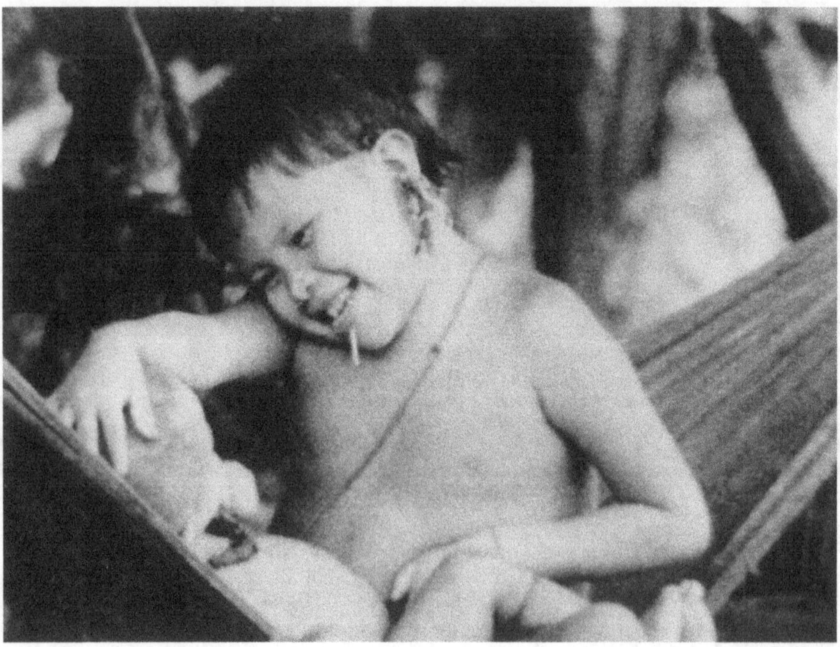

Figure 4.7 A Yanomami girl caressing a baby. The same expressions to the detail can be observed in the same context in our culture. The language of our motions belongs to our phylogenetic outfit. Still taken from a 16 mm film of the Shabono of the Ihiramaweteri (Alto Orinoko) made by the author.

(a)

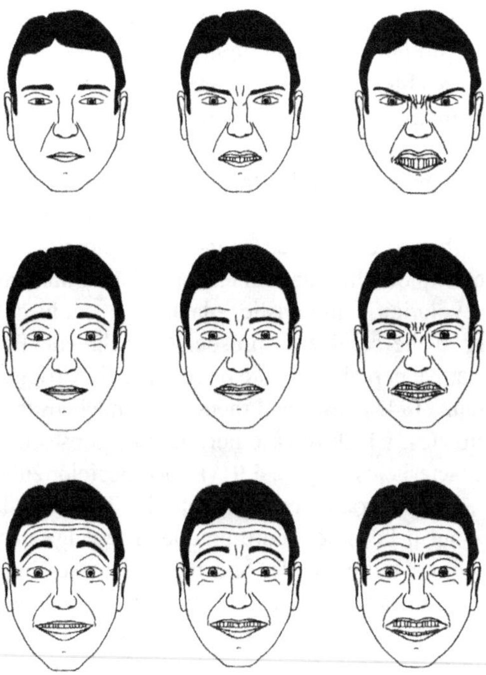

(b)

Figure 4.8 (a) Facial expressions of the dog resulting from the superimposition of fear (increasing top to bottom) and aggression (increasing left to right), each increasing from neutral, moderate to strong (source: Konrad Lorenz 1953) (b) Computer-generated superimposition of human approach and rejection expressions. The superimposition of affiliative, i.e. approach, (increasing top to bottom) and hostile rejection (increasing left to right) expressions, each from moderate to strong intensity. The result is an expression of insecurity (source: W. Musterle and O.E. Rössler 1986).

Childhood, curiosity and obedience

One characteristic of our species is the long childhood, characterized by a delay in physiological and morphological development. We can consider this as adaptation to acquire by learning the language the competence to use it in everyday life and in many ritualistic contexts: to acquire specific subsistence strategies; the myths explaining the origin of the group; the many customs that have to be observed; in short, the rich cultural knowledge that has to be learned. Were human children to mature as fast as gorillas, it would be impossible to acquire all the skills needed to survive as *Homo sapiens* – a cultural being by nature – since starting at early puberty they would prefer to follow own ways instead of obediently following instructions.

We know that pongids learn from their parents, playmates and other group members by observation, during play with others and by their own inquisitiveness. However, their inclinations to accept and even seek instruction fades away with puberty. Children of our species are in many ways prepared to seek information and to listen to and to follow instructions. A basic trust, if not abused, leads children to ask parents preferentially, by pointing at objects or bringing a found object or, if already capable, by asking “what is this”, “what is it good for”, “is it dangerous” and finally “why did he do this”, “why should I do – or not do – this” or “why does this look so …?” There is a special age, in German “das Fragealter”, in which children overburden their parents with such questions. In traditional societies, many questions are also addressed to playmates who serve as social models. Furthermore, children engage in exploratory behavior. Motivated by curiosity, they explore their natural and social environment.

During the course of evolution, mutualistic adaptations evolved between parents and their offspring in the service of prosocial attachment. Babies are characterized by features that we perceive as cute or cuddly. They trigger nurturant responses. Konrad Lorenz (1943) described them as “Kindchenschema” and refers to central innate templates, which release nurturant responses by the perception of certain baby characteristics (Figure 4.9) (Eibl-Eibesfeldt 2004). Once a baby becomes a toddler, its appearance changes rapidly. The child keeps its baby facial characteristics, but it becomes more gracile. The ridge of the nose develops and the body becomes more slender and the extremities longer. The voice is higher than the voices of adults. The child appears to us delicate in its static structures and its behavior seems charming. This seems to be a conditioned response, which superimposes an aesthetic bias over the innate one: Through sexual selection it could account for the persistence of infantile features into adulthood. In particular, this can be observed as a universal trait in females, which, in addition to sex-specific signals indicating maturity, show clear pedomorphic traits, particularly in the delicacy of their facial features and the gracefulness of their behavior. In caricatures these characteristics appear often exaggerated (Figure 4.10). Through these pedomorphic features women trigger nurturant, tender feelings in males. For further references see I. Eibl-Eibesfeldt and Christa Sütterlin (2007) and I. Eibl-Eibesfeldt (1989).

Figure 4.9 The cuteness graph. Top: side view of an infant's head in comparison with the profile of an adult. Below for comparison: on the left side, animals whose appearance trigger tender feelings of nurturance, i.e. desert jerboa, Pekinese dog, robin; on the right side, animals which do not appeal to us as cute, i.e. hare, hunting dog, golden oriole (source: drawings from Konrad Lorenz 1943).

Figure 4.10 A highly exaggerated presentation of the infant schema in a doll in a Japanese shop window.

The origin of nurturant care

The development of nurturant maternal care constituted a turning point in the evolution of terrestrial vertebrate behavior. Reptilian social behavior is based on dominance and submission. As the motivation for individualized nurturant care for offspring evolved along with a repertoire of fostering behaviors, such as feeding, grooming and protective behaviors, the offspring evolved a parallel motivation to seek protection and care, as well as developing the signals to trigger such responses in the parent. Finally, individual bonding evolved, i.e. the mutual capacity of parents and young to recognize each other and seek each other's proximity.

Individual bonding is in essence what we define as love. The relationship is characterized by a certain exclusivity. In precocial animals, mutual attachment takes place within a sometimes dramatically short time-span; in sheep, for example, it occurs within minutes of birth, in a process of flash learning which closely resembles imprinting. If a newborn lamb is left with its mother for five minutes, then separated for an hour and later returned to the ewe together with another lamb, the mother will accept her young and chase the foreign lamb away. However, were the newborn lamb to be taken away immediately after birth for one hour and then presented with another lamb to the ewe, she would chase away both and accept neither. Her sensitive period for adopting a newborn would have passed.[4]

Reptiles do not nurture their young, nor are they able to form individualized parent–child bonds. They therefore are unaware of any "we" and "others". Their social behavior is restricted to dominance and submission. The absence of nurturant interactions and individual bonding in lower vertebrates can be observed in the marine iguanas on the Galápagos Islands. Hundreds of these large reptiles bask on the rocky coast, lying side by side in apparently gregarious groups. Those familiar with birds and mammals know the rich repertoire of nurturant behavior present in both groups. Birds groom each other in friendly encounters, such as during courtship. They exchange gifts of nesting material during rituals of greeting and feed each other during courtship. Marine iguanas, however, do nothing of the sort. The only social behavior that can be observed consists of dominance displays, fights and submission. Males fight one another during the breeding season in a highly ritualized manner (Figure 4.11). Males also use dominance display in courtship. Females ready to copulate submit by accepting a flat position, whereupon the male grasps her at the nape of her neck with his jaws, pins her down, mounts, and copulates. If she is not ready, she simply runs as he approaches. Marine iguanas form aggregations, but they do not form groups of bonded individuals.

Nurturant, friendly relations amongst adults, as well as individualized bonding, became possible only after the motivational bases of individualized nurturant repertoire (the mother–child signals) and the nurturant behaviors had evolved. If we study the courtship behavior in birds and mammals as well as social interactions of already paired individuals living within groups, we can easily recognize that the patterns of friendly interactions are derived from these mother–child patterns, sometimes with little change (Figure 4.12). More often they became transformed into signals by a process called ritualization to serve the function of appeasement, bond establishment and suchlike.[5]

Similarly, in mammals nurturant behaviors such as grooming, mutual licking, feeding and defending, as well as infantile behaviors, serve the establishment and maintenance of a bond. Aggression between group members can be blocked by infantile behavior. The Galápagos Islands offer ample opportunity to observe how boobies present each other pebbles, feathers or sticks during courtship to cooperate in nest building (Figure 4.13a). Mood induction is one function of these rituals ("let's build a nest"). I was particularly fascinated by the flightless cormorants' brooding-relief ceremonies (Figure 4.13b). Whenever a mate returned to the bird sitting on its eggs, he carried in his beak seaweed, sticks or sometimes even a starfish as a symbolic present. It served as appeasement, since if one returned without this gift it was attacked by its mate. Human mothers feed their babies at an early age with premasticated additional food ("kiss-feeding", Figure 4.14). It is a widespread maternal behavior in our species and became ritualized as a sign of love, sympathy and in greetings as a sign of acceptance, like many of the patterns of sharing, giving and hosting derived from mutual sharing and giving within the

Figure 4.11 Ritualized fighting by head-butting in male marine iguanas. The loser surrenders, turning off his display by collapsing flat on his belly. The winner then stops fighting and gives the loser the chance to retreat. Drawing based on photographs taken by the author.

Figure 4.12 Nurturant courtship behavior is derived from mother–child patterns. Top left: The common tern feeding its young. Top right: a male tern with a fish, courting a female that is begging for food (source: A. Wickler 1969). Bottom left: a raven feeding its young. Bottom right: a raven pair during courtship feeding. Drawings based on photographs by E. Gwinner.

family (Figures 4.15–4.17). However, we also offer food in religious ceremonies, as well to objects (masks or figurines) serving as guardians (Figure 4.18a, b).

Individualized bonding in humans

In humans, the capacity for individualized bonding evolved in steps from maternal caretaking behaviors to the extended family. Patterns expressing affection, such as caressing, are clearly derived from maternal behaviors, as are embracing, kissing (derived from kiss-feeding) and baby talk in a voice raised by one octave. Individual acquaintance creates a relationship of trust, whereas a stranger is met with distrust (Figures 4.19 and 4.20). The first manifestation of distrust of strangers appears early in life and is well-known as the phenomenon of "stranger awareness" (or "fear of strangers"). Every healthy baby basic trust demonstrates during its first months of life; any approaching human being will be greeted with a smile. From approximately the age of three to six months onwards, the baby distinguishes between familiar persons and strangers. The baby may smile at a stranger, but usually after a few seconds it will turn toward its mother and hide its face. It will fluctuate between approach and withdrawal responses or show superpositions of these two responses. Should the stranger be insensitive and continue to approach, the baby usually clings to its mother and may start to cry in clear avoidance.

This is a universal pattern and does not depend on prior bad experiences with strangers. It persists throughout life as stranger awareness and finds its clear expression in ambivalent behaviors. It can be regarded as the first manifestation of an "us two" vs. perceived "others". It evolved to secure the mother–child bond in a species, which needs long childcare, and consequently it also provided a new potential for larger group formation. Through "familiarization" with others, behavior shifts along a continuum from mistrust to trust. Extended families and small individualized groups result, which demarcate themselves as "us" from "the others".

Figure 4.13a A male masked booby offers a pebble to a female during courtship.

Figure 4.13b Greeting ritual of a flightless cormorant approaching his nest to relieve his brooding female. As a greeting he passes a bushel of seaweed to her. Drawing based on photographs taken by the author on Fernandina, Galápagos.

Figure 4.14 A Himba grandmother and her grandson exchanging a candy through kiss-feeding. They did this in turns. Still from a 16mm film made by the author.

The ambivalence between affiliative and demarcative behavior tendencies is present in relationships within the group as well as between representatives of different groups. This is expressed in greetings rituals at festive occasions, where visitors as well as hosts combine dominance behaviors with friendly appeals (Figure 4.21). For example, the Nikobarese protect themselves against evil spirits with carved figurines showing threat display in combination with a board depicting scenes of their daily life (Figure 4.22). In this way, behavior patterns of bonding evolved by kin selection proved so efficient that individuals not directly blood-related could be adopted as fictive kin and bonded in such a way that the group could act as a unit in war. Supported by cultural techniques (e.g. identification via symbols, indoctrination), this enabled groups to become units of selection (Eibl-Eibesfeldt 1982). Bonding at all levels in humans is reinforced by relationships of mutual sharing and reciprocity, often called reciprocal altruism. The literature of the evolution of reciprocal altruism in ethology and its current expressions in anthropology is vast and beyond the scope of this chapter.

In sociobiological publications, the evolution of altruistic behavior is sometimes presented as a great puzzle. How could altruistic individuals get a foothold in a non-altruistic population? It did not come about this way. The evolution of nurturant individualized care for the young does not require complicated cost–benefit calculations. That considerable expenses are involved in the raising of their young can be explained on the basis of individual and kin selection. Once evolved, this capacity for individualized bonding, the nurturant motivations and

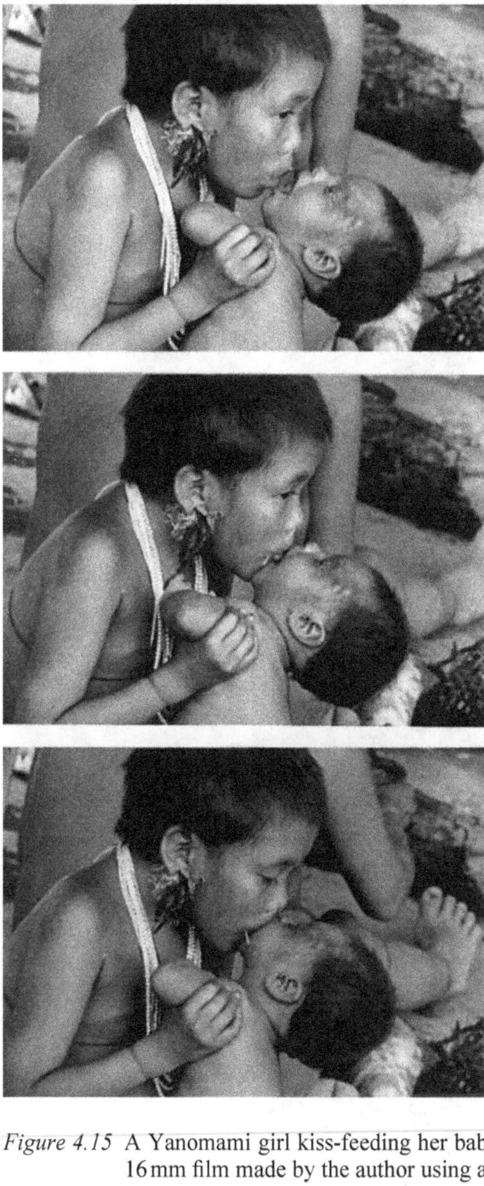

Figure 4.15 A Yanomami girl kiss-feeding her baby sister with saliva. Stills from a 16 mm film made by the author using a mirror lens.

behaviors including family defense became the raw materials for selection and proved to be pre-adaptations for adult bonding. In some mammals, and in our species in particular, they enabled the bonding of larger groups of individuals not closely related by blood to become units of selection. This process was enhanced by cultural means, as will be discussed later. Thus, cultural adaptation to a life in anonymous societies is in full swing.

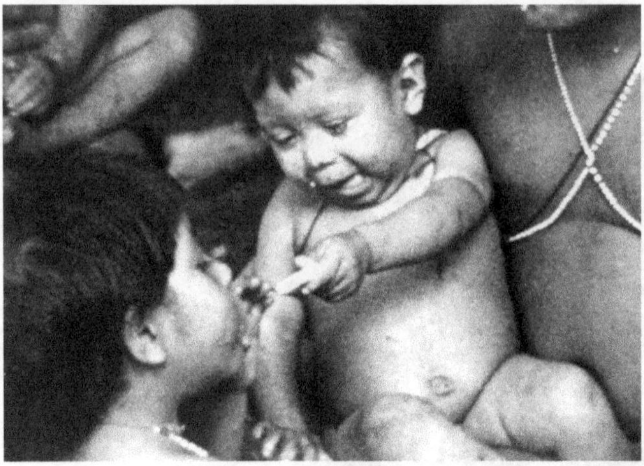

Figure 4.16 A Yanomami baby offers food to her elder sister. She opens her mouth while doing this, as mothers often do in our culture, when they feed their babies. Still from a 16mm film made by the author using a mirror lens.

Figure 4.17 The ceremony of initiation by tooth filing is concluded with a feeding ritual. The initiates, in this case brother and sister, united by a shawl, feed each other in turns with a sweet paste. Saba village in Bali.

Figure 4.18a Two masks of demons protect the entrance of the shrine of the God of the sea, Baruna, on the beach of Sanur in Bali. Offerings of rice are made by local people to keep them in good spirits and to do their service for the shrine.

Figure 4.18b The Bamileke in Cameroon protect their houses with masks, which are fed daily with millet directly pasted into mouth of the mask (source: A. Heymer).

Figure 4.19a, b Fear of strangers response of an infant of the In (in the Western Highlands of New Guinea). A visitor tries to pick the infant up, but it protests and flies to his father. Stills from a 16mm film made by the author using a mirror lens.

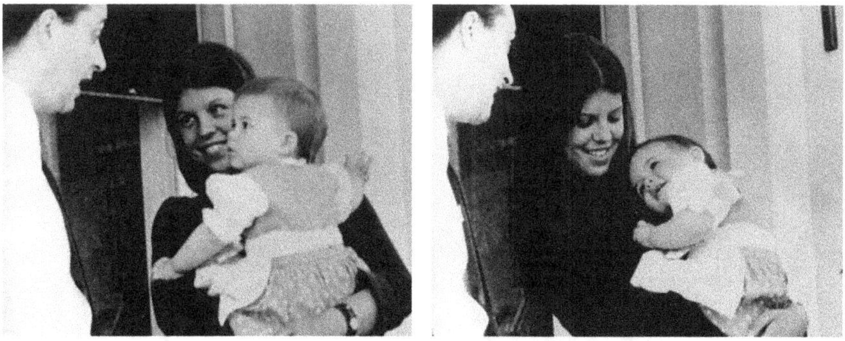

Figure 4.20a, b A little girl safe with her aunt looks at the stranger and, cuddling closer to her aunt, returns the friendly smile. Stills from a 16 mm film made by the author (direct).

Figure 4.21 The antithetic of display and appeasement in rituals of friendly greeting. The headman of a group invited for a feast dances around in the shabono (village) of his hosts. He displays aggressively with his weapons and dances, combining his display with that of his child who dances with him, carrying and waving green palm fronds in his hands.

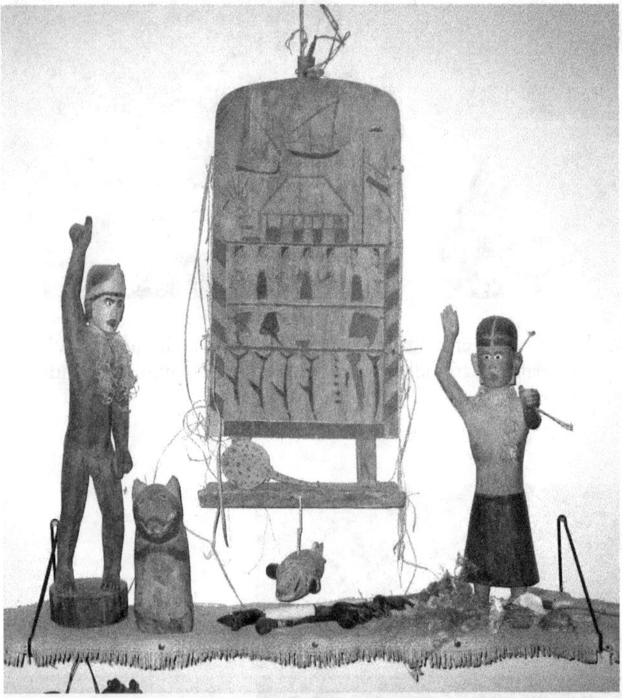

Figure 4.22 The Nikobarese of the Island Kondul (in Nikobar) ward off evil spirits with figurines showing a threat display. However, this is combined with a friendly appeal, as the board presents scenes of their daily life to appease the spirits hands.

Bonding in groups

Amongst the cultural mechanisms that enhance the biologically provided predisposition for kinship affiliation and reciprocity, ideology is of paramount importance. Human indoctrinability, in this context, plays an important role. Through indoctrination, a fixation to culture-specific standards of behavior, ethical concepts, values and other characteristics takes place, seemingly similar to the learning processes called "imprinting". Like imprinting, indoctrination proves to be quite resistant to therapy. Again, a predisposition for the evolution of this capacity first appeared in the mother–child relationship where it served to strengthen the bond by mutual fixation of both mother and child on individual characteristics of the other. This trait proved to be adapted to bond kin and then distant kin and finally other group members.

Indoctrinability seems to spring from various roots, and indoctrination thus draws on a variety of phylogenetic pre-adaptations. Besides those that enhance family bonding, another innate perceptive bias that seems, amongst others, to be responsible for the choice of a same-sex partner is the social model during childhood (Skrzipek 1978). This fits the observation that even without apparent cultural pressure boys in all cultures identify with their fathers and other males of their neighborhood while girls mimic female models. Boys accordingly tend to gang together in same-sex play groups and there can be little doubt that male bonding, culturally enhanced by symbols of identification (flags etc.) and shared beliefs, is of paramount importance for group defense and group solidarity, even in nation states.

Human indoctrinability as a specific learning disposition was enhanced by the advantage it brought in cementing existing bonds and cultural institutions, and in supporting social, economic and political institutions necessary for preserving harmony within the group (conflict management, rules for sharing and the like). This was accomplished by strengthening a sense of togetherness, building up loyalties and emphasizing contrasts to others by creating images of enemies. This was to the advantage of both the individual and the group, for in the face of fierce inter-group competition an individual had few chances outside of a strong group. Indoctrinability is a specific learning disposition allowing acceptance and identification with group characteristics and thus serves we-group demarcation. Once learned, these aspects of group identity seem to be rather resistant to extinction. Characteristics of group tradition are acquired early. Dialect stands out in this context, since the intonation and melody of voice remains for a lifetime and allows insiders to recognize one's group membership. It is very difficult to acquire such characteristics later in life. Identification with one's own family during childhood lies at the roots of human indoctrinability, with small local groups acting as quasi-familiar units.

We are also bonded to our home country and this type of "imprinting" may well be rooted in territoriality. Whether the affective bonding to home and country are of different origin and quality than the affective bonding to family and group, however, needs further investigation. Cultural indoctrination elicits group identity and love of one's native land in principle by the same means in tribal societies as in our western culture. Since values supporting group interests were advantageous when groups were competing in war, selection favored the disposition for indoctrination. Young males were indeed often willing to fight and take the risk of being killed in combat for their group. Once married and with family, however, family loyalty gains priority.

With the formation of the early state, ideologies promoted by state and religious leaders can assume an additional function as pacemakers of evolution by setting new goals and thus initiating new ways of acting and thinking. Ultimately, though, ideologies are measured against the yardstick of fitness.

Depending upon the subsistence strategy and the carrying capacity of the land, groups in pre-state societies ranged from a few dozen to a few hundred. In these societies, most groups split when they reach the size of 300–600. They usually split along kinship lines, ensuring that it is their closest kin whom they will help. Humans show a strong inclination to form such subgroups, which eventually distinguish themselves from others by dialect and other subgroup characteristics and go on to form new cultures. Erik Erikson (1966) aptly spoke of "cultural pseudospeciation".

If we examine the mechanisms employed to bond members or groups who are not close kin, we discover that they draw on the existing phylogenetic adaptations already mentioned. At the level of the kin-based society, one common means of bonding is through extension of kinship principles, terminology and accompanying behavior beyond the circle of close kin to more distant kin and, in some cases, non-kin. This is achieved by the creation of segmentary lineage systems and other systems of descent: groups that trace themselves to a common ancestor. These groups are held together on the basis of both kinship and reciprocity (Wiessner 1982).

In segmentary kinship societies, ideology thus calls on the metaphor of kinship to create fictive descent from mythical ancestors or creators, and such a belief bonds all as quasi-blood-relatives. Indeed, terms to address persons who are not blood relatives are often derived from those that characterize a familial relation, for example, sibling, sibling-in-law, or, if the person is much older "older-sibling", "father" or "mother". Thus, those not closely related are widely reclassified as close kin and the person accepted as a member of the group (Schiefenhövel 1998).

Familial ties are, of course, stronger than the ties between members of a single village, and the ties of the members of one village are in turn stronger than ties between the members of the different villages in a single valley. The feelings of obligation and loyalty are thus graded according to an inherited family bias.

The Eipo have myths that refer to their origin from a common ancestor or a bringer of culture. This created a feeling of shared descent and sense of belonging for all group members, but did not prevent the splitting up of the Mek into warring subgroups. However, upon pacification, the shared myth of origin acted as a medium of reunification (Eibl-Eibesfeldt and Heeschen 1998). In the communal mens-house of Munggona, the Eipo venerated an approximately two-meter-long, very old digging stick as a relic of this cultural hero. Whenever a new mens-house was built, this digging stick was moved to the new mens-house in a special ritual.

To live in groups that demarcate themselves from others is a basic feature of human nature. To blind ourselves to this reality would be unproductive and there is no need for such a denial. We are gifted with nurturance and bonding and we can sympathize even with non-kin. This may allow us to develop new strategies of coexistence. Difficulties derive from the fact that competition will continue to operate; but competition does not need to be red in tooth and claw (Eibl-Eibesfeldt *et al.* 1989)

The ethics of sharing and giving

Globalization changed the prospering countries of the European Union in a strange way into candidates for economic and social trust. The earnings of the lower income classes are approaching the poverty line, while the incomes of some managers reached gigantic proportions. The gap between rich and poor is widening, causing social strain.

"*The Blind Watchmaker*" as Richard Dawkins (1987) characterized evolution by random mutation and selection, produced not only marvelous, beautiful insects with fascinating adaptations, and friendly pets, but also monsters, such as the fly, *Lucilia silvarum*, whose maggots live in the nose cavity of frogs and toads. A related Brazilian species attacks the human face from within the nose cavity. Bacterial and viral diseases, and a great variety of parasites, plague all higher forms of life, and carnivorous vertebrates start to eat their prey often when still alive. Man in this respect does not differ so much in his modern ways of animal husbandry. However, there is something new: our species feels empathy even with its animal victims, experiences pangs of bad conscience and strives to improve their fate.

Evolution has thus provided us with an emotional outfit primarily, of course, to sympathize with other members of our species that allows us to civilize competition and thus achieve common welfare and internal peace, a prerequisite for peaceful international relations. Our urge to help has to do with an innate ethic of sharing and giving, associated with the feelings of empathy and love, which evolved in the context of nurturant maternal care. A great number of rituals of sharing, giving and hosting are universally used to establish and foster friendly relations. Even small toddlers know how to share and give as a way to win friends.

All over the world the transfer of morsels or other objects as gifts follows the same basic rules:

1 If a person wants to give, he or she must possess something. Moreover, possession is based on the rule of priority. "I had it first", is an argument that we often hear in disputes between children. And it is as a respected rule.
2 If a person wants to be given something, he or she should respect the ownership of the other person and not just demand to be given.
3 If a token is offered, it should be accepted, or a reason must be given to explain why it is refused, for example reference to a food taboo or an indisposition. However, without an excuse the refusal would be taken as an offence.
4 A person accepting a gift is expected to reciprocate. The reciprocation does not need to occur immediately. At the time of giving a friendly response such as the readiness for a chat or a game or simply thanking would do. Delayed reciprocation is often expected and reciprocation can be done in many ways.
5 Reciprocation should be balanced – not too little and not too much.

There are many cultural elaborations of the rituals of sharing, hosting and giving. The !Kung Bushmen of the central Kalahari, who represent a model for paleolithic foragers, had an elaborate system of sharing and giving (Wiessner 1977, 1982). Mainly women cultivated exchange partnerships with a number of persons spread over a larger area. In a reciprocal exchange, once a year they send their partners bracelets made from pierced disks of ostrich shells or beads, and they received the same from their partners as a token of friendship. This served as a sort of social security. The exchange partners were obliged to allow each other access to their hunting and foraging territories in cases of severe drought or other emergencies.

With the development of husbandry, agriculture division of labor and trading developed on the basis of balanced reciprocity. With the rise of anonymous societies, solidarity became diluted and exploitation entered the relation, which led to social unrest and even uprisings and civil war.

Trade is by its origin characterized as a friendly relation. Up to the present day, trade relations guarantee peace, as long as they are balanced. In ancient Greece the word "kattallateion" meant "establishing peace by trade" (A. v. Hayek, 1975). The threat to cut trading relations still serves as an efficient warning to behave.

The prosocial roots of collective aggression

Familial dispositions, as already pointed out, form the basis of humankind's prosociality. Their origin is rooted in the nurturant individualized parent–offspring relation. In this context, nurturant behaviors, the motivations of caretaking, mother–child signals and the capacity for individualized bonding evolved, with the mother–child bond being the first manifestation of the "us" versus the "others". These familial adaptations constitute pre-adaptations for living in larger anonymous communities, such as ethnicities, nation states and multinational federations. However, these pre-adaptations had to be welded by cultural experimentation. Since human beings are primarily adapted for a life in smaller face-to-face communities, ever since the transition into larger anonymous societies mankind has been faced with the problem of developing loyalties toward people unknown to him. If we look at the mechanisms employed to bond members of groups who are not close kin, we observe that they tap into existing adaptations of familial sociality. Culturally developed symbols of identification, toward which individuals get fixated and emotionally attached in an imprinting-like fashion, serve as bonding amongst others.

Ties of friendship and belonging bind members of the individualized group together in an atmosphere of basic trust. Innate and culturally elaborated rituals ensure that competitive fighting between group members does not escalate to manslaughter. Personal acquaintance effectively buffers aggression.

In contrast, strangers are met with suspicion. It is well-known that xenophobia is a universal phenomenon, but I want to emphasize that fear of strangers is not to be confused with hatred of strangers, which is a result of indoctrination. War unfortunately is an old "achievement", in part cultural but basically rooted in family defense (Eibl-Eibesfeldt, 1979), which explains its fierceness.

With the evolution of animal husbandry and agriculture, higher population densities became possible and competition over land, property and other resources became better organized and thus, also due to technical advances, more destructive, as history teaches us. Groups that, using social techniques, were able to recruit more manpower for attack and defense had an advantage over smaller groups.

Up to the present, competition between nations and other communities of humans, against all lip service, continues to be fairly merciless. War is still legitimized – of course only as a defensive measure, but excuses are easily constructed for preventive action. Killing on a large scale is permitted as long as one expresses regret for the civilian victims. An enormous amount of money is spent on armor, and fear is one prevailing motivation.

There is something special about collective aggression concerning its fierceness and emotionality. Under the umbrella of flags and other "sacred" insignia young people, especially men, experience the shudder of elatedness or enthusiasm, which is caused by the contraction of the musculus arrector pili. In an aroused readiness for group defense, we fluff a vestigial fur, get goose pimples and feel the shudder of being gripped by something out of our control. Marching music, hymns, folk songs and other melodies, which we associate with early social companionship and other positive communal experiences, carry us away, sometimes in a collective frenzy of enthusiasm.[6]

What makes collective aggression so dangerous, as well as heroic, is its being rooted in family defense. Collective aggression is by its nature prosocial aggression.

Accepting different levels of identification: an important step toward global peace

All over the world we are experiencing a resurgence of tribalism and ethnic conflict. This comes to many liberal intellectuals as a surprise. Instead of empirically searching for the causes of the worldwide manifestations of ethnocentrism and xenophobia, however, the problem is brushed aside as nonexistent: ethnicity is but a construct, we are told, and what is constructed can be deconstructed. The notion is not so new, nor is it original. During China's Cultural Revolution, Mao turned his back on ethnology and the ethnologists. "There is only one people of China" was the slogan. Ethnic minorities were defined away and their problems declared as nonexistent. "We have to crack the eggs of the nationalities in order to bake the omelette of a unified Nation" was one of Mao's sayings. The Namibian Government recently pursued similar goals. Somehow, it is worrying to see western intellectuals treading the same ideological pathways. True, ethnicity can be seen as a cultural construct, since ethnic groups are culturally defined. Nevertheless, they represent a social reality since Kurds, after all, define themselves as Kurds, and Armenians as Armenians, etc. And many are ready to sacrifice their lives to preserve their identity. One may argue: they are misled! However, this leads to questions such as: why are people all over the world so easily misled?

Previously, we provided some answers concerning the prosocial roots of ethnocentrism, racism and war, which mark man's history. The discussion of our century focused upon the question of how to overcome inter-ethnic violence and bloodshed. Should ethnicity be sacrificed? Many have proposed this solution. The idea of a classless homogenized humankind was perceived as one fascinating option by many intellectuals. Their intentions, I assume, were well-meaning. They failed, however, since all life strives toward diversity. Subspeciation and speciation are the "strategies" by which life secures its continuing existence in an ever-changing world. Only extremely repressive political systems could suppress this striving toward diversification. A forcefully homogenized world might be hell to live in, and the process of forceful homogenization of the existing multicultural world certainly meet with resistance, as the experiments by Stalin and Mao have demonstrated. Competition still continues along the ancient lines. Through indoctrination, people develop group identities that are elicited by the symbols of their community. For many, especially males, identity alone constitutes a readiness to respond to a threat to their identity with collective aggression, emotionally nourished from archaic parental motivations. The martyr who burned himself in protest against a dominating power in Prague is hailed as a hero. And it is not difficult to understand this universal trait, since being dominated certainly does not contribute to one's genetic fitness.

What could be done to protect group identities in accordance with the Statutes of UN and at the same time to promote world peace? First of all, we should not threaten the different levels of identity, which Europeans prize, as do non-Europeans. Besides identifying with family, kin and their local community, a high percentage of Europeans also identify themselves as Europeans. A recent Eurobarometer Study showed that 42% of the population of the 15 member states of the European Union said that they felt solely nationals of their own country, but 52% expressed an additional European identification. This implies that about 130 million adult citizens of the EU member states consider themselves as nationalists and 177 million as having multiple identities (Lutz *et al.* 2006).

In my hometown of Vienna, all of these identities are represented in the Denkmal Kultur (memorial culture), most within walking reach in the center of the city. We are also Europeans, and on a higher European level the parliament in Vienna refers to our Greek and Roman heritage. The building copies many elements of a Greek temple, with Pallas Athene, the protectoress of the cities, the fields, the Arts, the Sciences and the heroes on the facade (Figure 4.23).

We are extremely familial and thus prosocial beings and prepared to familiarize with others at different levels and within different circles as long as we are not forced to give up our identities stemming from family, kin and the local and ethnic "Heimat". If the nation state is dissolved or becomes too diverse, there is mounting evidence that this results in a loss of solidarity and endangers internal and in consequence external peace.

Loyalty with even larger groups can be built, tapping into the familial "we" by showing what we share in common. We can live with international ethnic diversity and identify with others at the highest levels. The more we know about others, the less we are inclined to foster negative images.

Finally, we should be aware that we have every reason, as Hans Hass expressed, to foster a spirit of comradeship for humankind, "since everything responsible for our human existence is due to an anonymous multitude of others who lived before us and whose achievements have been bestowed upon us as gifts" (Hass 1981).

Identification with others on different levels will also help to unite us in our attempts to solve the problems, which the "Hit of Evolution" faces due to its success. We have to adapt our population to the carrying capacity of our planet, but we value growth and this blinds our perception. We are definitely too many and should attempt to reach an optimum, which would allow a high standard of life including optimal conditions for the expression in the Arts and Sciences. Right now we are wasting the resources of future generations. We need an economically oriented market economy in a multi-ethnic world community bonded by sympathy and a shared concern for the future.

Last, but not least, we should not forget the dynamics behind collective aggression, which is driven by an easily instigated strong motivation. Here catharsis can be achieved with competitive games such as football championships or Olympic Games, which foster world companionship. Finally, there are enough tasks challenging the world community resulting from climatic changes, catastrophic events, overpopulation and the degradation of the social and ecological environment. We could jointly attack these problems and sink our teeth into them. In this context, it is always hopeful to experience how the world community hurries to help the victims of hurricanes, tsunamis, earthquakes and other catastrophes, regardless of the geographic region. Emotionally we are basically

Figure 4.23 The Austrian Parliament building with the Athena fountain in the foreground.

"good" as long as our families and kin and other superimposed levels of identity are not threatened. Our behavior toward our fellow men is ambivalent, oscillating between the friendly readiness to establish contact and our fear-motivated avoidance. Through emotion and reason, we are able to balance the scale toward prosociality. Able to contemplate and thus set free from restraints, we are the first species challenged to accept the responsibility for our future.

Summary and discussion

We appear to be an extremely successful species with high individual and cultural adaptability, especially salient when dealing with the greatest ingenuity, but we seem handicapped in solving many of our social problems and in keeping control of our inventions that often develop a dynamic of their own. Each discovery, each new invention changes our lives and, in addition to its beneficial effect, confronts us with unforeseeable consequences and challenges our adaptability. Some traits of our paleolithic heritage, however, hamper our efforts. Amongst others, we are a very competitive species with a strong urge to dominate others at the individual and group levels, programmed for the sprint to win right now, without much consideration for the future. We are prone to become caught in the trap of short-term thinking (Eibl-Eibesfeldt, 1998). All in all, the development has to be considered as progress, since without million societies there would be no universities, no large libraries, concert halls and other cultural institutions. However, overpopulation, poverty, hunger, war and environmental destruction plague our planet. We need to civilize ourselves, and this needs a better insight in the phylogenetic history of our functioning organism.

This chapter aims to provide such an understanding. It started with short introduction into the history of human ethology, pointing in this context to Darwin's contribution. In a summarizing way, the key term adaptation is discussed and the term "phylogenetic adaptation" defined.

Notes

1 empeiria (gr.) meaning experience, knowledge.
2 In the edelweiss, the petals of the flowers are a beautiful white in high altitudes. If the plants are transferred to low altitudes, the white filaments covering the petals as protection against the strong UV radiation vanish and they therefore appear green, which is advantageous for assimilation.
3 The left hemisphere also contains the modules which constitute the motor and acoustic language centers (Broca and Wernicke). The reference to objectivity, to talk and discuss "sine ira et studio" as well as the instrumental use of language by which we convince others and win their trust, supports the assumption that object manipulation and dexterity are important precursors for the development of speech.
4 We know that a hormonal reflex is responsible for the short sensitive period. The extension of the cervix during birth triggers oxytocin release. This hormone induces the readiness to accept an infant. In the course of evolution, these adaptations proved to be the pre-adaptations for many higher forms of social life.

5 During courtship many birds act alternately the role of the nurturant and the nurtured. The courting female woodpecker finch may behave like a fledging, uttering begging calls and engaging in begging behaviors like gaping and wing-fluttering, upon which her male partner may feed her. Shortly afterwards the male may in turn take on the infantile role. In the black-headed gull, both sexes exhibit a black facemask, a signal that triggers aggressive responses. When a female lands in the territory of a male in response to his beckoning call, she runs the risk of being attacked. To avoid this she approaches the male with the food-begging behaviors typical for the young, and thereby triggers feeding responses.

6 von griech. "Entheos", gottbegeistert ('carried off by Godly feelings').

References

Darwin, C. 1872. *The Expression of Emotions in Man and Animals* (London).

Dawkins, R. 1987. *The blind watchmaker* (W.W. Norton: New York, NY; London, UK).

Eibl-Eibesfeldt, I. 1950. Über die Jugendentwicklung des Verhaltens eines männlichen Dachses (*Meles meles L.*) unter bes. Berücksichtigung des Spieles, *Z. f. Tierpsychologie* 7:327–355.

Eibl-Eibesfeldt, I. 1975. *Ethology – The Biology of Behavior, 2nd edition* (Holt, Rinehart and Winston: New York, NY).

Eibl-Eibesfeldt, I. 1979. Human ethology: Concepts and implications for the science of man, *Behav. Brain Sci.* 2:1–57.

Eibl-Eibesfeldt, I. 1982. Warfare, Man's Indoctrinability and Group Selection. Zeitschrift f. Tierpsychologie, 60, 177–198.

Eibl-Eibesfeldt, I. 1989. *Human Ethology* (Aldine Transaction Publ: New Brunswick, NJ; London, UK). Paperback Edition 2008.

Eibl-Eibesfeldt, I. 1998. *In der Falle des Kurzzeitdenkens* (Piper: München, Germany) Paperback ed. 2000.

Eibl-Eibesfeldt, I. 2004. *Die Biologie des menschlichen* Verhaltens 5, Auflage (genehmigte Sonderausgabe), Vierkirchen-Pasenbach (BuchVertrieb Blank).

Eibl-Eibesfeldt, I. and Goodall, J. 1986. *Pan troglodytes (Pongidae) Termitenfischen. Film HF 194 – E 3012*, Encyclopaedia Cinematographica, Institut für den Wissenschaftlichen Film, Göttingen. Farbe, stumm, 233m, 20 min. Publ. Zu Wissensch. Filmen (Biologie) 21:89–100.

Eibl-Eibesfeldt, I. and Heeschen, V. 1998. *Eipo, West-Neuguinea, Zentrales Hochland: Demonstration des rituellen Pflanzens einer cordyline*, Film E 3035 von I. Eibl-Eibesfeldt. Publikationen zu wiss. Filmen Ethnologie. Sonderband 9:13–25. Institut f. den wissenschaftlichen Film, Göttingen.

Eibl-Eibesfeldt, I., Schiefenhövel, W. and Heeschen, V. 1989. *Kommunikation bei den Eipo*, Eine humanethologische Bestandsaufnahme (Dietrich Reimer: Berlin, Germany).

Eibl-Eibesfeldt, I. and Sütterlin, C. 2007. *Weltsprache Kunst. Zur Natur- und Kunstgeschichte bildlicher Kommunikation* (Brandstätter-Verlag: Wien, Austria).

Ekman, P. and W.V. Friesen. 1978. *Facial Action Coding System* (Consulting Psychologists Press Inc: Palo Alto, CA).

Erikson, E.H. 1966. Ontogeny of Ritualization in Man. Philosoph, Transact. *Roy. Soc. London B* 251:337–349.

Freedman, D. G. 1964. Smiling in blind infants and the Issue of Innate versus Acquired, *J. Child Psychol. Psychiat.* 5:171–184.

Hass, H. 1981. *Vorteil des Menschen; Das neue Erfolgs- und Karrierebuch für Erfolgs- und Führungskräfte* (Beste Unternehmensführung: Geretsried, Germany).

Hayek, F.A. von. 1975. *Die Irrtümer des Konstruktivismus,* Walter Eucken Institut, Vorträge und Aufsätze 51. J.C.B. Mohr (Pauls Siebeck: Tübingen, Germany).

Hooff, J.A.R.A.M. van. 1971. *Aspecten van Het Sociale Gedrag En De Communicatie Bij Humane En Hogere Niet-Humane Primaten. (Aspects of the social behaviour and communication in human and higher non-human primates.)* (Bronder-Offset n.v.: Rotterdam, The Netherlands).

Kortlandt, A. 1965. How do Chimpanzees use Weapons when Fighting Leopards, *Yearbook Amer. Philos. Soc.* 327–332.

Lorenz, K. 1935. Der Kumpan in der Umwelt des Vogels, *J. Ornithol.* 83:137–413.

Lorenz, K. 1943. Die angeborenen Formen möglicher Erfahrung, *Z. f. Tierpsychol* 5:235–409.

Lorenz, K. 1953. Die Entwicklung der Verhaltensforschung in den letzten 12 Jahren, *Zool. Anz. Suppl.* 16:36–58.

Lutz, W., S. Kritzinger and V. Skrzipek. 2006. The Demography of Growing European Identity, *Science* 314:425.

Markl, H. 1986. *Evolution, Genetik und menschliches Verhalten* (Piper: München, Germany).

Musterle, W. and O.E. Rössler. 1986. Computer Faces: The Human Lorenz Matrix, *BioSystems* 1919:61–80.

Pawlow, I.P. 1927. *Conditioned Reflexes* (Oxford).

Schiefenhövel, W. 1998. Indoctrination among the Eipo in the Highlands of New Guinea, in I. Eibl-Eibesfeldt and Frank Salter (ed.), *Ethnic conflict and Indoctrination. Altruism and identity in evolutionary perspective* (Berghahn: Oxford, UK; New York, NY), pp. 109–132.

Simpson, G.G. 1963. Biology and the nature of science, *Science* 138:81–88.

Skrzipek, K.H. 1978. Menschliche "Auslösermerkmale" beider Geschlechter. I. Attrappenwahluntersuchungen der Verhaltensentwicklung, *Homo* 29:75–88.

Tinbergen, N. 1951. *The study of Instinct* (Oxford University Press: London, UK; Toronto, Canada).

Wallhäuser, E. and H. Scheich. 1987. Auditory Imprinting leads to Differential 2-deoxyglucose Uptake and Dendritic Spine Loss in the Chick Rostral Forebrain, *Developmental Brain Res.* 31:29–44.

Wiessner, P. 1977. Hxaro*: A Regional System of Reciprocity for Reducing Risk among the !Kung San*, Ph.D. Dissertation, University of Michigan, Ann Arbor, Univ. Microfilms.

Wiessner, P. 1982. Risk, Reciprocity and Social Influences on !Kung San Economies, in E. Leacock and R. Lee (ed.), *Politics and History in Band Societies* (Cambridge University Press: Cambridge, London, UK), pp. 61–84.

5 The boat, the bay, and the museum

Significance of the 1905–1906 Galápagos expedition of the California Academy of Sciences

Matthew J. James

Introduction

The 1905–1906 Galápagos scientific collecting expedition achieved its success through careful planning and organization and by selecting competent fieldworkers as expedition members (Figure 5.1). The California Academy of Sciences (CAS) in San Francisco, California organized this crucial expedition. It shaped the history of Galápagos and the history of evolutionary thinking, particularly Neo-Darwinism. The determined organizational efforts of museum director and ornithologist Leverett Mills Loomis (1857–1928) (Bishop 1929) resulted in meticulous and methodical advance planning for the expedition. Its clearly defined goals were to collect a comprehensive set of specimens in the Galápagos Islands and return to San Francisco. These ends were met and exceeded Loomis's scientific expectations.

Loomis had both personal and professional goals invested in the expedition and its eight field collectors who served as sailor-scientists. He and the governing board of the Academy in San Francisco wanted to increase the scientific prestige of their institution, the oldest museum west of the Rocky Mountains. They hoped to obtain a level of international prestige, perhaps rivaling the American Museum of Natural History in New York City. Their path to success involved conducting extensive collecting expeditions to build up the size of their biological and geological collections. These new and enlarged collections would form the basis of scientific monographs to be published by the senior curatorial staff. As one of those senior curators at the museum, Loomis desired particularly to expand their holdings of seabirds, his personal taxonomic specialty, and to collect the giant tortoises that he and others believed were "fast disappearing".

The purpose of this chapter is to address a little known aspect of Galápagos history: the 1905–1906 Galápagos expedition of the CAS and its subsequent impact on advancing science. In particular, I look at the history of the young men who participated in the expedition and their boat – one of the last in the era of sail. A hallmark of the 1905–1906 expedition is the approximately 78,000 specimens brought back to San Francisco, which by today's standard is considered excessive. I study the historical reasoning that justified these large collections and the change in scientific focus from *ex situ* preservation in museums to *in situ* conservation and restoration over the last 100 years. Finally, I examine the significance of this vast collection of specimens in advancing Galápagos science over the last 100 years. This chapter extends current knowledge using reference to the original field notes, correspondence, and photographs taken during the expedition and housed in the CAS library and archives in San Francisco.

The title of this chapter, "The boat, the bay, and the museum", emphasizes three entities with strong Galápagos connections and all called "Academy". All three are part of or connected to the 1905–1906 Galápagos scientific collecting expedition of the CAS:

1 The CAS in San Francisco, California, founded in 1853, is the natural history museum that has become the center of specimen-based studies of Galápagos organisms, owing to the large collection of specimens brought back to San Francisco by the highly successful 1905–1906 expedition.
2 The 89-foot schooner *Academy*, which was named in honor of the museum, the CAS when it was rechristened in San Francisco on 27 June 1905, from the former U.S. Coast and Geodetic Survey and U.S. Navy vessel USS *Earnest*.

Figure 5.1 Members of the 1905–1906 California Academy of Sciences expedition to the Galápagos Islands, including the "eight young men" who served as sailor–scientists. From the left: Frederick T. Nelson, Alban Stewart, Ernest Samuel King, Rollo Howard Beck, Joseph Slayton Hunter, sitting J.J. Parker, Joseph Richard Slevin, Edward Winslow Gifford, Washington Henry Ochsner, Francis Xavier Williams. Not shown: James White, the expedition's cook (source: California Academy of Sciences, used with permission).

3 Academy Bay, the present-day port on the south coast of Isla Santa Cruz and location of the now-bustling town of Puerto Ayora, but which was completely uninhabited in 1905–1906. The bay was named by the crew of the schooner in honor of the schooner herself (not the museum), on 5 November 5 1905. In Spanish, the bay should be called Bahia Academy, not Bahia Academia, to preserve the original namesake.

Two notes of irony leading to success

To begin the story of the expedition, I would like to start at the end. Irony operates at several levels for the 1905–1906 Galápagos expedition, with two particularly ironic twists contributing to the ultimate success of the expedition. First, for nearly a year in 1904–1905, museum director Loomis could not charter or purchase a suitable sailing vessel on which to send the collecting party, headed by Rollo Howard Beck (1870–1950). Being unable to secure a suitable vessel meant that Loomis delayed departure for nine months from San Francisco from his original date of October 1904 until the actual departure date of late June 1905. Had the expedition departed as Loomis originally planned, they would have returned to San Francisco (after 17 months) in March of 1906. However, on 18 April 1906, a great earthquake devastated San Francisco and other cities in the greater San Francisco Bay Area (Fradkin 2005; Klett 2006; Winchester 2006). Thousands of Galápagos specimens that would have been stored in wooden museum cabinets would have all been destroyed. The three days of unstoppable fires that raged through San Francisco, and not the earthquake itself, would have demolished the specimens along with the building and other contents of the CAS (Gifford 1908).

The second irony, or perhaps near irony, occurred on the very last day of the expedition as the schooner full of specimens approached the then bridgeless entrance to San Francisco Bay on Thanksgiving Day, 29 November 1906. All the crewmembers were overjoyed about getting into harbor and having Thanksgiving dinner with their families. After sailing up to the entrance in light winds, the wind died and they were becalmed. Slowly they drifted through the headlands separating San Francisco from Marin County, and narrowly missed colliding with the pilot boat *Lady Mine*, another becalmed ship. Instead of their much-anticipated Thanksgiving family dinners, they settled for another tiresome meal of canned Alaska salmon. With insufficient leeway to come about without grounding on the rocks, they put out the ship's boat and attempted to row the schooner's bow around, away from the rocks. Unsuccessful in this sailing maneuver, they hailed a passing crab fisherman in his fishing smack, the *Louisa*, and for ten dollars the schooner hitched a tow to the quarantine station by 10:15 p.m. The trip had ended. The expedition party and boatload of specimens were safe. They had sailed non-stop for 65 days from their last Galápagos landfall at Culpepper Island, for a total of 519 days of the voyage (Slevin 1931).

The eight young men

For background on the expedition, I present in the list below the age of each of the sailor-scientists at the start of the expedition after their expedition title. Each man's age at death is given following his place of death. Names are presented in the same order as Slevin (1931: 6). The personnel aboard the schooner *Academy* consisted of 11 members, three crewmembers in addition to the "eight young men" who served as sailor-scientists, as follows:

Rollo Howard Beck, chief of party and master of the vessel, 34 years old. Born: 26 August 1870, Los Gatos, California. Died: 22 November 1950, Planada, California, 80 years old. Beck went on to lead several multi-year collecting expeditions and was widely viewed as *the* collector of his day (Pitelka 1986).

Washington Henry Ochsner, conchologist and geologist, 22 years old. Born: 4 July 1882, Wisconsin. Died: 11 April 1927, Portland, Oregon, 44 years old. Ochsner returned to Stanford University after the expedition and eventually found oil in the Kettleman Hills of central California, the fortune from which came in after his death.

Francis Xavier Williams, entomologist, 22 years old. Born: 6 August 1882, Martinez, California. Died: 16 December 1967, Chula Vista, California, 85 years old. Williams went on to a long career as an entomologist, which included many years working for the Hawaiian Sugar Planters Association.

Edward Winslow Gifford, ornithologist, 17 years old. Born: 14 August 1887, Oakland, California. Died: 16 May 1959, Paradise, Butte County, California, 71 years old. Was the last person in the US to become a full professor without even earning a bachelor's degree; he became director of the Lowie Museum of Anthropology and contributed to knowledge of migration in the Pacific through analysis of Lapita pottery.

Joseph Slayton Hunter, mammalogist, 25 years old. Born: 9 August 1879, Lincoln, Nebraska. Died: 20 January 1972, San Mateo, California, 92 years old. Hunter spent the next 42 years working for the California Fish and Game Commission and he became the head of the California State Bureau of Game Conservation.

Alban Stewart, botanist, 30 years old. Born: 14 January 1875, Wellington, Missouri. Died: 31 May 1940, Tallahassee, Florida, 65 years old. Stewart obtained his Ph.D. in botany in 1911 at the Gray Herbarium at Harvard University; until his death, he taught in the Department of Bacteriology at the Florida State College for Women, which later became Florida State University, in Tallahassee.

Joseph Richard Slevin, assistant herpetologist and second mate, 24 years old. Born: 13 September 1881, San Francisco, California. Died: 15 February 1957, San Francisco, California, 75 years old. Slevin went on to a long and distinguished career as the head herpetologist at the CAS until his death.

Ernest Samuel King, assistant herpetologist, 18 years old. Born: 16 December 1886, San Jose, California. Died: 1 July 1948, San Jose, California, 61 years old. King did not pursue science as a career, working for Kaiser Aluminum and Chemical Corporation until his death.

***Additional crew on the schooner* Academy**

Frederick T. Nelson, first mate, 28 years old. Born: 7 April 1877, Denmark. Died: 17 April 1938, Alameda, California, 61 years old. Nelson went on to a long career as a sea captain, remaining life-long friends with Ochsner.

Little biographical information is known about the expedition's navigator, J.J. Parker (who was put off the boat for incompetence late in the mission) or about the cook or steward, James W. White.

The boat: the schooner Earnest/Academy

The *Academy* was originally built as the schooner *Earnest* in 1875 in Baltimore, Maryland, in the William E. Woodall boatyard for the United States Coast Survey, founded by Congress in 1807 as the maritime equivalent of the Lewis and Clark expedition (1804–1806). She sank off Isle Au Haute, Maine in 1876, but was repaired and sailed around the Horn non-stop to San Francisco in 1878, passing 200 miles west of the Galápagos Island through one of the largest El Niño events on record (James 2003). The schooner *Earnest* remained in service with the Coast Survey (which became the U.S. Coast and Geodetic Survey in 1878) until 1901 and served in the San Juan Islands, Washington, and into Alaskan waters. While in a new role as a U.S. Navy training vessel in San Francisco Bay in March 1904, the most violent storm to hit San Francisco Bay in over a dozen years tossed the schooner ashore on Yerba Buena Island. She was beyond repair for the Navy, and was sold to the CAS for use as a scientific research vessel. She spent 17 months on the 1905–1906 Galápagos expedition of the CAS, and ultimately disappeared from maritime records on December 31, 1915, in Balboa, Panama, when sold after tragic events unfolded during an ill-fated gold-hunting expedition to Tierra del Fuego at the southern tip of South America.

The bay: Academy Bay

On the grounds of the Charles Darwin Research station, near the souvenir shop (tienda) at the little snack bar, a brass plaque was installed in 2005 by the CAS and the Charles Darwin Foundation "Commemorating 100 years of research and collaboration". Academy Bay, on the southern shore of Santa Cruz Island, was named on 5 November 1905 by crewmembers of the schooner *Academy* in honor of the schooner herself. The bay was uninhabited in 1905, but is today the location of the largest town in Galápagos, Puerto Ayora, and the headquarters of the Charles Darwin Foundation and the Galápagos National Park Service. The brass plaque reads,

> Near this site on November 5, 1905, members of the California Academy of Sciences' first Galápagos research expedition came ashore. Academy Bay is named for their ship, the *Academy*. This plaque celebrates the continued

collaboration between the Academy and the people of Ecuador to understand and conserve the islands' irreplaceable biological and historical treasures for humankind, now and forever. 3 June 2005.

The Museum: the California Academy of Sciences

The CAS began as a scientific organization in April 1853, during the flush years of the California Gold Rush. Seven prominent San Francisco gentlemen met under the dim glow of tallow candles in a poorly furnished room on Montgomery Street, near the heart of today's financial district, to form a fledgling society for the study of natural history. Their stated intention on 4 April 1853 was to organize "an association for the development of the natural sciences" (Hittell 1997). Their goal was accomplished, but it took many years to become a world-class museum, through strife and tragedy.

For most people familiar today with the city of San Francisco, the CAS is the big natural history museum in Golden Gate Park, right across from the de Young Museum of Art. Few visitors know that the Academy was not always located in Golden Gate Park, and fewer still know much about the early years of this venerable San Francisco institution. As people wander about the impressive museum building designed by Italian architect Renzo Piano, enjoying the Steinhart Aquarium, the Morrison Planetarium, and the numerous exhibits on natural history, there is little indication that over 150 years ago the Academy had a very modest beginning in downtown San Francisco. Few visitors know about the Academy's tumultuous history in the late nineteenth and early twentieth centuries. Despite its humble and unpretentious beginnings as a small, under-funded institution, the California Academy of Natural Sciences (as it was first called) proved ultimately to be one of the dominant forces in San Francisco's cultural history.

In 1873, as the Academy celebrated its twentieth year with a major windfall that propelled it toward permanent success. Mr James Lick (1796–1876), a San Francisco real estate mogul, entrepreneur, and philanthropist with land holdings dating from before the Gold Rush, contacted the Academy about a gift of land for a permanent museum. Lick donated a plot of land at the corner of Market and Fourth Streets in order to "promote the diffusion of Science and the prosperity and perpetuity of the Academy". With the Lick bequest, the Academy's star was certainly rising and it had become one of the wealthiest scientific societies in the United States. As a scientific institution, their future was secure and the Lick bequest ultimately allowed the Academy to build in 1891 a museum and an income-generating office building on Market Street, between Fourth and Fifth Streets, where it would remain for 15 years.

In the latter part of the nineteenth century, the CAS grew into a mature scientific institution: they acquired the museum building, built a respectable research collection of specimens and library, and employed a competent and energetic scientific staff. They were poised to expand, to flex their muscles, if you will, and the Galápagos Islands were the ideal agents of expansion. In those exotic isles, made famous half a century earlier by Charles Darwin, the Academy could obtain abundant specimens of rare plants and animals at minimal cost to boost the prestige of their collections. The Galápagos was their ticket to success. Little did they know it would also be their key to their survival.

Preservation in 1905 before modern-day conservation

Perhaps one of the surprising (and I would argue, incorrectly interpreted) aspects of this scientific expedition is the large number of Galápagos specimens collected (see Table 5.1) and the apparent disregard for conservation exhibited by the field collectors. In a historical context, however, their actions were scientifically justified. Their actions as field collectors cannot be judged by modern conservation standards, whose origins come from the 1950s. The reader must instead understand both the mindset of the state of scientific conservation in the early years of the twentieth century and the state of governmental protection of the Galápagos Islands in those same years (which was virtually nil).

To analyze this collection–conservation conundrum in greater depth I use the Galápagos example. The CAS and director Loomis decided on the Galápagos Islands because they were "made famous to every naturalist by Charles Darwin, whose account of the voyage of HMS *Beagle* has become a classic amongst students of nature" (See Grant and Estes 2009; Keynes 1979; Larson 2001). Loomis was further motivated by information he received from Rollo Howard Beck about the status of giant tortoises in the islands. Beck was a participant in an expedition to the islands in 1897–1898 financed by Walter Rothschild (1868–1937) of Tring, England, who wrote in 1899 in a letter to herpetologist Albert Günther (1830–1914), who was at the time President of the Linnaean Society: "It was lucky they went last year; in 3 years' time there will not be a

Table 5.1 Numbers of specimens collected of broad taxonomic groups on the CAS expedition of 1905–1906

Taxonomic group	*Number of specimens (based on Gifford, 1908; and B. West, pers. comm., 2011)*
Vertebrates	Reptiles 5,000 Birds 8,688 Eggs 2,000 Mammals 120 Sum = 15,808
Invertebrates	Land snails 29,975 Marine shells 8,967 Fossils *c.* 1,000 Insects *c.* 13,000 Sum = 52,942
Vascular plants	Plants *c.* 10,000
Expedition total	78,750

living giant Land Tortoise of any kind on the Galápagos Islands, 'What a damnable shame' is it not?" As a member of this Rothschild-financed expedition, Rollo Beck took a particular photograph (see Figure 9 in Fritts and Fritts 1982: 98; and Figure 1 in Dumbacher and West, 2010) that showed numerous tortoises on Albemarle (Isabella) Island that had been killed and their bodies boiled and rendered for oil, in much the same way whales were rendered for oil. The photograph itself showed, and the wider implications of current slaughter were, that extirpation of the tortoises was inevitable. This motivated Loomis and the CAS, which financially backed the 1905–1906 expedition to "make a thorough study of the status of the gigantic land tortoises and secure specimens of the various species before it proved too late" (Slevin 1931: 5; Van Denburgh 1914). The notion that time was running out gave a sense of urgency in San Francisco to organizing the expedition, arranging for a suitable schooner, hiring the eight young men to serve as sailor-scientists and, while in the islands, collecting as much as possible. If the organisms, especially the giant land tortoises, were on a collision course with extinction due to human depredation, then, the logic goes, the remaining tortoises were better off dead and preserved in a museum for scientific study than be killed for food or boiled for oil and lost forever to science.

Commenting on the large numbers of specimens that were taken by the *Academy* collectors during their year in the islands (especially the 266 giant tortoises), the entomologist Howard Evans cast their activity in a positive, if not with hindsight an illuminated, light. "This seems a considerable slaughter, but it should be remembered that at this time tortoises and other native animals were being devastated by visiting whalers and by the settlers, and goats and other introduced animals were destroying habitats rapidly. The work of the expedition provided basic knowledge on the fauna that ultimately led to successful conservation efforts" (Evans 1985: 207–208). It would take another generation, and a new perspective on conservation, before concrete efforts were made to preserve the biota of the Galápagos.

The small, uninhabited Barrington (Santa Fé) Island serves as a showcase, or microcosm, of the larger problems facing Galápagos organisms in 1905 when the *Academy* visited, and of the serious problems that continue today. In addition to the devastated land iguana colony, the tortoises of Barrington tell a parallel story. During the expedition, Slevin and the other men on the *Academy* met a fellow named Captain Thomas Levick (Latorre 1999: 137) who ran a schooner between the islands. Levick frankly informed them that "30 years ago tortoises were found scattered all over Barrington and that he had taken them off of there". (Fritts and Fritts 1982: 66) Rarely does one meet the actual person responsible for the extinction of a species, but the *Academy* crew seems to have crossed paths with one.

In terms of the mindset of scientists of the day, one can easily turn to the most prominent ornithologist at the end of the nineteenth century, whose influence extended into the early twentieth century, Elliott Coues (1842–1899) (last name is pronounced "cows"). After he died, the influence of his 1872 book *Key to North American Birds* was described in an obituary (Anonymous 1900) as having "probably done as much to advance the interests of ornithology in this country as any other work". In this landmark book on North American birds, which was very likely known to Rollo Beck, Joseph Hunter, and Edward Gifford (the field collectors whose primary emphasis was ornithology), Coues gives basic directions to amateur and professional ornithologists about how to conduct fieldwork and how to build a bird skin collection for personal or professional study. Coues opens the first section of the book with a description of "Field Ornithology: Being a Manual for Collecting, Preparing, and Preserving Birds". Coues begins this section (Coues 1894: 1) by proclaiming, "The double-barreled shotgun is your main reliance". Few birders today would even know how to use a shotgun, let alone want to use one.

Today, both amateur birders and professional ornithologists consider a good pair of binoculars as their "main reliance". So much so that a strong culture and market has developed about the relative merits of different specifications and brands. Coues recommended to birders over 100 years ago that they might possibly trap or snare birds to collect them, but such practices were "exceptions to the rule that you will shoot birds, and for this purpose no weapon compares to the one just mentioned [double-barreled shot gun]" (Coues 1894: 1). Coues' recommendation on how much to spend on a shotgun echoes what birders today consider when making a binocular purchase, "Get the best one you can afford to buy; go the full length of your purse in the matters of material and workmanship" (Coues 1894: 1).

Another series of statements by Coues is particularly insightful about the state of conservation thinking at the end of the nineteenth and early twentieth centuries. These statements aid in understanding why the 1905–1906 expedition field party collected so many specimens in general, and so many birds in particular. Coues advised birders to collect "all you can get", for example, "say fifty or one hundred of any but the most abundant and widely diffused species". His logic was that the widely diffused or common species could be collected at a later date. Coues went on to comment, "With a few possible exceptions … enough birds of all kinds exist to overstock every public and private collection in the world, without sensible diminution of their numbers" (Coues 1894: 13). Nature, as an inexhaustible source of specimens, removes restraint from the collector's mindset. For Coues, collecting did not permanently damage a species or the environment (Barrow 2000).

Coues was further convinced that collecting birds in the manner he recommended was actually good for the mental and physical health of the bird collector. He explained that, "It is Unnecessary to speak of the Healthfulness of a pursuit that, like the collector's occupation, demands regular bodily exercise, and at the same time stimulates the mind by supplying an object, thus calling the whole system into exhilarating action" (Coues 1894: 19). After a hard day of shooting specimens, the bird collector would be rejuvenated in mind, body, and spirit. Coues depicted field ornithology of the day as tantamount to an overall health regimen. Ornithology was good for what ailed you.

In summary, it is important to note that the field collectors on the 1905–1906 expedition (James 2010) were adhering to standard practice recommended by the most respected ornithologist of the day, and shared by contemporary prominent scientists. Even if today we do not agree with that perspective, it was in fact standard operating procedure at the time. Fortunately, museum specimens, such as those collected by the 1905–1906 expedition, are actively used for a variety of scientific studies, thus establishing the enduring legacy of the expedition. Recent examples of studies using century-old museum specimens are provided here (Beissing and Peery 2007; Desrochers 2010; Hofkin *et al.* 2004).

Immortalizing Darwin's finches

A measure of the expedition's success was an acknowledgement by ornithologist David Lack (1910–1973) that his statistical analysis of Darwin's finches was made possible by the extensive collection of specimens made during the 1905–1906 expedition (Lack 1945, 1961). Lack's first major publication on these birds was in 1945 through the CAS. Lack dedicated his book *Darwin's Finches* to the staff of the CAS. Arguably, without this large collection, Lack's work might have had a different outcome.

Another success of the large number of specimens collected during the 1905–1906 expedition was the taxonomic revision of the giant tortoises by John Van Denburgh (1872–1924) (Jennings 1997; Van Denburgh 1914). By having a large number of specimens at hand, and reference to other material, Van Denburgh was able to create a "family portrait" of the giant tortoises for the first time. His monograph on the group was the first treatment of all the extant and extinct species, and stands as a landmark achievement (Pritchard 1996). Without a complete suite of specimens in one museum, Van Denburgh would have needed to travel to numerous museums before completing his taxonomic work. Having the Galápagos study series under one roof afforded him the luxury of knowing from which island most specimens were collected and he figured them at standardized angles (Pritchard 1996).

Recent use of CAS specimens and observations

The specimens and observations from the 1905–1906 expedition have been an invaluable baseline for science and conservation in Galápagos, and have been used extensively. Examples include tissue samples collected from three tortoises on Pinta being used to determine evolutionary relationships of taxa in the *Geochelone nigra* group. This information has been used as guidance in finding a potential mate for Lonesome George (Caccone *et al.* 1999). Bollmer *et al.* (2006) used a single specimen of the now extinct population of the Galápagos hawk (*Buteo galapagoensis*) collected in San Cristóbal to describe phylogenic relationships and their colonization history. Specimens have also been used to help understanding animal responses to environmental variables over time. Based on a mechanistic understanding of individual performances of marine iguanas (*Amblyrhynchus cristatus*), Wikelski and Romero (2003) predicted an evolutionary increase in maximum body size caused by global warming trends. Comparing modern specimens with those collected during 1905 validated this prediction.

Published observations from the expedition have also been used to reconstruct extinction events. Grant *et al.* (2005) show that the warbler finch (*Certhidea fusca*) was uncommon in 1905–1906, and searches since 1979 have been unable to detect their presence. Published observations and samples have been used to reconstruct the history of introduction of invasive species under current management including feral donkeys (*Equus asinus*) and feral pigs (*Sus scrofa*) (Carrion *et al.* 2007; Cruz *et al.* 2005). Patton *et al.* (1975) used allozyme analysis of a number of specimens, including those collected by CAS, to show that the black rat (*Rattus rattus*) had been introduced to the archipelago in at least three separate events between 1600 and 1945. Parker *et al.* (2011) used samples from CAS and the Zoologisches Staatssammlung Muenchen to reconstruct the introduction of avipoxvirus into Galápagos. Using histopathology and viral genotyping they concluded that this virus was introduced late in 1890s and was dispersed among islands by a variety of mechanisms, including regular human movements among colonized islands. Changes in the endemic land snail fauna, a more extensive diversification of species than Darwin's finches, has been documented by Parent and Crespi (2006) and Parent *et al.* (2008) using specimens from the CAS collections.

In summary, "the boat, the bay, and the museum" have great significance to Galápagos science: the specimens are long dead but their legacy continues.

Acknowledgements

I thank Matthias Wolff for inviting me to participate in the 20–24 July 2009 Galápagos Science Symposium organized by the Charles Darwin Foundation. Valuable editorial comments from Mark Gardener greatly improved the manuscript, along with those from my Sonoma State University faculty writing group (Kathy Charmaz, Tom Rosen, Noel Byrne, Nicole Myers, Rebecca Bryan, and Diana Grant). I thank Mark Gardener and Matthias Wolff for their patience during the editorial process. Tom Poulsom was very helpful with logistics during the 2009 symposium.

References

Anonymous. 1900. A Great Ornithologist [Elliot Coues], *The Outlook* 64:98.

Barrow, M.V., Jr. 2000. The Specimen Dealer: Entrepreneurial Natural History in America's Gilded Age, *Journal of the History of Biology* 33:493–534.

Beissinger, S.R. and M.Z. Peery. 2007. Reconstructing the historic demography of an endangered seabird, *Ecology* 88(2):296–305.

Bishop, L.B. 1929. In Memorium: Leverett Mills Loomis, *The Auk* 46(1):1–13.

Bollmer, J.L., R.T. Kimball, and N.K. Whiteman. 2006. Phylogeography of the Galápagos hawk (*Buteo galapagoensis*): a recent arrival to the Galápagos Islands, *Molecular Phylogenetics and Evolution* 39:237–247.

Caccone, A., J.P. Gibbs, V. Ketmaier, E. Suatoni, and J.R. Powell. 1999. Origin and evolutionary relationships of giant Galápagos tortoises, *Proc. Nat. Acad. Sci.* 96:13223–13228.

Carrion, V., C.J. Donlan, K. Campbell, C. Lavoie, and F. Cruz. 2007. Feral donkey (*Equus asinus*) eradications in the Galapagos, *Biodiversity and Conservation* 16: 437–445.

Coues, E. 1894. *Key to North American Birds Containing a Concise Account of Every Species of Living and Fossil Bird at Present Known from the Continent North of the Mexican and United States Boundary, Inclusive of Greenland and Lower California* (Estes and Lauriat: Boston, MA).

Cruz F., C.J. Donlan, K. Campbell, and V. Carrion. 2005. Conservation action in the Galapagos: Feral pig (*Sus scrofa*) eradication from Santiago Island, *Biological Conservation* 121:473–478.

Desrochers, A. 2010. Morphological response of songbirds to 100 years of landscape change in North America, *Ecology* 91(6):1577–1582.

Dumbacher, J.P. and B. West. 2010. Collecting Galápagos and the Pacific: How Rollo Howard Beck Shaped Our Understanding of Evolution, *Proceedings of the California Academy of Sciences, Series 4*, 61 (suppl. I):211–243.

Evans, H.E. 1985. *The Pleasures of Entomology: Portraits of Insects and the People Who Study Them* (Smithsonian Institution Press: Washington, DC).

Fradkin, P.L. 2005. *The Great Earthquake and Firestorms of 1906 – How San Francisco Nearly Destroyed Itself* (University of California Press: Berkeley, CA).

Fritts, T.H. and P.R. Fritts. 1982. Race With Extinction: Herpetological field notes of J.R. Slevin's journey to the Galapagos 1905–1906, *Herpetological Monographs* 1:i–viii; 1-98.

Gifford, E.W. 1908. The rehabilitation of the California Academy of Sciences, *The Condor* 10(2):95–96.

Grant, K.T. and G.B. Estes. 2009. *Darwin in Galápagos: Footsteps to a New World* (Princeton University Press: Princeton, NJ).

Grant, P.R., B.R. Grant, K. Petren, and L.F. Keller. 2005. Extinction behind our backs: the possible fate of one of the Darwin's finch species on Isla Floreana, Galápagos, *Biological Conservation*, 122(3):499-503.

Hittell, T.H. 1997. *The California Academy of Sciences – A Narrative History: 1853–1906*, A.E. Leviton and M.L. Aldrich (ed.) (CAS: San Francisco, CA).

Hofkin, B.V., A. Wright, J. Altenbach, K. Rassmann, H.M. Snell, R.D. Miller, A.C. Stone, and H.L. Snell. 2004. Ancient DNA gives green light to Galápagos Land Iguana repatriation, *Conservation Genetics* 4(1):105–108.

James, M.J. 2003. Did Galápagos experience and El Niño in 1878? *Noticias de Galápagos* 62:30–32.

James, M.J. 2010. Collecting Evolution: The Vindication of Charles Darwin by the 1905–06 Galápagos Expedition of the California Academy of Sciences, *Proceedings of the California Academy of Sciences, Series 4*, 61(Suppl. II):197–210.

Jennings, M.R. 1997. John Van Denburgh 1872–1924, pioneer herpetologist of the American West, in Theodore W. Pietsch and William D. Anderson, Jr. (ed.). *Collection Building in Ichthyology and Herpetology. American Society of Ichthyologists and Herpetologists, Special Publication (3)*, pp. 323–350.

Keynes, R.D. 1979. *The* Beagle *Record: Selections from the original pictorial records and written accounts of H.M.S.* Beagle (Cambridge University Press: Cambridge, UK).

Klett, M. 2006. *After the Ruins 1906 and 2006 – Rephotographing the San Francisco Earthquake and Fire* (University of California Press (with the Fine Arts Museums of San Francisco): Berkeley, CA).

Lack, D.L. 1945. The Galapagos Finches (Geospizinae): A Study in Variation, *Occasional Papers of the California Academy of Sciences* 21:1-159.

Lack, D.L. 1961. *Darwin's Finches* (Cambridge University Press: Cambridge, UK).

Larson, E.J. 2001. *Evolution's Workshop: God and Science on the Galapagos Islands* (Basic Books: New York, NY). See especially Chapter 5, California Stakes Its Claim.

Latorre, O. 1999. *El Hombre en las Islas Encantadas: La Historia Humana de Galápagos* (s.n.:Quito, Ecuador).

Parent, C.E., A. Caccone, and K. Petren. 2008. Colonization and diversification of Galápagos terrestrial fauna: a phylogenetic and biographical synthesis, *Philosophical Transactions of the Royal Society, B* 363:3347–3361.

Parent, C.E. and B.J. Crespi. 2006. Sequential colonization and diversification of Galápagos endemic land snail genus Bulimulus (Gastropoda, Stylommatophora), *Evolution* 60:2311–2328.

Parker, P.G., E.L. Buckles, H. Farrington, K. Petren, N.K. Whiteman, R.E. Ricklefs, J.L. Bollmer, and G. Jiménez-Uzcátegu. 2011. 110 Years of Avipoxvirus in the Galapagos Islands, *PLoS ONE* 6:e15989, doi:10.1371/journal.pone.0015989

Patton, J.L., S.Y. Yang, and P. Myers. 1975. Genetic and morphologic divergence among introduced rat Populations (Rattus rattus) of the Galapagos Archipelago, Ecuador, *Systematic Zoology* 24:296–310.

Pitelka, F.A. 1986. Rollo Beck – Old-school collector, member of an endangered species, *American Birds* 40(3):385–387.

Pritchard, P.C.H. 1996. *The Galápagos Tortoises – Nomenclatural and survival status* (Chelonian Research Monographs 1).

Slevin, J.R. 1931. *Log of the Schooner "Academy" on a voyage of scientific research to the Galapagos Islands 1905–1906* (Occasional Papers of the California Academy of Sciences XVII). Darwin/Beagle quote page 5.

Van Denburgh, J. 1914. The Gigantic Land Tortoises of the Galápagos Archipelago, *Proceedings of the California Academy of Sciences 2* Part 1:203–374.

Wikelski M. and L.M. Romero. 2003. Body size, performance and fitness in Galapagos marine iguanas, *Integrative and Comparative Biology* 43:376–386.

Winchester, S. 2006. *A Crack in the Edge of the World: America and the Great California Earthquake of 1906* (Harper Perennial: New York, NY).

6 Part I summary

The evolutionary context

Matthias Wolff and Mark Gardener

This first chapter provides the reader with an overview of the research in Galápagos – or related to the archipelago – that is aimed at understanding the evolutionary principles that shape animal and human societies.

William Durham asks what Charles Darwin found most convincing from his time in the Galápagos Islands during the Beagle Voyage, and puts forward the hypothesis that Galápagos data – once confirmed, interpreted and expanded with input from experts back in England – persuaded Darwin of two key anomalies that challenged the dominant paradigm of divine creation of life on Earth. The "affinity anomaly" is concerned with the similarity between the biota of oceanic islands and neighboring continental areas and the "replacement anomaly" is concerned with a pattern in space or in time whereby similar species appear to succeed one another. He showed that the mockingbirds of Galápagos more than any other species, and certainly more than the famous finches named after Darwin, provided crucial data for the young naturalist to allow the rejection of the static, divinely created species concept.

In their overview on evolutionary research in Galápagos over the past 50 years *Carlos Valle and Patricia G. Parker* show how island ecosystems and their organisms offer a unique opportunity to study fundamental principles of evolution, including natural selection, adaptation, speciation and evolutionary radiation. They summarize the pioneering work that was conducted on the evolutionary ecology of endemic species of Galápagos, with emphasis on the patterns and mechanisms of adaptation. One long-term study on the Darwin's finches specifically addressed the issue of ecological competition and natural selection and was able to demonstrate natural selection and adaptive (micro)evolutionary changes in a natural population of these birds. The authors emphasize that nowadays the study of speciation and evolutionary radiation (adaptive and non-adaptive) found on oceanic archipelagos like the Galápagos, can be reconstructed in both time and space owing to the development of modern molecular techniques and their application to the study of phylogeny (or molecular phylogeny) and biogeography (or phylogeography).

In the following contribution, *Patricia G. Parker and Noah K. Whiteman* give Galápagos examples of the co-evolution of parasites and their hosts. They categorize pathogens of Galápagos birds into functional groupings in terms of their evolutionary histories with their hosts. From this they propose the hypothesis that a host's time since exposure to a functional group of pathogens correlates negatively with the impact caused by a novel exposure to that group. They present a detailed example of the co-evolutionary relationships between the Galápagos hawk (*Buteo galapagoensis*) and ectoparasite lineages that accompanied its colonization. Each of these species has been reported from *Buteo swainsoni* or other raptors on the mainland. Using a molecular clock, the split between *B. galapagoensis* and *B. swainsoni* was estimated at less than 250,000 years ago, showing that this top predator has only very recently speciated. Using mitochondrial DNA data of ectoparasites, the authors found highly structured populations between islands and significant patterns of isolation by distance. The population divergence times of the Galápagos hawk and the louse *D. regalis*, based on mtDNA data, were positively and significantly related after correcting for geographic distance between islands, suggesting that *D. regalis* moves with hawk genes in contemporary (ecological) time in the form of recent inter-island gene flow, so the colonization histories of the two species are linked. Their study showed that ecological and life history traits believed to underlie macroevolutionary patterns, such as co-speciation in hosts and parasites, are important at the microevolutionary scale, providing a link between microevolutionary processes and macroevolutionary patterns. This also underscores the importance of conserving co-evolutionary units in the Galápagos, including native symbionts and parasites, for their own sakes and for what they can tell us about their hosts.

Eibl-Eibesfeld – co-founder of the Charles Darwin Research Station in 1959 and one of the first scientists to describe the social behavior of marine iguanas in the context of the evolution of vertebrate behavior – gives us a fascinating description of human behavior and its roots in vertebrate phylogeny. He starts with a short introduction into the history of human ethology referring to Darwin's cross-cultural studies based on observations as well as on questionnaires with natives in different parts of the world. The basic human expressions were found to be universal. In addition, he points at the similarity in animals across different taxa including man, which reveal basic laws of perception. For example, in aggressive encounters many animals make themselves appear larger and thus stronger: fish by spreading their fins, birds their feathers and man by showing off bearskin hats, feather crowns or other artificial display organs. He also mentions Darwin's "antithesis", illustrating it with the well-known drawings of a dog displaying anger and fear and of a swan defending his territory. Eibesfeld follows Hubert Markl's characterization of our species as a "hit" of evolution, which populated the world with million societies and developed a technical civilization, which within a century jetted us into the electronic age with telecommunication and space travel. Whether we continue as a hit, however, is questionable and people ponder about our future. Natural resources cannot match our growth and competition is getting increasingly stronger. Eibesfeld emphasizes that a new generation focused on a survival ethos, which takes into consideration the welfare and happiness of future generations, is needed. In order to achieve such a goal, more needs to be learned about our endowments and handicaps, much of them rooted in our phylogenetic past.

Matthew James describes another milestone: the expedition of the California Academy of Sciences (CAS) to the Galápagos 70 years after Darwin's visit. It lasted for 17 months (June 1905 to November 1906) and lead to the collection of some 75,000 specimens. A key to the success of this expedition was that each of the "eight young men" had their own scientific collecting specialty: birds, reptiles, plants, insects, fossils, rocks, mammals and seashells. During the expedition there was a series of "firsts" for Galápagos: the first sighting of tool use by the woodpecker finch, the first (and only) tortoise from Fernandina Island, and the naming of Academy Bay (after the schooner *Academy*). The enduring legacies of the 1905–1906 expedition are these well-curated specimens housed at the CAS. These form an important historical baseline for conservation efforts by the Charles Darwin Foundation, the Galápagos National Park Service, and other researchers. The specimens collected are actively used in evolutionary and taxonomic studies; biogeography studies that examine how species distributions have changed over time; and as a baseline for conservation efforts to restore plant and animal populations; and in the reconstruction of exotic invasions.

Part II

Biodiversity assessment and monitoring of change

7 Monitoring the Galápagos ecosystem

Challenges, pitfalls and a vision for the future

James P. Gibbs and Bryan Milstead

Introduction

The Galápagos requires, but currently lacks, an integrated system for tracking the biological, social, economic and cultural characteristics of the islands. A continual flow of monitoring information is critical to the adaptive management of the archipelago because monitoring provides the information feedback loop required to distinguish human impacts from natural changes and thereby guide conservation management and policy (Gibbs *et al.* 1999). Two stellar examples from Galápagos illustrate the critical role that monitoring data play in the adaptive management loop: co-management of the Marine Reserve (Heylings and Bravo 2007) and large-scale removal of introduced hoofed mammals (Campbell and Donlan 2005). Although monitoring of some critical ecosystem components occurs in the physical realm (e.g. volcanism – Thomas *et al.* 2009; sea temperatures and productivity – Garcés-Vargas *et al.* 2005; Banks 2003), the biological realm (e.g. infectious disease – Bataille *et al.* 2009; bird populations – Vargas *et al.* 2006; Gibbs *et al.* 2003; plant communities – Hamann 1993; invasive insects – Causton *et al.* 2005; subtidal rocky reef communities – Edgar *et al.* 2009) and the human social realm (e.g. human migration – Bremner and Perez 2002), it is remarkable that an integrated system for tracking the status of the entire Galápagos ecosystem is lacking. Galápagos' highly endemic biological diversity is at stake but, as importantly, so is the welfare of over 30,000 human residents because their fates are intimately tied together. This is because virtually all of Galápagos' human economy is linked to its lucrative ecotourism industry (Kenchington 1989). The connection between human welfare and biological health is stark in Galápagos; perhaps nowhere else on Earth do so many people rely on their government to make good decisions about conserving biodiversity, both for the biota's sake and for their own.

There remains great potential to develop an exemplary, integrated system for monitoring the Galápagos ecosystem, for several reasons. The first is that vast amounts of scientific information have been gathered in the Galápagos archipelago over the last 50 years (Snell *et al.* 1996) that together provide useful baselines for many indicators. The second is that a propitious institutional environment exists, at least in theory, to close the adaptive management loop in Galápagos. More specifically, a constitutionally defined relationship between a scientific advisory body – the Charles Darwin Foundation – and a management authority – the Galápagos National Park Service – has created a science-management partnership unlike any on Earth that could streamline the process of generating and harvesting scientific monitoring data and implementing it in decision-making. Third, chronic underfunding is always the bane of monitoring efforts, yet from a funding perspective the archipelago is of international significance and receives extraordinary financial support from both the federal government of Ecuador as well as from international donors; there exist many funding streams that could provide a stable funding situation for monitoring change in the Galápagos ecosystem.

In this review, we attempt to offer fresh perspectives on what is required to build an integrated system for monitoring Galápagos. First, we review lessons learned elsewhere over the last 50 years of ecosystem monitoring in order to review characteristics of successful and unsuccessful large-scale programs for monitoring and thereby point out pitfalls to avoid. Second, we turn to the constraints unique to making monitoring "work" in Galápagos and identify obstacles to integrated monitoring that have arisen specifically in the Galápagos context. Third, we integrate these perspectives in the form of a preliminary vision of a system for integrating scientific data for facilitating management in Galápagos.

Lessons learned elsewhere

Ecosystem-level monitoring has reached a maturation point after having been practiced for over the last five decades around the world. There are now many examples of successful programs that have ultimately become indispensable to decision-makers and therefore enjoy their continual support. There are even more examples of failed programs whose promise never materialized. These have been reviewed by, among others, Lindenmayer and Likens (2010), Lovett *et al.* (2007) and Fancy *et al.* (2009). Based on these reviews and our own perspectives as individuals long involved in environmental monitoring (e.g. Gibbs *et al.* 1999), we offer the following key perspectives that should be considered in the process of developing an integrated monitoring system for Galápagos.

Justify the monitoring

"Monitoring for monitoring's sake" rarely yields useful data: only monitoring designed around clear and compelling scientific and management questions furthers management goals. Many monitoring programs involve a jumble of nonessential, "pet" indicators measured at great cost and whose utility baffles end users, including management authorities and politicians.

Build adaptive capacity into the monitoring

The guiding questions that initiate a monitoring program will change over time; therefore, the monitoring process should continually involve revising those questions and evaluating the utility of the data. The capacity to adapt to changing questions and incorporate changing technology without losing the continuity of core measurements is critical to sustained monitoring programs. This presents a real conundrum. Monitoring can be backward looking, i.e. always referencing current conditions back to baseline conditions established previously, or forward-focused, i.e. comparing current conditions to a constantly evolving vision of where stakeholders think the environment should be. The challenge is to develop a program that enables stakeholders see in both directions, i.e. incorporating baselines while enabling the assessment of current status to evolve alongside our ever-improving understanding of how ecosystems work as well as changing the vision of a desired future state that stakeholders seek for an ecosystem.

Choose carefully the variables to be monitored

A monitoring program cannot succeed without a careful choice of the variables needed to capture the changes of interest. The selection of variables is best done through a consensus process involving a cadre of experts and stakeholders. An automobile's "dashboard" provides a surprisingly useful metaphor for guiding choice using a few indicators that provide useful and readily accessible information about the performance and functioning of an inherently complex system. Core measurements selected for a monitoring program should be important as indicators of system function, barometers of change, or variables of particular societal interest. Variables should be chosen with low per-measurement costs because overall costs mount rapidly with each repetition of the program and overall costs often determine long-program viability. Joint development of a model of the ecosystem under focus forces all stakeholders to come to an understanding of the system to be monitored, identifies critical indicators and generates a clear rationale for what is ultimately chosen to be monitored (Lookingbill *et al.* 2007).

Identify triggers and thresholds and sample accordingly

In designing a monitoring system, it is important to specify the degree of change sufficient to trigger a management response. Only by identifying such thresholds can sampling targets be developed to ensure an effective sampling design is elaborated that generates enough data to capture that level of change at an ecologically appropriate level of statistical power. This is where ecological models re-enter the picture. Through them can be identified which thresholds of change are significant and which are not. The early years of any monitoring program should be regarded as a period to refine the sampling regime so that it becomes progressively more efficient, as well as to understand background levels of natural variability that must be accommodated through sufficient sampling to capture the relevant thresholds of change, should they occur.

Anticipate the inevitability of personnel change

Program continuity is dependent on maintaining quality and consistency of the data despite inevitable changes in personnel. Clearly articulated and carefully documented standard operating procedures are critical to sustaining consistent data streams over extended periods involved in long-term monitoring. Development of such protocols is a significant undertaking (Oakley *et al.* 2003) and requires its own set of resources but is essential to reduce "method drift". Arbitrary changes in monitoring methods should be avoided, but if necessary should involve an extended period of overlap between new and old methods to establish comparability.

Recognize that monitoring is expensive

Monitoring programs often fail because of inadequate and unrealistic budgeting. More specifically, it is common that only costs of field data collection are budgeted prior to initiation of monitoring. Yet it is a poorly appreciated and ultimately painful truth that the costs of compilation, data reduction, analysis, archiving and presentation typically equal or exceed costs of data collection. It is critical to develop a budget for any monitoring program that covers costs of data collection and analysis to avoid a program's initial efforts joining the legacy of unanalyzed, prematurely terminated datasets.

Realize that the value of monitoring data changes through time

Stable funding is needed to support monitoring over a sufficient duration to allow changes to be detected over the natural temporal fluctuations that inevitably occur in any ecosystem. Notably the initial years of monitoring can be the most difficult to support because few insights can be generated until a sufficient baseline is built to permit temporal trends to be evaluated. This said, after conclusion of the initial period many monitoring programs undergo a rapid transition to "indispensable" status once the baseline materializes and insights accrue. Ensuring financing is in place to usher a monitoring program through its difficult "growing" years is critical; ten years is a sensible minimum target for base funding.

Sharing the data

Policies of confidentiality, data ownership, and data holdback times must be articulated early in the monitoring process. After several iterations of monitoring, many outside parties typically seek access to the data. Different models of data sharing should be evaluated carefully. The typical, conservative model of extended holdback is often short-sighted; releasing the data quickly to the broader community can generate many spin-offs in the form of publications and analyses that would otherwise not be possible under the monitoring program's own funding umbrella; the spin-offs can add considerable value to the overall monitoring effort and expand its base of support.

Consider carefully the reporting schedule

Only through frequent analysis and presentation of monitoring data will interest in the monitoring be sustained. Policy-makers are often operating on, at most, an annual basis for their decision-making process. Scientists often operate on, at least, a five-year turn-around time from project inception to publication. Reporting annually and in synchrony with planning schedules of policy-makers will ensure interest in the program. Frequent and early analysis further ensures that errors in the design can be identified and can be corrected while the opportunity remains to do so (Reid 2001).

Design the monitoring to maximize scientific value

Monitoring is usually denigrated as not being "science" because most monitoring data are correlational in nature and thus can fail to explicitly establish "cause and effect". Without engaging in the debate, correlational data are nevertheless extremely valuable for highlighting compelling questions for research programs to then focus upon. The scope for generating scientific insights through correlational monitoring data is greatly expanded by co-locating measurements of multiple indicators at the same sampling stations to permit inter-variable correlations to be examined.

Monitoring needs to be collaborative

As they say, "Too many chefs often spoil the soup", yet no one chef can make a soup that will please everyone. Including a suite of chefs from government agencies, conservation NGOs, and researchers in academic institutions in the design process will insure that useful ecosystem-level monitoring programs are developed. Although individual chefs may lack long-term funding or sufficient resources to ensure sampling designs with high statistical power, a suite of chefs can maximize economies of scale and increase access to decision-makers. Collaborative relationships among government personnel, researchers and managers are crucial to the success of monitoring and their largely separate professional cultures, different goals and different reward systems must be recognized to maintain collaborations.

Involve non-experts

Large-scale monitoring increasingly involves innovative approaches that can generate vast amounts of useful monitoring data via engagement with "citizen scientists". Many insights about environmental change are in fact only available through involvement of amateur scientists who bring strength in numbers (vast sample sizes) and broad geographical coverage not feasible with the staff devoted directly to the monitoring. Understanding the strengths, limitations and process of engaging the public as data collectors is a vital consideration for modern-day large-scale monitoring efforts (e.g. Braschler 2009).

In conclusion, ecological monitoring is unjustifiably expensive if it is poorly designed or not explicitly linked to management objectives. In contrast, properly designed and implemented monitoring costs little relative to the value of the resources it protects, particularly in such places as Galápagos with its biodiversity-based ecotourism economy. Lessons learned elsewhere can help government agencies, NGOs and researchers collaborate to avoid pitfalls others have stumbled upon.

Challenges to monitoring in the Galápagos context

A formal, integrated cross-institutional system for monitoring the status of the Galápagos ecosystem has not materialized for many reasons. The first is institutional. Although historically the Galápagos National Park (GNP) Service and the Charles Darwin Foundation (CDF) have been the primary institutions working together to manage the Galápagos ecosystem, an increasing number of agencies, both governmental and non-governmental, are now involved in conserving the spectacular wild life of the archipelago and ensuring the well-being of its human inhabitants. A cluttered institutional landscape makes it increasingly difficult to coalesce stakeholders and find a common vision for monitoring.

A second set of challenges are intellectual. More specifically, the conceptual domain of what is regarded as important to monitor must be broadened. Despite several long-established programs for tracking biophysical resources of Galápagos, there is currently a critical need to develop new capacities for gathering and integrating socio-economic and cultural information with ecological data. This integration is needed to support planning and envisioning by the governmental entities mandated to do so, particularly the municipal authority (Consejo de Gobierno), in conjunction with the National Park, who together face the extraordinarily difficult task of maintaining the health of the archipelago's wild life while meeting the needs and aspirations of its human inhabitants. Moreover, there exists a degree of intellectual snobbery about what constitutes valid information and who should collect it. For example, over 170,000 tourists passed through the islands in the year 2009 and this vast population of intent observers leaves without ever having an opportunity to share its observations. Harnessing ecotourist-derived observations through carefully designed citizen science programs represents a golden yet completely unrealized opportunity for tracking components of the Galápagos ecosystems. Citizen science data are critical for guiding decision-making by management agencies elsewhere (Bonney *et al.* 2009), so why not in Galápagos? As significantly, local residents would benefit from being engaged in science via monitoring. In doing so, they would have more opportunity to learn about the environment in which they live and hence have more incentive for conserving it.

A third set of challenges is technical. Remarkably, there is a complete lack of common information-handling infrastructure for coordinating data gathering, management and communication among the many institutions involved. Data loss and leakage is rampant. Furthermore, managing information collection in Galápagos – a widely scattered archipelago of many small islands – is an inherently spatial problem that is site specific and spread across a vast area. Yet access to usable geographic information management software among institutions responsible for Galápagos is highly variable. Some institutions have access to professional grade software but limited capacity to use it. Others are rich in data but lack software. Among all institutions there is simply no system whatsoever in place to share information. Thus, there is an acute need in Galápagos for managing information in general and spatial information in particular.

Other technical challenges relate to secure data storage, rapid reporting, cross-institutional integration, and information mobilization to enhance communication. Currently there exist a wealth of observations on the biology, geology, sociology, economics and history of the archipelago. Unfortunately, there are no standard procedures for how these data are recorded, archived, documented and shared. Indeed, much of the available information is still not in digital format and there is no central archive system. As a result, it is very difficult to compile data into useable information for the many stakeholders that are involved in the management, conservation, research and enjoyment of these islands.

Steps toward improving monitoring of the Galápagos ecosystem

There are a number concrete steps that can be taken to start to build the kind of monitoring system Galápagos needs to facilitate informed decision-making. The first step relates to information management, which in Galápagos is in substantial disorder. The Galápagos ecosystem is clearly anomalous in being a world-famous United Nations-designated Biosphere Reserve and the focus of a vast and lucrative ecotourism activity oriented around a unique flora and fauna, yet lacking an integrated system for tracking status, impact and management effectiveness. A great deal is at stake and Galápagos needs a system in which information about it can be mobilized quickly into different forms to suit the needs of particular Galápagos stakeholders (Figure 7.1). For example, base data in its raw form may be of particular interest to researchers, in summary form to managers, and in synoptic and perhaps primarily graphical form be most useful to the public, press and donors. Ensuring scalability of information to its most appropriate application is the essence of the inverse relationship indicated here between data resolution and user group.

The creation of a well-designed and adequately funded information management system is critical for preserving existing data and will serve as a template to guide the acquisition of new data. For maximum effectiveness, this new system will need to be integrally tied to a well-developed geographical information system (GIS) and a taxonomic database. At a minimum, the GIS will include spatial data, remote sensing images and consistent naming conventions for islands and sites. The taxonomic database must be designed to include current and historical naming conventions for all taxa, as well as information on populations and genotypes. From this base all existing scientific, economic, sociological and monitoring data can be closely coordinated via a system of common location and species identifiers, and could be readily scaled and mobilized as appropriate to a target audience. This capacity would greatly enhance the Galápagos scientific enterprise as well as the communication, administration and funding of it. Notably, the technologies for developing the proposed information management system are readily available and 40 years of existing data are by and large ready for integration. The resources are simply needed to catalyze the system and thereby propel the Galápagos into an up-to-date state of capacity for acquisition, management and communication of scientific information.

It is critical to assemble all relevant stakeholders to collectively envision what form an integrated management system for Galápagos should take and elaborate accordingly upon its technical details. Stakeholders should be simultaneously combined with technical experts so that vision and practicality remain compatible. Group members would include those from (1) the technical side (hardware, programming, data capture and analysis); (2) the application side (leaders from exemplary sites where the sort of data integration and reporting, and integration with policy making envisioned for Galápagos has already been achieved); (3)

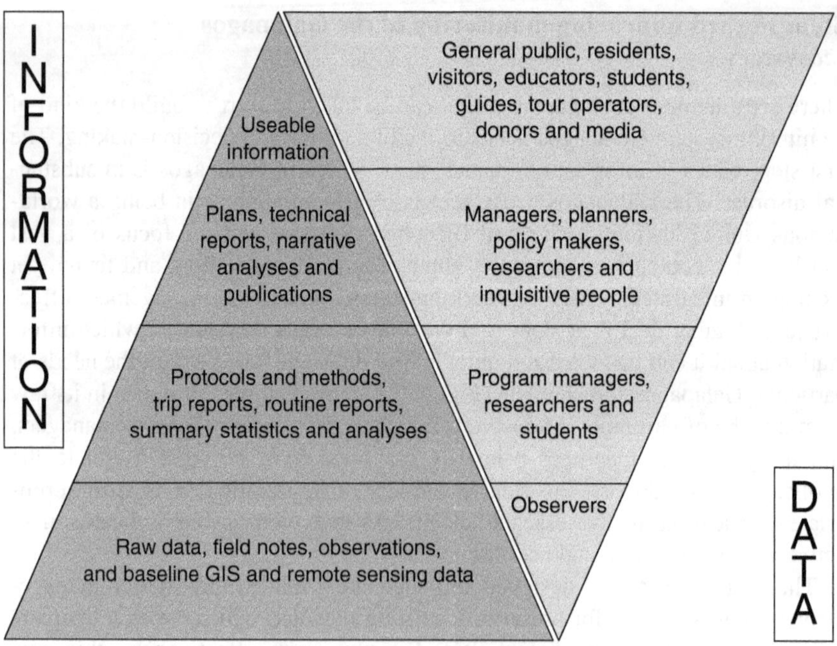

Figure 7.1 Critical aspects of the scalability of information that must be considered in envisioning an integrated monitoring program for Galápagos.

key Galápagos stakeholders (representatives from Galápagos institutions both generating and using monitoring data); and (4) potential donors and industry collaborators. The primary outcome of the envisioning exercise would be well-refined vision document outlining the structure of a useful and up-to-date information management system for Galápagos, an agreement among chief stakeholders to support its development and a set of concrete steps for realizing both the technical side of the effort and funding the initiative over its first ten years. A follow-up series of workshops would involve technical experts to develop a robust and defensible model of the Galápagos human–natural coupled ecosystem and identify the key indicators of it that should be measured. This would then lead to the elaboration of sampling designs and ultimately to cost estimations.

Key personnel to support an integrated monitoring program for the Galápagos ecosystem are a group leader, a spatial database technician, a web programmer, two assistants for data entry/manipulation, and a technical writer or science translator. Data servers and a place of work could be located in Galápagos or elsewhere; in fact, there are significant advantages to physically basing the enterprise elsewhere (e.g. reliability of internet connection and power supply, attraction of qualified personnel and perceived political neutrality of hosting entity). In close consultation with the National Park, the CDF, local decision-makers and scientists, the group leader would be in charge of the overall vision, planning and preparation of an information management plan as well as seeking funding to sustain the program. The group leader would also be responsible for spearheading development of the information management plan upon which experts would design databases for the storage and retrieval of information. Database experts would work with scientists currently active in Galápagos to make sure all data collected are entered into a shared database structure. These databases would be capable of rapidly generating standard reports and summary statistics. The technical writer would produce digested summaries of the information written at a level tailored to target audiences (public, donors, managers or visiting scientists). The web programmer would be responsible for developing ways to both input and retrieve this information via the internet. Finally, two assistants would provide hand digitization of important older datasets or importing existing digital datasets. Aside from personnel, support is required for software, physical equipment and operating expenses. Because all data everywhere are increasingly becoming spatially explicit and because Galápagos is inherently spatial, partnerships with entities that specialize in mobilizing geographic data are particularly important to the success of this project.

We have assembled an extensive list of existing and potential databases (Appendix 1) to serve as a starting point for discussion among stakeholders about how to advance the development of the integrated monitoring and information management system Galápagos needs. Integrating these databases using modern information management methods could mobilize information instantly through widely available platforms that would be of tremendous value to the policy-makers in Galápagos, who need such information for effective decision-making. Moreover, the information would benefit the millions of past and future visitors to Galápagos, as well as those who are simply curious about the archipelago. Similarly, it would be of great value to researchers and professionals who could access the data for management and study purposes. Moreover, it would be of enormous value to local residents for better understanding their environment and building their support for conservation of it. With such a system in place, the potential of monitoring to provide the information feedback loop required to distinguish human impacts from natural changes and thereby guide conservation management and policy could finally be realized in Galápagos.

Appendix 1: proposed elements of an integrated monitoring information management system for facilitating conservation management in Galápagos

- **Observations Database** that would compile geographically referenced observations made by researchers, managers, visitors and guides on native and introduced species occurrence, abundance and health status across the archipelago. In addition to biological data other observations, such as the number of visitors at each site, fishing activity and environmental information could also be collated.
- **Samples Database** that organizes the immense amount of sampled material taken from the Archipelago (e.g. blood samples) relies on a species identifier (link to Species database), location (link to Island database), specimen type, sample location, preservation method and other data as deemed useful (link to People database).
- **Field Data Database** would compile and document the vast amounts of raw scientific data gathered across the multitude of research projects undertaken in Galápagos and make sure these data are archived and shared appropriately.
- **Marked Animals and Plants Database** to coordinate among studies the rich datasets compiled in Galápagos on marked individuals (e.g. banded finches or tagged cacti) to permit long-term tracking of individuals and the extraordinary insights therein permitted, by organizing individual identifiers and corresponding marks, type of mark, date of marking, person that marked (with link to People database) and supporting data (size, age, etc.).
- **Wild Species Database** that would integrate information on authoritative determination of species and subspecies nomenclature, distribution by island (and population where appropriate) and origin where known, as well as habitat affiliation and International Union for the Conservation of Nature (IUCN) status (which is frequently used in status assessments).
- **Domestic Animal Database** in collaboration with government authorities to compile information about domestic animal import, numbers, distribution, health status and current preventive health practices to minimize emerging pathogen threats to native fauna.

- **Islands Database** that would serve as a critical base for organizing geographically all data collected within the archipelago. Currently there are over 240 island, islets and rocks registered in the CDF–GNP database. Most of the larger islands have at least four commonly used names. Additionally, there are thousands of unregistered names for specific locations within the islands themselves. This database will develop a set of unique island and site identifiers to keep track of names and enable proper identifications of physical locations within the archipelago.
- **Risk Assessment Database** that would integrate state-of-the-science estimates of species status and extinction probability.
- **Management Options Database** that would directly link species and ecosystems information to management-relevant information, including known management approaches both in Galápagos and elsewhere; the information source; how particular management actions can be used to mitigate for particular risks (explicit link to Risk Assessment database); and a supporting bibliography.
- **Management Actions Database** that would track and archive specific management events in Galápagos by recording identifiers for management event; island and site, species and ecosystems affected; date undertaken; personnel involved and their contact information; the specific management action undertaken; and the result of the effort (e.g. success or failure). This database will be explicitly linked to the Wild Species and Island databases for rapid cross-referencing.
- **People Database** to compile information about exactly who is involved in gathering information in Galápagos, including an identifier, name, contact details and specific association with the CDF.
- **Socio-economic Database** that would integrate information about human society in Galápagos, including, for example census data, economic activity and multidimensional social data on health and welfare of the archipelagos human inhabitants. These data would be amalgamated across institutions:
  - INEC/National Census Bureau
    - Detailed census data for the human population
  - The National Park Service
    - “Entrance card” data including:
      - Sex and age
      - Dates of arrival and departure
      - Lodging (i.e. hotel, vessel, private home, other)
      - Activities
    - Informe de Guias
    - Data on cupos
    - Vessel Park/concession/permit fees
    - Value and distribution of entrance fees
    - Budget and number of employees
    - Visitor Site Usage
    - Number of visitors by month and year

  - List of guides by class that are active and non-active
  - Number of employees
- INGALA/CONSEJO DE GOBIERNO
  - Sector subsidies
  - Consumer Price Index
  - Number and duration of temporary work permits issued
  - Number of Galápagos active and non-active cedulas/residency cards
  - Employment by sector
  - Extraction of building material
  - Number of vehicles and motorcycles
  - Opinion polls
  - Number of employees
  - Number of commercial and private flights and passengers
  - Amount and type, if possible, of cargo transported
- Port Captains/DIGMER
  - Number of voyages by cargo ships and type of cargo (arriving and leaving) such as fuel, etc.
  - Dates and number of passengers on each cruise by each tourist vessel.
  - Budget and number of employees
- Subsecretariat of Fisheries or National Fisheries Institute/INP
  - Number and types (by gear) of fishing vessels
  - Number of registered fishermen
  - Quantity, value and effort of landings
  - Estimates of local fish consumption, exports and imports
  - Budget and number of employees
- Ministry of Agriculture and Cattle/MAG
  - Amount of land available for agriculture and ranching
  - Land use (i.e. area planted, in pasture, forested, etc.)
  - Number of farms, ranches and employees
  - Quantity and value of local agricultural and ranch production
  - Agricultural imports and exports
  - Budget and number of employees
- The three municipalities
  - Number and grades of students
  - Existing infrastructure
  - Pending projects
  - Budgets, expenditures (published in La Lupa Fiscal) and number of employees
  - Number and types of businesses and their number of employees
  - Number of residential dwellings
  - Pending building permits
  - Zoning and construction regulations
  - Energy consumption/electrical output
  - Waste management

- The Ministry of Tourism
  - Number of hotels, beds and employees by island
  - Number of restaurants, bars, night clubs and their employees by island
- SICGAL
  - Number of introduced Species
  - Budget and number of employees
- CDF and NGOs
  - Budgets
  - Number of employees

- **Bibliographic Database** that organizes and links the extraordinary wealth of published materials about Galápagos, including a unique identifier for each item, the full citation, information about the material and, when possible, a digital facsimile of the item itself.
- **Museum Database** that would record the huge number of museum and herbarium specimens taken from Galápagos and dispersed all over the world.
- **Photo Database** that compiles images of Galápagos through recording of source of image, location, description and the image itself (lots of links here too).
- **"Galapedia"**, a wiki to serve as a compendium of moderated, contributed and evolving pieces about the archipelago, for example, focused on island descriptions and species descriptions, in multiple languages, to provide general information on Galápagos to its many visitors.
- **E-Galápagos** that would serve to assemble unstandardized but nevertheless useful observations collected by guides, residents, tourists and fisherman, and even scientists and park guards with, minimally, a species, location and count identifier.

References

Banks, S. 2003. SeaWiFS satellite monitoring of oil spill impact on primary production in the Galapagos Marine Reserve. *Marine Pollution Bulletin* 47:325–330.

Bataille, A., A.A. Cunningham, V. Cedeño, M. Cruz, G. Eastwood, D.M. Fonseca, C.E. Causton, R. Azuero, J. Loayza, J.D. Martinez and Goodman S.J. 2009. Evidence for regular ongoing introductions of mosquito disease vectors into the Galapagos Islands, *Proceedings Of The Royal Society B: Biological Sciences* 276:3769–3775.

Bonney, R, C.B. Cooper, J. Dickinson, S. Kelling, T. Phillips, K.V. Rosenberg and J. Shirk. 2009. Citizen Science: A developing tool for expanding science knowledge and scientific literacy, *Bioscience* 59:977–984.

Braschler, B. 2009. Successfully implementing a citizen-scientist approach to insect monitoring in a resource-poor country, *Bioscience* 59(2):103–104.

Bremner, J. and J. Perez. 2002. A case study of human migration and the sea cucumber crisis in the Galapagos Islands, *Ambio* 31:306–310.

Campbell, K. and C.J. Donlan. 2005. Feral goat eradications on islands, *Conservation Biology* 19:1362–1374.

Causton, C.E., C.R. Sevilla and S.D. Porter. 2005. Eradication of the little fire ant, *Wasmannia auropunctata* (Hymenoptera: Formicidae), from Marchena Island, Galapagos: On the edge of success?, *Florida Entomologist* 88:159–168.

Edgar, G.J., S. Banks, M. Brandt, R.H. Bustamante, A. Chiriboga, S.A. Earle, L. Garske, P.W. Glynn, J. Grove, S. Henderson, C.P. Hickman, K.A. Miller, F. Rivera and G.M. Wellington. 2009. El Niño, grazers and fisheries interact to greatly elevate extinction risk for Galapagos marine species, *Global Change Biology*. doi: 10.1111/j.1365–2486. 2009.02117.x.

Fancy, S.G., J.E. Gross and S.L. Carter. 2009. Monitoring the condition of natural resources in US national parks, *Environmental Monitoring and Assessment* 151:161–174.

Garcés-Vargas, J., W. Schneider, R. Abarca del Río, R. Martínez and E. Zambrano. 2005. Inter-annual variability in the thermal structure of an oceanic time series station off Ecuador (1990–2003) associated with El Niño events, *Deep-Sea Research Part I-Oceanographic Research Papers* 52:1789–1805.

Gibbs, J.P., W.G. Shriver and H. Vargas. 2003. An assessment of a Galapagos Rail population over thirteen years (1986 to 2000), *Journal Of Field Ornithology* 74:136–140.

Gibbs, J.P., H.L. Snell and C.E. Causton. 1999. Effective monitoring for adaptive wildlife management: Lessons from the Galapagos Islands, J*ournal Of Wildlife Management* 63:1055–1065.

Hamann, O. 1993. On vegetation recovery, goats and giant tortoises on Pinta Island, Galapagos, Ecuador. *Biodiversity and Conservation* 2:138–151.

Heylings, P. and M. Bravo. 2007. Evaluating governance: A process for understanding how co-management is functioning, and why, in the Galapagos Marine Reserve, *Ocean and Coastal Management* 50:174–208.

Kenchington, R.A. 1989. Tourism in the Galapagos Islands – the dilemma of conservation, *Environmental Conservation* 16:227–232.

Lindenmayer, D. and G.E. Likens. 2010. *Effective ecological monitoring* (CSIRO Publishing: Collingwood, Vic).

Lookingbill, T.R., R.H. Gardner, P.A. Townsend and S.L. Carter. 2007. Conceptual models as hypotheses in monitoring urban landscapes, *Environmental Management* 40:171–182.

Lovett, G.M., D.A. Burns, C.T. Driscoll, J.C. Jenkins, M.J. Mitchell, L. Rustad, J.B. Shanley, G.E. Likens and R Haeuber. 2007. Who needs environmental monitoring?, *Frontiers in Ecology and the Environment* 5: 253–260.

Oakley, K.L., L.P. Thomas and S.G. Fancy. 2003. Guidelines for long-term monitoring protocols, *Wildlife Society Bulletin* 31:1000–1003.

Reid, L.M. 2001. The epidemiology of monitoring, *Journal of the American Water Resources Association* 37: 815–820.

Snell, H.M., H.L. Snell, G. Davis-Merlen, T. Simkin and R.E. Silberglied. 1996. *Bibliografía de Galápagos, 1535–1995* (Fundación Charles Darwin: Quito, Ecuador).

Thomas, H.E., I.M. Watson, C. Kearney, S.A. Carn and S.J. Murray. 2009. A multi-sensor comparison of sulphur dioxide emissions from the 2005 eruption of Sierra Negra volcano, Galapagos Islands, *Remote Sensing of Environment* 113:1331–1342.

Vargas, F.H., S. Harrison, S. Rea and D.W. Macdonald. 2006. Biological effects of El Niño on the Galapagos penguin, *Biological Conservation* 127:107–114.

8 The neglected majority

Biodiversity inventories as an integral part of conservation biology

Frank Bungartz, Frauke Ziemmeck, Nathalia Tirado, Patricia Jaramillo, Henri Herrera and Gustavo Jiménez-Uzcátegui

Introduction

Towards a new concept of biodiversity science

Global biodiversity is in crisis. Celebrating the *2010 Year of Biodiversity* is, sadly, an ironic exercise: while the majority of species remain unknown, scientists unambiguously agree that humans are currently causing a mass extinction of unprecedented proportions (Dunn *et al.* 2009; Pimm *et al.* 1995; Reid 1995; Wake and Vredenburg 2008). Yet at the same time, taxonomy, the science of describing and inventorizing biodiversity, faces an equally unprecedented crisis.

Eighteen years after the 1992 Rio Summit and despite political commitments like the Convention on Biological Diversity (CBD, www.cbd.int), the Darwin Declaration (www.environment.gov.au/biodiversity/abrs/publications/other/darwin/index.html), or the Global Taxonomy Initiative (GTI, *www.cbd.int/gti*), scientists still have but a mere idea of the organisms with which we share this planet. At a time when ecologists and conservation managers urgently need taxonomic expertise, biodiversity collections are neglected or abandoned, and taxonomists, like their objects of interest, are found on the "endangered species list" (Kim and Byrne 2006).

What happened?

1. *Biodiversity is overwhelming*: Dealing with the sheer number of species in any given ecosystem requires enormous resources, yet the demand to reduce this complexity is challenged by poorly known yet ecologically important taxa that continue to be neglected.
2. *Taxonomy and ecology have become alienated from each other*: Taxonomists focus on phylogenies as an objective means to delimit taxa while the description of species lags behind. As a result, ecologists fail to see practical applications of taxonomy for their own studies.

This chapter is divided into two parts. First, a general overview addresses the challenges of biodiversity research and how in recent years taxonomy and ecology have become increasingly alienated. Then, the Galápagos biodiversity assessment is presented as a case study, where, despite more than 50 years of research, a large part of the native biodiversity continues to be neglected.

The functional dilemma: towards an ecology without species?

It is not uncommon that conservationists focus on few *emblematic species*. It is much easier to fundraise for the last remaining tiger, for beautiful butterflies, and majestic eagles. It is almost impossible to draw attention to rare grasses, endangered spiders, or poorly known fungi. If done well, conservation biologists will use iconic species to promote ecosystem restoration and combat habitat loss. Ideally, they will design strategies that also benefit less conspicuous taxa.

This goal presents, however, a considerable challenge (Clark 2002). Assessing the role of individual species within an ecosystem soon reaches numerical limits: complex ecosystems are characterized by enormous diversity. Science is always an exercise in abstraction, reducing complexity without losing information. In conservation science prioritization mechanisms are, however, highly problematic. They are almost all strongly biased in favor of a few, well-known species groups (Clark 2002; Dunn 2005; Dunn *et al.* 2009). In Galápagos, many iconic species like the giant tortoises have been saved from extinction, but on inhabited islands these astounding animals today typically survive in highly degraded, agriculturally dominated systems where the original diversity of the native ecosystems is lost. While single species may thus be preserved, conservation of complex ecosystems continues to face considerable challenges.

Biodiversity is overwhelming. Even simple, relatively species-poor ecosystems are characterized by magnitudes of species numbers that are difficult to grasp. As this case study of Galápagos demonstrates, the number of species even on an isolated archipelago easily numbers thousands.

Confronted with this diversity ecologists naturally ask if it is not possible to reduce the sheer numbers of species to a few functional groups? Why go through a meticulous exercise of taxonomic "bean-counting"? Would it not be easier to deal only with few representative species without the necessity for comprehensive taxonomic inventories?

Here it is argued that this is a false assumption, one that may be best summarized by the demagogy of "the post office and the stamp collector": while an individual rare stamp is highly prized by a collector, any post office continues to function without this precious specimen. The obsession to collect stamps is therefore redundant for a postal service to continue to function.

But ecosystems are *not* post offices. Taxonomists are *not* stamp collectors. Biodiversity is more than the sum of its elements: species interact, they compete, they evolve and adapt. Each species is characterized by a complex, specialized biology that is distinct from other species in that same system. Members of one species function together within populations, they share an evolutionary history and are characterized by similar adaptations. Each species is necessarily a functional component of its ecosystem. Once all principal components are known it might become possible to reduce complexity. However, the opposite is not true: knowing few species that are far from representative leads to a simplistic, reductionist view. Being able to name and identify at least the basic components of any system is a prerequisite to better understand an entire system. Biodiversity inventories are an essential and integral part of conservation biology. We cannot protect and preserve natural systems without knowing their most basic elements – the species.

Biodiversity assessments: can we reduce the complexity that we need to deal with?

Among the most commonly used prioritization tools in conservation are *red lists* (Baillie *et al.* 2004). Ironically, these lists include an inherent bias. The idea of establishing a ranking system of endangered species creates an "aristocracy of species" where the best studied, not necessarily the most threatened ones, inhabit the upper ranks (Régnier *et al.* 2009). To be fair, red list criteria provide tools to account for uncertainties and in theory permit even poorly known species groups to be evaluated (IUCN 2001, 2003). The bias is thus not inherent in the assessment procedure, but any cursory glance reveals that red lists feature well-known species groups much more prominently. Ironically, donors sponsoring conservation management will be tempted to save the "last of its kind" rather than the "least known of its kind".

Even in places that have received much scientific attention, most species groups have never been evaluated according to International Union for the Conservation of Nature (IUCN) criteria. In Galápagos, red lists exist only for very few species groups (vertebrates, vascular plants, butterflies, terrestrial snails, corals, macroalgae; Bungartz *et al.* 2010). Assessing which species are threatened is thus not a viable mechanism to reduce ecosystem complexity and it does not permit focusing management on a few priority species.

As an alternative, the *umbrella species concept* suggests that conservation science can a priori identify species presumed to be most important for any ecosystem (Groom *et al.* 2006; Ozaki *et al.* 2006). Focusing conservation on these species assumes that all others will equally benefit. To be useful, umbrella species by design only include common, widely distributed, representative taxa (Seddon and Leech 2008). The basic presumption, that conservation of these common, well-known species automatically also benefits rare, endangered ones has, however, rarely been empirically tested (Roberge and Angelstam 2004). The concept appears almost contradictory by design: a rare *and* widely distributed species is an oxymoron. Unique, specialized, rare species are more likely to be threatened and almost by definition fall "between the cracks of this concept".

How then do we know when ecosystems are in trouble? Can we focus only on functional components instead of individual species?

Functional concepts are clearly one of the most attractive approaches to reduce system complexity but they do not absolve ecologists from studying individual components of each system. The theoretical framework behind the *keystone species concept*, for example, assumes that ecosystems remain intact as long as species providing essential ecosystem services continue to be present (Paine 1969, 1995). Even if such a system loses individual, less important species, it will remain functional as long as key components are not lost. It has been argued that conservation biology should therefore not so much strive to preserve individual "objects" but ultimately to "preserve the processes of life" (Bowen 1999).

This is an elegant theory and it is essentially impossible to argue against it: as long as a basic functional framework persists, the system is by definition in no danger of collapsing. However, arguing this concept to its abstract extreme, any native species being only a functional component of the system could easily be replaced by any equally adapted, but non-native species. This is of course absurd: it implies that the functionality of a system prevails while its unique elements are gone!

How does one tropical archipelago, say in East Asia, actually compare to another one off the coast of Africa, or indeed to the Galápagos? Provided that abiotic conditions are comparable, any ecosystem is characterized by similar habitats. Therefore, should all these islands be inhabited by functionally similar organisms? This is not clearly the case: geographically disjunct ecosystems differ significantly by their own, regionally characteristic suite of individual and often endemic species. These species correspond to different taxonomic groups, all with their distinct biology and with unique, individual adaptations. While they share some functional characteristics, individual species are not at all ecologically identical. Though abiotic factors in different parts of the world are comparable, biogeography convincingly illustrates how rather different ecological systems have developed in what might essentially be regarded as very similar, if not identical environments. Similar systems that are inhabited by a different suite of taxonomic groups are also functionally different.

Of course, on a macro scale, at a certain level of abstraction any system could be reduced to fit a few identical types. However, this is beside the point: if conservation science strives to preserve the unique character of individual ecosystems it needs to take into account why and how the species that characterize these systems differ.

How can any ecologist discard the importance of certain species whose functional role remains unknown? Different taxonomic groups are characterized by distinct biologies. As a "one size fits all" approach, the continued neglect of taxa fosters an ecological dogmatism that is based on the misconception that all species can be reduced to few functional roles.

Studying ecosystems in detail, the ecology of each singular species is not incompatible with modeling ecosystem complexity. Both are complementary! Both are necessary, important aspects of conservation science. The more that is known about the individual biology of species and how they function as integral parts of their ecosystem, the more sophisticated models can be designed.

The necessity to reduce complexity but not to ignore differences becomes ultimately a circular argument: on the one hand, the attempt to halt biodiversity loss clearly cannot afford to wait until all species are named and certainly not until their ecological roles are known in detail. Yet, to presume we already know all the "key players in the game" is hubris. Models that reduce complexity are necessary, but they need to be tested in the real world (Piraino *et al.* 2002).

The taxonomic dilemma: the "tree of life" versus an "inventory of life"?

The neglected majority: why do we still know so little?

The majority of all species are microscopically small. It is not surprising that we are most curious about what we can see, a common, almost natural constraint. Nevertheless, the fact that bacteria will easily survive without us (Nee 2004) is beyond the point. True, the macroscopic world that we can see with our own eyes is only a small, almost negligible side branch of evolution. To us this branch is vitally important, yet we do not even know most species it represents (Clark 2002; Clark *et al.* 2002; Dunn 2005; Dunn *et al.* 2009; Pawar 2003; Rohde 2010). At the same time, we are witnessing mass extinction on an unprecedented scale (Dunn *et al.* 2009; Pimm *et al.* 1995; Reid 1995; Wake and Vredenburg 2008).

A phylogenetic bias of modern taxonomy?

Giving names to organisms is not a trivial task. For the biological sciences, nomenclature serves as a common language with species names as a universally accepted currency. Every single name represents a hypothesis, a suggestion that this taxon is real, that it is an evolutionary ecological unit in time, that members of this species share common ancestry, an evolutionary history, that their populations have evolved in response to their environment, and that their traits represent adaptations to environmental constraints imposed by the habitat they inhabit.

Identifying diagnostic descriptive differences as evidence for this hypothesis has been the "bread and butter" of classical taxonomy. This is a cumbersome, meticulous craft and until Willi Hennig (1950, 1966) established the first, hypothesis-driven framework for classification, taxonomy could be blamed to be driven by a mentality of indiscriminately collecting sheer numbers of arbitrarily delimited species. Ironically, when Hennig revolutionized taxonomy by proposing a phylogenetic taxonomy, he could himself not have foreseen a fatal side-effect: any taxonomist whose primary goal was not to establish a phylogeny suddenly stood accused of not working scientifically. Yet this accusation is based upon a misconception. The exercise of assembling the *Tree of Life* is not just one of "pruning" and then placing branches where they belong. Equally important is the necessity of detecting new branches or species.

Deciphering the tree of life, the way species are related, is today unambiguously accepted as the *only* principle for scientific classification. Modern, molecular phylogeny has revolutionized this task, yet Hennig could not have imagined that his methodological criticism would have contributed to an ongoing polemic against descriptive taxonomy and thus almost to the demise of his own "species", the taxonomist.

Species description and species identification was no longer the focal point of biological nomenclature. Instead phylogeny became the primary, all too often the *only*, objective of modern taxonomy (Boero 2005, 2010; Smith 2004; Wheeler 2004). Ironically, while modern taxonomy thus began to address the origin of life, finally capable of deciphering the tree of life (http://tolweb.org/tree/), the discovery and description of new species suddenly lagged behind (Kim and Byrne 2006).

In competition with molecular taxonomy, descriptive taxonomy lost the fight for funding and taxonomy began to cannibalize itself (Boero 2005). The classical taxonomist capable of describing and distinguishing species was being portrayed as digging through shelves of specimens gathering dust while molecular taxonomists were busy resolving their discipline's principal question: the phylogeny of life.

But ecologists continue to need tools for species identification. Without these, they lack the resources to do their assignment. Taxonomists have a mandate to distinguish and describe. Ecologists need this descriptive framework to identify key components of the systems that they study.

Phylogeny and nomenclature: accuracy versus pragmatism?

What is the most important aspect of biodiversity? The phylogeny of a species?

For any ecologist it may be helpful to know how species are related, but he would certainly argue that phylogeny is but an insubordinate aspect of the ecosystem. To an ecologist it is most important to understand how biodiversity functions (Boero and Bonsdorff 2007), including population dynamics, species interaction, energy flows, trophic relationships, and deciphering how ecosystems work. Ecologist will undoubtedly agree that understanding functionality is more important than phylogeny.

Although phylogeny is the guiding principle for establishing a natural classification, it is not the basic principle that shapes the diversity of life. The driving forces that impose shape and structure upon any organism, and requires individual members of a population to adapt or perish, are only to a minor degree based on phylogenetic constraints. The environment, not the ancestry, determines the survival of any organism. Ironically, this aspect of biodiversity is well illustrated by the multitude of examples of convergent evolution. Again and again the environment has forced structural adaptations upon organisms of very different origins.

For any ecologist identifying a species is a means to an end, not the principal goal of his science. From his view-point, deciphering the tree of life remains an academic exercise until it translates into reliable identification. For a taxonomist, however, species represent hypotheses. Establishing their phylogeny is a necessary task of his discipline. False hypotheses result in false identifications, which is ultimately not in an ecologist's interest either.

For the sake of other disciplines, nomenclature has nevertheless to be pragmatic: any ecological study that cannot distinguish one cryptic species from another is forced to accept experimental fuzziness, which is inherently undesirable. When a species can no longer be recognized even by specialists, ecologists and taxonomists lose their common ground. If taxonomists fail to provide efficient tools for species identification, they must not be surprised to be marginalized. Ecologists on the other hand must concede that taxonomic studies provide a necessary basis for their own discipline.

New technologies to the rescue?

If the biodiversity of species is overwhelming but cannot be ignored, how do scientists, taxonomists, and ecologists alike, best deal with this paradox?

Despite being starved for resources, taxonomists have made enormous advances in cataloging biodiversity, yet their discipline continues to be criticized as not up-to-speed with today's information age (Godfray 2002, 2007). A new, electronic alpha-taxonomy is proclaimed as a modern solution to overcome this "taxonomic impediment" (Mayo *et al.* 2008). In a global extinction crisis with fewer taxonomists available, technology offers the tempting "quick and dirty way out". However, even "biodiversity inventories done differently" (Webb *et al.* 2010) require resources and programmers developing database solutions that ironically often compete for funding with their "primary producers", the taxonomists who contribute raw data.

Undoubtedly, modern databases can be utilized efficiently in managing large taxonomic data sets (e.g. the World Register of Marine Species (WoRMS) www.marinespecies.org/; Index Fungorum, www.indexfungorum.org/; Myconet, www.fieldmuseum. org/myconet/outline.asp; FishBase, www.fishbase.org/); The Encyclopedia of Life (EoL), www.eol.org/). Many natural history collections now provide free access to their collection data (Global Biodiversity Information Facilities (GBIF), www.gbif.org/; Symbiota, http://symbiota.org/tiki/tiki-index.php; The Californian Academy of Sciences (CAS), www.calacademy.org/search.php?q=collections; The Smithsonian Natural History Museum, http://collections.nmnh.si.edu/; and The Charles

Darwin Foundation (CDF), www.darwinfoundation.org/datazone/collections/collections_index.php). As elegant as these systems are, all data sets need to be critically assessed because they potentially refer to collections with outdated nomenclature and unverified identifications (Lücking *et al.* 2011) and there are inherent limitations to extrapolating ecological information from these records (Newbold 2010).

Even though modern databases have become an increasingly valuable resource for taxonomists, they do not provide ecologists with a rapid, reliable means of species identification. Genetic barcoding has been proposed as an alternative to classic specimen collections for cataloging species uniquely identified by characteristic genetic sequences (or molecular operational taxonomic units, MOTUs; Blaxter 2004; Hebert and Gregory 2005; Stoeckle *et al.* 2004). Presumably, once the majority of species is barcoded, MOTUs will permit any unidentified taxon to be checked against a universal register. However, currently no magic "tricoder" exists and assembling a gigantic barcode database requires an immense effort (Lücking 2009). Taxonomists are strongly divided as to what extent this effort will be useful (Smith 2004, 2005), a principal objection being that genetic barcodes cannot substitute for descriptive taxonomy (Ebach and Holdrege 2005; Will *et al.* 2005). Any code is as ecologically non-informative as a species name: both are *only labels*. Although an inherent part of an organisms' DNA, for the barcode sequence to be informative, it needs to correspond to a *known* taxon.

Generally speaking, new technology can only ever be a tool to overcome *technical* impediments. Species names need to correspond to biologically meaningful hypotheses. "Simply increasing the rate of species descriptions … will not ameliorate the 'crisis' – taxa that correspond to incorrect hypotheses … compromise the reliability of systematic information" (de Carvalho *et al.* 2008). A "quick and dirty" approach to taxonomy cannot be the answer for a scientific discipline that continues to be starved of its most important resource: educated, professional taxonomists (Cotterill and Foissner 2010; de Carvalho *et al.* 2007; Will *et al.* 2005).

What is necessary is a *paradigm shift*: the atomization of biological disciplines has led biologists astray. Over the past 20 years, biology shifted from a holistic view of organisms to the dominance of narrowly focused technological and molecular concepts (Lücking 2009; Lücking *et al.* 2011) causing an alienation of its fundamental disciplines: ecology and taxonomy. New technologies will reverse this trend only if the necessity for comprehensive species accounts is again unambiguously acknowledged. Assembling what has been called the *natural history of a species* must again become the focal point of joint efforts of taxonomy *and* ecology.

For this paradigm shift, biodiversity inventories require fundamental investments, providing *all* necessary taxonomic resources (Boero 2001). Such investments include better infrastructure (collections, DNA banks, barcode registers, specimen databases) and logistics (funding for field surveys and expeditions) but much more importantly, *training of new professional taxonomists* capable of re-establishing a basis for a new, comprehensive modern biodiversity science.

Galápagos: a case study

The Galápagos Islands are a classic example of why taxonomy and ecology again need to become an integral part of conservation biology. The archipelago is amongst the most intensely studied tropical island ecosystems in the world. In 2009 the Galápagos National Park and the CDF celebrated their fiftieth anniversaries: 50 years of conservation management and ecological research in Galápagos.

One might assume that this long history of scientific research would have permitted sufficient time to assemble a representative overview of species diversity throughout the archipelago. Traditionally, biologists were indeed well aware of this necessity. Their first expeditions shared the principal objective of making an inventory of the biodiversity of Galápagos. When a permanent research station was founded, some of the earliest studies were species inventories of major taxonomic groups. The necessity for such accounts was not challenged and today ecologists still benefit from these "science classics", tomes like *Flora of the Galápagos* by Wiggins and Porter (1971).

Yet today, knowledge of Galápagos biodiversity remains strongly discrepant and biased against small, inconspicuous species (Tables 8.2. and 8.3.). Ironically, with the advance of taxonomy into a new phylogenetic era the description of inconspicuous, non-emblematic taxa now lags behind. The interest to describe the lesser known species of the archipelago also dwindled and the need for taxonomic baselines is increasingly questioned. In the face of immense conservation challenges, it becomes increasingly difficult to argue why basic biodiversity inventories remain a necessity.

Towards an all species inventory: compiling what is known

The first attempt to establish an inventory of all *known* species from the archipelago was started as late as 2008, when the CDF finally began to compile its first comprehensive online register for all Galápagos species (Bungartz and Gardener 2009). This exercise proved a difficult challenge: it was evident from the start that records for different taxonomic groups were very incomplete. Instead of truly documenting which species were known, the first version inadvertently highlighted that a majority had never been investigated, or that research on a particular group was not readily accessible. Compiling the data clearly demonstrated the immense challenge to find "existing" information.

Reports of Galápagos species in different taxonomic groups today are scattered across the literature. Older publications typically follow a taxonomy that is outdated and historic collections are distributed widely around the world. These collections are rarely well documented, locality data for specimens are scant, they lack geo-references, and very few historic collections are cataloged at all (e.g. CAS, www.calacademy.org/search.php?q=collections; The Smithsonian Natural History Museum, http://collections.nmnh.si.edu/). Observational and monitoring data cited in the scientific literature or maintained in CDF databases are of disparate quality: species that are difficult to identify in the field should be referenced in CDF collections, where these records can be verified. Nevertheless, such careful documentation has regularly been neglected. Quality control of species records, tracking the annotation history of taxonomic identifications, and updating outdated taxonomy represent significant obstacles towards the documentation of known Galápagos species.

The first version of Galápagos species published online in December 2008 was necessarily far from complete. It was based on static information hastily compiled in spreadsheets. In a second phase, a database was designed and the information migrated. Finally a significantly technically more advanced updated online version was released in May 2010, but more taxonomic records still continue to be added (Table 8.1; Bungartz *et al.* 2010).

Current state of knowledge of Galápagos biodiversity

The total number of all species ever reported for the Galápagos is here estimated between 18,000 and 25,000 names. This rough estimate includes synonyms and erroneous reports and suggests that between 45% and 63% of these names are currently in the CDF database (a total of 11,305, of which 6,484 correspond to accepted names, the remaining ones being synonyms, or names rejected because reports are based on misidentifications; see Table 8.1).

When the CDF inventory began, first estimates suggested that as much as 60–80% of all Galápagos species were possibly still unknown (Bungartz and Gardener 2009). Revising this original assessment, more conservative estimates still suggest that at least 50% of the species continue to remain unknown. This would suggest that a realistic total number of Galápagos species could be as high as 16,200, possibly more (Tables 8.2 and 8.3). An objective assessment continues to be extremely difficult. Many different methods to develop realistic estimates have been proposed for different taxonomic groups (e.g. Bebber *et al.* 2007; Colwell and Coddington 1995; Dolphin and Quicke 2001; Feuerer and Hawksworth 2007; Gaston and Blackburn 1997; Koslow *et al.* 1997; Mueller and Schmit 2007; Peck 2001; Unterseher *et al.* 2008). No single method is universally accepted and even within the same group estimates vary considerably.

A relatively simplistic scale is used here, assuming that a more or less realistic assessment can be based upon what is currently known about the biodiversity of a particular species group (Table 8.2). For this assessment, species numbers published in the literature were compared to names entered to date into the CDF collection database. This database includes names from taxonomic identifications of more than 84,000 specimens and taxon names from a review of 1,242 literature references (checklists, monographs, identification manuals, etc.; Sept. 2010). Using these numbers a subjective assessment is presented as to whether a particular species group is *well*, *moderately* or *poorly known* (Table 8.2.). Extrapolation from these assessments remains difficult. Peck (2001), for example, compares three extrapolation methods (insect–host, species–area, and direct count) to estimate insect species numbers for Galápagos. His direct count

Table 8.1 Progress of the CDF biodiversity inventory

Milestones	*Names of all taxa* included in the CDF database (i.e., including both taxonomic synonyms and species erroneously reported from Galápagos)*	*Names of taxa* currently accepted (i.e., excluding synonyms and erroneous reports)*	*Percentage of accepted names*
Phase 1: First compilation of all data in different formats (written catalog, herbarium database, marine monitoring database, invertebrate collection database)			
December 2008	8,069	4,202	52%
Phase 2: Migration of data from different formats into one single database; re-design of collection database:			
November 2009	8,207	4,773	58%
December 2009	8,932	4,996	56%
January 2010	8,943	5,224	58%
March 2010	9,496	5,315	56%
April 2010	10,004	5,601	56%
Phase 3: Dynamically updated online checklist (www.darwinfoundation.org/datazone/checklists/) and online search of collection database (www.darwinfoundation.org/datazone/collections/collections_index.php):			
May 2010	10,554	5,879	56%
August 2010	10,951	6,203	57%
06 September 2010	11,199	6,413	57%
10 September 2010	11,305	6,484	57%

Notes

*numbers include species, subspecies, varieties and forms, taxa above species rank are not counted.

Table 8.2 Assessment of current Galápagos biodiversity (bacteria not included)

1	*2*	*3*		*4*	*5*	*6*		*7*	
Checklist	*Literature reviews*	*CDF checklists (September 2010)*		*Estimate of known species*	*Current knowledge*	*% known species*		*Total species number*	
	No. of names	*No. of accepted names*	*No. of all names*			*High*	*Low*	*Min.*	*Max.*
TOTAL (without pathogens)	7,319	6,595	11,082	8,080				16,208	42,815
ANIMALS									
Vertebrates				537		96	88	565	631
Actinopterygii and Chondrichthyes	550	249	253	550	good–excellent	90	80	611	688
Amphibia	1	2	5	2	excellent	90	90	2	2
Reptilia	50	48	100	50	excellent	100	90	50	56
Aves	176	179	273	179	excellent	100	90	179	199
Mammalia	57	55	67	57	excellent	100	90	57	63
Marine Invertebrates				1,908		32	23	4,424	7,108
Annelida (marine)	192	24	54	192	moderate	50	40	384	480
Arachnida (marine)	not reviewed	39	41	39	poor	20	10	195	390
Chordata (non-vertebrates)	not reviewed	10	13	10	poor	20	10	50	100
Cnidaria	42	87	123	87	poor	20	10	435	870
Crustacea	238	238	313	238	poor–moderate	30	20	793	1,190
Ctenophora	not reviewed	0	2	0	poor	20	10	0	0
Echinodermata	200	89	100	200	moderate	50	40	400	500
Ectoprocta	not reviewed	12	23	12	poor	20	10	60	120
Mollusca (marine)	833	861	1,259	861	moderate–good	60	50	1,435	1,722
Nematoda (marine)	not reviewed	2	4	2	poor	20	10	10	20
Platyhelminthes (marine)	not reviewed	48	64	48	poor–moderate	30	20	160	240

Porifera	not reviewed	6	73	6	poor	20	10	30	60
Other small marine invertebrate groups	not reviewed	8	11	8	very poor	10	1	80	800
Interstitial fauna	not reviewed	109	130	109	good	90	80	121	136
Zooplankton	not reviewed	96	198	96	poor–moderate	30	20	320	480
Terrestrial Invertebrates				2,850		52	48	6,141	10,926
Acari	308	0	0	308	moderate–good	60	50	513	616
Annelida (terrestrial)	9	9	10	9	very poor	10	1	90	900
Arachnida (terrestrial)	184	162	308	184	good	90	80	204	230
Chilopoda	7	7	7	7	moderate	50	40	14	18
Coleoptera	487	435	602	487	good	90	80	541	609
Collembola	35	42	81	42	poor	20	10	210	420
Dermaptera	7	6	9	7	good–excellent	90	80	8	9
Dictyoptera	1	17	20	17	good	90	80	19	21
Diplopoda	7	4	7	7	poor	20	10	35	70
Diptera	267	246	423	267	poor–moderate	30	20	890	1,335
Gastropoda (terrestrial)	120	125	198	125	good	90	80	139	156
Hemiptera	459	267	410	459	good	90	80	510	574
Hymenoptera	295	43	274	295	poor	20	10	1,475	2,950
Lepidoptera	319	295	332	319	good	90	80	354	399
Malacostraca (terrestrial)	38	5	9	38	moderate	50	40	76	95
Myxozoa	not reviewed	0	1	1	poor	20	10	5	10
Neuroptera	8	8	9	8	good	90	80	9	10
Nematoda (terrestrial)	100	4	10	100	poor	20	10	500	1,000
Odonata	8	10	11	10	good–excellent	90	80	11	13
Onychophora	1	1	1	1	excellent	100	90	1	1
Orthoptera	33	33	50	33	moderate–good	60	50	55	66
Platyhelminthes (terrestrial)	not reviewed	2	2	2	poor	20	10	10	20
Psocoptera	40	40	76	40	poor	20	10	200	400
Thysanoptera	50	33	70	50	moderate	50	40	100	125
Other small terrestrial invertebrate groups	34	34	44	34	poor	20	10	170	340

continued

Table 8.2 continued

1	*2*	*3*		*4*	*5*	*6*		*7*	
Checklist	*Literature reviews*	*CDF checklists (September 2010)*		*Estimate of known species*	*Current knowledge*	*% known species*		*Total species number*	
	No. of names	*No. of accepted names*	*No. of all names*			*High*	*Low*	*Min.*	*Max.*
PLANTS									
Algae				362		40	30	900	3,050
Chlorophyta	42	48	72	48	moderate	50	40	96	120
Heterokontophyta	46	55	83	55	moderate	50	40	110	138
Rhodophyta	228	237	361	237	moderate	50	40	474	593
Other algal groups (mostly microscopic, e.g. Bacillariophyta, Chrysophyta, Cryptophyta, Haptophyta, Sagenista)	not reviewed	0	22	22	very poor	10	1	220	2,200
Bryophytes				282		60	53	313	353
Anthocerotophyta and Hepatophyta	150	115	312	150	good	90	80	167	188
Musci	132	116	267	132	good	90	80	147	165
Vascular Plants	1,426	1,426	1,744	1,426	excellent	100	90	1,426	1,584

FUNGI									
True Fungi				713		22	16	2,419	18,963
Chytridiomycota	n/a	0	0	1	very poor	10	1	10	100
Zygomycota	n/a	1	1	1	very poor	10	1	10	100
Glomeromycota	n/a	0	0	1	very poor	10	1	10	100
Ascomycota (non-lichenized)	95	42	121	95	very poor	10	1	950	9,500
Basidiomycota (non-lichenized)	85	34	172	85	very poor	10	1	850	8,500
Lichenized and Lichenicolous Fungi	509	530	1,851	530	good	90	80	589	663
Other "fungi"				2		7	1	20	200
Myxomycota, Labyrinthulomycota, Acrasiomycota, etc.	not reviewed	0	4	1	very poor	10	1	10	100
Oomycota, Hyphochytridiomycota, etc.	not reviewed	1	2	1	very poor	10	1	10	100
OTHERS (not included in the total)									
Diseases	not reviewed	72	100	72	poor–moderate	30	20	240	360
TOTAL (without diseases)	7,319	6,595	11,082	8,080				16,208	42,815

Notes

Column (1) CDF checklists currently online. Column (2) numbers of species names reported in the literature; column (3) numbers currently included in the online checklist. Column (4) estimates of currently known species using (2) and (3) as references. In some cases numbers included in the checklists are more accurate, but for most species groups data entry is ongoing. The total number of known and unknown Galápagos species is assessed using a simple scale of percentage classes: very poor (only 0–10% of species known), poor (10–20%), poor to moderate (20–30%), moderate (40–50%), moderate to good (50–60%), good (70–80%), good to excellent (80–90%), excellent (90–100%). The lower range of these percentages was used to calculate a conservative estimate (minimum total species number); the higher percentages to calculate the highest estimate (maximum total species number). Table 8.3 summarizes results.

includes at least 1,558 species, both other estimates are significantly higher (up to 5,000) and he concludes that a conservative estimate of no more than 2,000 species might be most realistic. This would imply that as much as 77% of all insect species are already known: estimates presented here are more cautious.

Overall, although the archipelago is one of the best studied tropical island ecosystems, the state of knowledge among different species groups is fraught with enormous discrepancies and the progress of entering and verifying taxonomic records remains slow (Table 8.1).

Most obvious is the discrepancy between known terrestrial species and marine ones. Peck (1997, 2001) suggests that terrestrial diversity of Galápagos *known* species is only slightly higher than marine diversity. With the data presented here, this assessment has become inaccurate: numbers of currently *known* terrestrial species are almost three times greater than marine ones. This ratio can be ascribed to the challenge of surveying the marine environment, even though it also reflects that to some extent marine species are still incompletely databased. Wilson (1992) suggested global terrestrial biodiversity to be two times larger than marine diversity. If "his" ratio is applied to Galápagos, the "true" total number of species could easily be more than 16,000, and even as high as 42,000 (Table 8.3.)! Assuming that this ratio is incorrect and that marine and terrestrial species numbers are indeed approximately equal (according to Peck 2001), the total number of Galápagos species could still be higher. Globally, the Census of

Table 8.3 Estimates of species currently known from Galápagos, and minimum and maximum estimates of the species that possibly occur in the archipelago

Groups	*Total number of species currently known*	*Total species number (conservative estimate)*	*Total species number (high estimate)*
ANIMALS			
Vertebrates	537	565	631
Marine invertebrates	1,908	4,424	7,108
Terrestrial invertebrates	2,850	6,141	10,926
PLANTS			
Algae	362	900	3,050
Bryophytes	282	313	353
Vascular plants	1,426	1,426	1,584
FUNGI			
True fungi	713	2,419	18,963
Other "fungi"	2	20	200
Total	8,080	16,208	41,815
of these:			
Terrestrial species	5,810 (72%)		
Marine species	2,270 (28%)		
percentage all known species		49%	19%
percentage all unknown species		51%	81%

Marine Life (www.coml.org/) even indicates that reverse ratios could be imagined, with marine species numbers being significantly higher than terrestrial ones: entire phyla of organisms are today only known in the sea, where life originated and has had significantly more time to evolve (Carr *et al.* 2003).

Overall, the best known Galápagos species groups today are terrestrial and marine vertebrates, and vascular plants (almost 100% of species known). This is not surprising since these organisms are all macroscopic, among them the most conspicuous and attractive iconic species: giant tortoises, Darwin's finches, marine iguanas, blue-footed boobies, endemic daisy trees, hammerhead and whale sharks, dolphins, sea lions…

Very poorly known are marine (20–30%) and terrestrial invertebrates (*c.*50%, with insects up to 70%), and algae (30–40%). Of all organisms, fungi (10–20%) remain the least studied group despite their important ecological role in nutrient cycling in any terrestrial ecosystem! Not only do all lesser known groups belong to the least visible and inconspicuous taxa, they are also generally among the most numerous groups. Without these species, Galápagos ecosystems would cease to function. Incomplete knowledge is a major factor for why it is currently impossible to objectively assess Galápagos biodiversity and better understand ecosystem functionality.

Lost paradise: where are we headed?

Galápagos species inventories: can they provide a novel perspective on restoration?

Historic efforts to understand Galápagos ecology understandably centered on a few, well-documented and typically iconic taxa. Exploitation of tortoises and whales was real and happened on an unimaginably drastic scale. Success to save Galápagos' most famous icons from the brink of extinction has been immensely successful. Yet today we have few excuses except for sheer ignorance if this single-species approach to conservation continues. The focus on iconic taxa has inadvertently resulted in a "gardener's" approach to conservation, preserving few emblematic species but else failing to preserve entire ecosystems.

One example is the humid highlands of the inhabited islands that today are all highly disturbed, agricultural areas. Here, iconic species like the giant tortoise still survive. On farms, plantations of the famous endemic *Scalesia* trees have become a visitor attraction, while less than 1% of the original forests prevail. Even in these fragments of the original vegetation, the composition of the flora and fauna has long been considerably altered.

Ironically, as little as is known, classic management policies nevertheless tried to restore the Galápagos ecosystem to a presumed original, pristine state. As a result, management practices focused primarily on the eradication and control of invasive species, perceived to be the highest threat to the Galápagos natural systems (Snell *et al.* 2006). Overall, these programs have shown little success (Gardener *et al.* 2010). Apart from large mammals, most species, once introduced, are here to stay (for a detailed review: see Atkinson *et al.* 2011).

The idea to restore supposedly primeval, pristine ecosystems is at least to some extent based on a romanticized presumption that "natural" ecosystems are intrinsically better than anthropogenic "artificial" ones. Yet, this dualism is not only flawed because humans are an integral part of nature, it is also fraught with methodological challenges. Ecosystems are by nature dynamic. In most parts of the world, human civilizations have altered ecosystems since the Stone Age. With the passage of time, it is rarely possible to deduct and establish a realistic historic baseline of a presumed "primeval pristine" state perceived not to be negatively impacted by human disturbance.

Of course, it might be argued that perhaps no other tropical archipelago was settled as late as the Galápagos, which as a result remained one of the few archipelagos in the world untouched by humans for millennia. However, realistic assessments today must admit that only a few generations of inhabitation have irrevocably altered all Galápagos natural systems! For example, there are currently 515 native (indigenous and endemic) vascular plant species reported, but as many as 834 plant species have been introduced to Galápagos, of which 326 species are already naturalized (CDF collection database, Sep 2010; also see Guézou *et al.* 2010).

While it remains an intriguing challenge to investigate how the Galápagos landscape might have looked before humans arrived, restoring this presumed "pristine" state is evidently no longer realistic. Today, humans are here to stay and so are the majority of organisms that they brought along with them.

Modern restoration biology and biodiversity assessments: towards a realistic scenario

Even in Galápagos, restoring ecosystems can no longer mean to recreate a "paradise lost". Restoration ecology must set realistic, pragmatic goals of managing diverse, but "novel" ecosystems that are essentially "hybrids" of the original biodiversity and alien newcomers. Once it is known how management practices affect both original and alien species, strategies can be developed to *minimize biodiversity loss*.

Ironically, these strategies are not necessarily identical to the goal of *maximizing* biodiversity. Disturbed, altered ecosystems are often characterized by high species numbers. Some cultural landscapes managed for centuries by traditional agriculture practices are well known to have matured today into diverse secondary ecosystems.

The Galápagos terrestrial ecosystems have not yet matured into cultural landscapes, but represent novel, hybrid ecosystems where, despite all control efforts, alien species will continue to coexist alongside native and endemic ones. These systems have become a pragmatic management reality. To preserve Galápagos' original biodiversity, management must focus on (1) identifying remaining biodiversity hot spots and (2) developing rigorously tested restoration recipes to (3) ensure that effects of management practices are well understood and (4) that they do not contribute to further biodiversity loss from natural refugia. Restoration of an unknown original landscape remains an illusion; the prime objective must be to better understand the consequences of ecosystem management!

For this strategy, biodiversity inventories are indispensible. Only surveys of a wide range of diverse groups permit objective assessments of both the status quo and the outcome of different management practices. A good example where such an approach is *not* employed is the *Scalesia* remnant forest at Los Gemelos in Santa Cruz Island. Here the forest understory is today dominated by highly invasive blackberry (*Rubus niveus*) and it has become routine to control this invasive weed with regular herbicide treatments. Yet no studies examine the effect of these regular herbicide applications. Preliminary studies suggest that macrofungi diversity in these forests is as low as in forests entirely composed of invasive trees (Arturo-López 2008), diversity of lichenicolous fungi is extremely low (Ertz, personal communication), and the breeding success of Warbler finches appears to have been negatively affected (Kleindörfer, personal communication). Multi-species inventories of such forests could provide a tool to assess management practices.

Conclusions: where are we headed?

How can taxonomy and ecology better complement each other to meet the biggest global crisis of modern times: can we halt extinction of the majority of species with whom we share this planet?

The Galápagos Islands have been called a natural laboratory of evolution. It now needs to become a model of Noah's Ark. In this small insular ecosystem scientists have a unique opportunity to "understand" biodiversity. A Census of Galápagos Species Diversity has the unique chance to showcase how taxonomy and ecology can be integrated to better understand species diversity and ecosystem functionality.

Tourists visiting the Galápagos are typically told that the islands remain unique as the best-preserved tropical island ecosystem of the world, with more than 95% of its originally reported species still present (Bensted-Smith 2006). Galápagos thus continues to be celebrated as *the most pristine island ecosystem in the world*!

It is a sad fact, however, that this statement might even be correct – if we compare the Galápagos with most other, even more degraded tropical archipelagos. However, as we are barely capable of overseeing Galápagos diversity, how can it be argued that this ecosystem continues to be pristine?

Until recently a centralized CDF register of Galápagos species did not exist, but even if the above cited 95% estimate were correct for *known* taxa, the CDF database unequivocally illustrates that the majority of species-numerous groups, all providing essential ecosystem services, have almost entirely been neglected! Of course, building up such a taxonomic, centralized register can only be a first step. Presently the CDF online checklist includes little ecological information on the functional roles that different species play within their Galápagos ecosystems.

An analogy comes to mind: A doctor who prescribes an antibiotic is well aware that the drug kills bacteria and heals infections. At a time when bacteria were not known, doctors still attempted to cure diseases and for any patient it would have been disastrous had they not tried. Nevertheless, no one would suggest today that the discovery of infectious bacteria and the search for drugs to eliminate them was not a useful scientific exercise.

Improving our knowledge of Galápagos biodiversity for a wide range of species groups and assessing existing ecosystems are not mutually exclusive. Using multi-species inventories to assess how management affects ecosystems is one of the most objective, although cumbersome and costly, approaches to monitor restoration success. Yet, to better understand Galápagos ecosystems it is essential to establish this broad, objective overview of biodiversity.

Galápagos has long been opened to the world. While it remains a high priority to avoid further species introduction, conservation science must finally accept that new species have become an integral part of its ecosystems. Galápagos can only learn to deal with newcomers if scientists continue to investigate *all* unique elements of the original biodiversity setup of this archipelago. This includes groups that no longer must be ignored: the *neglected majority of species*.

Acknowledgements

The CDF Galápagos Species Checklist (available online at www.darwinfoundation.org/ datazone/checklists/) is a huge, multi-authored project. The case study discussed here relies heavily on this large data set. It would not be possible without the contributions of CDF staff scientists and collaborators worldwide. Authors, contributors, and donors are too numerous to be named individually here but all are cited on this website and they deserve all the credit for making this project a reality. The project relies on more than 50 years of research in Galápagos and all data now available online are a result of this long tradition. One person in particular should not go unnamed, though: Anna Dolma Alonso has been a volunteer programmer at the CDF who donated many, many months of her time programming the interface and dynamic database that now drives the online checklist. Without her skills, this information would still not be accessible and analyses like the case study presented here would be impossible. Another team of volunteer programmers needs to be mentioned: Robin and Paul Schroeder (of SegiSoft) have re-designed the CDF collection database, and Samuel Clarke has made this specimen database available online. Finally, this project would not have been possible without continued strong support by Mark Gardener, the former CDF Director of Terrestrial Sciences, who during his tenure early on recognized the fantastic potential of the data available and accumulated at the CDF and had the vision to lobby tirelessly for this project to become a reality. Of course, no research in Galápagos would be feasible without the Ecuadorian government having realized that this unique world heritage site continues to be in danger as a result of human activity, and the Ecuadorian Galápagos National Park Service has a long tradition of supporting conservation science in the archipelago and mitigating human impact. Without their continued support and vision recognizing the importance of fundamental biodiversity research, Galápagos today would be another sad example among the multitude of tropical archipelagos that have been hard hit by enormous extinction waves. It can only be hoped that this vision and courage continues.

References

Arturo-López, X. 2008. *Inventario de la Diversidad de Macrohongos del Orden Agaricales en un bosque de* Scalesia pedunculata *Hook. f., localizado en la zona alta de la Isla Santa Cruz, Galápagos, Ecuador*. Licenciatura, Universidad Central del Ecuador, Quito. www.darwinfoundation.org/english/pages/interna.php?txtCodiInfo=96

Atkinson, R., M. Gardener, G. Harper, and V. Carrion. 2011. 50 years of eradication as a conservation tool in Galapagos: what are the limits?, *Galapagos Report 2009–2010*, 14.

Baillie, E.M., C. Hilton-Taylor, and S.N. Stuart (ed.). 2004. *2004 IUCN Red List of Threatened Species. A Global Species Assessment* (IUCN: Gland).

Bebber, D.P., F.H. C. Marriott, K.J. Gaston, S.A. Harris and R.W. Scotland. 2007. Predicting unknown species numbers using discovery curves, *Proceedings of the Royal Society B* 274:1651–1658.

Bensted-Smith, R. 2006. *A biodiversity vision for the Galapagos Islands* (Charles Darwin Foundation and World Wildlife Fund,: Quito, Ecuador).

Blaxter, M.L. 2004. The promise of a DNA taxonomy, *Philosophical Transactions of the Royal Society* 359:669–679.

Boero, F. 2001. Light after dark: the partnership for enhancing expertise in taxonomy, *Trends in Ecology and Evolution* 16:266.

Boero, F. 2005. Lots of biodiversity research services but… for whom?, *MarBEF Newsletter* 2:27.

Boero, F. 2010. The Study of Species in the Era of Biodiversity: A Tale of Stupidity, *Diversity* 2:115–126.

Boero, F. and E. Bonsdorff. 2007. A conceptual framework for marine biodiversity and ecosystem functioning, *Marine Ecology* 28:134–145.

Bowen, W.B. 1999. Preserving genes, species, or ecosystems? Healing the fractured foundations of conservation policy, *Molecular Ecology* 8:5–10.

Bungartz, F. and M. Gardener. 2009. *List of all known species from the Galapagos Islands – Lista de todas las especies conocidas de las Islas Galápagos*, online repository of the Charles Darwin Foundation/Fundación Charles Darwin. www.darwinfoundation.org/checklists/

Bungartz, F., H.W. Herrera, P. Jaramillo, N. Tirado, G. Jiménez-Uzcátegui, D. Ruiz, A. Guézou, and F. Ziemmeck. 2010. *List of all known species from the Galapagos Islands – Lista de todas las especies conocidas de las Islas Galápagos* (Charles Darwin Foundation/Fundación Charles Darwin: Puerto Ayora, Galápagos).

Carr, M.C., J.E. Neigel, J.A. Estes, S. Andelman, R.R. Warner, and J.L. Largier. 2003. Comparing marine and terrestrial ecosystems: implications for the design of coastal marine reserves, *Ecological Applications* 13:90–107.

Carvalho, M.R., de, F.A. Bockmann, D.S. Amorim, and C.R. Brandão. 2008. Systematics must embrace comparative biology and evolution, not speed and automation, *Evolutionary Biology* 35:150–157.

Carvalho, M.R., de, F.A. Bockmann, D.S. Amorim, C.R.F. Brandão, M. De Vivo, J.L. De Figueiredo, H.A. Britski, M.C.C. De Pinna, N.A. Menezes, F.P.L. Marques, N. Papavero, C.E.M., C.J.V., J.D. Mceachran, R.C. Schelly, J.G. Lundberg, A.C. Gill, R. Britz, Q.D. Wheeler, M.L.J. Stiassny, L.R. Parenti, L.M. Page, W.C. Wheeler, J. Faivovich, R.P. Vari, L. Grande, C.J. Humphries, R. Desalle, M.C. Ebach and G.J. Nelson. 2007. Taxonomic Impediment or Impediment to Taxonomy? A Commentary on Systematics and the Cybertaxonomic-Automation Paradigm, *Evolutionary Biology* 34:140–143.

Clark, D.E. and R.M. May. 2002. Taxonomic Bias in Conservation Research, *Science* 297:191–192.

Clark, J.A., J.M. Hoekstra, P.D. Boersma, and P. Kareiva. 2002. Improving U.S. Endangered Species Act Recovery Plans: Key Findings and Recommendations of the SCB Recovery Plan Project, *Conservation biology* 16:1510–1519.

Colwell, R.K. and J.A. Coddington. 1995. Estimating terrestrial biodiversity through extrapolation, *Philosophical Transactions of the Royal Society of London B* 345:101–118.

Cotterill, F.P.D. and W. Foissner. 2010. A pervasive denigration of natural history misconstrue how biodiversity inventories and taxonomy underpin scientific knowledge, *Biodiversity Conservation* 19.

Dolphin, K. and D.J. Quicke. 2001. Estimating the global species richness of an incompletely described taxon: an example using parasitoid wasps (Hymenoptera: Braconidae), *Biological Journal of the Linnean Society* 73:279–286.

Dunn, R. 2005. Modern insect extinctions, the neglected majority, *Conservation biology* 19:1030–1036.

Dunn, R.R., N.C. Harris, R.K. Colwell, L.P. Koh and N.S. Sodhi. 2009. The sixth mass coextinction: are most endangered species parasites and mutualists?, *Proceedings of the Royal Society B* 276:3037–3045.

Ebach, M.C. and C. Holdrege. 2005. DNA barcoding is no substitute for taxonomy, *Nature* 434: 697.

Feuerer, T. and D.L. Hawksworth. 2007. Biodiversity of lichens, including a world-wide analysis of checklist data based on Takhtajan's floristic regions, *Biodiversity Conservation* 16:85–98.

Gardener, M.R., R. Atkinson and J.L. Renterı́a. 2010. Eradications and People: Lessons from the Plant Eradication Program in Galapagos, *Restoration Ecology* 18:20–29

Gaston, K.J. and T.M. Blackburn. 1997. How many birds are there?, *Biodiversity and Conservation* 6:615–625.

Godfray, H.C.J. 2002. Challenges for taxonomy, *Nature* 417:17–19.

Godfray, H.C.J. 2007. Linnaeus in the information age, *Nature* 446:259–269.

Groom, M.J., G.K. Meffe and C.R. Carroll. 2006. *Principles of Conservation Biology* (Sinauer Associates: Sunderland, MA).

Guézou, A., M. Trueman, C. Buddenhagen, S. Chamorro, A.M. Guerrero, P. Pozo and R. Atkinson. 2010. An extensive alien plant inventory from the inhabited areas of Galapagos, *PLoS ONE* 5:e10276. doi:10210.11371/journal.pone.0010276.

Hebert, P.D.N. and T.R. Gregory. 2005. The Promise of DNA Barcoding for Taxonomy, *Systematic Biology* 54:852–859.

Hennig, W. 1950. *Grundzüge einer Theorie der phylogenetischen Systematik* (Deutscher Zentralverlag: Berlin, Germany).

Hennig, W. 1966. *Phylogenetic Systematics* (University of Illinois Press: Urbana, IL).

IUCN 2001. *IUCN Red List Categories and Criteria: Version 3.1* (IUCN Species Survival Commission: Gland).

IUCN 2003. *Guidelines for Application of IUCN Red List Criteria at Regional Levels: Version 3.0* (IUCN Species Survival Commission: Gland).

Kim, K.C. and L.B. Byrne. 2006. Biodiversity loss and the taxonomic bottleneck: emerging biodiversity science, *Ecological Research* 21:794–810.

Koslow, J.A., A. Williams and J.R. Paxton. 1997. How many demersal fish species in the deep sea? A test of a method to extrapolate from local to global diversity, *Biodiversity and Conservation* 6:1523–1532.

Lücking, R. 2009. Taxonomy: a discipline on the brink of extinction. Are DNA barcode scanners the future of biodiversity research? *Arch. Sci.* 61.

Lücking, R., E. Rivas Plata, A. Mangold, H.J.M. Sipman, A. Aptroot, R. Miranda González, K. Kalb, J.L. Chavez, N. Ventura and R.E. Esquinel. 2011. Natural history of Nash's Pore Lichens, Trinathotrema (Ascomycota: Lecanoromycetes: Ostropales: Stictidaceae) *Bibliotheca Lichenologica* 106.

Mayo, S.J., R. Allkin, W. Baker, V. Blagoderov, I. Brake, B. Clark, R. Govaerts, C. Godfray, A. Haigh, R. Hand, K. Harman, M. Jackson, N. Kilian, D.W. Kirkup, I. Kitching, S. Knapp, L. G.P., P. Malcolm, E. Von Raab-Straube, D.M. Roberts, M. Scoble, D.A. Simpson, C. Smith, V. Smith, S. Villalba, L. Walley and P. Wilkin. 2008. Alpha e-taxonomy: responses from the systematics community to the biodiversity crisis, *Kew Bulletin* 63:1–16.

Mueller, G.M. and J.P. Schmit. 2007. Fungal biodiversity: what do we know? What can we predict?, *Biodiversity Conservation* 16:1–5.

Nee, S. 2004. More than meets the eye. Earth's real biodiversity is invisible, whether we like it or not, *Nature* 429:804–805.

Newbold, T. 2010. Applications and limitations of museum data for conservation and ecology, with particular attention to species distribution models, *Progress in Physical Geography* 34:3–22.

Ozaki, K., M. Isono, T. Kawahara, S. Iida, T. Kudo and K. Fukuyama. 2006. A mechanistic approach to evaluation of umbrella species as conservation surrogates, *Conservation biology* 20:1507–1515.

Paine, R.T. 1969. A note on trophic complexity and community stability, *The American naturalist* 103:91–93. .

Paine, R.T. 1995. A conversation on refining the concept of keystone species, *Conservation biology* 9:962–964.

Pawar, S. 2003. Taxonomic chauvinism and the methodologically challenged, *BioScience* 53:861–864.

Peck, S.B. 1997. The species scape of Galapagos organisms, *Noticias de Galápagos* 58:18- 21.

Peck, S.B. 2001. *Smaller orders of insects of the Galapagos islands, Ecuador: Evolution, Ecology and Diversity*. (NRC Research Press: Ottawa, Canada).

Pimm, S.L., G.J. Russell, J.L. Gittleman and T.M. Brooks. 1995. The future of biodiversity, *Science* 269:347–350.

Piraino, S., G. Fanelli and F. Boero. 2002. Variability of species' roles in marine communities: change of paradigms for conservation priorities, *Marine Biology* 140:1067–1074.

Régnier, C., B. Fontaine and P. Bouchet. 2009. Not knowing, not recording, not listing: numerous unnoticed mollusk extinctions, *Conservation biology* 23:1214–1221.

Reid, W.V. 1995. Reversing the loss of biodiversity: An overview of international measures, *Aridlands Newsletter* 37.

Roberge, J.-M. and P. Angelstam. 2004. Usefulness of the Umbrella Species Concept as a Conservation Tool, *Conservation biology* 18:76–85.

Rohde, K. 2010. *How many species on Earth?:The present state of our knowledge of biodiversity on Earth.* http://knol.google.com/k/klaus-rohde/how-many-species-on-earth/xk923bc3gp4/43.

Seddon, P.J. and T. Leech. 2008. Conservation short cut, or long and winding road? A critique of umbrella species criteria, *Oryx* 42:240–245.

Smith, V.S. 2004. *Twenty-first century taxonomy: perspectives on taxonomy's industrial age*, unpublished manuscript. http://vsmith.info/DNA-Barcoding.

Smith, V.S. 2005. DNA Barcoding: Perspectives from a "Partnerships for Enhancing Expertise in Taxonomy" (PEET) Debate, *Systematic Biology* 54:841–844.

Snell, H.L., A. Tye, C.E. Causton, and R. Bensted-Smith. 2006. The status and threats to terrestrial biodiversity, in R. Bensted-Smith (ed.) *A biodiversity vision for the Galapagos Islands*, , pp. 43–59 (Charles Darwin Foundation and World Wildlife Fund: Puerto Ayora, Galapagos).

Stoeckle, M., P. Waggoner and J. Ausubel. 2004. Barcoding life: ten reasons, in *Consortium for the barcode of life* (ed.), pp. 1–2.

Unterseher, M., M. Schnittler, C. Dormann and A. Sickert. 2008. Application of species richness estimators for the assessment of fungal diversity, *FEMS Microbiological Letters* 282:205–213.

Wake, D.B. and V.T. Vredenburg. 2008. Are we in the midst of the sixth mass extinction? A view from the world of amphibians, *PNAS* 105:11466–11473.

Webb, C. O., J.W.F. Slik and T. Triono. 2010. Biodiversity inventory and informatics in Southeast Asia, *Biodiversity Conservation* 19:955–972.

Wheeler, Q.D. 2004. Taxonomic triage and the poverty of phylogeny, *Philosophical Transactions of the Royal Society of London B* 359:571–583.

Wiggins, I.L. and D.M. Porter. 1971. *Flora of the Galapagos Islands* (Stanford University Press: Stanford, CA).

Will, K. W., B.D. Mishler and Q.D. Wheeler. 2005. The perils of DNA barcoding and the need for integrative taxonomy, *Systematic Biology* 54:844–851.

Wilson, E.O. 1992. *The diversity of life* (Norton & Co: New York, NY).

9 The power of long-term monitoring to understand mechanisms of ecosystem change

The case of the Galápagos Marine Reserve

Stuart Banks, Rodrigo Bustamante, Diego Ruiz, Natalia Tirado, Mariana Vera and Franz Smith

Introduction

History, location, and dynamics have led in the Galápagos Islands to a complex mix of tropical and temperate marine and coastal ecosystems. Across the 133,000 km^2 of the Galápagos Marine Reserve (GMR) entire marine communities can shift significantly within and between years, strongly influenced by the productive water masses that drive and define them. Straddling the equator and bathed by westward flowing surface currents and nutrient rich upwelled water, the GMR represents a particularly fascinating oceanographic microcosm, a significant sanctuary zone from the effects of industrial fishing and forms over 90% of the Marine Managed Area (MMA) within the Eastern Tropical Pacific (ETP) region. It is often scrutinized by the global community, constantly subject to a diversity of interests, acclaimed for insights into natural science, and more recently valued for inference into synergies between ecosystem services and the human condition. As a result, the GMR has been driven by necessity to the frontier of applied conservation science as an example and test-bed for management practice in largely pristine oceanic islands.

Following its official designation in 1998 the GMR entered a new management paradigm. While Park managers and stakeholders discussed mechanisms to protect biodiversity and preserve the very resources that should sustain local fisheries and tourism livelihoods, it became imperative to rapidly identify those areas, habitats, and species requiring particular levels of protection. That demanded a substantial field time investment (largely dive work) to jump-start the marine species inventory, document the otherwise inaccessible, largely unseen and unregistered marine biota, and characterize oceanography, new fisheries, and tourism interactions. Limited by research resources that never quite matched the scope of the challenge, baseline information nonetheless accrued through complementary monitoring programs, key collaborations with Park and science groups through systematic inventories and directed searches for rare and threatened species (Figure 9.1). Those coastal areas intensively used by local fisheries and tourism were prioritized for mid- to long-term evaluation within a prototype coastal zoning scheme against protected low impact sites. Consequently, sampling emphasis in the early years was across rocky reef habitat in the coastal zone – an area integrated from the sub-littoral to the 40 m isobath comprising >85% of near coast habitat.

Placing a finger on the pulse of the Reserve

Despite the changeable nature of the Reserve, it was obvious that a comprehensive baseline should be the first step to quantify change in two senses. First, any long-term monitoring program would require an appreciation of spatial heterogeneity in marine communities in order to select sites both representative and informative of the larger dynamic of the GMR. Biogeography cited by Harris (1969) based upon ~300 discrete sea surface temperature measurements and seabird breeding success had been adapted by others (Jennings *et al.* 1994; Wellington *et al.* 2001) yet due to the sheer size of the Reserve still lacked a synoptic overview that considered multiple marine taxa and the interactions therein. Second, it would permit a posterior analysis of broad scale shifts across marine communities in a before–after comparison between management extractive and sanctuary subzones. Over time, it gives an important reference point given El Niño Southern Oscillation (ENSO) changes in climate, modalities, and intensity of human use. With local diver training, program continuity, and institutional memory afforded by the Charles Darwin Foundation (CDF) and Galápagos National Park Service (GNPS) this would become a reproducible methodology for meaningful comparisons in the future (Figure 9.2).

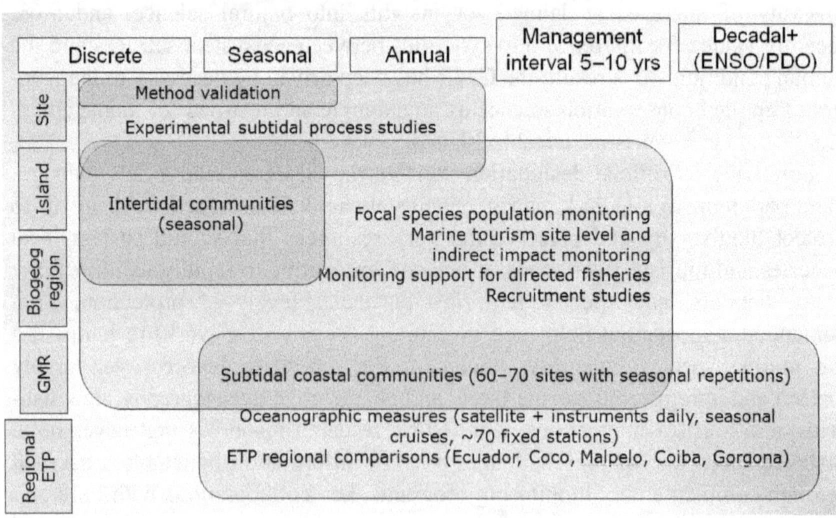

Figure 9.1 Conceptual schematic of CDF research and monitoring programs spanning a range of space and time scales.

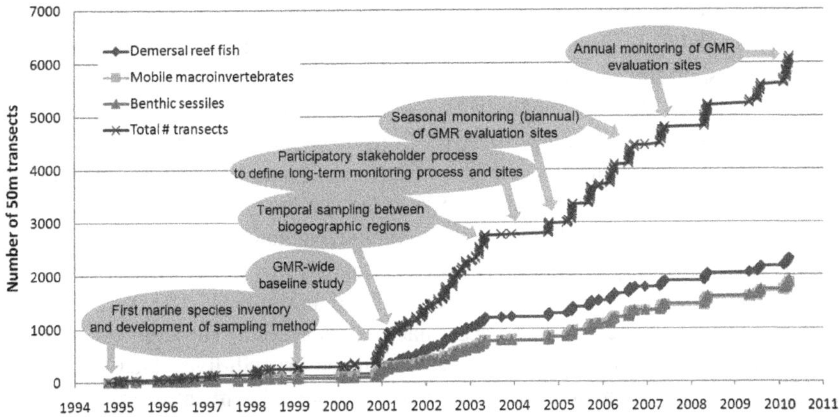

Figure 9.2 Monitoring sampling effort 1994–2010 for subtidal marine communities over 6 m and 15 m depth strata. Sampling campaigns and milestones are indicated.

Diver surveys from 1994 to 1999 worked towards a standardized monitoring methodology over subtidal depth strata for mobile macroinvertebrates, benthic macroinvertebrates, algae, and demersal reef fish, providing early quantitative information across entire subtidal communities. The newly established GMR in 1998 created an unprecedented opportunity to intelligently manage the multi-use 1,750 km coastal reserve, yet required rapid expert input into the proposed coastal zoning process from all stakeholders, including the science sector. Driven by a mix of technical input, local knowledge, compromise, and validation by stakeholders, the resulting scheme provided a first draft towards a functional MMA.

In the aftermath of the 1999 coastal zoning agreement, considerable research effort was invested in a synoptic registry of the entire near-shore reserve leading to the GMR biodiversity baseline publication (Danulat and Edgar 2001). Diver sampling from 2000 to 2001 covered >250 sites, many of which were part of tri-monthly or seasonal case studies with repetitions between take and no-take zones in particular islands. Follow-up 2001–2003 surveys in the wake of the Jessica oil spill examined the extreme differences between marine communities in the northerly tropical islands of Wolf and Darwin and upwelling western isles of Isabela and Fernandina. These observations, and those across well-studied sites such as Floreana Island, extended the time series subtidal record for the archipelago (Bustamante *et al.* 2004; Banks *et al.* 2003). Further refinements to the subtidal monitoring protocol, a new information management system to improve data quality during field campaigns and a two year multi-Park and multi-NGO process within stakeholder forums (2004–2006) selected for a subset of >60 monitoring sites across the Reserve with clustered replicates within management subzones and two further years of repeated seasonal data. Multidimensional Scaling (MDS) analysis across the three principal monitoring groups and oceanographic regime distinguished a distinct biogeography between three macrozones that characterize sessile organisms (Bustamante *et al.* 2004) and 3–5 macrozones for mobile fish and macroinvertebrate species (Figure 9.3), as described in detail by Edgar *et al.* (2004). Biogeographic domains guided the selection of sampling clusters to inform upon broader ecological function and diversity between discrete GMR habitats (Banks *et al.* 2006). Monitoring has continued successfully through to 2010, considering over 1,100 species in the coastal zone and summing (since 1994) >300 km of linear transects equivalent to ~11,000 diver hours, yet covering just 5% of the coastal reserve.

Recognizing that the small-scale oceanographic dynamic explains a great degree of biological variability, a parallel research campaign was designed to investigate the defining role of the upwelling Equatorial Undercurrent (EUC), to both complement and contextualize the biological macrofauna record. Through 2004–2007 CDF–GNPS oceanographic surveys were conducted through five 11-day seasonal cruises over 1,500 nautical miles cruise tracks coupled with a sparse in-water mooring array of instruments. This data, along with hyperspectral registries, served to ground truth algorithms for synoptic satellite overpass data collected as part of both the NASA–SeaWiFS (Sea Wide Angle of View Field Sensor) and MODIS–AQUA sensors. Covering 3,000 km wide continuous swathes on a daily basis, accessible remotely sensed data has hugely changed how we perceive the Reserve. A High Resolution Picture Transmission (HRPT) collection station installed at the Charles Darwin Research Station (CDRS) marine lab from 2001–2005 collected overpasses of high resolution ocean color data (derived chlorophyll-a) which now collected onboard the satellites are available online to projects and updated on a daily basis. Such continuity of ocean data parameterized a first small-scale ocean

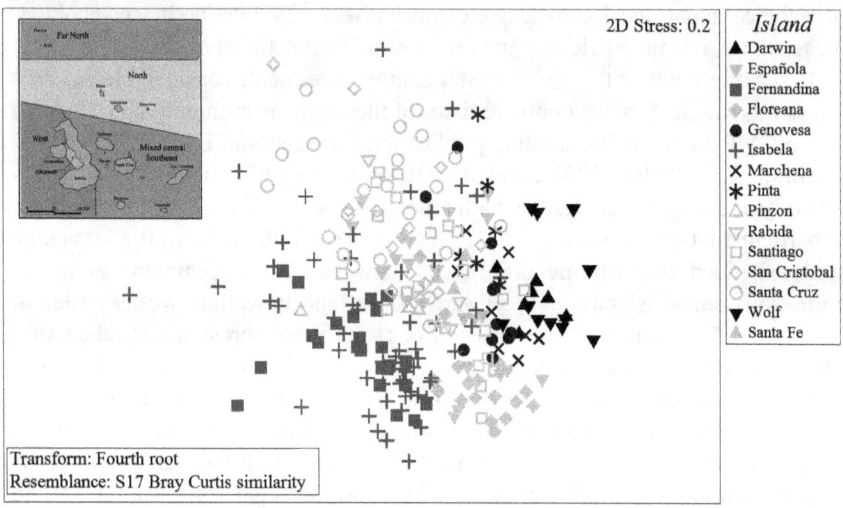

Figure 9.3 Multidimensional Scaling (MDS) of the relative abundance of 225 fish species in 2000–2010. The data highlights differences between the compositions of marine communities across 235 sites used to distinguish regional biogeographic units (inset after Edgar *et al.* 2004).

circulation model for the islands (the Hybridized Coordinate Model, HyCoM) recently extrapolated against future IPCC (International Panel for Climate Change)-predicted global climate change scenarios using Hadley data (Xie *et al.* 2009).

Determining causality behind any observed changes is a core objective of the monitoring program and substantiates any inference into future trends. It requires integration of community data with fisheries pre- and post-stock monitoring programs, GNPS–CDF fisheries observer programs, GNPS tourism records, and an understanding of broader ocean-climate shifts impacting the archipelago. Some relationships are reasonably straightforward. Fisheries biomass extraction, for example, shows a clear correlation with the most productive regions (Figure 9.4a, b). In contrast, trophic and behavioral responses to shifts in productivity, ocean regimes, tourism, and fishing patterns demand synthesis of many directed observations and modeling exercises to approach any meaningful conjecture (Witman and Smith 2003; Okey *et al.* 2004; Ruiz and Wolff 2011; Edgar *et al.* 2009).

Such inferences and their application for conservation are usually the product of complementary initiatives. Baseline inventories of high-risk fragmented coral reef habitat promoted low impact anchorage installations. Taxonomic work for rocky reef macrobiota improved the GMR biodiversity registry, helping inform national Convention on Biological Diversity (CBD) obligations and provide relevant information and education for the local community. Trophic models of generalized rocky reef and productive upwelling zones populated with field data reduce levels of uncertainty for fisheries predictions. An International Union for the Conservation of Nature (IUCN) red-listing process highlighted the sensitivity of habitat-forming algae and coral species, creating benchmarks for their protection. Risk analysis exercises began to qualify functional resilience before perturbations such as overfishing and climate stress. Field observations guided predictive mapping of species distributions. Biota fragility at recreational dive sites became criteria towards reduced-impact boat itineraries. The list continues.

Research upon marine focal species has shifted over the years and currently includes shark telemetry, *Chelonia mydas* marine turtle nesting trends, pinniped research, population viability assessment for Galápagos penguins and cormorants, to name just a few. Work continues in many aspects of fisheries stock analysis for sea cucumber, lobster, wahoo, the endangered endemic demersal grouper *Mycteroperca olfax*, with new emphasis upon evaluation of fisheries alternatives in largely undescribed open water habitat.

Given the life histories of many marine species spanning the Pacific, it became apparent that part of the key to local conservation involves protecting wider MPA (Marine Protected Areas) networks influencing and influenced by Galápagos. The subtidal protocol was extended to facilitate ETP region-wide analysis, helping to compare and characterize rocky reef systems between adjacent and partially analogous MMAs such as Malpelo (Colombia), Coco Island and Gorgona (Costa Rica), Coiba (Panama) and Machalilla (mainland Ecuador). The data also extends to a wider global evaluation of marine management effectiveness, contrasting managed areas in the Galápagos with those in the US, Panama, Belize, Brazil, Fiji, and the Solomon Islands.

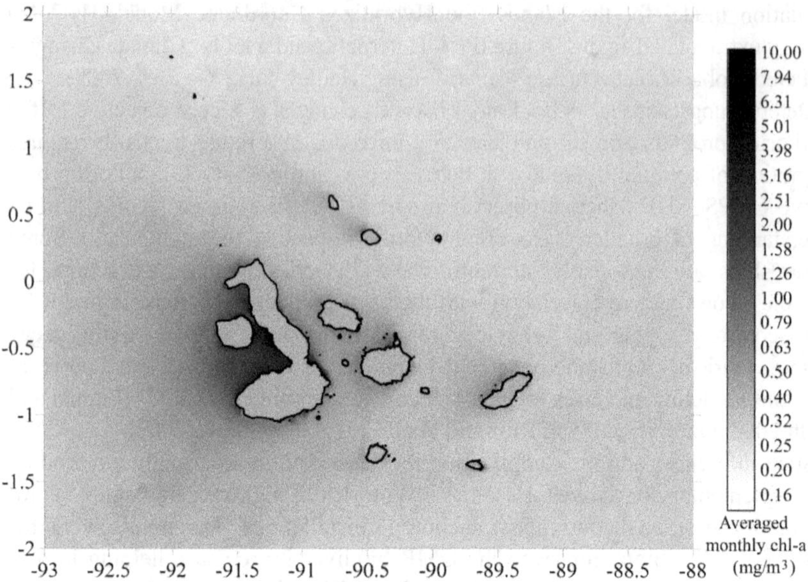

Figure 9.4a Average monthly chlorophyll values derived from SeaWiFS/MODIS–AQUA sensors (1997–2009).

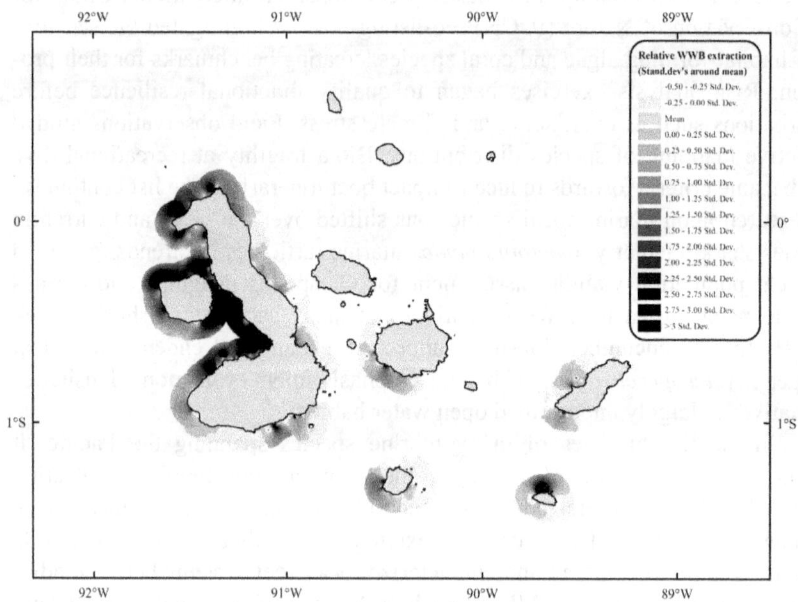

Figure 9.4b Relative wet weight biomass extractions of sea cucumber *Isostichopus fuscus* by artisanal fishermen in 1999–2003. Data extrapolated from GNPS–CDF fisheries monitoring database shows a high correlation with zones of high primary productivity across western shores.

Approaching variability

As an interconnected three-dimensional living space for well over 3,155 near coastal and marine species, the Reserve spans varied and productive habitats. These include fragmented coral reefs, cold upwelling cells over thick algae beds, mangrove stands, gorgonian- and barnacle-studded vertical walls, to little explored abyssal oligotrophic platforms and hydrothermal vents (Table 9.1). Sheer bathymetric drop-offs from the intertidal fringe to 3,500 m down at the abyssal plain are extremely abrupt in the far west of the archipelago and also form submarine chasms between some islands such as northeastern Isabela and the west coast of Santiago. This tends to bring pelagic species into close contact with inshore fauna over the 200–500 m Galápagos platform, mixing unlikely combinations such as carangid jacks, scombrid tuna, and even oceanic sunfish (*Mola mola*) with Galápagos cormorants, coral communities, reef sharks, and sea lions.

Certain sites, such as Caleta Tagus in Isabela, represent shoaling of deeper geological features that funnel cold water from continental drop-offs directly into the coastal zone, occasionally bringing deep water species into upwelling bays. In contrast, zones to the southeastern and central part of the islands have shallow platforms extending several kilometers out from the coast. Inshore seamounts rising from 500 m to 200 m across the Galápagos platform occasionally approach the surface and are well recognized productive areas important to local open water fisheries (Figure 9.5). The far northerly islands of Wolf and Darwin south of the Galápagos Spreading Center form oceanic pinnacles surrounded by deep oceanic waters and deep water seamounts subject to open ocean

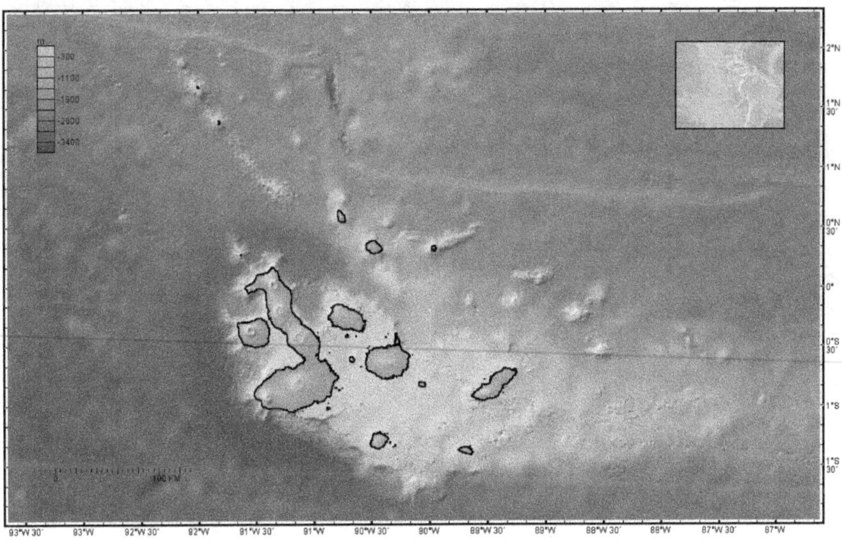

Figure 9.5 The bathymetry of the Galápagos platform (data source: Global Multi-Resolution Topography (GMRT), Marine Geoscience Data System).

Table 9.1 Principal GMR habitat types

Habitat type or community	*Brief description*
Rocky intertidal	The predominant shoreline habitat (>80%), subject to intense heating and immersion during the semi-diurnal tidal period across lava substrate.
Rocky subtidal reef	A relatively stable and extensive lava substrate habitat (>80% of near shore reserve), with much variation in structural complexity and gradient creating diverse exposed and cryptic habitat. Distinct current regimes sustain diverse community assemblages with notable climate driven shifts in benthic die off and colonization between ENSO years.
Soft bottom sediments	Near shore (>20%) and deep water sand banks harbor unique species assemblages and in-fauna and are important foraging areas for many rocky reef residents. Sheltered bays favor build up of benthic diatoms and deep water bacterial mats in some craters.
Vertical walls	More than 19 vertical walls of importance for dive tourism are regularly visited. These sites, usually subject to strong currents sustain a rich benthic fauna that encourages rich diversity and by virtue of their profile, pelagic species. Turnover of filter feeding species such as barnacles under strong upwelling is exceptionally high across these localities (Witman *et al.* 2003) driving a particularly dynamic ecology.
Coral communities	Greatly restricted in distribution after the compounding effects of two of the strongest El Niño events in recent history to the northern islands, with fragmented patches across particular sites in the central-southern archipelago. The last extensive formation covers little more than 500 m extensions in Wolf and Darwin, although some of the oldest reefs remaining in Galápagos were recently discovered to the west of Darwin with 3–7 m extensions for a single *Porites* colony. Marchena in contrast harbors the greatest extension of *Psammacora* coral fields (a loose carpet of coral), whereas the last known colonies of free-living corals such as *Cycloseris* and *Diaseris* are in very restricted localities in Floreana and Española respectively.
Macroalgae beds	Thick macroalgae beds disappeared over a few months during the 1982–1983 ENSO event drastically changing intertidal and subtidal ecosystems. The last remaining microalgae representing nursery and productive habitat persisted in very restricted sites between Fernandina and Isabela and some other cold water pockets of habitat upon western shores of other central southern islands. A significant endemic deep water kelp habitat 4–6 × more productive than analogous macroalgae habitats (M. Graham per. comm.) thought near extinction was recently rediscovered (2004 and 2007) in certain sites in Fernandina and Western Isabela.

Mangroves	Important, highly productive if spatially restricted nursery habitats for many marine species, including sharks, turtles and rays.
Sandy beaches	Biogenic and volcanic in origin, these areas are shifting. Reduction of protective reef frameworks along the coastal fringe after the last strong ENSO events may be accelerating erosion processes.
Coastal lagoons	Important land–sea interfaces and home to many endemic invertebrates, marine birds and mangrove stands. *Talapia* infestations, *Scinax* tree frog introduction and salinity issues in populated areas present significant conservation problems.
Open water pelagic	Over 126,000 km^2 of open water continuous 3D habitat. Surrounding and connecting the coastal zone it encourages mixing of Pacific open water and near-shore species in various stages of their lifecycle and from different hemispheres. A dynamic mesoscale oceanography generates significant biophysical structuring of the water column where subsurface current filaments are forced over and around the Galápagos platform.
Seamounts	Largely unexplored deep and shallow water marine mountains, which influence local ocean circulation promoting productivity, and act as stepping stones for many marine populations. Fish aggregations drawn to high benthic and pelagic productivity attract a range of predators to forage across such areas, including marine birds, sea lions, sharks and of course fishermen. Other sharp bathymetric features include, gorges, canyons and vast pits formed by transform faults recently documented through geophysical surveys.
Hydrothermal vents	Deep water ephemeral and volatile habitats that come right into the coastal zone in the west of the islands, and encourage development of pockets of unique hot water microcosms (with a unique water chemistry and microbial environment) in otherwise cold water ecosystems.
Abyssal plain	Deep water 3,000–4,000 m abyssal habitat with unique unexplored species assemblages sometimes brought up into the coastal zone by virtue of the sharp bathymetry and strong currents.
Galápagos platform and continental shelf (>100–3,000 m)	The Galápagos platform shelves up to the northeast and the Galápagos spreading center and falls with an abrupt rapid drop to the abyssal plain in the west of the archipelago. Across these inshore waters constituting the interior of the GMR, tidal currents are particularly strong, and open water offshore species tend to mix to some extent with coastal species.

currents >40–60 cm/s in the surface. In contrast, across the central topography of islands wind effects around volcanic formations can generate mesoscale eddies and refraction patterns in surface waters. Hence, transitions in the bathymetry, direction, and magnitude of prevailing water masses often create variable features.

The entire archipelago is also subject to periodic passage of eastward propagating internal waves trapped in the equatorial plane, adding another layer of complexity to diurnal tidal and seasonal cycles. Strong diurnal solar heating under the equatorial sun and variations in heat transport both vertically and horizontally can generate strong gradients in temperature in the near coast that, when influenced by internal wave shallowing of the thermocline, can result in episodes of heat stress in excess of 12°C within as little as six days and strong convection currents (Witman *et al.* 2010).

Phytoplankton productivity across the archipelago is patterned from kilometer up to archipelago-wide scales. Over large areas, productivity can occasionally increase under the influence of the upwelling ETP cold tongue extending out from the coast of South America along the equator, unqualified aeolian dust fertilization, and possibly volcanic plumes. The small-scale productive regime however is dictated by easterly EUC subsurface flow interacting with bathymetry, surface water masses, island topography, and wind contours around volcanoes. Physical collision of EUC water shoaling and refracting against the edge of the Galápagos platform and around western lineaments creates a series of filaments that later regroup at depth to the east. The resulting nutrient enrichment into coastal surface waters tends to generate spatially consistent, yet temporally ephemeral, zones of elevated productivity. Plankton also remains entrained in mesoscale gyres and oceanic fronts between tropical and temperate water masses. Large blooms are often observed passing to the west along the shear jets that cut across the northern and southern tips of Isabela Island and delineate the passage of large tropical instability waves into the central equatorial Pacific (Chavez *et al.* 1999; Sweet *et al.* 2009). Where productivity is ephemeral across the central archipelago, the western area of Elizabeth Bay and Bolivar Channel are typically highly productive throughout the year, supporting large plankton feeders such as baleen whales and a particularly high biomass. The broad scale character of the physical and productive environment sets the stage for a distinct spatial gradation in the composition of marine communities.

The upwelling west and far northern islands stand out as having very different species assemblages, with the former dominated by algae and species of Peruvian and Chilean distributions and the latter with species of largely Panamic circumtropical and Indo-Pacific distributions. Interestingly, there are similarities between these two regimes at smaller sites located in the central and southeastern part of the archipelago. In part, this reflects the partial expression of upwelling cold water cells and filaments that generate the cold water refuge "pockets" particularly evident along western shores. Extreme examples of this effect include recruitment points such as Caleta Iguana in Isabela, consistently colder than other sites in the west (Kuhn 2010), demonstrating first signs of recovery of species such as the sea star *Heliaster cumungii* heavily impacted by the strong ENSOs, or a small inlet in Playa Tortuga Negra (Isabela), the only know population represented in large numbers of a formerly widespread but now endangered solitary coral *Tubastrea taguensis*. Heterogeneity is also partly explained by the seasonal shift in westward flowing surface currents from the northeast and southeast increasing the potential for displacement of communities and larval dispersal across the confines of the archipelago from Mesoamerican and Peruvian provinces. As a result, the mixed central region shows increased inshore species richness due to greater heterogeneity of habitat correlated with small-scale (typically 1–50 km) oceanographic patterning (Figure 9.6). As a result of the high connectivity afforded by confluent water masses, the overall magnitude of variation in subtidal marine communities across the Galápagos region (~3°) was found to be of the same order as that across the entire 10° latitudinal span of continental sites from Coiba (Panama) to Machalilla (Ecuador). Wolf Island in particular shows high sessile biotic similarity to sites in Coiba and Gorgona (Colombia), whilst Wolf, Darwin, Isla Coco (Costa Rica), and Malpelo (Colombia) show high affinity in fish assemblages from Panamic and Indo-Pacific provinces (Edgar *et al.*, in revision 2010).

The marine biodiversity record over time (as distinct from the subset ~1,100 species within regularly monitored subtidal groups) reflects in large measure the sampling effort and geographic extent of research campaigns, as well as the

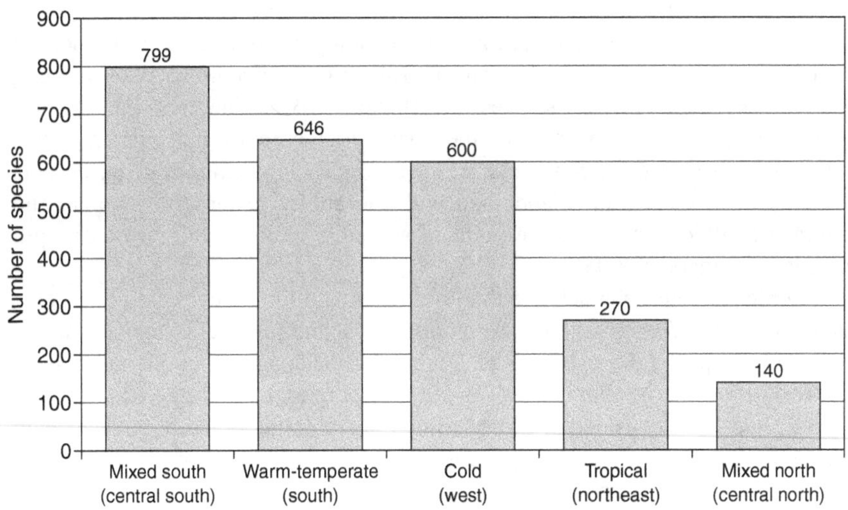

Figure 9.6 Diversity in Galápagos regional species assemblages. Early in the monitoring process it became apparent that regional species assemblages showed increased diversity across the variable central and southern regions as a result of the mixture and connectivity between western cold water and tropical northern habitats (reported from literature and sampling records after Bustamante 1994–2000).

taxonomic expertise available. Numbers of species have steadily risen since the 1970s with the inclusion of new taxa, depth strata, and habitats (Table 9.2). Mostly concentrated around collections in near coast hard bottom communities, over 22% of recorded species by taxa are insular endemics, although recent surveys suggest that some species thought to be endemic are likely shared with mainland Ecuador. Geographically located in the tropics, but with also a temperate and upwelling character subject to strong peaks in warm–cold conditions and productive and oligotrophic episodes, the system lends itself to a relatively rapid turnover of species through local extinction and colonization events. Transient visitors such as butterfly and triggerfish tend to establish with flow reversal from the Western Pacific during strong ENSO years, and then disappear. Occasionally, the recruiting slipper lobster *Parribacus scarlatinus* gains a brief foothold in the far northern islands of Wolf and Darwin. Biodiversity seems closely coupled to the extreme natural variation (ENSOs) and the continual opportunities for extant and novel species shifts during the succession it engenders. Following moderate–strong El Niño events, cold productive La Niña switches foster rapid recovery of some species, such as subtidal barnacles, with *Ulva* and *Enteromorpha* species competing with coral and other established sessile macrofauna. Some species, such as the normally voracious sea star corallivore *Acanthaster planci*, remain uncommon in Darwin, possibly held in check by periodic cold water incursions after warm events. Coralline encrusting algae also likely play an important persistent role in reef accretion during and after such episodes. For sessile productive species such as corals, encrusting and foliose algae, and barnacles, the subtidal war for space and resources is moderated by urchin eroders and grazers reducing bottom rugosity, schools of herbivorous fish, and levels of control from higher predation. Where strong associations exist between species, the character of marine communities presumably shifts commensurate to the changing nature of those interactions. Apertures also open for novel marine invasives such as *Caulerpa* sp., an alga recently observed in the islands and with the ability to rapidly establish and degrade benthic systems to the point of something comparable to an oil spill response (Anderson 2005).

In order to better characterize the level of threat to marine species, a sizeable undertaking between IUCN, conservation NGOs, and regional scientists worked to greatly improve the marine Red Listing for Galápagos. Traditionally, since the early 1960s, large characteristic marine vertebrates, birds, cetaceans, and pinnepeds had been considered, groups which are now periodically updated with new information (with the latest change being the Galápagos sea lion *Zalophus wollebaeki* now considered as endangered; Aurioles and Trillmich 2008). Other marine reptile, ray, and shark groups were added from the early 1980s onwards. In 2007 the addition of habitat-forming coral and macroalgae groups effectively doubled the number of species considered threatened (with vulnerable, endangered, or critically endangered criteria) (Figure 9.7).

Forty-five Galápagos marine species currently fulfill IUCN Red Listing threatened criteria: five mammals; six birds; six fish; one echinoderm; seven corals; six brown algae; and nine red algae. At least two species, the black spotted damselfish *Azurina euplama* and the 24-rayed sea star *Heliaster solaris*, are probably extinct. Since no marine fish has been registered by IUCN or otherwise as extinct, this is particular noteworthy.

The highest densities of threatened marine species with restricted ranges are to be found in the western part of Isabela and Fernandina Islands. Using modified Key Biodiversity Area (KBA) vulnerability and irreplaceability criteria, recent studies indicate that an estimated 30% of threatened species fall within unprotected areas (Edgar *et al.* 2008). Defined as where >1% of the population permanently or seasonally resides, the review suggests that the extinction risk could be reduced with a 2% minimum increase in protected coastal coverage. Seven IUCN red-listed species extending into the coastal fringe were also useful in the KBA process owing to their regular occurrence and discrete distributions: Galápagos penguins (*Spheniscus mendiculus*); the flightless cormorant (*Phalacrocorax harrisi*); the whale shark (*Rhincodon typus*); the Galápagos sea lion (*Zalophus wollebaeki*) and the Galápagos fur seal (*Arctocephalus galapagensis*;

Table 9.2 Number of GMR marine species in major taxonomic groups (after Bustamante *et al.* 2002; Hickman 2009)

Taxonomic groups	*No. species*	*No. endemics*	*% endemics*	*Species richness*	*Level of study*
Gorgonians	14	10	71.4	Intermediate	Poor
Sponges	66	37	56.1	Intermediate	Low
Sea pens	4	2	50	Low	Poor
Corals, Ahermatypic	43	17	39.5	Intermediate	Poor
Algae	333	130	39	High	Poor
Amphipods	50	19	38	Intermediate	Good
Opisthobranchs	49	18	36.7	Low	Poor
Marine Birds	19	5	26.3	High	Good
Polychaetes	192	50	26	Intermediate	Poor
Barnacles	18	4	22.2	Low	Moderate
Porcelain crabs	14	3	21.5	Low	Moderate
Brachyurans	120	23	19.2	Intermediate	Poor
Bryozoans	184	34	18.5	High	Poor
Molluscs	780	141	18.1	Low	Moderate
Echinoderms	200	34	17	Low	Moderate
Caridea and Stenopods	65	10	15.4	High	Poor
Hydroids	96	14	14.5	High	Moderate
Sea anemones	15	2	13.3	Low	Poor
Fishes	447	51	11.4	Intermediate	Moderate
Mammals	24	2	8.3	High	Good
Corals, Hermatypic	23	0	0	Low	Good
Cerianthids	2	0	0	Low	Poor
Zoanthids	7	Unknown	Unknown	Low	Poor
Soft bottom communities	390	Unknown	Unknown	High	Poor
Total	3,155				
Total (excl. soft bott.)	2,758	606	21.97		

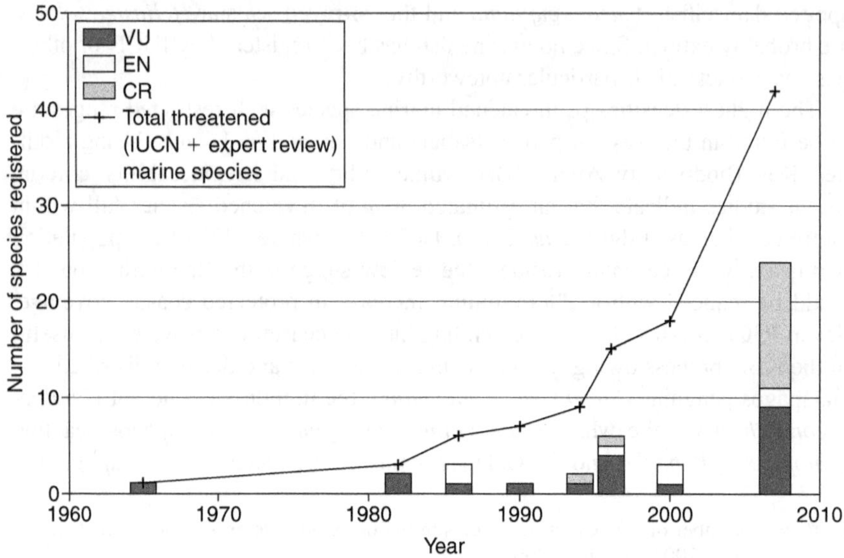

Figure 9.7 GMR coastal marine threatened species. Risk assessment of taxa from specific expert workshops and red-listing processes over recent years have added important habitat forming groups, such as corals and macroalgae, to sharks, turtles, and marine mammals, effectively doubling the number of species registered in Galápagos that are considered threatened under IUCN criteria.

the mangrove finch (*Camarhynchus heliobates*) and the lava gull *Larus fuliginosus*. The presence of the first two marine birds also showed an indirect correlation with other cryptic marine endemics, suggesting aggregated conservation benefits when prioritizing any shifts or improvements to protected zones in western Isabela and Fernandina.

Role of El Niño

The ENSO in the region represents perhaps the greatest significant perturbation to the Galápagos system, driving considerable interannual variability against a backdrop of global climate change effects. A flux of invasive species to the islands, patterns of overfishing, and illegal activities such as shark finning since the 1980s coincided with two particularly strong El Niño events (1982–1983 and 1997–1998) that through bottom-up food deprivation and heat stress rapidly restructured entire marine coastal communities. The compounding interactions between climate and local human intervention are particularly relevant to marine conservation. For example, subsequent overfishing of natural reef predators during and following El Niño episodes (otherwise controlling urchin herbivory in the coastal fringe) appears to have negatively affected the recovery of climate impacted habitat-forming species such as corals and macroalgae in recent years (Edgar *et al.* 2009). Increased stress over natural populations at such times also tends to increase susceptibility to disease. In particular, many species with Peruvian, Chilean, and local endemic cold water associations in the upwelling western isles of Isabela and Fernandina tend to be negatively affected by warm ENSO events and are considered particularly vulnerable. They fall under some of the strongest thermal anomalies ever recorded in the Pacific (Figure 9.8). Part of the reason for that dubious distinction is the

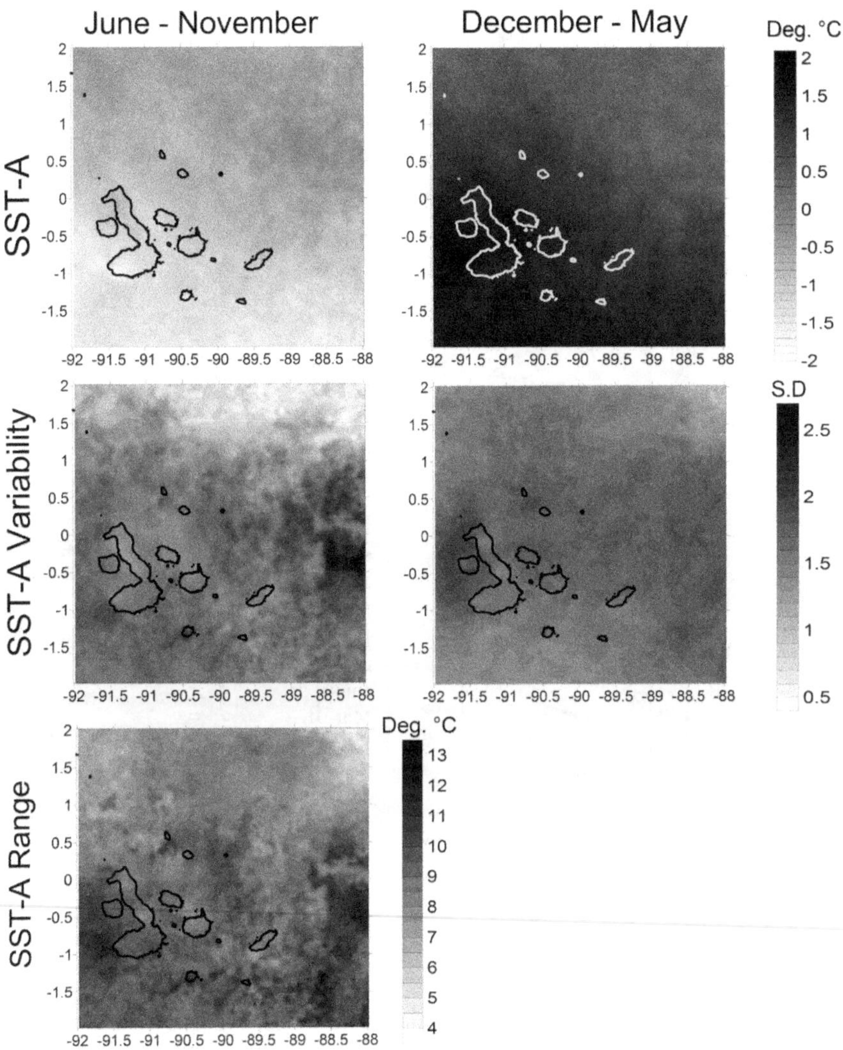

Figure 9.8 MODIS–AQUA-derived SST anomalies. Residuals from monthly 4 km^2 resolution cells averaged 2003–2008 show clear NE–SW temperature gradients and variability associated with the propagation of the cold tongue to the east of the islands and the EUC upwelling on the exposed western coast.

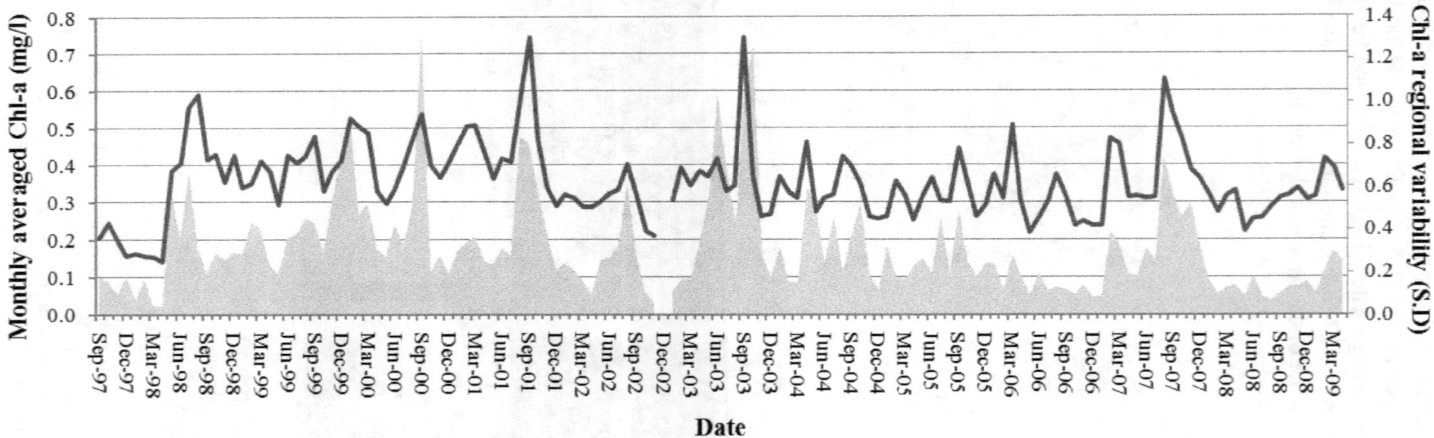

Figure 9.9 Monthly averaged SeaWiFS/MODIS–AQUA-derived chlorophyll-a time series within an 88–93°W by 2°S–2°N boundary. Periodic mean phytoplankton enrichment (La Niña) and deprivation events (El Niño) and seasonal strengthening of overall productivity are shown.

influence of otherwise cold upwelling of deep water brought up from the Galápagos platform, which through nutrient enrichment keeps the near-shore surface water primed with soluble iron – a micronutrient that otherwise limits the uptake of nitrates by phytoplankton from their surroundings. During strong warm ENSO events, depression of the thermocline reducing the vertical mixing of upwelled deep water into the euphotic coastal zone causes a drastic reduction in standing stock biomass of phytoplankton across the reserve (Figure 9.9).

The magnitude and frequency of temperature change can also herald significant changes. Cold water shock (through internal wave propagation rapidly pushing segregated deep water over the Galápagos platform and exposed oceanic pinnacles into the solar heated mixed surface layer) is as much a stress to subtidal environments as gradual warming. Exaggerated temperature differentials and rates of temperature change have caused extensive bleaching responses. A moderate El Niño event in early 2007 followed by sharp cold upwelling transitions of 11°C over 10 m depth subtidal reef over six days paved the way into a La Niña that compounded extensive cold water bleaching of *Porites* and *Pocillopora* corals (Glynn *et al.* 2009; Witman and Smith 2003; 2010) as the cold season developed into late 2007. Both the interval between strong ENSO events and rate of change from ENSO SST (Sea Surface Temperature) maxima to minima as well as generating a strong bleaching response, presumably also indirectly impact the level of bioerosion of the reef following strong events and the aperture for coral framework recovery (Figure 9.10.).

Recently rediscovered deep water kelp such as *Eisenia galapagensis* (Graham *et al.* 2007) and *Desmarestia tropicana* join the ranks of the 15 algae species identified through IUCN review as threatened. Dependent upon the cold upwelling

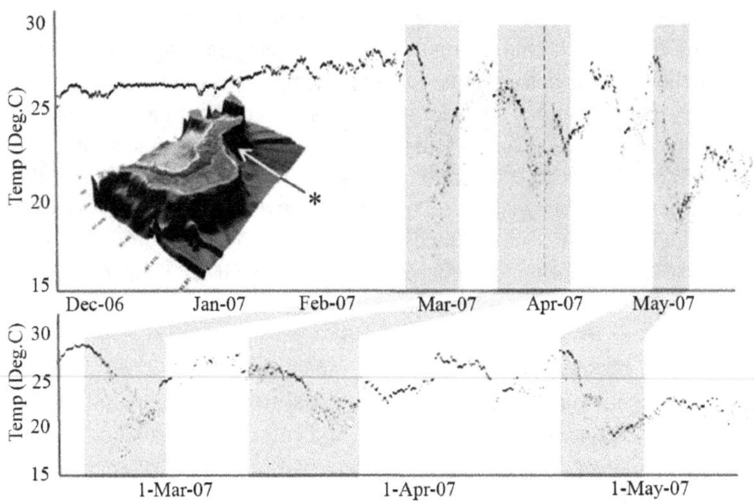

Figure 9.10 Subtidal temperature loggers at 10 m depth in Bahia Tiburon. The sharp transition between a mild El Niño and a strong La Niña with >10°C temperature shock in as little as six days over the subtidal coral reef, as internal waves pass around the oceanic pinnacle, is captured (Wolf Island inset, indicated *).

dynamic and depth limited by light penetration in often turbid productive water, they provide significant habitat (if unexpected upon the equator) for a host of invertebrate and fish assemblages, yet are susceptible to both heat stress under ENSO and increased urchin grazing. Other intertidal algae, such as the fucoid *Bifurcaria galapagensis* reported in surveys by Wellington (1975), have not been recorded since the 1982–1983 El Niño and are very probably extinct. Galápagos penguins *Spheniscus mendelus* are another example of a charismatic endemic highly dependent upon the upwelling dynamic. Their limited foraging range around nesting zones is further impacted by surface heating around supra-littoral nesting caves. Starvation effects coincide with drops in hatching success when productivity falls around those sites (Matamoros *et al.* 2006). Such rapid shifts within a year between productive and thermal regimes can alter the patterning of environmental envelopes, changing niche boundary conditions across a range of space scales. In cases where endemic species with restricted distributions exhibit low tolerance to stress and/or an inability to adapt alternative foraging behaviors extinction risk can greatly increase. As a result, they tend to be more susceptible to episodic heating compared to existing and novel invasive species.

The rocky road to sustainability

Although the current zoning system has yet to ride out the effects of a full-blown El Niño event, observations from previous episodes strongly suggest that wide-scale habitat modification can occur depending upon the preceding recuperation and the extraction during the event. Photographic surveys both before and after the 1982–1983 event and in recent years indicate that recovery of habitat formers has not been significant and is a slow process largely compromising broad regime shifts to persistent low diversity urchin barrens. Hence, current Galápagos MPAs are expected to ameliorate, but not prevent, ecosystem impacts during strong ENSO disturbances. Key considerations include an appropriate moderation of visitation and fishing in the coastal zone around sensitive communities. There is an aperture for improved protected coverage of particularly sensitive areas, especially in the upwelling west and far northerly islands. Current protected area zoning covers 16% of the Reserve (including 10% non-extractive tourism areas) and ideally should be increased to ~18–25% to better safeguard representative GMR habitat. Further investigation is required into the role of nursery zones that could be considered within existing fisheries areas to complement spillover from the smaller MPAs, as well as ordination of new low impact extraction modalities such as "pesca vivencial" (tourists accompanying fishers) with the potential to alleviate pressure upon higher reef predators if properly defined, assessed, and enforced in local legislature.

Effective MPAs that encourage spillover are shown to be at least several kilometers in length. Although most large Galápagos "sanctuary" blocks exceed these dimensions, an apportioned extension of 26 km has been suggested by Edgar *et al.* (2008) across all existing MPAs to improve their relative effectiveness, incorporating aforementioned unprotected sites harboring unique threatened endemics. Allowance should also be made to spatially plan multiple use port areas in the three main populated islands of San Cristobal, Santa Cruz, and Isabela. Under regular human influence, they accommodate a suite of alternative interests and uses for education, tourism, and intertidal fisheries not traditionally reflected in the wider coastal zoning.

Tourism is concentrated around species-rich areas with many endemics; hence, conservation and nature-based tourism tend to select for the same areas. They also have the advantage of assigning an economic value distinct from fisheries and lend a kind of passive vigilance, reducing infractions in popular sites. There is incentive to respect zone use as growing market awareness and advocacy for "best tourism practices" become selling points for nature-based tourism agencies and these ideals are appropriated by Galápagos naturalist guides. Although difficult to quantify, illegal line fishing from tourism vessels has presumably reduced in recent years. On-site impact is considered to be low, although anchor damage, continuous small hydrocarbon spills, and pollution through constant visitation are increasingly problematic. Threatened ahermatypic corals requiring additional levels of protection are often associated with the tourism sites that were chosen for their exposed high current and headland character that attracts a range of tourism target species, in particular pelagic animals. Where tourism zones appear to capture areas of higher endemism, some biasing probably exists owing to the higher levels of diver visitation throughout recent years drawing attention to uncommon species in those areas.

Based upon historical and current observations that imply probable post-El Niño extinctions (Edgar *et al.* 2009), the prospect of future biodiversity loss of threatened marine species seems likely unless "climate conscious" adaptation measures are employed to reduce compounding risk presented by human activity in the coastal zone. Since low impact scenarios based on past ENSO patterns have already been implicated in significant marine habitat restructuring and in extinction risk, ecosystem diagnostics for benthic resilience should be employed to monitor and better respond to future climate shifts, coupled with directed management measures designed to ameliorate the Galápagos human footprint. In many cases, this implies the continuation and evaluation of ongoing invasive species prevention and where feasible eradication programs – intertidal predation by introduced mammals, transfer of existing and novel diseases by insect vectors, and ecological displacement of native species during climate shifts can seriously threaten reduced Galápagos populations.

Widespread reduced habitat complexity (reef to rubble) seems a reasonable indicator of a regime shift symptomatic of compromised resilience – a consequence of bioerosion and overgrazing making urchin barrens ubiquitous across the reserve since the last strong ENSO events of 1982–1983 and 1997–1998. The pencil urchin *Eucidaris galapagensis*, for example, doubled in numbers from 1982 to 1984 (pseudo-photoquadrat data standardized from marine photos). Major ecosystem-level changes occurred during these periods as a result, and populations do not appear to have recovered (Edgar *et al.* 2009). Patterns of benthic cover from photographic surveys show remarkable a correlation in 1984 and 2004, yet are these distinctly different from 1982, emphasizing that despite the absence of other data during the period, changes in habitat-forming species were very significant. Nonetheless, in intervening years there are some signs of recuperation in the 1–5% of reef frameworks that persisted. Glynn reports recovery of bleached tissue in certain northern reefs since 2000 and new recruits from the same locality in the most extensive Darwin reef with a largely intact accreted framework.

There is likely a threshold level of urchin abundance (principally *Eucidaris*) at which re-establishment of coral and macroalgal habitat is limited, resulting in a semi-permanent regime shift. We have yet to determine those thresholds as indicators of a regression to a lower diversity habitat state. An averaged 3.2 individuals/m^2 abundance seems indicative of urchin barren development in the central islands, while densities <1 individuals/m^2 in the far northern islands suggest a different functional balance over the remaining coral systems (Edgar *et al.* 2008).

Galápagos coral also resides amidst one of the naturally highest CO_2 environments recorded globally. Since naturally high-CO_2 reefs persist near the distributional threshold limiting aragonite formation in Galápagos, they represent a "canary in the coalmine" for Pacific corals and are expected to be among the first and most highly affected by ocean acidification (Manzello *et al.* 2010). Weaker cementation will make corals more susceptible to bioerosion and physical abrasion, also restricting recruitment (Colgan 1990). In response, pilot schemes are underway for wider implementation of low impact fixed anchorages to reduce anchor damage in the few remaining source areas with reasonable extensions of continuous coral growth. Other calcifying benthos, such as coralline algae otherwise supporting reef cohesion, would also be affected. This does not bode well for the future of associated Galápagos tropical marine communities – restricted range and fragmented coral populations in the far north exhibit a range of health anomalies (23.9% across 973 sampled colonies from 2005–2007 (Vera and Banks 2009)) in addition to routine cold water and warm water bleaching stress, exceeding that documented for many other impacted regions.

Although many ENSO impacts are reasonably well documented, important information gaps relating to the Galápagos ocean-climate dynamic still exist. Particularly relevant is the determination of threshold levels for switches in the Galápagos climate system (i.e. at which point does a NOAA-defined El Niño in the EN3 zone become a Galápagos El Niño with cascading trophic deprivation effects; what degree of thermocline depression prevents Equatorial Undercurrent upwelling into sunlit surface water and over what scales, etc.). Ongoing climate research aims to determine which interactions are the most sensitive and applicable as indicators, and what is the spatial variability at small scales relevant to conservation management and protection of small threatened species populations.

In practice the islands represent a yardstick against which to measure climate impacts, and an immense opportunity to gauge the effectiveness of marine management strategies that confront the seemingly intangible specter of climate change predictions, conserve natural resilience, improve food security, and reduce the chance that exacerbating activities compromise the recovery capacity of the natural system. Despite a lot of groundwork, Galápagos still requires an information management system appropriately feeding back to management based around an ecosystem-level and robust monitoring framework. Importantly it will requires coordination, communication and continuity – with a "legacy" mechanism in place to ensure adherence to management milestones over time and emphasis upon best use of competencies between local institutions.

Given past observations and ongoing research, monitoring, if structured correctly to answer relevant conservation questions, presents us a window of opportunity to lend valuable management insight encouraging proactive adaptation and avoiding the erosion of natural resilience. Given the immutable presence of people interacting constantly with the local ecosystem and the practicalities therein, the answer by necessity involves a careful appraisal of interdependencies and a consensus definition of what an "acceptable" human footprint represents for the culture, biodiversity, and economy of a future Galápagos.

References

Anderson, L. 2005. California's Reaction to *Caulerpa taxifolia*: A Model for Invasive Species Rapid Response, *Biological Invasions* 7:1003–1016.

Aurioles, D. and F. Trillmich. 2008. *Zalophus wollebaeki*, in IUCN 2010, IUCN Red List of Threatened Species, Version 2010.1. www.iucnredlist.org.

Banks, S.A and M. Trueman. 2009. *Galapagos and climate change: technical report*, Charles Darwin Foundation.

Banks, S., M. Vera, M. Toscano, D. Ruiz and N. Tirado. 2006. *Monitoreo ecológico de la zona costera para la evaluación de la zonificación provisional consensuada (ZPC). Resumen de actividades octubre 2004 – septiembre 2006* (Informe de avances para USAID: Fundación Charles Darwin, Santa Cruz, Galápagos, Ecuador), pp. 1–34.

Banks, S., D. Wiedenfeld and A. Loose. 2003. *Ecological monitoring of the Galapagos Marine reserve: an integrated approach*, Final report to the Heinz Sielmann Stiftung (August 2003) (Charles Darwin Foundation: Santa Cruz, Galápagos, Ecuador), pp. 1–68.

Bustamante, R.H. (2004). *Ecological Monitoring Of The Galapagos Marine Reserve: Evaluating The Zoning scheme In A Participatory Manner To Achieve*, Report to Pew Fellow Program In Marine Conservation (September 2004).

Chavez, F., P. Strutton, G. Friederich, R. Feely, G. Feldman, D. Foley, and M. McPhaden. 1999. Biological and chemical response of the equatorial Pacific Ocean to the 1997–98 El Niño, *Science* 286:2126.

Colgan, M. 1990. *El Niño and the history of eastern Pacific reef building. Global ecological consequences of the 1982–1983 El Niño-Southern Oscillation* (Elsevier: Amsterdam, The Netherlands), pp. 183–232.

Edgar, G., S. Banks, R. Bensted-Smith, M. Calvopiña, A. Chiriboga, L. Garske, S. Henderson, K. Miller, S. Salazar, and W. Foundation. 2008. Conservation of threatened species in the Galapagos Marine Reserve through identification and protection of marine Key Biodiversity Areas, *Aquatic Conservation: Marine and Freshwater Ecosystems* 18:955–968.

Edgar, G., S. Banks, M. Brandt, R. Bustamante, A. Chiriboga, S. Earle, L. Garske, P. Glynn, J. Grove, and S. Henderson. 2009. El Niño, grazers and fisheries interact to greatly elevate extinction risk for Galapagos marine species, *Global Change Biology*. d oi:10.1111/j.1365–2486.2009.02117.

Edgar, G., S. Banks, J. Fariña, M. Calvopiña, and C. Martinez. 2004. Regional biogeography of shallow reef fish and macro-invertebrate communities in the Galapagos archipelago, *Journal of Biogeography* 31:1107–1124.

Glynn, P.W., B. Riegl, A.M.S. Correa, and I.B. Baums. 2009. Rapid recovery of a coral reef on Darwin Island, *Galapagos Research* 66:6–16.

Graham, M., B. Kinlan, L. Druehl, L. Garske, and S. Banks. 2007. Deep-water kelp refugia as potential hotspots of tropical marine diversity and productivity, *Proceedings of the National Academy of Sciences* 104:16576.

Harris, M.P. 1969. Breeding season of sea-birds in the Galapagos Islands, *J. Zool. (Lond)* 159:145–165.

Jennings, S., A. Brierley, and J. Walker. 1994. The inshore fish assemblages of the Galápagos Archipelago, *Biological Conservation* 70:49–57.

Kuhn, A. M. 2010. *Incidencia de la Temperatura del Mar en las Comunidades Rocosas Submareales de la Reserva Marina de Galápagos*, Tesis de licenciatura. Escuela Superior Politécnica del Litoral, Guayaquil.

Manzello, D. 2010. Ocean acidification hot spots: Spatiotemporal dynamics of the seawater CO2 system of eastern Pacific coral reefs, *Limnol. Oceanogr* 55:239–248.

Matamoros, Y., H. Vargas, B. Lacy, O. Byers, E. Travis, and Montoya, G. (ed.). 2006. *Taller para Anàlisis de Viabilidad de Poblaciòn y Hàbitat para el Pingüino de Galápagos, Informe Final Parque Nacional Galápagos, Puerto Ayora, Santa Cruz, Galápagos, Ecuador* (8–11 de febrero, 2005).

Okey, T.A., Banks, S., Born, A.F., Bustamante, R.H., Calvopiña, M., Edgar, G.J., Espinoza, E., Fariña, J.M., Garske, L.E., Reck, G.K., Salazar, S., Shepherd, S., Toral-Granda, V., Wallen, P. 2004. A trophic model of a Galápagos subtidal rocky reef for valuating fisheries and conservation strategies. *Ecological Modeling* 172: 383–401.

Ruiz, D. and Wolff, M. 2011. The Bolivar Channel Ecosystem of the Galapagos Marine Reserve: Energy flow structure and role of keystone groups. *Journal for Sea Research* 66: 123–134.

Sweet, W.V., J.M. Morrison, Y. Liu, D. Kamykowski, B.A. Schaeffer, L. Xie and S. Bank. 2009. Tropical instability wave interactions within the Galápagos Archipelago, Deep Sea Research Part I, *Oceanographic Research Papers* 56(8):1217–1229. doi:10.1016/j.dsr.2009.02.005

Vera, M. and S. Banks. 2009. Health status of the coralline communities of the northern Islands; Darwin, Wolf and Marchena of the Galápagos Archipelago, *Galapagos Research* #66.

Wellington, G., A. Strong, and G. Merlen. 2001. Sea surface temperature variation in the Galápagos archipelago: A comparison between AVHRR nighttime satellite data and in situ instrumentation(1982–1998), *Bulletin of marine science* 69:27–42.

Wellington G.M. 1975. *The Galapagos coastal and marine environments*. Department of National Parks and Wildlife, Quito.

Witman, J., M. Brandt, F. Smith, A. Altieri, and O. Rhoades. 2010. *Asymmetric, large-scale community responses to ENSOs in Galapagos subtidal ecosystems*, in abstract to the 95th ESA Annual Meeting, Pittsburg 4 August 2010.

Witman, J., and F. Smith. 2003. Rapid community change at a tropical upwelling site in the Galapagos Marine Reserve, *Biodiversity and Conservation* 12:25–45.

Xie L, Yanyun Liu, and J. Morrison. 2009. *A 100-year simulation of the ocean circulation around the Galapagos from 1951 to 2050 using a nested grid hybrid coordinate ocean circulation model, NCSU and UNC*, in Workshop of Assessment of the Vulnerability of Biodiversity and Related Human Well-Being in the Galapagos Islands to Climate Change, 20–23 April, 2009, Santa Cruz Galápagos.

10 Wildlife health monitoring and disease management

Protecting the biodiversity of Galápagos

Patricia G. Parker and Sharon L. Deem

Introduction

There is little doubt that biological extinctions are strongly associated with human contact, as paleoecology links periods of widespread animal extinctions with human colonization (Burney and Flannery 2006). Much effort has addressed the relative impacts of drivers of extinction, including attempts to measure the consequences of invasive species: (1) invasive predation; (2) invasive competition; (3) invasive habitat alteration; and (4) invasive pathogens (IUCN 2001). Clavero *et al.* (2009) show that these categories are more strongly associated with extinction risks than other drivers. However, distinguishing their individual effects is challenging. For example, introduction of mammals is strongly associated with avian extinctions on oceanic islands (Blackburn *et al.* 2004), but analyses including other parameters show that intrinsic island factors (e.g. size and isolation) have an even stronger association with avian extinction risk (Karels *et al.* 2007). Assessments of impacts of disease alone have lagged behind. However, increasing awareness of emerging infectious diseases (Daszak *et al.* 2000) has led to recognition of the impact of pathogens in populations with limited or no previous exposure and thus high susceptibility (Smith *et al.* 2006, 2009). These studies point to the urgent need to understand the identity, abundance, and impact of pathogens in wildlife populations, especially in populations that are perpetually small, such as those on remote islands.

Emerging infectious diseases of high conservation concern include fibropapillomatosis in sea turtles, chytridiomycosis in amphibians, canine distemper in a number of carnivores, and Ebola virus in humans and animals (as reviewed in Anderson *et al.* 2004; Daszak *et al.* 2000; Kuiken *et al.* 2005). These diseases can have impacts that occur on multiple scales, affecting individuals (fitness costs), populations (population size and connection), communities (changes in species composition), and ecosystems (structure, function, and resilience) (Deem *et al.* 2008). Additionally, disease has been a direct cause of extinction (Cunningham and Daszak 1999; Schloegel *et al.* 2006; Warner *et al.* 1968). Other species are on the brink of extinction with diseases suspected as a primary cause in their decline (e.g. black-footed ferrets and Tasmanian devils) (McCallum *et al.* 2007; Thorne and Williams 1988).

Nowhere are anthropogenic impacts as drivers of disease more evident than for island ecosystems. For our studies of the health of Galápagos endemic birds, the most relevant examples of extinctions by disease come from the honeycreepers of Hawaii. The family Drepaniidae comprises more than 50 described species of endemic Hawaiian honeycreepers. Of these species, fewer than 20 went extinct between first human contact by Polynesians and European contact in the late 1700s. Since then more than 20 additional species have disappeared. This rapid extinction over 200 years is largely attributed to the invasive drivers mentioned earlier: predation, competition, habitat alteration, and disease. For many honeycreepers, the final push to extinction came with exposure to two pathogens: avian malaria caused by *Plasmodium relictum*, and avian poxvirus (Atkinson *et al.* 2005; van Riper *et al.* 1986; van Riper *et al.* 2002; Warner *et al.* 1968). The colonization and introductions of invasive species in Galápagos resembles the early years of European colonization of Hawaii, and it is the sad fate of Hawaii's honeycreepers that must be avoided for Galápagos endemics.

Infectious disease depends on the interaction of the disease-causing agent, the host, and the environment. For vector-borne diseases, such as avian malaria, characteristics of the vector are also important. Although infectious disease agents are ubiquitous in the lives of wild animals and represent a major component of biological diversity (Price 1980), the conservation threats posed by these agents are increasingly complex.

We must know the health status of populations, and what agents are present, if we are to determine the significance of a disease in the future. Thus, we must have baseline health data for future comparisons. Disease and health status may change rapidly, making this task more difficult and mandating immediate health monitoring in biodiversity sensitive spots and for endangered species.

Monitoring for health and disease in populations may include: (1) field studies; (2) modeling; and (3) risk assessments. The collection of data from wildlife in their natural habitats is an essential first step to understand current disease/health status. These data are necessary both for modeling (providing real data for model parameters) and for risk assessments (the evaluation of the likelihood and consequences of entry, establishment, or spread of a pathogenic agent). Our work in Galápagos began in 2001 with baseline monitoring which has now encompassed more than half of the resident, breeding bird species. Some of these studies will be summarized below. The next important steps will be modeling and risk assessments that build on this foundation.

Avian health monitoring in Galápagos: an example of disease monitoring and management

As one example of health monitoring and disease management in Galápagos, we present the collaborative consortium, The Center for Avian Health in Galápagos, a partnership of the University of Missouri–Saint Louis; the WildCare Institute, Saint Louis Zoo; the Galápagos National Park; and the Charles Darwin Foundation. Our work began with a three-pronged approach: (1) monitoring of key bird populations, assessing the presence/absence of a suite of pathogens; (2) sampling of introduced birds, the domestic chicken and rock pigeon; and (3) focused studies on particular pathogens that we already knew occurred in the archipelago. In addition, we conducted a series of basic science studies of the interactions between the birds and their parasites, providing additional information for interpreting patterns of arrival and movement of pathogens in the archipelago.

Baseline monitoring

We began by conducting baseline health monitoring on populations on which we had long-term demographic monitoring already underway (Parker *et al.* 2006): the Galápagos dove *Zenaida galapagoensis* (Padilla *et al.* 2004); the waved albatross *Phoebastria irrorata* (Padilla *et al.* 2003); the Galápagos penguin *Spheniscus mendiculus* (Travis *et al.* 2006a); the flightless cormorant *Phalacrocorax harrisi* (Travis *et al.* 2006b); and the Galápagos hawk *Buteo galapagoensis*. In addition, we monitored a set of co-occurring seabird species on the island of Genovesa (Padilla *et al.* 2006). While these surveys established baseline levels of blood chemistries and cell counts in apparently healthy birds, they included serological tests, genetic tests by the polymerase chain reaction (PCR), and microscopy tests for a variety of common pathogens. These tests led to our discovery of blood parasites previously undescribed in doves (Padilla *et al.* 2004; Santiago-Alarcon *et al.* 2006; Santiago-Alarcon *et al.* 2010; Valkiunas *et al.* 2010) and the Plasmodium parasite in penguins (Levin *et al.* 2009). Monitoring of additional species of wild birds has been done in association with studies on the potential transmission from domestic birds to wild birds, and in association with studies of particular pathogens.

Because baseline samples are geographically widespread and attempt to cover the range of each species, we have used them to provide useful information during follow-up studies. A single drop of bird blood produces enough DNA to conduct dozens of tests. We have conducted studies of the population genetic structure of each of the focal endemic species, discovering that some have a flat genetic structure across their geographic range, meaning that there is little or no genetic distinctiveness of the different island populations and suggesting that the birds are moving easily among islands. This is true in particular for the Galápagos dove (Santiago-Alarcon *et al.* 2006) and the Galápagos penguin (Nims *et al.* 2008), both of which appear to move in an unrestricted manner across the islands in their range. The waved albatross is by nature highly philopatric, endemic to the island of Española. Nonetheless, different breeding colonies show no evidence of genetic structure, suggesting common movements among colonies (Huyvaert and Parker 2006). In contrast, other species show extreme levels of genetic structure, or high levels of genetic distinctiveness between islands, such as the Galápagos hawk (Bollmer *et al.* 2005) and the flightless cormorant (Duffie *et al.* 2009). Each of the eight island populations of the Galápagos hawk is genetically distinct, and even within islands almost all cormorant colonies are significantly genetically distinct, except for immediately adjacent colonies

(Duffie *et al.* 2009). These data are critical for studies of particular pathogens, or for future risk analyses, as they indicate which species may be moving their pathogens and genes among islands.

Domestic and introduced birds

It is a logical expectation that wild mammals may be susceptible to diseases of domestic mammals (Pederson *et al.* 2007), and likewise for birds. Domestic poultry are common on four of the five human-inhabited islands, and we have tested them for the presence of avian pathogens on three of those islands (Gottdenker *et al.* 2005; Soos *et al.* 2008; Deem *et al.* 2011), revealing a list of avian pathogens, some that have caused serious declines in wild bird populations elsewhere, such as paramyxovirus 1 (Newcastle Disease; Banerjee *et al.* 1994) and *Mycoplasma gallisepticum* (Hartup *et al.* 2001). Wild birds associated with the same farms were also tested, and have shown evidence of exposure to these pathogens (Deem *et al.*, in press).

We were able to sample rock pigeons (*Columba livia*) during their eradication in 2001 and 2002. They tested positive for a number of pathogens, such as *Trichomonas gallinae* (Padilla *et al.* 2004), which had previously been reported in the Galápagos dove (Harmon *et al.* 1987). A new blood parasite species in the Galápagos dove (Santiago-Alarcon *et al.* 2008; Valkiunas *et al.* 2010) was also found in a number of other South American dove species; one explanation is that the parasite was widespread in South American dove species and was introduced to the endemic Galápagos dove with the multiple introductions of rock pigeons during the 1970s (Santiago-Alarcon *et al.* 2010). Thus, the eradication of this introduced species did not occur soon enough to prevent the transmission of its pathogens to the endemic dove.

Focus on particular pathogens

Poxvirus

As the avipox virus was reported on the islands long before we began our survey (e.g. Vargas 1987), we initiated an ongoing study of the virus and its impacts. First, we characterized the poxvirus present in the wild birds (Figure 10.1) as two variants of canarypox virus and that in the chickens as fowlpox virus (Thiel *et al.* 2005).

As canarypox virus is common throughout the world in passerine birds, and as the fowlpox virus in the chickens was genetically identical to fowlpox virus reported elsewhere, we concluded that the pox viruses in Galápagos represent at least two independent colonizations, one of the fowlpox virus infecting the chickens, and an independent colonization of the canarypox virus infecting the wild birds. We are now working to characterize the patterns of susceptibility of Galápagos species to each poxvirus, and its geographic distribution (Jiménez-Uzcátegui *et al.* 2007). Further, we have initiated studies to understand the role of biting insects in transmission of the virus, which can be mechanically vectored through any break in the skin.

Figure 10.1 Galápagos mockingbird (*Mimus parvulus*) with cutaneous lesions caused by the avipox virus (Copyright: Sharon L. Deem).

Plasmodium

Because of its role in the extinction of Hawaiian birds (Atkinson *et al.* 2005), Plasmodium was one pathogen that we hoped to never detect in Galápagos birds. We were dismayed to find it in Galápagos penguin samples collected in 2004–2005 (Levin *et al.* 2009). As the penguins move around (Nims *et al.* 2008), we cannot infer the site where the infection originated from the geographic location at which an infected bird was sampled. We are now testing birds along the coasts where penguins gather to see whether other species are also infected, and to identify the reservoir population(s) from which the infections are transmitted by mosquitoes to the penguins. We are also attempting to identify the mosquito vector of the Plasmodium parasite. Unlike the poxvirus, which is spread mechanically through any small openings in the skin, including by biting insects, the Plasmodium parasite undergoes life stages within the vertebrate host, alternating with required life stages within an insect host. The insect host is necessary for sexual reproduction of the parasite. In Hawaii, the *Plasmodium relictum* parasite responsible for honeycreeper extinctions is vectored by the mosquito *Culex quinquefasciatus*. This mosquito was first documented in Galápagos in the 1980s (Whiteman *et al.* 2005). Although we suspect it is the vector of the Plasmodium found in the penguins, this has yet to be confirmed. Additionally, we lack data on the impact that this parasite is having on the penguin population, but we are now attempting to measure fitness costs. Since our samples of the Galápagos penguins were collected at fairly benign times (e.g. mild climate conditions), we are concerned that this parasite may prove more pathogenic when penguins suffer stresses of the kinds associated with El Niño events when their numbers decline due to reduced food availability (Vargas *et al.* 2006). With the prospect of climate change and more serious or frequent El Niño events, the urgency of understanding the dynamics of this parasite is high.

Toxoplasma gondii

In 2008 we initiated a study to better understand the epidemiology of *Toxoplasma gondii*, a common protozoan parasite of warm-blooded animals. Since members of the Felidae family are the only definitive hosts of this pathogenic parasite, we suspected that (1) *T. gondii* was introduced into Galápagos with the arrival of domestic cats (*Felis catus*); (2) wildlife species in Galápagos are exposed to this parasite; and (3) endemic Galápagos species, naïve to this pathogen, are highly susceptible to disease following infection. Supporting our prediction is a study finding 63% of cats in Puerto Villamil, Isabela with antibodies to *T. gondii* (Levy *et al.* 2008). Second, we used blood samples collected as part of our baseline health studies (Travis *et al.* 2006a, 2006b) and confirmed exposure to *T. gondii* in Galápagos penguins and flightless cormorants (Deem *et al.* 2010). To better understand the impact of these infections, we will continue long-term monitoring efforts to provide data on longevity of *T. gondii*-exposed versus non-exposed birds. Currently, we are exploring routes of transmission of *T. gondii* to penguin and cormorant populations. A land to sea transmission of oocysts in cat feces reaching coastal waters has received considerable study in California due to toxoplasmosis-related mortality in California sea otters (Conrad 2005). A similar mode of transport may be occurring in Galápagos. Therefore, our studies are directed at testing water sources for the highly durable infectious oocysts. Results from this study will be instrumental in our understanding of the epidemiology of this parasite.

Our disease monitoring studies in Galápagos avifauna have recognized three general infectious agent categories (Parker 2009): (1) Those that appear to have colonized with their avian hosts and have long histories with those hosts (e.g. several ectoparasites of hawks, Whiteman and Parker 2005; Whiteman *et al.* 2006, 2007); (2) those that have switched hosts from one native species to another since their colonization (e.g. the microfilarid nematodes in penguins and cormorants, Merkel *et al.* 2007); and (3) those that are more recent arrivals since human colonization and which have the potential for the largest negative impacts (e.g. the avipox virus, Thiel *et al.* 2005, or the *Plasmodium* parasite, Levin *et al.* 2009). We are combining all of these perspectives in testing an overarching hypothesis that the impact of a novel pathogen on a host depends on the number of generations that the host lineage has been isolated without exposure to a pathogen of that type. For example, a host that co-evolves with a parasite will develop immunity to the parasite, allowing the agent and host to coexist. For most infectious agents, the agent evolves toward some optimum reproductive rate (R_0, see below) with a host that allows it to replicate itself efficiently without killing the host. However, if this same host is exposed to an infectious agent to which it is naïve and thus has no innate immunity (e.g. Darwin finches that come in contact with avipox virus for the first time) the possibility of clinical disease is high. In many species and geographical locations, when hosts encounter pathogens with which they have no immunologic "experience", the result can be catastrophic (Warner 1968). We already know, for example, that both the Galápagos penguin and Galápagos hawk have the lowest genetic variability at major histocompatibility complex (MHC) loci yet measured in their respective taxonomic groups (Bollmer *et al.* 2007; Bollmer *et al.* 2011), meaning they are pre-adapted to deal with very few pathogens. Testing this hypothesis will require the accumulation of estimates of colonization dates for both hosts and pathogens; many of these estimates are already in hand.

Galápagos National Park management decisions

Begun in 2001, many of the Center's achievements in disease monitoring have been translated into disease management. For example, the documentation of avian disease pathogens present in the expanding domestic poultry industry on the islands (Gottdenker *et al.* 2005; Soos *et al.* 2008) led to recommendations for increased biosecurity measures on poultry farms. In a separate study, we demonstrated that there is a population genetic influence on the health status of the endemic Galápagos hawk, with populations on smaller islands having decreased immunologic status and higher parasite loads (Whiteman *et al.* 2006). Based on the hawks' lower immunocompetence on smaller islands, we made recommendations to the Galápagos National Park (GNP) to limit tourist visitations on those smaller islands with Galápagos hawk populations that would be more susceptible to introduced pathogens. Lastly, the documented exposure of penguins and cormorants to *Toxoplasma gondii* (Deem *et al.* 2010) reinforces the harm done by feral cats, as cats are the only definitive host of this parasite.

The Center for Avian Health in Galápagos may serve as a template for additional health programs in Galápagos to better understand the health status of the fauna and flora, disease threats to the endemic animals and plants of the archipelago, and measures to manage diseases.

Conclusions and the future

Historically, the management of wildlife diseases was directed at those diseases that were either zoonotic (shared between animals and humans), diseases in wildlife that threatened the health of domestic animals (e.g. foot and mouth disease), or diseases that fit into both categories (e.g. rabies, brucellosis). However, today there are few species that have not been influenced by some form of human intervention, primarily in a negative way (Redford and Richter 1999; Vitousek *et al.* 1997), and the management of diseases may now be imperative for many species on the brink of extinction (Berger *et al.* 1998; McCallum *et al.* 2007).

The management of disease in wildlife may be categorized into (1) prevention; (2) control; or (3) eradication. These strategies can be directed at the host, disease agent, environment, or vector (Table 10.1). In the context of Galápagos, one example is the recent law requiring spraying for insects (disinsection) on airplanes en route to Galápagos to prevent entry of disease vectors (e.g. mosquitoes). Other preventive measures may include reducing exposure of animals to pathogens (e.g. quarantine) or exposure to toxins (e.g. regulations for oil disposal). The control of disease in wildlife is the most common management strategy, with implementation following the detection of disease in a population. For example, in Galápagos an estimated 1,500 introduced species have been recorded in the archipelago, necessitating control efforts (Bungartz *et al.* 2009). One of these introduced species is a parasitic fly, *Philornis downsi*, that can cause up to 95% mortality in Darwin finch nestlings, and a fitness cost to surviving nestlings (Fessl and Tebbich 2002; Dudaniec *et al.* 2006). The need to control this fly should be a priority management measure owing to possible consequences, including species extinctions.

Control of an infectious agent attempts to reduce the basic reproductive rate (R_0) of that agent. R_0 is defined as the number of secondary infections produced by the first infective individual to appear in the population (Anderson and May 1982). When R_0 is less than unity the pathogen ceases to maintain itself and declines to local extinction. In contrast, when R_0 is greater than one, an epidemic outbreak occurs. Controlling disease thus includes methods employed to reduce R_0 below one. Methods that may do this include limiting the number of susceptibles by vaccinating or treating infected individuals to reduce duration or intensity of the infectious period, thus reducing the number of infectious individuals. This form of disease control may be the least acceptable in Galápagos

Table 10.1 Interaction of three disease management approaches (prevention, control, and eradication) with the components of the epidemiologic triad of host, disease-causing agent, and environment. In this case, we consider vectors separately from the environment

	Prevent	*Control*	*Eradicate*
Host	Prevent exposure of animals by quarantine	Vaccination Decrease number of reservoir hosts	Eradicate introduced reservoir hosts
Agent	Prevent entry into Galápagos	Biocontrol	Eliminate parasite/ pathogen immediately following introduction
Environment	Limit where tourists travel	Create barriers between agents and hosts	
Vector	Prevent introductions Light modifications	Spray and control in key areas	Eradicate immediately following introduction

owing to the need to use invasive procedures (e.g. vaccination) on wild animals. However, the use of vaccination of domestic animals to protect wildlife (e.g. canine distemper virus vaccination of domestic dogs to protect Galápagos sea lions) may be an alternative that requires no handling of wildlife species.

Other possible control methods target the host species directly. Measures such as the dispersal of aggregating animals (e.g. a flock of birds) during a known non-infectious disease event (e.g. toxin spill) can be an effective control measure without direct handling of wildlife. Additionally, culling of introduced species such as cats, dogs, or anis can be very effective in removing a reservoir of infection, thus reducing or eliminating exposure to wildlife species.

Environmental controls aim to reduce contact between diseased and susceptible animals or the spread of infectious agents. Good examples of this form of management are already operating in Galápagos and include: (1) limiting the number of tourists per site and tourists sites near vulnerable wildlife; (2) establishing barriers where tourists cannot go; and (3) vector control by changing the types of lights on boats to decrease the number of insects moved between islands.

The last disease management method, eradication, is extremely difficult. The only diseases known to have been eradicated globally are smallpox in humans and rinderpest in animals. On islands it may be possible to extirpate an agent especially if that agent (or vector) is a recent arrival, but this is only a reasonable option when the dynamics of the pathogen are understood, it has not yet spread, and managers have successful histories of eradication efforts, such as in Galápagos (see Chapter 3). More often, by the time an agent is recognized, it is too late. Preventing the arrival of new infectious agents to Galápagos is far less complicated than controlling them after arrival.

Effective conservation mandates healthy habitats and species. Our program provides an example of one way to monitor and manage diseases but some limitations exist today. After ten years we have not even surveyed every bird species, not to mention the other vertebrate taxa. We recommend further programs across taxa and expansion into domestic animals and other invasive species not yet eradicated. Further, we would like to expand our own baseline studies to include immune studies, which we have barely begun (Bollmer *et al.* 2007; Whiteman *et al.* 2006), and to add surveillance for environmental toxins.

The GNP should be proud of its record of conservation of endemic species. However, the challenges will only continue to grow as human pressures on the archipelago escalate with increased human activity. It is imperative to integrate health monitoring and control along with other disciplines to be successful in our biodiversity conservation efforts in the archipelago.

Acknowledgments

Our work in Galápagos represents a partnership between our home institutions (University of Missouri–St. Louis and the Saint Louis Zoo) and our local partners, the GNP and the Charles Darwin Foundation. We acknowledge the support and guidance of Washington Tapia and Victor Carrion at the GNP, and Felipe

Cruz and Sonia Cisneros at the Charles Darwin Foundation. Drs Marilyn Cruz and Virna Cedeño have been important participants in this work. From the Saint Louis Zoo, Jane Merkel and Drs Eric Miller, Mary Duncan, Luis Padilla, Erika Travis, Nicole Gottdenker, and Catherine Soos have provided veterinary expertise. From UMSL, Patty Baiao, Jenny Bollmer, Caroline Duffie, Jenni Higashiguchi, Kate Huyvaert, Iris Levin, Jane Merkel, Ben Nims, Diego Santiago-Alarcon, Eloisa Sari, Shane Siers, and Noah Whiteman assumed responsibility for individual studies summarized here. Gediminas Valkiunas provided critical guidance in the assessment of avian blood parasites.

References

Anderson, P.K., A.A. Cunningham, N.G. Patel, F.J. Morales, P.R. Epstein, and P. Daszak. 2004. Emerging infectious diseases of plants: pathogen pollution, climate change and agrotechnology drivers, *Trends in Ecology and Evolution* 19:535–544.

Anderson, R.M., and R.M. May. 1982. Coevolution of hosts and parasites, *Parasitology* 85:411–426.

Atkinson, C.T., J.K. Lease, R.J. Dusek, and M.D. Samuel. 2005. Prevalence of pox-like lesions and malaria in forest bird communities on leeward Mauna Loa volcano, Hawaii, *The Condor* 107:537–546.

Banerjee, J., W.M. Reed, S.D. Fitzgerald, and B. Panigrahy. 1994. Neurotropic velogenic Newcastle Disease in cormorants in Michigan: Pathology and virus characterization, *Avian Diseases* 38:873–878.

Berger, L., R. Speare, P. Daszak, D.E. Green, A.A. Cunningham, C.L. Goggin, R. Slocombe, M.A. Ragan, A.D. Hyatt, K.R. McDonald, H.B. Hines, K.R. Lips, G. Marantelli, and H. Parkes. 1998. Chytridiomycosis causes amphibian mortality associated with population declines in the rain forests of Australia and Central America, *Proceedings of the National Academy of Sciences of the United States of America* 95:9031–9036.

Blackburn, T.M., P. Cassey, R.P. Duncan, K.L. Evans, and K.J. Gaston. 2004. Avian Extinction and mammalian introductions on oceanic islands, *Science* 305:1955–1958.

Bollmer, J.L., J.M. Hull, H.B. Ernest, J.H. Sarasola, P.G. Parker. 2011. Reduced MHC and neutral variation in the Galapagos Hawk, an island endemic. *BMC Evolutionary Biology* 11: 143 doi:10.1186/1471-2148-11-143.

Bollmer, J.L., F.H. Vargas, and P.G. Parker. 2007. Low MHC variation in the endangered Galápagos penguin (*Spheniscus mendiculus*), *Immunogenetics* 59:593–602.

Bollmer, J.L., N.K. Whiteman, M.D. Cannon, J.C. Bednarz, T. de Vries, and P.G. Parker. 2005. Population genetics of the Galápagos Hawk (*Buteo galapagoensis*): Genetic monomorphism within isolated populations, *The Auk* 122:1210–1224.

Bungartz, F., H.W. Herrera, P. Jaramillo, N. Tirado, G. Jiménez-Uzcátegui, D. Ruiz, A. Guézou, and F. Ziemmeck. (ed.) (2009). *List of all known species from the Galapagos Islands – Lista de todas las especies conocidas de las Islas Galápagos*, Online repository of the Charles Darwin Foundation/Fundación Charles Darwin, Puerto Ayora, Galapagos. www.darwinfoundation.org/checklists/ (last updated 08 Mar 2010).

Burney, D.A. and T.F. Flannery. 2006. Fifty millennia of catastrophic extinctions after human contact. *Trends in Ecology and Evolution* 20:395–401.

Clavero, M., L. Brotons, P. Pons, D. Sol. 2009. Prominent role of invasive species in avian biodiversity loss. *Biological Conservation* 142:2043–2049.

Conrad, P.A., M.A. Miller, C. Kreuder, E.R. James, J. Mazet, H. Dabritz, D. Jessup, F.

Gulland, and M. Grigg. 2005. Transmission of *Toxoplasma*: Clues from the study of sea otters as sentinels of *Toxoplasma gondii* flow into the marine environment, ***International Journal of Parasitology*** 35: 1155–1168.

Cunningham, A.A., and Daszak, P. 1999. Extinction of a species of land snail due to infection with a microsporidian parasite, *Conservation Biology* 12:1139–1141.

Daszak, P., A.A. Cunningham, and A.D. Hyatt. 2000. Emerging infectious diseases of wildlife–threats to biodiversity and human health, *Science* 287:443–449.

Deem, S.L., M. Bedon Cruz, J.M. Higashiguchi, and P.G. Parker. Diseases of poultry and endemic birds in Galapagos: Implications for the reintroduction of native species. Doi/10.1111/j.1469-1795.z011.00489.x/pdf, Animal Conservation.

Deem S.L., V.O. Ezenwa, J.R. Ward, and B.A. Wilcox. 2008. Research frontiers in Ecological Systems: Evaluating the Impacts of Infectious Disease on Ecosystems, in R.S. Ostfeld, V.T. Eviner, and F. Keesing (ed.), *Infectious Disease Ecology: Effects of Ecosystems on Disease and of Disease on Ecosystems*, pp. 304–318 (Princeton University Press, Princeton, NJ).

Deem, SL, J. Merkel, L. Ballweber, F.H. Vargas, M.B. Cruz, and P.G. Parker. 2010. Exposure to *Toxoplasma gondii* in Galapagos penguins (*Spheniscus mendiculus*) and flightless cormorants (*Phalacrocorax harrisi*) in the Galapagos Islands, Ecuador. *J. Wildl Dis.* 46:1005-1011.

Dudaniec, R.Y., S. Kleindorfer, and B. Fessl. 2006. Effects of the introduced ectoparasite Philornis downsi on haemoglobin level and nestling survival in Darwin's small ground finch (*Geospiza fuliginosa*), *Austral Ecology* 31:88–94.

Duffie, C.V., T.C. Glenn, F.H. Vargas, and P.G. Parker. 2009. Genetic structure within and between island populations of the flightless cormorant (*Phalacrocorax harrisi*), *Molecular Ecology* 18:2103–2111.

Fessl, B. and S. Tebbich. 2002. *Philornis downsi* – a recently discovered parasite on the Galapagos archipelago – a threat for Darwin's finches? *Ibis* 144:445–451.

Gottdenker, N.L., T. Walsh, H. Vargas, J. Merkel, G. Jiménez, R.E. Miller, M. Dailey, and P.G. Parker. 2005. Assessing the risks of introduced chickens and their pathogens to native birds in the Galápagos Archipelago, *Biological Conservation* 126:429–439.

Harmon, W.H., W.A. Clark, A.C. Hawbecker, and M. Stafford. 1987. Trichomonas gallinae in Columbiform birds from the Galapagos Islands. *Journal of Wildlife Diseases* 23:492–494.

Hartup, B.K., A.A. Dhondt, K.V. Sydenstricker, W.M. Hochachka, and G.V. Kollias. 2001. Host range and dynamics of mycoplasmal conjunctivitis among birds in North America, *Journal of Wildlife Diseases* 37:72–81.

Huyvaert, K.P. and P.G. Parker. 2006. Absence of population genetic structure among breeding colonies of the waved albatross, *Condor* 108:441–446.

IUCN 2001. *IUCN Red List categories and criteria – version 3.1*, IUCN-SSC. www.redlist.org/info/categories.criteria2001.html.

Jiménez-Uzcátegui, G., D.A. Wiedenfeld, and P.G. Parker. 2007. Viruela aviar en especies silvestres (Passeriformes) en la isla Santa Cruz, Galapagos, Ecuador, *Brenesia* 67:29–34.

Karels, T.J., F.S. Dobson, H.S. Trevino, and A.L. Skibiel. 2007. The biogeography of avian extinctions on oceanic islands, *Journal of Biogeography* 35:1106–1111

Kuiken, T., F.A. Leighton, R.A.M. Fouchier, J.W. LeDuc, J.S.M. Peiris, A. Schudel, K. Stöhr, and A.D.M.E. Osterhaus. 2005. Pathogen surveillance in animals, *Science* 309:1680–1681.

Levin, I.I., D.C. Outlaw, F.H. Vargas, P.G. Parker. 2009. *Plasmodium* blood parasite found in endangered Galapagos penguins (*Spheniscus mendiculus*), *Biological Conservation* 142:3191–3195.

Levy, J.K., P.C. Crawford, M.R. Lappin, E.J. Dubovi, M.G. Levy, R. Alleman, S.J. Tucker, and E.L. Clifford. 2008. Infectious diseases of dogs and cats on Isabela Island, Galapagos, *Journal of Veterinary Internal Medicine* 22:60–65.

McCallum, H., D.M. Tompkins, M. Jones, S. Lachish, S. Marvanek, B. Lazenby, G. Hocking, J. Wiersma, and C.E. Hawkins. 2007. Distribution and impacts of Tasmanian devil facial tumor disease, *EcoHealth* 4:318–325.

Merkel, J., H.I. Jones, N.K. Whiteman, N. Gottdenker, H. Vargas, E.K. Travis, R.E. Miller, and P.G. Parker. 2007. Microfilariae in Galápagos Penguins (*Spheniscus mendiculus*) and Flightless Cormorants (*Phalacrocorax harrisi*): Genetics, Morphology and Prevalence, *Journal of Parasitology* 93:495–503.

Nims, B., H. Vargas, N. Gottdenker, and P.G. Parker. 2008. Low genetic diversity and lack of population structure in the endangered Galápagos penguin (*Spheniscus mendiculus*), *Conservation Genetics* 9:1413–1420.

Padilla, L.R., K.P. Huyvaert, J.F. Merkel, R.E. Miller, and P.G. Parker. 2003. Hematology, Plasma Chemistry, Serology, and Chlamydophila status of free ranging adult waved albatrosses (*Phoebastria irrorata*) on Española, Galápagos Islands, *Journal of Zoo and Wildlife Medicine* 34:278–283.

Padilla, L.R., D. Santiago, J.F. Merkel, R.E. Miller, and P.G. Parker. 2004. Survey for *Trichomonas gallinae, Chlamydophila psitacci, Salmonella* spp. and *Haemoproteus* organisms in Columbiformes from the Galápagos Islands, *Journal of Zoo and Wildlife Medicine* 35:60–64.

Padilla, L., N.K. Whiteman, J.F. Merkel, K.P. Huyvaert, and P.G. Parker. 2006. Health assessment of seabirds on Genovesa, Galápagos Islands, *Ornithological Monographs* 60:86–97.

Parker, P.G. 2009. Parasites and Pathogens: Threats to native birds, in T. de Roy (ed.), *Galapagos: Preserving Darwin's Legacy*, pp. 177–183 (Firefly Books: Ontario).

Parker, P.G., N.K. Whiteman, and R.E. Miller. 2006. Conservation Medicine in the Galápagos Islands: Partnerships among Behavioral, Population and Veterinary Scientists, *The Auk* 123:625–638.

Pedersen, A.B., K.E. Jones, C.L. Nunn, and S. Altizer. 2007. Infectious diseases and extinction risk in wild mammals, *Conservation Biology* 21:1269–1279.

Price, P.W. 1980. *Evolutionary biology of parasites* (Princeton University Press, Princeton, NJ).

Redford, K.H., and B.C. Richter. 1999. Conservation of biodiversity in a world of use. *Conservation Biology* 13: 1246–1256.

Riper, C.S. van, III, S.G. van Riper, M.L. Goff, and M. Laird. 1986. The epizootiology and ecological significance of malaria in Hawaiian land birds, *Ecological Monographs* 56:327–344.

Riper, C.S. van, III, S.G. van Riper, and W.R. Hansen. 2002. Epizootiology and effect of avian pox on Hawaiian forest birds, *The Auk* 119:929–942.

Santiago-Alarcon, D., D.C. Outlaw, R.E. Ricklefs, and P.G. Parker. 2010. Phylogenetic relationships of haemosporidian parasites in New World Columbiformes, with emphasis on the endemic Galapagos dove, *International Journal of Parasitology* 40:463–470.

Santiago-Alarcon, D., S.M. Tanksley, and P.G. Parker. 2006. Morphological variation and genetic structure of Galápagos Dove (*Zenaida galapagoensis*) populations: issues in conservation for the Galápagos bird fauna, *Wilson Journal of Ornithology* 118:194–207.

Santiago-Alarcon, D, N.K. Whiteman, R.E. Ricklefs, P.G. Parker, and G. Valkiunas. 2008. Patterns of parasite abundance and distribution in island populations of Galapagos endemic birds, *Journal of Parasitology* 94:584–590.

Schloegel, L.M., J.-M. Hero, L. Berger, R. Speare, K. McDonald, and P. Daszak. 2006. The decline of the sharp-snouted day frog (*Taudactylus acutirostris*): the first documented case of extinction by infection in a free-ranging wildlife species? *Eco-Health* 3:35–40.

Smith, K.F., K. Acevedo-Whitehouse, and A.B. Pedersen. 2009. The role of infectious diseases in biological conservation, *Animal Conservation* 12:1–12.

Smith, K.F., D.F. Sax, K.D. Lafferty. 2006. Evidence for the role of infectious disease in species extinction and endangerment, *Conservation Biology* 20:1349–1357.

Soos, C., L. Padilla, A. Iglesias, N. Gottdenker, M. Cruz Bedon, A. Rios, and P.G. Parker. 2008. Comparison of pathogens in broiler and backyard chickens on the Galapagos Islands: Implications for transmission to wildlife, *The Auk* 125: 445–455.

Thiel, T., N.K. Whiteman, A. Tirape, M.I. Baquero, V. Cedeno, T. Walsh, G. Jimenez-Uzcategui, and P.G. Parker. 2005. Characterization of Carnarypox-like viruses infecting endemic birds in the Galapagos islands, *Journal of Wildlife Diseases* 41:342–353.

Thorne, E.T. and E.S. Williams. 1988. Disease and endangered species: the black-footed ferret as a recent example, *Conservation Biology* 2:66–74.

Travis, E.K., F.H. Vargas, J. Merkel, N. Gottdenker, R.E. Miller, and P.G. Parker. 2006a. Hematology, serum chemistry, and serology of the Galápagos Penguin in the Galápagos Islands, Ecuador, *Journal of Wildlife Diseases* 42:625–632.

Travis, E.K., F.H. Vargas, J. Merkel, N. Gottdenker, R.E. Miller, and P.G. Parker. 2006b. Hematology, plasma chemistry, and disease serology of the Flightless Cormorant (*Phalacrocorax harrisi*) in the Galápagos Islands, Ecuador, *Journal of Wildlife Disease* 42:133–141.

Valkiunas, G., D. Santiago-Alarcon, I.I. Levin, T.A. Iezhova, and P.G. Parker. 2010. A new Haemoproteus species (Haemosporida: Haemoproteidae) from the endemic Galapagos dove Zenaida galapagoensis, with remarks on the parasite distribution, vectors, and molecular diagnostics, *J. Parasitology* 96:783–792.

Vargas, F.H. 1987. Frequency and effect of pox-like lesions in Galapagos mockingbirds, *Journal of Field Ornithology* 58:101–102.

Vargas, F.H., S. Harrison, S. Rea, and D.W. Macdonald. 2006. Biological effects of El Niño on the Galapagos penguin, *Biological Conservation* 127:107–114.

Vitousek, P.M., H.A. Mooney, J. Lubchenco, and J.M. Melillo. 1997. Human domination of Earth's ecosystems, *Science* 277:494–499.

Warner, R.E. 1968. The role of introduced disease in the extinction of the endemic Hawaiian avifuana, *Condor* 70:101–120.

Whiteman, N.K., S.J. Goodman, B. J. Sinclair, T. Walsh, A.A. Cunningham, L.D. Kramer, and P.G. Parker. 2005. Establishment of the avian disease vector *Culex quinquefasciatus* Say, 1823 (Diptera: Culicidae) on the Galápagos Islands, Ecuador, *Ibis* 147:844–847.

Whiteman, N.K., R.T. Kimball, and P.G. Parker. 2007. Co-phylogeography and comparative population genetics of the Galápagos Hawk and three co-occurring ectoparasite species: Natural history shapes population histories within a parasite community, *Molecular Ecology* 16:4759–4773.

Whiteman, N.K., K.D. Matson, J.L. Bollmer, and P.G. Parker. 2006. Disease ecology in the Galápagos Hawk (*Buteo galapagoensis*): Host genetic diversity, parasites, and natural antibodies. *Proceedings of the Royal Society of London B* 273:797–804.

Whiteman, N.K. and P.G. Parker. 2005. Using parasites to infer host population history: A new rationale for parasite conservation, *Animal Conservation* 8:175–181.

11 Part II summary

Biodiversity assessment and monitoring of change

Mark Gardener and Matthias Wolff

Part II covers the many challenges of developing baseline biodiversity inventories, based on collections like those of Charles Darwin and the California Academy of Sciences described in Part I. These baseline inventories form a central part in monitoring programs. Monitoring programs help us to detect and understand ecosystem change with time and its causes. This ability to detect change can act as early warning systems to conservation managers.

Frank Bungartz and his team discuss the central role of biodiversity inventories in conservation science and the challenges to collect and catalog all biodiversity, not just iconic species. Whilst the Galápagos Islands are one of the best studied tropical archipelago ecosystems, many important taxonomic groups have been neglected. Part of this negligence is a result of an increasing alienation between taxonomists and ecologists. Ecologists and conservation managers use iconic and/or indicator species to make decisions and assume that these species are surrogates for overall biodiversity and reflect ecosystem health. Another factor in these incomplete inventories is the taxonomists themselves. Many of them have gone away from the painstaking work of describing new species and now focus on classification or the construction of phylogenic trees made possible with the advent of easy-to-use molecular techniques. As in most parts of the world, the Galápagos vascular plants and vertebrates are best known, while invertebrates are much less studied, and some groups like fungi are mostly ignored. In 2010, there were about 7,000 accepted taxa in the inventory but the authors estimated that the total biodiversity would be between 17,000 and 42,000. To minimize biodiversity loss and design efficient conservation strategies for entire ecosystems, conservation managers, ecologists and taxonomists have to look beyond the scope of their own bias and better integrate their research.

James Gibbs and Bryan Milstead discuss the pitfalls of designing biological monitoring programs including unclear objectives, not being explicitly linked to management and being unjustifiably expensive. In contrast, properly designed and implemented monitoring costs little relative to the value of the resources it protects, particularly in such places as Galápagos with its biodiversity-based ecotourism economy. Furthermore, for all monitoring systems there is a need to evaluate the scalability of data obtained; the true status of the target organism(s);

the reasons for their decline or increase; and the management effectiveness. The need for a knowledge management system in Galápagos is identified as a priority to facilitate informed decision-making. The authors point out that a propitious institutional environment already exists in Galápagos to close the adaptive management loop: a constitutionally defined relationship between a scientific advisory body – the Charles Darwin Foundation (CDF) – and a management authority – the Galápagos National Park Service. This has enabled the creation of a science-management partnership unlike any on Earth that can streamline the process of generating, collecting and implementing scientific monitoring data in decision-making. Since the archipelago is of international significance and receives extraordinary financial support from both the federal government of Ecuador and international donors, the authors see great opportunities for a stable funding situation for monitoring change in the Galápagos ecosystem.

Stuart Banks and co-workers use an example of a marine monitoring program running since 2000, which has clear objectives, is linked directly to management and is cost effective. The CDF–Galápagos National Park (GNP) subtidal monitoring program has had many useful outcomes, including biodiversity inventories, risk assessments to identify IUCN threatened species, and, most importantly, it has provided a long-term data set whose results are used to manage the zoning scheme. Ongoing evaluations under the adaptive management paradigm propose that minor amendments to zoning are necessary to protect key biodiversity areas from over-exploitation; to better manage commercial species; and to better understand the role of climatic variability (ENSO, climate change). The CDF–GNP bi-institutional ecological monitoring program consists of a systematic array of 64 subtidal sites, >60 oceanographic stations and remote sensing collections that evaluate ecosystem status and trend of biophysical indicators over time. The program thus follows GMR vital signs to detect the effects of the interplay between environment (ENSO, climate change) and such human uses (exploitation, introductions and disturbances) that could lead to or perpetuate system-wide shifts, loss and extinctions of Galápagos marine biodiversity. The authors also emphasize the need for a Galápagos information management system, which appropriately feeds back to management and which is based around an ecosystem level and robust monitoring framework. Importantly this system will require coordination, communication and continuity – with a "legacy" mechanism in place to ensure adherence to management milestones over time and the best use of competencies between local institutions.

Patricia G. Parker and Sharon Deem's chapter discusses another developing monitoring program, that of wildlife pathogens in Galápagos, and illustrates how this program can detect immerging threats. By reviewing the literature, they show that nowhere are anthropogenic impacts as drivers of disease more evident than in island ecosystems. The most poignant example of extinctions by disease comes from the honeycreepers of Hawaii. Their rapid decline over a 200-year period is largely attributed to predation and competition from invasive species, habitat alteration and disease. For many honeycreepers, the final push to extinction came with exposure to two pathogens: avian malaria caused by *Plasmodium relictum* and avian pox virus. According to the authors' perceptions, colonization and introductions of invasive species in Galápagos resemble the early years of European colonization of Hawaii. Based on these past experiences, and in the face of growing international concerns over the impact of emerging diseases on wildlife populations in island systems, the authors have undertaken a ten-year survey of pathogens in Galápagos birds, including the Galápagos dove, the waved albatross, the Galápagos penguin, the flightless cormorant and the Galápagos hawk. They identified a number of emerging threats including transmission from domestic animals to wild birds, bird pox and avian malaria, and show that the knowledge of transmission dynamics is essential for effective management. This management can be categorized into (1) prevention, (2) control or (3) eradication, and strategies can be directed at the host, disease agent, environment or vector. The authors recommend further monitoring programs across taxa, including other domestic species. They further propose to expand their baseline studies to include immunological studies and survey for environmental toxins.

Part III

A systemic approach

Modeling and restoration

12 Fifty years of eradication as a conservation tool in Galápagos

What are the limits?

Rachel Atkinson, Mark Gardener, Grant Harper and Victor Carrion

Introduction

In Galápagos, invasive species present the largest threat to terrestrial biodiversity (Snell *et al.* 2002). Introduced species were first noted in Galápagos in the seventeenth century, increasing steadily since the 1830s and rising most rapidly in the last 50 years (Causton and Sevilla 2008; Deem *et al.* 2008; Jimenez-Uzcátegui *et al.* 2008; Tye 2007b). In 2008, the tally of introduced terrestrial species was 1,445 including 870 plants, 536 invertebrates, 30 vertebrates and ten diseases (Table 12.1). Of these introduced species, many have invaded native ecosystems. Vertebrate invasions were the first to cause impact and alarm in the latter half of the twentieth century. These have been followed by plant and invertebrate invasions that now cover huge areas, particularly in the highland regions of the inhabited islands (Causton *et al.* 2006; Watson *et al.* 2009) and further invasions are expected in the future (Trueman *et al.*, in press)

For a conservation manager, the ultimate goal of any action against introduced species should be to preserve or re-establish native biodiversity and ecosystem function (Genovesi 2007). Once introductions and invasions have occurred, the main options for management are eradication, containment or long-term control (McNeely *et al.* 2001). A fourth option would be to take no action at all.

Table 12.1 Number of introduced, invasive and potentially invasive species in Galápagos (data from Causton *et al.* 2006; Jiménez-Uzcátegui *et al.* 2008; Trueman 2008)

Taxon	*Number of species*		
	Introduced	*Invasive (subset of introduced)*	*Potentially invasive (subset of introduced)*
Plants	870	32	447
Invertebrates	536	6	52
Vertebrates	30	22	8
Diseases*	>10	?	?

Note
*a comprehensive analysis of the invasiveness of introduced diseases recorded in Galápagos has yet to be ascertained.

Eradication is the complete removal of all populations of an introduced species from a defined area, by means of a time-limited campaign. A consideration of four main criteria is necessary before deciding to attempt eradication: (1) strategic/operational; (2) biological; (3) economic; and (4) socio-political (Bomford and O'Brien 1995; Panetta and Timmins 2004). Some important considerations are as follows:

1 An eradication operation should not be attempted if reintroduction cannot be prevented.
2 The rate of removal must exceed the rate of population increase.
3 Species with limited distributions, that are easily detectable, with a short-lived dormant stage (e.g. a seed or egg bank), and that have a known control method for reproductive individuals are prime candidates for eradication.
4 Eradications, especially when carried out at the early stages of invasion, are cost effective and theoretically neat solutions to prevent the future or current impact of invasive species. Mack and Forster (2009) use the analogy that an eradication operation is like a single lump sum payment, with no further instalments required. Whilst attractive, this analogy neglects two important points. First, the value of the lump sum may be large or hard to predict (Panetta 2009). Second, there will always be an annual cost associated with monitoring and preventing the reintroduction of the eradicated species. Additionally, eradications should not be started if there is insufficient funding to address unforeseen consequences of the operation on ecosystem dynamics (Zavaleta *et al.* 2001). Another frequently overlooked requirement is the need for governmental and public support for all aspects of the project from the start in order to ensure that there are no barriers to the program from beginning to end (Mack and Forster 2009).

The objective of this chapter is to assess the 50-year history of eradication projects in Galápagos in order to inform future decision-making for invasive species management. We discuss the rationale and effectiveness of eradication projects, identify the main reasons for eradication failures, introduce new eradication projects and discuss alternative options for invasive species management.

Invasive species eradications in Galápagos

Eradication has been used as a tool for invasive species management in Galápagos since 1961 when goats were removed from the 12 ha islet of South Plaza. During the intervening 50 years there have been 57 eradication operations on 27 species of which 27 have been successful, 20 unsuccessful and ten are ongoing (Table 12.2). The target species were chosen either because of actual impact or because of potential future impacts, as shown by invasive behaviour in other parts of the world. The outcomes of these attempts show that eradications of large vertebrates such as goats and donkeys have been increasingly successful on bigger islands as the technology has improved. Small vertebrate eradication such as rats has only recently become viable on larger islands because of improved technology. Eradications of invertebrates and plants have been largely unsuccessful, except for a few cases when the invasion area was small and well defined. We outline the eradication projects below and in the following section we discuss the effect of successful eradications on ecosystem recovery.

Vertebrates

Goats (*Capra hircus*) were first recorded in Galápagos in 1685, donkeys (*Equus asinus*) in 1834 and pigs (*Sus scrofa*) in the mid-1850s. Large populations of these herbivores were noted as early as 1875, but consequences on the ecosystem were not realized until much later. Introduced herbivores have been extremely destructive to native vegetation in Galápagos (Hamann 1975; Henderson and Dawson 2009). It was estimated that 55–60% of the 194 endemic plant species were threatened by goats (IUCN 2001). Concern was also raised of competition for food with the giant tortoise populations (MacFarland 1991), and there is evidence of significant changes in invertebrate community structure during the time of maximum goat density in northern Isabela (Desender *et al.* 1999). Over the last 50 years there has been an increasingly concentrated effort to reduce and finally remove goats from islands. Prior to 2000, the largest island where goats were eradicated in Galápagos was 6,000 ha. Under a multi-million dollar initiative, "Project Isabela", using new technology (such as helicopters, Judas goats, and geographic information systems), goats have now been eradicated successfully from 11 islands and islets, and remain only on Santa Cruz and San Cristóbal (Campbell *et al.* 2007; Cruz *et al.* 2009). Similarly, pigs have an impact on invertebrates and on eggs and hatchlings of giant tortoises, sea turtles and petrels (Coblentz and Baber 1987; Cruz and Cruz 1987). Pigs have been eradicated from Santiago (Cruz *et al.* 2005) and donkeys from northern Isabela and Santiago (Carrion *et al.* 2007).

Black rats (*Rattus rattus*) were introduced to Galápagos at some point in the seventeenth century. By the 1830s they had been recorded in Santiago, Floreana and Isabela, and by the Second World War in Santa Cruz and Baltra (Clark 1978). They are now known from 35 islands and islets (Carrion and Harper, in press). Although the impacts of black rats in Galápagos have not been studied exhaustively, their predation of eggs is held responsible for preventing recruitment of the tortoise population on Pinzon Island (MacFarland *et al.* 1974). They prey on the young of many bird species, including the endangered medium tree finch (*Camarhynchus pauper*), the dark-rumped petrel (*Pterodroma phaeopygia*) and the mangrove finch (*Camarhynchus heliobates*) (Jody O'Connor, personal communication; Cruz and Cruz 1987; Fessl *et al.* 2010), as well as on other reptile species and may also have an impact on the recruitment of plants through seed predation. It is also believed that they displace the endemic rice rats. Only four of seven rice rat species (*Oryzomys* and *Nesoryzomys* spp.) remain, of which only one occurs on an island with black rats, coexisting at low densities

Table 12.2 List of 57 eradication projects including species, area of distribution (or of island if not known), year of first recorded introduction, years of eradication attempts, outcome and reason for failure. Island names follow Snell *et al.* (1996). Reason for failure is categorized according to groupings provided by Panetta and Timmins (2004). (Reason for failure: socio = socio-political, op = operational, bio = biological, econ = economic; n/a = not applicable)

Scientific name	*Island*	*Area (ha)*	*Year of introduction*	*Year of eradication*	*Outcome*	*Reason for failure*
VERTEBRATES						
Capra hircus	Mariela Sur	1.3	1990	?	successful	
Capra hircus	Plaza Sur	12	?	1961	successful	
Capra hircus	Wolf	130	2009	2009	successful	
Capra hircus	Rabida	499	1971	1971–1975	successful	
Capra hircus	Santa Fe	2,413	1905*	1971	successful	
Capra hircus	Baltra	2,619	1900	2008	successful	
Capra hircus	Pinta	5,940	1954	1971–2003	successful	
Capra hircus	Española	6,048	1905	1978	successful	
Capra hircus	Marchena	12,996	1967*	1979–2002	successful	
Capra hircus	Floreana	17,253	1832	2009	successful	
Capra hircus	San Cristóbal	55,808	<1880s	n/a	in progress	
Capra hircus	Santiago	58,465	1920s	2006	successful	
Capra hircus	Southern Isabela	218,812	1897	2006	in progress	
Capra hircus	Northern Isabela	240,000	1968	2008	successful	
Columba livia	San Cristobal, Santa Cruz, Isabela	?	1972	2005	successful	
Equus asinus	Santiago	58,465	<1875	2004	successful	
Equus asinus	Northern Isabela	74,103	<1880s	2006	successful	
Felis catus	Baltra	2,619	1940	2004	successful	
Oreochromis niloticus	San Cristóbal	5	2006	2008	in progress	
Rattus rattus	Mariela Norte	0.2	?	1998–2009	successful	
Rattus rattus	Pitt	0.4	1983	1989	successful	
Rattus rattus	Mariela Sur	1.3	?	1998–1999	successful	
Rattus rattus	Mosquera	4.6	?	2007	successful	
Rattus rattus	Lobos	6.7	?	2002	unsuccessful	op
Rattus rattus	Venecia	13.3	?	1980s	unsuccessful	op
Rattus rattus	Banbridge islets	38.3	?	2002	unsuccessful	op
Rattus rattus	Seymour norte	184	?	2007–2009	successful	

Rattus rattus	Pinzon	1,815	?	1988	unsuccessful	op
Sus scrofa	Santiago	58,465	1875	1970–2000	successful	
INVERTEBRATES						
Solenopsis geminata	Las Marielas	1.2	?	?	unsuccessful	bio
Solenopsis geminata	Champion	9.5	?	n/a	in progress	
Wasmannia auropunctata	Isla Mao	1.2	?	n/a	in progress	
Wasmannia auropunctata	Santa Fe	3	?	1994	successful	
Wasmannia auropunctata	Marchena	21	?	1988	unsuccessful	op
Wasmannia auropunctata	Northern Isabela #	35	?	n/a	in progress	
Wasmannia auropunctata	Northern Isabela #	196	?	n/a	in progress	
PLANTS						
Acacia nilotica	Santa Cruz	1	1950s	2006–2007	unsuccessful	socio
Aristolochia odoratissima	Santa Cruz	40	1970	2002	unsuccessful	bio
Cenchrus pilosus	Santa Cruz	1	2002	2005	successful	
Citharexylum gentryi	Santa Cruz	330	1950	2000–2007	unsuccessful	socio
Citrus spp.	Santiago	20	?	2006–2010	unsuccessful	op
Cryptostegia grandiflora	Santa Cruz	1	?	2006–2007	unsuccessful	op, econ
Furcraea hexapetala	Floreana	5	?	2007–2010	in progress	
Leucaena leucocephala	Floreana	6	1980s	2007–2010	in progress	
Persea americana	Santiago	1	?	2003–2010	unsuccessful	op
Pueraria phaseoloides	Santa Cruz	1	1996	1996	successful	
Rubus adenotrichos	Santa Cruz	1	1995	1999	successful	
Rubus adenotrichos	Isabela	1	1960	2001–2007	unsuccessful	op, econ
Rubus glaucus	Santa Cruz	40	1970	2000–2007	unsuccessful	op, econ
Rubus megalococcus	Santa Cruz	1	1983	2000	successful	
Rubus niveus	Santiago	105	<2001	2006–2010	unsuccessful	bio
Rubus niveus	Floreana	140	<2001	2007–2010	unsuccessful	bio
Rubus niveus	Isabela	200	1980s	1998–2007	unsuccessful	bio
Rubus ulmifolius	Santa Cruz	2	1930s	2002–2007	unsuccessful	op, econ
Sapindus saponaria	Santiago	1	?	2003–2007	unsuccessful	op
Solanum quitoensis	Santiago	4	?	2006–2010	unsuccessful	op
Syzygium jambos	Floreana	1	1920s	2007–2010	in progress	

Notes
* Multiple introductions.
# site based, not whole island.

on Santiago (Dowler *et al.* 2000). Ground-based rat eradication operations have taken place on 12 islands or islets, of which five were successful on the first attempt and two were successful when a second operation was carried out (Carrion and Harper, in press). At 184 ha, North Seymour is the largest islet free of rats to date.

Feral cats (*Felis catus*) are also widespread across the archipelago. Baltra was chosen for an eradication operation to protect the large colony of land iguanas there, terminating successfully in 2004 (Phillips *et al.* 2005). The rock pigeon (*Columba livia*) was targeted for archipelago-wide eradication due to its potential for disease transmission including *Trichomonas gallinae*, a fatal disease of endemic pigeons and poultry. It was eradicated in 2005 and is one of the few successful bird eradications in the world (Victor Carrion, personal communication). The fish tilapia (*Oreochromis niloticus*) is known worldwide to be highly invasive, decimating populations of native species. It was first recorded in El Junco Lake, the largest body of freshwater in Galápagos, in 2006. The lake contains no native fish but at least 24 native invertebrates, of which at least nine are endemic (Miriam Steinitz Kannan, personal communication). In 2008 a non-specific fish poison "rotenone" was used but further applications are necessary to remove the remainder of the population (Victor Carrion, personal communication).

Invertebrates

The little fire ant (*Wasmannia auropunctata*) and the tropical fire ant (*Solenopsis geminata*) are known to have a serious impact on biodiversity, most significantly on native invertebrates, as well as on young reptiles and birds. Their sting is also an annoyance to humans. The first official record of *W. auropunctata* in Galápagos is from 1905 and it is now known from nine large islands and at least six islets. Genetic analysis suggests that there was a single introduction of an inseminated female to the archipelago (Mikheyev and Herrera, unpublished data).

Wasmannia auropunctata was successfully eradicated from Santa Fé in 1994 where it had infested 3 ha (Abedrabbo 1994) and from the near pristine Marchena where it had colonized approximately 21 ha. At the time, this was the largest known attempted ant eradication in the world (Causton *et al.* 2005). However, another infestation on the island was found in 2008 about 2 km from the original site and covering 67 ha. It is likely that this is an old infestation that was not detected during island-wide surveys; Funding was limited and an intensive search outside the area of eradication was not possible. This project is still in progress. *Solenopsis geminata* is known from seven islands and six islets (Herrera and Causton 2008, unpublished data) and eradication has been attempted at two penguin breeding colonies and at one of the two remaining populations of the critically endangered Floreana mockingbird. However, the proximity of these sites to other islands infested with ants has made eradication difficult owing to the species' winged dispersal stage.

Plants

Plant species were chosen for eradication using the precautionary principle of eliminating recent introductions (either to the archipelago or to islands within the archipelago). Thirty projects were chosen, based on an extensive risk analysis, and 21 projects (18 species) were begun, the earliest in 1996. Only four of the eradication projects were successful, all on Santa Cruz: *Rubus adenotrichos* and *R. megalococcus* (Buddenhagen 2006); *Pueraria phaseoloides* (Tye 2007a); and *Cenchrus pilosus*. Each of these species covered less than 1 ha in net area, had no seed bank and was on land with a single owner (Gardener *et al.* 2010).

Effectiveness of eradications in Galápagos

Eradication of widespread invasives can change the system dynamics and alter interactions between species. The result can be positive, reversing population declines and degradation processes, but it can also lead to unexpected and unwanted secondary consequences, which, if not monitored, can cause problems as difficult and expensive to reverse as the initial eradication operation (Bergstrom *et al.* 2009; Zavaleta *et al.* 2001). Long-term monitoring post-eradication is rarely carried out well (Hoffmann 2009) but is an important part of any operation in order to increase our understanding of ecological processes, to identify emerging problems and enable appropriate mitigation. In Galápagos, some post-eradication monitoring of threatened species and vegetation has been undertaken. These are reviewed below.

Threatened species recovery

Donlan *et al.* (2007) observed ten-fold increases in densities of Galápagos rail (*Laterallus spilonotus*) in the highlands of Santiago after goat and pig eradication. The effect of these eradications on the Galápagos hawk (*Buteo galapagoensis*) population on Santiago has also been monitored (Parker 2009). For the first two years following the eradications (2005–2006), there was almost no juvenile survival, and adult survivorship also declined slightly. However, this situation was reversed by 2009. For seven of nine threatened plant taxa monitored on Santiago and Floreana, the number of known populations has increased, and six of the species show a marked increase in total population size (Atkinson *et al.* 2008). There is also evidence of a mass recovery of the Pinta endemic *Scalesia bauri* ssp. *hopkinsii* following goat eradication there (Hamann 1993).

There have also been some studies on the impact of rat eradication from the nearly successful operation on Pinzón. Observed effects on native wildlife included increases in numbers of juvenile marine iguanas (*Amblyrhynchus cristatus*) (Cayot *et al.* 1994), endemic Pinzón lava lizards (*Microlophus duncanensis*) and Galápagos doves (*Zenaida galapagoensis*). Successful giant tortoise nesting was also recorded. In contrast, there was an apparent decrease in the population of Galápagos hawks (*Buteo galapagoensis*) and short-eared owls (*Asio flammeus*) (Muñoz 1989), presumably owing either to secondary poisoning or a decline in food availability.

Vegetation recovery

As expected, rapid and vigorous vegetation recovery has been noted on Pinta (Hamann 1993), Santiago and Alcedo (unpublished, Charles Darwin Foundation (CDF)) through the monitoring of permanent vegetation plots following herbivore eradications. Invasive plants have also been released from herbivory, especially the mora or Mysore raspberry (*Rubus niveus*). This species is a serious problem in the highlands and agricultural zone of San Cristóbal, Santa Cruz and Isabela, and is increasing in abundance on Santiago and Floreana (Atkinson *et al.* 2008; Gardener *et al.* 2010).

Lessons learned from species eradications

An analysis of the eradication operations carried out in Galápagos over the last 50 years shows that they have been increasingly successful, and have developed in scale, scope and species. It is however useful to analyse the failures in order to help understand their cause and determine when eradication is the most appropriate tool to manage a particular invasive species problem as indicated in Table 12.2. The reason for failure for each of the 20 projects that could not be completed was: operational (9); biological (5); operational and economic (4) and; socio-political (2), following the groupings used by Panetta and Timmins (2004). We discuss these reasons below.

Operational failures

Some eradications failed owing to the operational problem of finding the last individuals of an invasive species, especially in some of the early attempts at goat eradication. For example, the first eradication attempts on Pinta (1971–1982) failed because just a few goats remained. Eradication was finally achieved in 2003 using technological advances, such as "Judas" goats to find the last individual, better systematic planning and tracking, which was not possible before the advent of cheap hand held radio tracking, and GPS technology (Campbell *et al.* 2004). These tools opened the door for larger scale operations, where island size and technology were no longer a constraint for goat eradication campaigns in Galápagos.

Delimitation of distribution has also been a problem in some operations. For example, the single *Wasmannia auropunctata* colony targeted for eradication on Marchena was falsely assumed to be the only colony on the island because there were not enough funds to carry out an initial survey across the whole island. A single colony seemed feasible because this species has no winged dispersal stage and no other colonies were detected using an equidistant point sampling method around the known colony (Causton *et al.* 2005). The recently discovered 67 ha colony at a different site on Marchena suggests that the distribution had not been fully delimited before the project started.

Failures due to species biology

Before eradication is attempted, it is essential that the species biology and life history is understood well. Species such as rats and goats are targeted on islands worldwide for eradication, and have been studied for years. However other species may only be problems locally and are less well understood, or may simply have life histories that are not amenable to eradication. One example is *Rubus niveus*, a species that was thought eradicable on newly colonized islands in Galápagos, leading to operations that were started before a real understanding of the species biology had been obtained. The rapid life cycle, ease of seed dispersal, longevity of the seed bank, ability to reproduce vegetatively and difficulty in finding plants before they are of reproductive age are all factors that have made this species very difficult to manage (Gardener *et al.* 2010).

Failure from lack of resources

While the large-scale eradications of vertebrates on Santiago and Isabela were much more cost effective than any before them (Lavoie *et al.* 2007), the total project cost was estimated at 8.5 million US$. This level of funding has so far only been obtainable for the eradication of large herbivores but is difficult to obtain for other organisms. For example the proposed 8 million US$ and ten-year-long eradication strategy for the red quinine tree (*Cinchona pubescens*) on Santa Cruz (Buddenhagen and Yanez 2005) has never received interest from donors.

Socio-political failure

On uninhabited islands, human involvement in an eradication operation may be restricted to scientists and conservation managers (Donlan 2003). On inhabited islands, the human dimension can neither be ignored nor manipulated if the aim is a long-term solution. Invasive species are a human issue, with a human cause and a human solution, and as such it is not simply the mechanical removal of the species that leads to a successful eradication. Other human-related factors are extremely important, such as the prevention of human-mediated reinvasion. An example is the eradication of goats from Marchena Island. There have been several intentional reintroductions by disgruntled fishermen, who use the goats as a food and an alternative source of income. These reintroductions have led to the need for further costly eradication operations.

There are two overarching obstacles to eradications. One is the lack of an eradication ethic in many of these projects. Searching for the final individuals and the monitoring to ensure success requires planning for years or decades. This requires that management authorities consider and maintain these projects as funding priorities. The second is the understanding that eradication is not a one-off event. Once a species has been removed it needs to be kept out. This is not a passive activity, but involves annual investment to ensure that the costly eradication operations remain successful – eradication operations are useless without effective biosecurity measures. The substantial number of small boat journeys between islands by locals and tourists can easily result in reinvasion. Without effective biosecurity, social acceptance (local community buy-in) and knowledge of the necessity for this, eradication is not necessarily the most appropriate tool. It could be argued that none of these measures are yet to be adequately implemented in Galápagos.

Future of invasive species management in Galápagos

Eradication is one potentially feasible method in a tool kit available to restoration and conservation managers, and its use needs to be considered within the contexts discussed above. Bearing those issues in mind, there are four eradication operations planned for the next five to ten years in Galápagos:

1. Black rat eradication on Pinzón and Rábida islands. Following a workshop held in 2007, Plan Pinzón was launched with the aim of achieving three goals: (a) to eradicate rats from Rábida and Pinzón; (b) to plan subsequent and larger whole island eradications of rats; and (c) to enhance technical and management capacity in Galápagos to carry out the work (CDF and Galápagos National Park (GNP) 2007).
2. Cat eradication on Floreana Island. As part of a whole island restoration project, and in order to prepare the island for the reintroduction of the critically endangered Floreana mockingbird (*Mimus trifasciatus*), it is envisaged to eradicate cats from Floreana using new bait formulae and toxins being developed in Australia.
3. Eradication of feral donkeys from the GNP areas on the inhabited islands. Large populations of feral donkeys still exist on San Cristóbal and Santa Cruz, with smaller numbers of Isabela. Using the techniques developed under Project Isabela, it is planned to eliminate these populations over the next five years.
4. The Mediterranean fruit fly (*Ceratitis capitata*) is a serious citrus pest and has caused significant economic damage to the citrus industry in many parts of the world. It was first detected in Galápagos in 2008 in San Cristóbal and Santa Cruz. Citrus is an important seasonal crop for farmers and the discovery of the fly led to the suspension of movement of fruit between the islands. In collaboration with experts in the United States it has been decided to release sterile males, aiming to eliminate the species from the island.

For more intractable species invasions, a suite of other non-eradication options are being used or developed:

Biological control

The invasive cottony cushion scale (*Icerya purchasi)*, was first discovered in the Galápagos in 1982, and has spread to at least 15 islands in the archipelago.

Infestations damage plants, restricting their growth or killing individuals. The sugary waste also attracts invasive ant species which guard the scales from predators and transport them between trees. The problem is particularly critical for threatened plant species with restricted ranges, and specialist insects that feed on them. Following intensive non-target testing, the Australian ladybird (*Rodolia cardinalis*), a predator of the scale insect, was released on 11 different islands in 2002 (Causton *et al.* 2006). Evaluations carried out in 2009 indicated that the ladybird was still present, keeping the scale under control and showing no adverse impacts (Hoddle *et al.* 2009).

This success has led to interest for other projects including the development of a biological control agent for *Rubus niveus* (Atkinson *et al.* 2009). The project to identify and rigorously test control agents is estimated to cost USD one million and take up to ten years.

New technology

The larvae of the fly *Philornis downsi* are parasitizing young chicks of native and endemic finches and have been estimated to cause up to 95% of nestling mortality (Fessl *et al.* 2006). It is a species with an elusive life cycle that has proven complicated to study. One option for control is to develop pheromone traps that would lure the flies to their death in areas of importance during the breeding season.

Localized control operations

Intensive and temporally constrained control may be the preferred management option in situations where management is necessary over a spatially and temporally defined area. For example, rat control around the last stronghold of the mangrove finch is carried out only during the breeding season and over an area of about 20 ha. This relatively inexpensive management has resulted in a 170% increase in the fledgling success of this critically endangered species (Fessl *et al.* 2010).

Containment

Containing species to prevent their spread may be the only viable management solution for several newly establishing weed species. For example, *Rubus niveus* on Santiago at present covers 105 ha, divided into three main infestations in an overall area of 1,000 ha. Current control every three months of the three main infestations and continued and systematic searching of the surrounding area throughout the year is helping to prevent further spread of this species. Containment requires continuous presence but it may be effective in keeping the species under control until a more economically viable solution, such as biological control, is developed (Atkinson *et al.* 2009).

Living with invasives

One of the most pressing conservation problems in Galápagos is restoration of the degraded highlands of the inhabited islands (Bensted-Smith *et al.* 2002). The system has so many different invasive species and is so altered ecologically that the removal of one species is likely to result in replacement by another invasive, making eradication an unlikely tool. For example, *Cinchona pubescens* management facilitates invasion of *Rubus niveus* (Jäger *et al.* 2009). In addition, the socio-political willingness and value attached to many of the invasives or potential future invasives would prevent such actions. It is unclear, however, what management action is most appropriate; long-term control programs in key habitat areas have not led to an improvement in habitat quality or a reduction in the invasive species problem (Gardener *et al.*, in press). The lack of success is at least partly because we do not adequately understand system function to be able to develop an effective restoration strategy. If we wish to optimize the use of limited resources for both research and management to maintain bigger natural areas that retain ecological function, then we need to accept the endpoint as a functional and mixed system of native and invasive species rather than one composed only of native biota (Hobbs *et al.* 2006). Whilst there are significant knowledge gaps that prevent us proceeding effectively with this task, some of these gaps are being addressed in current research projects.

Conclusion

Nearly half of all eradication projects in Galápagos have been successful. These successes all met a strict set of criteria including: (1) a pragmatic methodology in which all individuals of all life stages were susceptible to a control method; (2) reinvasion was prevented; (3) there were sufficient resources to see the project to the end; and (4) there were clear lines of authority to take all necessary actions.

Experiences from 50 years of eradication programs in Galápagos have allowed for a much better understanding of the complex problems related to species invasions and have elucidated the important role of scientific research for achieving success in restoration activities. Many of the lessons learned from this experience are transferable to other island ecosystems around the world. The effective and efficient management of invasive species for Galápagos requires an integrated approach, determining the most appropriate solution for each invasive species problem that is economically realistic, socially acceptable, maximizes biodiversity and allows better ecosystem function. Eradication is one potential tool to achieve this goal, and although in theory it is a technical solution applicable to all introduced species, it is often not the most suitable tool, owing to ecological, social or economic reasons. It is important that invasive species management has a solid scientific basis. The tools chosen for each restoration task must be applied with planning and followed through to their conclusion through an adaptive management approach. Such future projects require tight communication and collaboration between scientists, managers and the community.

References

Abedrabbo, S. 1994. Control of the little fire ant *Wasmannia auropunctata* on Santa Fe Island in the Galapagos Islands. pp. 219–227 in D.F. Williams (ed.) *Exotic ants: Biology, impact and control of introduced species*, Boulder, CO.

Atkinson, R., J.L. Rentería, and W. Simbaña. 2008. The consequences of herbivore eradiation on Santiago: are we in time to prevent ecosystem degradation again? pp. 121–124 in L. Cayot (ed.) *Galapagos Report 2007–2008*. Charles Darwin Foundation, Galapagos National Park and INGALA, Puerto Ayora, Galapagos, Ecuador.

Atkinson, R.J., A. Guézou, J. Rentería, D. Rueda, and G. M.R. 2009. *Diagnostico y planificacion para el desarrollo de un agente de control biológico para* Rubus niveus *en las islas Galápagos*. Fundacion Charles Darwin y Servicio Parque Nacional Galápagos, Puerto Ayora, Galapagos.

Bensted-Smith, R., G. Powell, and E. Dinerstein. 2002. Planning for the ecoregion. pp. 11–16 in R. Bensted-Smith (ed.) *A Biodiversity vision for the Galapagos Islands*. Charles Darwin Foundation and World Wildlife Fund, Puerto Ayora, Galapagos, Ecuador.

Bergstrom, D.M., A. Lucieer, K. Kiefer, J. Wasley, C. Belbin, T.K. Pedersen, and S.L. Chown. 2009. Indirect effects of invasive species removal devastate Word Heritage island. *Journal of Applied Ecology* 46:73–81.

Bomford, M., and P. O'Brien. 1995. Eradication or control for vertebrate pests? *Wildlife Society Bulletin* 23:249–255.

Buddenhagen, C.E. 2006. The successful eradication of two blackberry species *Rubus megalococcus* and *R. adenotrichos* (Rosaceae) from Santa Cruz Island, Galapagos, Ecuador. *Pacific Conservation Biology* 12:272–278.

Buddenhagen, C.E., and P. Yanez. 2005. The cost of quinine *Cinchona pubescens* control on Santa Cruz Island, Galapagos. *Galapagos Research* 63:32–36.

Campbell, K., C.J. Donlan, F. Cruz, and V. Carrion. 2004. Eradication of feral goats *Capra hircus* from Pinta Island, Galápagos, Ecuador. *Oryx* 38:1–6.

Campbell, K.J., G.S. Baxter, P.J. Murray, B.E. Coblentz, and C.J. Donlan. 2007. Development of a prolonged estrus effect for use in Judas goat. *Applied Animal Behaviour Science* 102:12–23.

Carrion, V., C.J. Donlan, K. Campbell, C. Lavoie, and F. Cruz. 2007. Feral donkey (*Equus asinus*) eradications in the Galapagos. *Biodiversity and Conservation* 16:437–445.

Carrion, V., and G.A. Harper. In press. Introduced rodents in the Galapagos: colonisation, removal and the future in C. R. Veitch, M.N. Clout, and D.R. Towns (ed.) *Island invasives: Eradication and management*. IUCN, Gland, Switzerland.

Causton, C.E., S.B. Peck, B.J. Sinclair, L. Roque-Albedo, C.J. Hodgson, and B. Landry. 2006. Alien insects: threats and implications for the conservation of the Galápagos Islands. *Annals of the Entomological Society of America* 99:121–143.

Causton, C., and C. Sevilla. 2008. Latest records of introduced invertebrates in Galapagos and measures to control them. pp. 142–145 in CDF (ed.) *Galapagos Report*, Puerto Ayora, Galapagos.

Causton, C.E., C.R. Sevilla, and S.D. Porter. 2005. Eradication of the little fire ant, *Wasmannia auropunctata* (Hymenoptera: Formicidae) from Marchena Island Galapagos: on the edge of success? *Florida Entomologist* 88:159–168.

Cayot, L.J., K. Rassmann, and F. Trillmich. 1994. Are marine iguanas endangered on islands with introduced predators? *Noticias de Galapagos* 53:13–15.

Charles Darwin Foundation and Galapagos National Park 2007. *Project Pinzon: Ecosystem restoration of the Galapagos Islands through introduced rodent removal*. Puerto Ayora, Galapagos.

Clark, D.E. 1978. *Population biology of two rodents of the Galápagos islands, Rattus rattus and Oryzomys bauri*. PhD thesis, University of Wisconsin-Madison.

Coblentz, B.E., and D.W. Baber. 1987. Biology and control of feral pigs on Isla Santiago, Galapagos, Ecuador. *Journal of Applied Ecology* 24:403–418.

Cruz, F., V. Carrion, K.J. Campbell, C. Lavoie, and C.J. Donlan. 2009. Bio-economics of large-scale eradication of feral goats from Santiago Island, Galapagos. *Journal of Wildlife Management* 73:191–200.

Cruz, F., and J.B. Cruz. 1987. Control of black rats (*Rattus rattus*) and its effect on nesting dark-rumped petrels in the Galapagos Islands. *Vida Silvestre Neotropical* 1:3–13.

Cruz, F., C.J. Donlan, K. Campbell, and V. Carrion. 2005. Conservation action in the Galapagos: Feral pig (*Sus scrofa*) eradication from Santiago Island. *Biological Conservation* 121:473–478.

Deem, S.L., M. Cruz, G. Jimenez-Uzcátegui, B. Fessl, R.E. Miller, and P.G. Parker. 2008. Pathogens and parasites: an increasing threat to the conservation of Galapagos avifauna, *Galapagos Report 2007–2008*, pp. 125–130 (CDF: Puerto Ayora, Galapagos).

Desender, K., L. Baert, J.P. Maelfait, and P. Verdyck. 1999. Conservation on Volcan Alcedo (Galapagos): Terrestrial invertebrates and the impact of introduced feral goats. *Biological Conservation* 87:303–310.

Donlan, C. 2003. Islands, exotic herbivores, and invasive plants: Their roles in coastal California restoration. *Restoration Ecology* 11:524–530.

Donlan, C.J., K. Campbell, W. Cabrera, C. Lavoie, V. Carrion, and F. Cruz. 2007. Recovery of the Galapagos rail (*Laterallus spilonotus*) following the removal of invasive mammals. *Biological Conservation* 138:520–524.

Dowler, R.C., D.S. Carroll, and C.W. Edwards. 2000. Rediscovery of rodents (Genus *Nesoryxomys*) considered extinct in Galapagos. *Oryx* 34:109–117.

Fessl, B.J., B. Sinclair, and S. Kleindorfer. 2006. The life cycle of *Philornis downsi* (Diptera:Muscidae) parasitizing Darwin's finches and its impacts on nestling survival. *Parasitology* 133:739–747.

Fessl, B., G.H. Young, R.P. Young, J. Rodrigues-Matamoros, M. Dvorak, S. Tebbich, and J.E. Fa. 2010. How to save the rarest Darwin´s finch from extinction: the mangrove finch on Isabela Island. *Philosophical Transactions of The Royal Society of London B: Biological Sciences* 365:1019–1030.

Gardener, M., R. Atkinson, D. Rueda, and R. Hobbs. In press. Optimizing restoration of the degraded highlands of Galapagos: a conceptual framework. *Galapagos Report*, Puerto Ayora, Galapagos.

Gardener, M.R., R. Atkinson, and J.L. Renteria. 2010. Eradications and people: lessons from the plant eradication program in Galapagos. *Restoration Ecology* 18:20–29.

Genovesi, P. 2007. Limits and potentialities of eradication as a tool for addressing biological invasions. *Ecological studies analysis and synthesis* 193:385–400.

Hamann, O. 1975. Vegetational changes in the Galapagos Islands during the period 1966–1973. *Biological Conservation* 7:37–59.

Hamann, O. 1993. On vegetation recovery, goats and giant tortoises on Pinta Island, Galápagos, Ecuador. *Biodiversity and Conservation* 2:138–151.

Henderson, S., and T.P. Dawson. 2009. Alien invasions from space observations: detecting feral goat impacts on Isla Isabela, Galapagos Islands with the AVHRR. *International Journal of Remote Sensing* 30:423–433.

Hobbs, R.J., S. Arico, J. Aronson, J.S. Baron, P. Bridgewater, V.A. Cramer, P.R. Epstein, J.J. Ewel, C.A. Klink, A.E. Lugo, D. Norton, D. Ojima, D.M. Richardson, E.W. Sanderson, F. Valladares, M. Vila, R. Zamora, and M. Zobel. 2006. Novel ecosystems:

theoretical and management aspects of the new ecological world order. *Global Ecology and Biogeography* 15:1–7.

Hoddle, M.S., C.D. Hoddle, R.G. Van. Driesche, and C. Causton. 2009. *Progress report on the classical biological control of cottony cushion scale (el Pulgon) with Rodolia cardinalis (la Mariquita) in the Galapagos Islands.* Charles Darwin Foundation, Puerto Ayora, Galapagos.

Hoffmann, B.D. 2009. Ecological restoration following the local eradication of an invasive ant in northern Australia. *Biological Invasions* 12:959–969

IUCN. 2001. *IUCN Red List Categories: Version 3.1* IUCN, Gland.

Jäger, H., I. Kowarik, and A. Tye. 2009. Destruction without extinction: long-term impacts of an invasive tree species on Galápagos highland vegetation. *Journal of Ecology* 97:1252–1263.

Jiménez-Uzcátegui, G., V. Carrión, J. Zabala, P. Buitrón, and B. Milstead. 2008. Status of introduced vertebrates in Galapagos, *Galapagos Report*, pp. 136–141 (CDF: Puerto Ayora, Galápagos).

Lavoie, C., F. Cruz, V. Carrion, K. Campbell, C. Donlan, S. Harcourt, and M. Moya. 2007. *The thematic atlas of Project Isabela.* Charles Darwin Foundation, Puerto Ayora.

MacFarland, C. 1991. Goats on Alcedo Volcano in the Galápagos Islands: Help needed. *Conservation Biology* 5:6–7.

MacFarland, C.G., J. Villa, and B. Toro. 1974. The Galapagos giant tortoises (*Geochelone elephantophus*). Part I. Status of the surviving populations. *Biological Conservation* 6:118–133.

Mack, R.N., and S.K. Forster. 2009. Eradicating plant invaders: combining ecologically-based tactics and broad-sense strategy. pp. 35–60 in Inderjit (ed.) *Management of invasive weeds*. Springer.

McNeely, J.A., H.A. Mooney, L.E. Neville, P. Schei, and J.K. Waage (ed.). 2001. *A global strategy on invasive alien species.* IUCN Gland, Switzerland and Cambridge, UK.

Muñoz, E.A. 1989. *Control experimental de la rata negra (*Rattus rattus*) en la zona de anidación de los Galápagos (*Geochelone elephantopus*). Isla Pinzón.* Undergraduate thesis, Universidad de Cuenca, Cuenca.

Panetta, F.D. 2009. Seed persistence of the invasive aquatic plant, *Gymnocoronis spilanthoides* (Asteraceae). *Australian Journal of Botany* 57:1–5.

Panetta, F.D., and S.M. Timmins. 2004. Evaluating the feasibility of eradication for terrestrial weed incursions. *Plant Protection Quarterly* 19:5–11.

Parker, P.G. 2009. *2005–2009 Survey for Galapagos Hawks (*Buteo galapagoensis*) on Islas Santiago and Española, Galapagos, Ecuador*. University of Missouri–St. Louis and Saint Louis Zoo, St Louis.

Phillips, R.B., B.D. Cooke, K. Campbell, V. Carrion, C. Marquez, and H.L. Snell. 2005. Eradicating feral cats to protect Galapagos land iguanas: methods and strategies. *Pacific Conservation Biology* 11:57–66.

Snell, H. M., P. A. Stone, and H. L. Snell. 1996. A summary of geographical characteristics of the Galápagos Islands, *Journal of Biogeography* 23:619–624.

Snell, H.L., A. Tye, C.E. Causton, and R. Bensted-Smith. 2002. Current status and threats to the terrestrial biodiversity of Galápagos. pp. 30–47 in R. Bensted-Smith (ed.) *A biodiversity vision for the Galapágos Islands*. Charles Darwin Foundation and World Wildlife Fund, Puerto Ayora.

Trueman, M. 2008. *Minimising the risk of invasion into the Galapagos National Park by introduced plants from the inhabited areas of the Galapagos Islands*, MSc thesis, Charles Darwin University, Darwin.

Trueman, M., R. Atkinson, and A. Guézou. in press. Residence time and human-induced propagule pressure at work in the alien flora of Galapagos. *Biological Invasions*.

Tye, A. 2007a. Cost of rapid-response eradication of a recently introduced plant, tropical kudzu (*Pueraria phaseoloides*), from Santa Cruz Island, Galapagos. *Plant Protection Quarterly* 22:33–34.

Tye, A. 2007b. The status of the endemic flora of Galapagos: the number of threatened species is increasing. Pages 97–103 in L. Cayot, editor. *Galapagos Report 2006–2007*. Charles Darwin Foundation, Galapagos National Park and INGALA, Puerto Ayora, Galapagos, Ecuador.

Watson, J., M. Trueman, M. Tufet, S. Henderson, and R. Atkinson. 2009. Mapping terrestrial anthropogenic degradation on the inhabited islands of the Galápagos archipelago. *Oryx* 44:79–82.

Zavaleta, E.S., R.J. Hobbs, and H.A. Mooney. 2001. Viewing invasive species removal in a whole-ecosystem context. *Trends in Ecology and Evolution* 16:454–459.

13 Food web structure of the Galápagos Marine Reserve after a decade of protection

Insights from trophic modeling

Matthias Wolff, Cesar Peñaherrera-Palma and Annika Krutwa

Introduction

The Galápagos Islands and their surrounding large marine reserve are world-renowned for their unique biological diversity, as a natural laboratory of evolution and speciation, and as a major stimulus to Darwin's Theory of Natural Selection. The archipelago represents the top of eroded volcanoes that surfaced the ocean 4–5 million years ago, but with a geological history of more than 10–15 million years (Christie *et al.* 1992; Mitchell and Reading 1969).

Different ocean currents and water masses converge around the archipelago, providing a unique and complex oceanographic setting. This is reflected in characteristic coastal biogeographic zones, a rich diversity of habitats, and a flora and fauna with an exceptionally high percentage of endemics both on land and in the sea (Edgar *et al.* 2004). Over 95% of its original species composition remains extant (Watkins and Cruz 2007), mostly due to the late arrival of humans and to the archipelago's inhospitable conditions, which discouraged rapid population expansion in early colonization days. As a UNESCO World Heritage Site and Biosphere Reserve, it is of exceptional value as the most ecologically intact large, complex, and diverse oceanic archipelago remaining today.

The open waters surrounding Galápagos were subjected to heavy industrial fishery from the 1930s onwards. The main target species were tuna, with catches that ranged from 412 tonnes in 1933 to more than 23,00 tonnes in 1940 (Shimada and Schaefer 1956), but also many bait species, like sardines and salemas, were heavily exploited (IATTC 1956, 1960, 1961, 1963). During the period 1995–1997, about 16 industrial fishing boats were operating and catching around 40,000 tonnes of yellowfin, bigeye, and skipjack tuna (Bustamante 1999). Industrial fishing was banned in 1998 with the declaratory of the Special Law for Galápagos (SLG) and the creation of the Galápagos Marine Reserve (GMR). This law allows only artisanal fishing with locally based, small boats and simple gear. Since then, fin fish catches have decreased greatly in the GMR to a few tens of tonnes annually.

In the first years following the SLG, local fishermen were mainly exploiting benthic lobsters and sea cucumbers to lucrative export markets. However, owing to the current overexploited state of these benthic fisheries (Hearn 2008; Castrejón 2008), fin fishery is regaining importance in the GMR and fishermen are strongly interested in its further development. At the moment the artisanal pelagic fishery targets mainly yellowfin tuna and wahoo using mainly speed pulled hand lines, as well as oceanic hand lines with several hooks at their ends (Peñaherrera, 2007). Fixed Fish Attracting Devices (FADs) are experimentally used to aggregate large pelagic fish near the shore to enable higher catch rates. Long lines were also suggested as an alternative to enhance catch rates (after their use was banned in 1998), but records from "experimental fishing" performed inside the GMR revealed a high by-catch of sharks and sea turtles that served as a basis for its final prohibition (Murillo *et al.* 2004).

Over the last decades, management in the GMR has mainly been focused on the benthic target species with emphasis on population monitoring and single-species stock assessments (Coello 1989; Granda 1995; Nicolaides *et al.* 2002). Recently, the other fisheries within the GMR were described by Peñaherrera (2007) and Castrejón (2008), clearly showing the great need for further assessment. An ecosystem approach to fisheries management in the GMR has been advocated by the Charles Darwin Foundation (CDF) and the Galápagos National Park for some time (PNG 2005), to consider the trophic interrelations between the fishery resources and the other ecosystem compartments and to explicitly incorporate the effects of fisheries exploitation on the system. A first step into this direction was a risk assessment of the demersal fishery, conducted by Peñaherrera and Hearn (2008).

The complex and large open ocean ecosystem of the GMR is part of the Eastern Tropical Pacific (ETP), which contains some of the most productive waters of the world's oceans (Barber and Chavez 1986). The top levels of the pelagic food web comprise several toothed and baleen whales, dolphins, large tunas, sharks, billfishes, and other species. Outside the GMR, many of these predators are still targeted by, or are by-catches of large international fisheries. Data from these fisheries are the principal sources of information about the pelagic ecosystem and provided the basis for modeling the trophic interactions of the large ETP ecosystem (Olson and Watters 2003).

The objectives of this chapter are to: (1) construct a trophic model of the state of the GMR Pelagic Ecosystem during the decade of 1990s prior to the banning of the industrial fishery in 1998 in order to (a) identify the main functional groups of the GMR and their biological elements and to integrate the available ecological and fishing information of this system, (b) provide an integrated holistic description of the energy flows among the different groups identified, (c) to compare statistics of the flow structure of the GMR with those of other tropical systems to identify the particularities of the GMR, and (d) to identify keystone groups of the system and to explore their relative impact on the system; (2) use catch reports from the time prior to 1998 and thereafter to simulate ecosystem changes following the substantial changes from an industrial fishery for large pelagic fish to an exclusive artisanal small-scale multi-species fishery after 1998; (3) use published data on the decrease in primary production in the GMR during the strong El Niño event 1997–1998 to simulate ecosystem response to these changes and to compare simulated changes with observed population changes during this event reported in the literature (i.e. Valle *et al.* 1987).

We hypothesized that 12 years of banning of industrial fishing in the GMR should have induced visible changes to the ecosystem trophic structure, especially when an El Niño warming event hit GMR immediately after its closure to industrial fisheries. Top predatory groups (like sharks, tuna, and other pelagic fish) and most of their prey species are largely protected and should be more abundant than elsewhere in the ETP, where heavy industrial fishing is still going on.

Material and methods

Brief oceanographic description of the Galápagos Marine Reserve

The GMR and our model area covers approximately 138,000 km^2 circumscribed by 1°N–2°S, 90–92°W (Figure 13.1). It is comprised of an insular shelf area, where the main islands are surrounded by deep oceanic waters (>2,000 m) and several sea mounts in the south, east and north areas, some of which are emergent as small islands such as Wolf and Darwin (Figure 13.1).

The Galápagos climate and oceanography is shaped mainly by the influence of the warm Panama and cold Humboldt currents, coming from the northeast and southeast, respectively (Banks 2002). Primary productivity, in contrast, is driven mainly by nutrient supply from the Equatorial Upwelling (EU) and "topographic upwelling" where the Equatorial Undercurrent (EUC) collides with the archipelago on its western margin (Chavez and Brusca 1991). The resulting mixing causes a drop in temperature in near surface waters and greatly elevates macronutrient concentrations (Pennington *et al.* 2006). As a consequence,

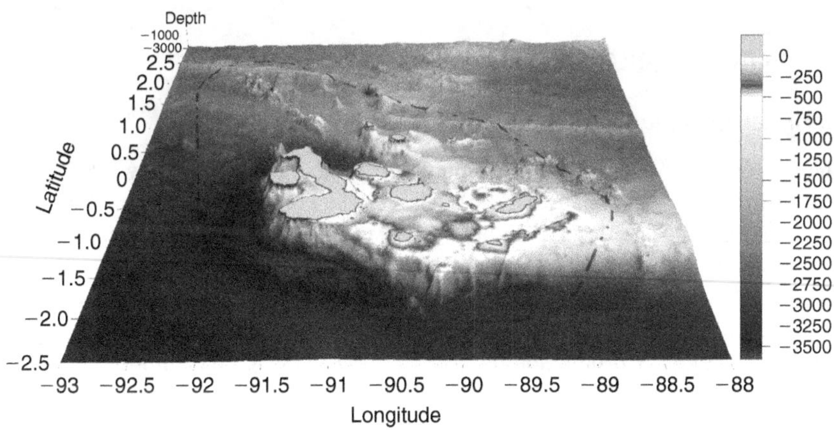

Figure 13.1 Illustrative third-dimensional map of the bathymetry and extension of the Galápagos Marine Reserve (depths are exaggerated four times for illustrative purpose) (source: CDF/NASA).

phytoplankton biomass and primary production are about twice as high as in the remainder EUC region or in any open ocean regions, except for the Pacific Central Upwelling. Although the EUC region in general is dominated by small solitary cells characteristic of the subtropical gyre (Chavez *et al.* 1998), diatoms and other large phytoplankton cells are important contributors to the Galápagos productivity (Pennington *et al.* 2006).

The resulting oceanographic setting in Galápagos allowed scientist to recognize five distinct biogeographic regions (Edgar *et al.* 2004). These, mainly based on benthic and invertebrate surveys, are congruent with marine currents influence on the archipelago. Nevertheless, partitioning the open water environment into several regions corresponding to Edgar and co-authors' work would create a problem in adequately representing pelagic animals and their mobility range. Several of the species and functional groups move between zones, but there is no information on the amount of time or on the amount of energy these animals consume in each province.

El Niño affects Galápagos and the EUC region by weakening or reversing easterly trade winds, deepening the thermocline, weakening the South Equatorial Current, and weakening or causing the disappearance of the EUC. Most important to biological production is the thermocline deepening and disappearance of the EUC, which result in substantial decreases in euphotic zone nutrient supply (Barber and Chavez 1983). Subsequently, nutrient limitation leads to shifts in the phytoplankton community, from larger diatoms to picoplankton species more typical of open ocean areas (cyanobacteria and prochlorophytes; Chavez 2005). Warm water species, such as rare and solitary oceanic dinoflagellates, are moved onshore and polewards into the normally productive near-shore environments (Avarıa and Muñoz 1987; Ochoa and Gomez 1987). These changes disrupt food webs and lead to death or emigration of higher trophic level animals dependent on phytoplankton production (Chavez 2005, and references therein).

The modeling approach

Construction of the Ecopath model

The basic model was constructed using the Ecopath module of the EwE 6.0 software (Christensen and Walters 2004), which is based on two equations for each functional group: one describing how ingested food is divided into respiration, non-assimilated food, and production; and the other dividing the biomass production of each group into fractions leading to predators, the fishery, and non-predatory losses. Required input for each functional group are wet weight biomass (*B*, $t \cdot km^{-2}$), production/biomass ratio (*P/B*, y^{-1}), consumption/biomass ratio (*Q/B*, y^{-1}), catch (*C*, $t \cdot km^{-2} \cdot y^{-1}$), and diet composition (*DC*). Unknown parameters (*B*, *P/B*, *Q/B*, or *EE*) are estimated when solving the system of linear equations (for more details see Christensen and Walters 2004).

Our final version of the model (GMR) had 34 model groups (Table 13.1), comprising emblematic species such as sharks, penguins and flightless cormorants, principal exploited species and their main prey, sea turtles, marine mammals and other seabirds, as well as several phytoplankton and zooplankton groups. Since sharks, dolphins, and tuna are often observed to feed in productive near-shore areas where they overlap with semi-demersal grouper and other demersal fish, a "benthic fish" group was also included in our model. Some taxa were segregated into size group components because of considerable changes in trophic ontogeny, resulting in their inclusion in different prey components of the model during their life history. In defining the model components, we grouped taxa on similarity of size, food, and predators. When only little information was available for some taxa, we lumped similar taxa into functional groups (e.g. scombrids and other small pelagic predators). Ecotrophic efficiency ($0<EE<1$) and gross efficiency ($0<GE<0.35$) served as constraints for balancing the model. During the balancing procedure the biomass of the small pelagic, mesopelagic, and cephalopod groups had to be increased to satisfy the food requirements of their predators.

Ecosystem summary statistics and network indicators

We computed several summary statistics and network indicators as explained in the result and discussion section (see Table 13.2)

Using Ecosim to simulate system impacts due to changes in fishing and oceanographic conditions (El Niño)

In Ecosim, the biomass dynamics of all ecosystem components that occupy trophic levels higher than 1.0 are determined by:

$$\frac{\partial B_i}{\partial t} = g_i \sum_{j-1}^{k} c_{ji}(B_i, B_j) - M_i B_i - F_i B_i - \sum_{j-1}^{k} c_{ij}(B_i, B_j) \tag{1}$$

The change in biomass of component i (B_i) per unit time (t) equals biomass accumulation less three types of losses. Biomass accumulation is the sum of the predation by component i on its prey (indexed by j) multiplied by the gross efficiency gi of component i. The function c_{ji} (B_i,B_j) predicts the consumption of component j by component i from their respective biomasses (see Walters *et al.* 1997 for the details of this function). Losses are from non-predation natural mortality (M_i), fishing mortality (F_i), and the consumption of component i by its predators. In Ecosim, the biomass of component i that is vulnerable to predation by component j (V_{ij}) is a function of a vulnerability rate (v).

$$\frac{\partial V_{ij}}{\partial t} = v(B_i - V_{ij}) - vV_{ij} - a_{ij}V_{ij}B_{ij} \tag{2}$$

where a_{ij} is the effective rate at which predator j searches for prey i. The vulnerable biomass increases from exchange with a pool of invulnerable biomass, v ($B_i - V_{ij}$), and decreases when prey return to the invulnerable condition (vV_{ij}) or

Table 13.1 Description of the final groups for the GMR model and their elements

No	*Group*	*Elements*
1	Boobies, frigates and others	Frigate birds, boobies, terns, shearwaters, petrels.
2	Cormorants and penguins	*Phalacrocorax harrisi* and *Spheniscus mendiculus*.
3	Sea turtles	*Chelonia mydas, Eretmochelys imbricata, Lepidochelys olivácea* and *Dermochelys coriacea.*
4	Sea lions and seals	*Zalophus wollebaeki* and *Arctochepalus galagoensis*
5	Dolphins	Common dolphins, Bottlenose dolphins, *Stenella* spp, pilot whales.
6	Sperm whales	Sperm whales and dwarf sperm whales.
7	Killer whales	*Orcinus orca*, *Pseudorca crassidens* and pilot whales
8	Baleen whales	*Balaenoptera musculus*, *B. edeni* and *B. borealis*
9	Large zooplankton feeders	*Manta birostris, Mobula munkiana, Rhincodon typus*
10	Juvenile sharks	Juveniles of black tip, white tip, Galápagos and hammerhead sharks
11	Benthopelagic sharks	Galápagos sharks (*Carcharhinus galapagensis*), tiger sharks (*Galeocerdo cuvier*), silver tip (*C. albimarginatus*) and black tip sharks (*C limbatus*)
12	Large pelagic sharks	Blue (*Prionace glauca*), threashers (*Alopias vulpinus*, *A. pelagicus*), mako (*Isurus oxirhincus*, *I. paucas*), oceanic sharks (*Carcharhinus longimanus*) and silky sharks (*C. falciformis*)
13	Hammerhead sharks	Primary *Sphyrna lewini*
14	Marlins	*Makaira* spp. and *Tetrapturus audax*
15	Swordfish	*Xiphias gladius*
16	Sailfish	*Istiophorus platypterus*
17	Wahoo	*Acathocybium solandri*
18	Dorado/Dolphinfish	*Coryphaena hypurus*

19	Thunnus spp.	*Thunnus albacares* and *T. obesus*
20	Benthic fish	Primary: Serranid spp. and Labridae spp.
21	Small benthopelagic fishes	Haemulidae (*Anisostremus interruptus*, *Haemulon scudderii*, *Xenichthys agassizi*, *Xenocys jessiae*), mullets, Lujanidae spp., *Paranthias colonus, Caulolatilus affinis* and *C. princeps*, *Mulloidichthys dentatus*, Sparidae spp. and rays
22	Small pelagic fishes	Clupeidae, Nomeidae, Balistidae, Ostraciidae, Tetraodontidae, Diondontidae, Engraulidae, pelagic Mugillidae, Carangidae (*Trachinotus stilbe* and *Alectis ciliaris*), *Chanos chanos*, pelagic mullets, flying fishes (Exocoetidae spp.)
23	Small pelagic predator	*Scomberomonus sierra, Auxis rochei, Katsuwomus pelamis, Euthyneus lineatus, Scomber japonicus, Sarda orientalis*, jacks (*C. lugubris, C. sexfasciatus, C. caninus*), *Elagatis bipinnulata*, *Seriola peruna*, *S. rivoliana. Sphyraena idiastes, Lepidocibyum flavobrunneum* (Gempylidae), juvenile tunas (*Thunnus alalunga, T. obesus* and *T albacares*) and juvenile of billfishes (Istiphorid and Xiphiidae spp.)
24	Mesopelagic fishes	Primary: Phosichthydae, Myctophidae
25	Macrobenthos	Crustaceans, sea cucumbers, sea stars, bivalves
26	Cephalopods	Octopuses and squids
27	Gelatinous plankton	Primary: Siphonophores, hidromedusa, scyphomedusa, tunicates and apendicularia
28	Pelagic decapods	Penaeoidae,Caridae
29	Mesozooplankton (copepods) (2000 μm)	Euphausids, Chaetognaths, Ostracods Copepods
30	Microzooplankton (<200 μm)	Flagellates, Ciliates, other
31	Macrophytes	Macrocystis spp. Sargassum spp. Ulva. spp.
32	Dino- and silicoflagellates	Several species
33	Diatoms	Several species
34	Detritus	

Table 13.2 Summary statistics computed for the GMR Model

Name of index	*Meaning*	*Value*
Finn's Cycling index	Fraction of an ecosystem's throughput that is recycled	**8.12**
Predatory cycling index	Corresponds to the cycling index but excluding detritus groups	**2.35**
Connectance index	The ratio of the number of actual links to the number of possible links. Feeding on detritus (by detritivores) is included in the count, but the opposite links (i.e. detritus "feeding" on other groups) are disregarded	**0.1772268**
System omnivory index	The average omnivory index of all consumers weighted by the logarithm of each consumer's food intake. It is a measure of how the feeding interactions are distributed between trophic levels. An omnivory index is also calculated for each consumer group, which is a measure of the variance of the trophic level estimate for the group	**0.1956564**
Trophic transfer efficiencies (TE)	Calculated for a given trophic level as the ratio between the sum of the exports plus the flow that is transferred from one trophic level to the next, and the throughput on the trophic level. The transfer efficiencies are used for construction of trophic pyramids, and others.	**11.5%**
Primary production required (PPR)/catch	To estimate the PPR to sustain the catches and the consumption by the trophic groups in an ecosystem all cycles are removed from the diet compositions, and all pathways in the flow network are identified using the method suggested by Ulanowicz (1995). For each pathway the flows are then raised to primary production equivalents using the product of the catch, the Q/P ratio of each path element times the proportion the next element of the path contributes to the diet of the given path element.	**4381.77**
Ascendency (A)	EwE includes a number of indices related to the ascendency measure described in detail by Ulanowicz (1986). Ascendency is seen as a measure of ecosystem growth and development.	**25.1%**
Gross efficiency of the fishery	Denotes the relation of fish catch to net primary production; usually decreases with the trophic level of the resource.	**0.00243%**
Mean trophic level of catch	Derived from the trophic level of all resources.	**3.848**
Total system throughput	Sumo of all flows; considered a measure for system size.	**10061.05**
Total biomass	Sumo of biomass of all system compartments (excluding detritus).	**33.1** (tonnes km^{-2})
Total catches	Sumo o all catches.	**0.09078** (tonnes km^{-2} $year^{-1}$)
PP/R	Total production over total respiration.	**2474.723**

by predation ($a_{ij}V_{ij}B_j$). When v is small, the flows between predators and prey are controlled mostly by variations in prey biomass, i.e. control is bottom-up. When v is large, these flows are controlled mostly by variations in predator biomass, i.e. control is top-down. We used the default vulnerability value ($v = 2.0$), given in EwE, since longer time series of observed group biomass values were not available for applying the "vulnerability search routine" of EwE.

Simulations

We used our Ecopath base model (pre-1998) and decreased the fishing effort of the industrial fishery by 90% (allowing for 10% of clandestine fishery still operating in the GMR; Piu, 1998; Altamirano and Aguiñaga 2002). For the simulations we estimated for each species/group the lifetime fraction spend within the borders of the GMR (see Appendix 13.3), which was subtracted from the reference fishing mortality (F_{ref}) (prior to 1998) and the population response was simulated. In a second simulation, the reference model was subjected to the strong El Niño event of 1997–1998 by reducing primary productivity by 50% for a ten-month period (September–June) (Robinson and del Pino 1985; Schaeffer *et al.* 2008). In a third run, the combined effect of El Niño and the ban on industrial fishery (after 1997–1998) was explored, with emphasis on those groups considered emblematic for Galápagos, such as penguins and flightless cormorants, green sea turtles, marine mammals, swordfish, marlins, and sharks.

Data used

P/B and *Q/B* input values, as well as diet data, were gathered from diverse published and unpublished sources (Appendix 13.1). Catch values of the artisanal fishery were obtained from the participatory fishery monitoring database for the artisanal long line fishery catches (1998–2002), from Nicolaides *et al.* (2002), Castrejón (2008), and from data assembled by Bustamante (1999) for industrial tuna fishery prior to the year 1998.

For calculating phytoplankton biomass and production we used the following approach: first, we considered average surface water (<80 m) Chlorophyll a (Chla) concentration of 0.3–0.4 mg Chla m^{-3} as reported by Pennington *et al.* (2006) and then used the authors' mean depth integrated primary production of 642 mg C m^{-2} d^{-1}. Then, wet weight phytoplankton biomass and production was calculated using the following conversion factors from Brush *et al.* (2002): Chla – C (1:40) and C – wet weight biomass (1:14.25). Thus, phytoplankton biomass would be 13.7–18.2 g m^{-2} and production of about 3,339.2 g m^{-2} y^{-1} giving a range of an annual P/B rate of 183–243. These values were used as first input to our model.

Catches and biomasses for the resources of industrial fishery (tuna, swordfish, marlins, and sharks), were calculated as follows. First, catch values of Bustamante (1999) for yellowfin tuna caught within the GMR during the years 1995–1997 were used and an exploitation rate of $E = 0.5$ (full exploitation) was assumed to estimate biomass using Sekharam's formula (Sekharam 1974), by dividing annual yield (Y) by fishing mortality (F). Second, data of the artisanal long line fishery of the Galápagos (from 1998 to 2002) were used for estimating the percentage of the different groups of large pelagic fish and sharks landed during this period. Third, these percentages together with the reported tuna catch for the period 1995–1997 were used to extrapolate the catches of large fish and sharks during this period. Finally, we assumed strong but not full exploitation (E=0.3) for these groups and calculated their biomass using Sekharam's formula. The final input parameters used for the model are given in Table 13.3; the diet matrix is shown in Appendix 13.2.

Table 13.3 Input parameters for the balanced model

	Group name	*TL*	*B*	*P/B*	*Q/B*	*EE*	*P/Q*
1	Boobies, frigates, others	3.624	0.032	0.15	60	0.354	0.002
2	Cormorants and penguins	3.790	0.001	0.2	50	0.960	0.004
3	Sea turtles	2.184	0.043	0.15	3.5	0.965	0.043
4	Sea lions and seals	4.036	0.070	0.15	35	0.973	0.004
5	Dolphins	4.257	0.040	0.04	16.5	0.825	0.002
6	Sperm whales	4.494	0.024	0.02	6.8	0.917	0.003
7	Killer whales	4.703	0.002	0.02	11	0	0.009
8	Baleen whales	4.384	0.017	0.02	9.1	0.647	0.002
9	Mantas and whale sharks	3.427	0.025	0.1	7	0.958	0.014
10	Juvenile sharks	3.718	0.017	0.5	6	0.984	0.083
11	Benthopelagic sharks	4.176	0.013	0.25	4	0.761	0.062
12	Large pelagic sharks	4.742	0.012	0.2	3	0.489	0.067
13	Hammerhead sharks	4.440	0.016	0.15	3	0.698	0.050
14	Marlins	4.222	0.003	1	7.8	0.678	0.128
15	Swordfish	4.511	0.015	0.44	7.8	0.406	0.056
16	Sailfish	4.632	0.011	1.15	8	0.779	0.144
17	Wahoo	4.092	0.014	1.7	10	0.475	0.170
18	Dolphinfish	3.897	0.031	1.2	21.9	0.394	0.055
19	*Thunnus* spp.	4.034	0.065	0.95	12	0.900	0.079
20	Benthic fish	2.775	0.550	1	3.5	0.988	0.286
21	Jacks and other small benthopelagic fishes	3.571	0.380	1.4	4	0.956	0.350
22	Small pelagic fishes	2.502	1	7	18	0.673	0.389
23	Scombrids and other small pelagic predators	3.665	0.660	1.35	5	0.996	0.270
24	Mesopelagic fish	3.256	1.100	1.4	14	0.979	0.100
25	Macrobenthos	2	1	1.5	7	0.978	0.214
26	Cephalopods	3.697	0.450	4.3	12	0.928	0.358
27	Gelatinous plankton	2.839	1.600	3	100	0.416	0.030
28	Pelagic decapods	2.432	2.800	19.1	80	0.965	0.239
29	Copepods	2.105	5	35	200	0.754	0.175
30	Microzooplankton	2.053	3	200	800	0.443	0.250
31	Benthic macroalgae	1	0.11	18	0	0.921	0.002
32	Dinoflagelates	1	7	260	0	0.578	0.004
33	Diatoms	1	8	240	0	0.712	0.043
34	Detritus	1	0.1			0.388	0.004

Mixed trophic impact (MTI): sensitivity of model groups

The MTI routine implemented in Ecopath is based on an approach of Ulanowicz and Puccia (1990) built on the concept of the Leontief matrix originally created to assess the direct and indirect interactions in the economy of the USA. In Ecopath, the routine assesses the effect that changes in the biomass of a group will have on the biomass of the other groups in a system. In this sense, it is a form of a sensitivity analysis, allowing the identification of those groups for which slight changes in biomass greatly impact other groups of the system. When calculating the host compositions the fishing fleets are included as "predators". In the visual presentation of the MTI results (Figure 13.3) the black circles indicate positive impacts, while the open circles show negative impacts. The impacts are relative, but comparable between groups.

Results and discussion

General system properties: the GMR prior to 1998

System biomass is dominated by trophic levels one and two, with the groups of *phytoplankton*, *zooplankton*, and *macrobenthos* dominating (Figure 13.2). Significant biomass is also accumulated around trophic level 3, with small pelagic and mesopelagic fish, gelatinous plankton, and benthic fish representing the prominent groups. Energy from these groups is distributed to *birds*, *mammals*,

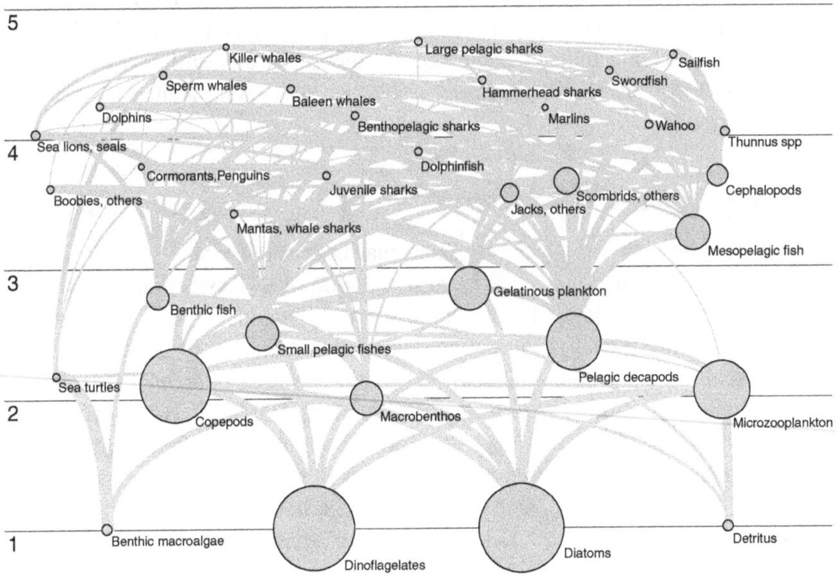

Figure 13.2 Flowchart of the GMR model (pre-1998); size of circles are scaled to group biomass and width of linkages are scaled to the amount of flow; trophic level is given on the y-axis.

large pelagic bony fish, and *shark* groups, for which biomass pools are smaller. However, overall biomass of high trophic level groups (TL>4.0) is with 0.33 tonnes km^{-2} still quite high representing 6.5% of overall system biomass (excluding *plankton* groups).

The summary statistics given in Table 13.2 describe a system, which in terms of size (throughput, *T*) lies between eastern boundary upwelling and open ocean or shelf systems (Christensen and Pauly 1993; Taylor and Wolff 2007; Wolff *et al.* 1996; Wolff *et al.* 1998). It is interesting to note that during the strong El Niño event of 1997–1998 *T* dropped by 58.7% for the Humboldt Current system (HCS), where upwelling was greatly reduced (Tam *et al.* 2008). Our estimated 50% reduction in primary production alone reduces *T* by about 30%, suggesting that the El Niño effect on the GMR was comparable. Gross efficiency of the fishery is with 0.0024% about two orders of magnitude lower than for the HCS and the mean trophic level of the catch with 3.85 about one step higher. This is also reflected in the low overall catch volumes in the GMR (0.09 tonnes km^{-2} y^{-1}), which lie between average catches of oceanic and shelf systems (Christensen 1996). Olsen and Watters (2003) found catch and biomass values for their large ETP Model to be six and three times lower than the values for the GMR model, which indicates that the GMR is significantly more productive and biomass rich than the surrounding open ocean. The PPR:catch ratio is very high when compared to upwelling or other coastal regions, where catches are one to two orders of magnitude higher and the PPR:catch ratio is significantly lower. The transfer efficiency (11.5%) is near the average reported for aquatic systems in the literature (Christensen and Pauly 1993) and at the high end for eastern boundary systems, where most reported values are <10% (Taylor and Wolff 2007). The values for the cycling indices calculated for the GMR are similar (<±10%) to those reported for the HCS by Tam *et al.* (2008), suggesting a similar coupling of trophic groups.

Most sensitive groups

The MTI analysis (Figure 13.3) revealed that both tooth whale groups (*sperm whales* and *killer whales*) have the highest potential overall system impact owing to their role as warm-blooded top predators with high consumption rates, which prey upon a great diversity of prey, including fish, mammals, birds, reptiles, and invertebrates. Small annual changes in biomass can thus be expected to cause important changes in these prey groups. A biomass change of *small pelagic fish* and *cephalopods* as well as *pelagic decapods*, *scombrids* and *Thunnus* spp. also causes higher than average system impact due to their central role as prey of mammals, several bony fish, sharks, and birds. Predation mortality is very high on these groups and a small reduction in their stock sizes (e.g. as observed through the El Niño impact, see discussion below) may greatly affect their predators.

Figure 13.3 also reveals those groups to be most susceptible to any change occurring on other groups of the system (sum of the circles in the vertical plain

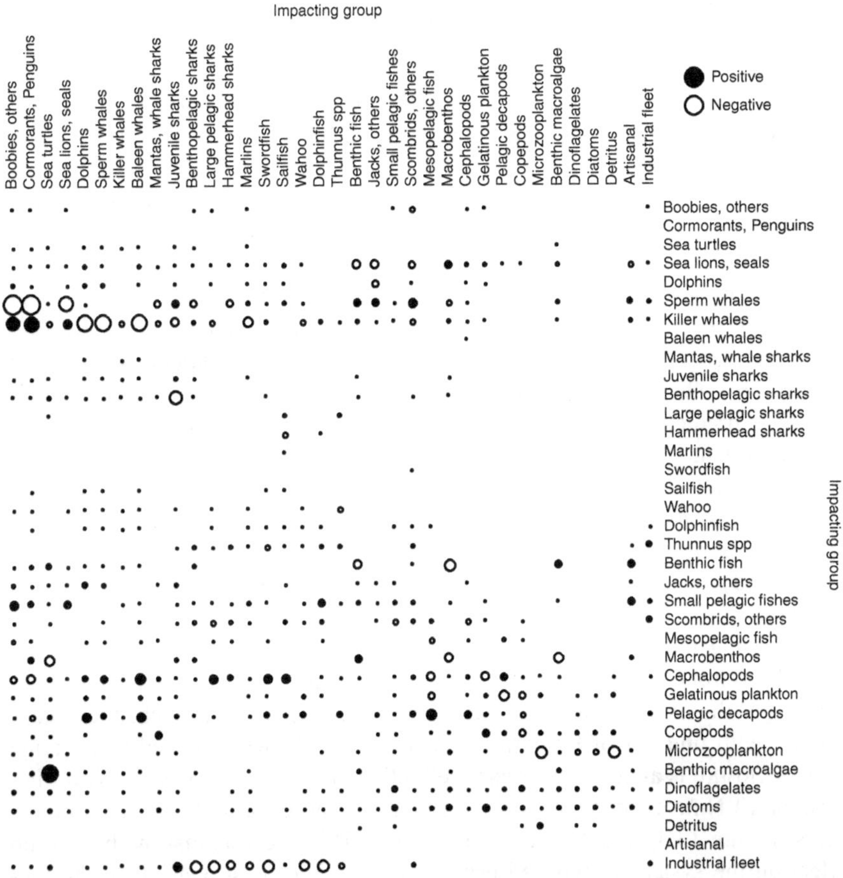

Figure 13.3 Mixed trophic impact analysis showing the impact of each model group over the other groups in the ecosystem.

of Figure 13.3). These are, in rank order, *cormorants and penguins*, *sea turtles*, *juvenile sharks*, *baleen whales*, *dolphins* and *sperm whales*. Their susceptibility to changes can be explained mainly by their small population sizes (in the case of *cormorants and penguins*), their control by *killer whales* and different sharks (all groups), and their large food requirements of *cephalopods* and *small pelagic fish* (in the case of whales and dolphins), which they share with many other species.

Effect of El Niño and the ban of the fishery

Our simulations revealed a strong El Niño impact on all groups; the effect of the reduced primary production clearly cascades up the food web to the high trophic levels. While we do not have biomass time series for the period 1997–2010 for the bony fish and shark groups of our model, there are published series from the CDF monitoring for *penguins and cormorants*, *sea lions and seals* and marine reptiles, which include the 1997 event (some data even extend to the 1983 El Niño). The *penguins and cormorants* monitoring data show great reductions in population numbers during the El Niño events of 1982–1983 and 1997–1998. Valle-Castillo (1985) reports decreases of 45% and 78% for *cormorants and penguins* respectively during the 1982–1983 El Niño, and during the 1997–1998 El Niño reported population reductions were similar (Vargas *et al.* 2005). The model simulations showed a substantial reduction in stock size, which strongly suggests that an El Niño-induced food shortage was the main reason for the increased mortalities within both populations (Valle-Castillo 1985; Vargas *et al.* 2005). *Sea turtle and marine iguana* populations decreased during the 1997–1998 El Niño (unpublished CDF monitoring data) and this was also predicted by our model simulations. A similar decrease was also reported for the 1982–1983 El Niño by Laurie (1985), who attributed it to the great reduction of macroalgae, which form the basis of the reptilian food chain. The marine seals and sea lions monitoring time series also show a significant decrease during the El Niño event of 1997–1998 (by as much as 50%; Salazar 2002–2003), which is, but to a lesser extent, also suggested by our model simulations.

According to our simulations, most large pelagic fish would have – under normal environmental conditions – attained 10–20% stock increase only two years after the fishery ban (Figure 13.4, upper graph). This rapid change is concordant with findings of Halpern and Warner (2002), who showed that marine reserve closure is almost immediately effective in less than two years. Nevertheless, the El Niño event suppressed this rapid response for a further two to three years (Figure 13.4, middle and lower graphs). This suggests that the bottom-up effect on the system of reduced primary productivity is stronger than the top-down effect from the release of fishing pressure. The first predicted to surpass the pre- El Niño reference level is the tuna, followed by *wahoo*, *dolphin fish* and *sailfish*. Due to their slow turnover, sharks follow later. *Juvenile sharks* are predicted to maintain reduced biomass throughout the time due to strong control by increased top predator. *Sea lions*, *cormorants and penguins*, and *sea turtles* needed the whole period of 12 years to rebuild their populations. It is interesting to note that the disruption of the system by the El Niño impact led in the medium term (3–9 years), to higher biomasses of large pelagic fish predators, than occurred under the same fishery conditions without the El Niño impact. It thus seems that since predator biomass is reduced during the El Niño, prey populations find an "open loophole" (Bakun and Weeks 2008) to proliferate first and are then followed by their predators in a Lotka–Volterra fashion. It then takes several years for the system to normalize.

The predicted biomass increase over the 12 years period following the fishery ban for the large pelagic fish and sharks is very substantial and was based on our estimates of residence times for the different species (Appendix 13.3). Since

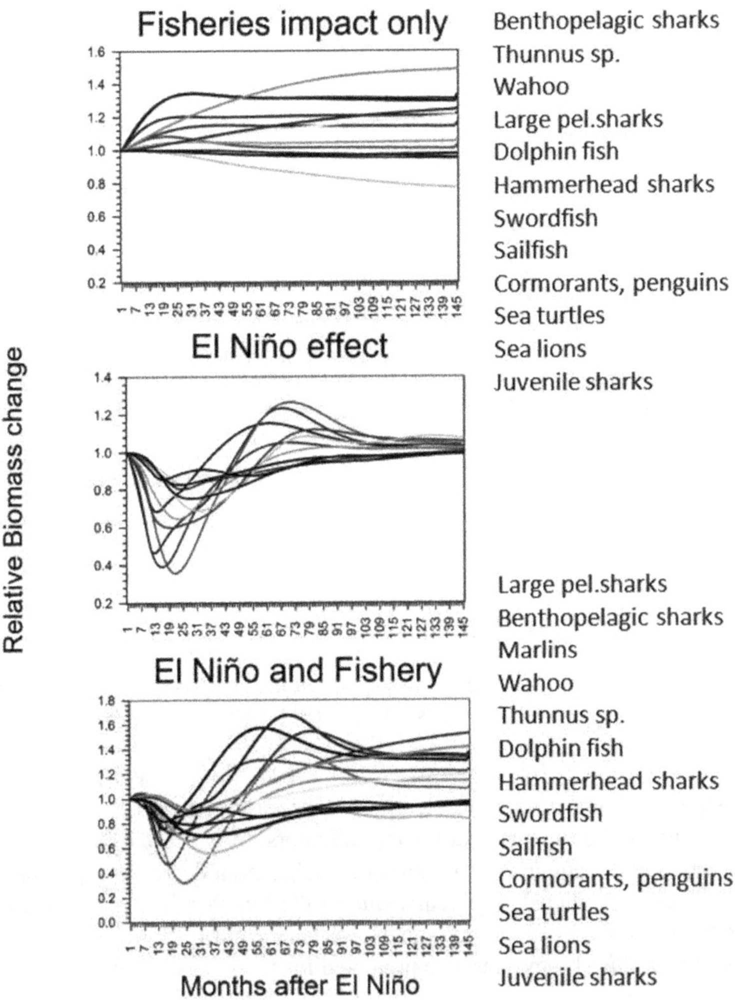

Figure 13.4 Effect of environmental factors on marine species populations. Effects of fishery ban (upper graph), El Niño impact (middle graph) and the combination of El Niño and the reduction in fishery (lower graph) on the different groups of sharks, large pelagic fish and sea lions, cormorants and penguins, and sea turtles.

these estimates were derived from only a few observational data, we explored the effect of different residence times on the biomass changes of the resource groups (Figure 13.5). It is seen that even at lower than assumed values the predicted biomass increase is still substantial for most groups.

The model predicts no substantial changes for the *benthic fish*, *jacks*, and *small pelagics* groups after the closure of the fishery, which indicates that the

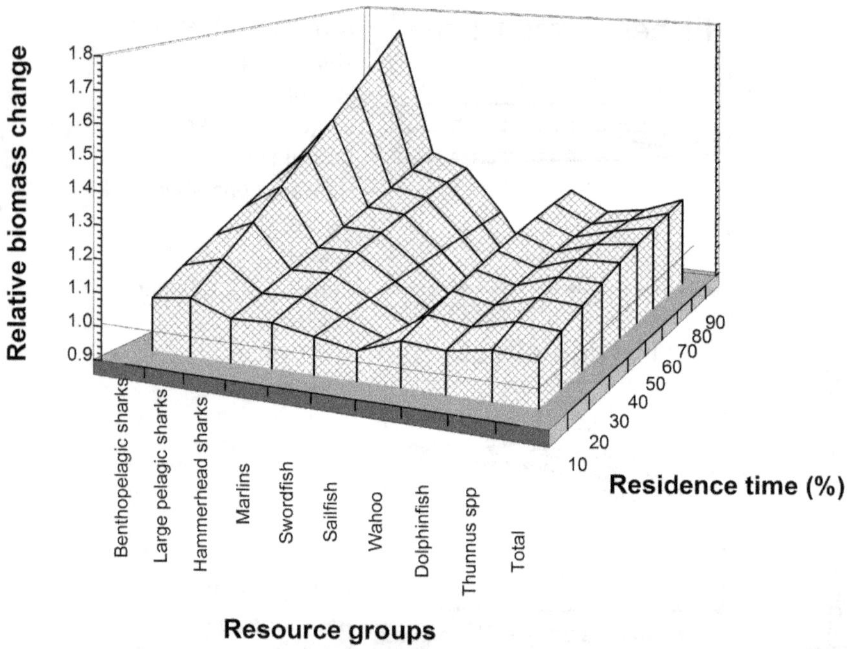

Figure 13.5 Biomass increase over the 12 year period following the ban on industrial fishery as a function of residence time (RT) of resources in the GMR.

release in fishing pressure is compensated by the increase in predation on these groups through population increase of the top predators. In the case of the *scombrids* and other *small pelagic predators* groups, a substantial decrease in population biomass is even predicted, apparently due to the biomass increase of their predators, which remove more biomass than the fishery did prior to the ban. A small decrease in *sailfish* biomass is also predicted for the same reason.

Caveats and future directions of research

The model and simulations presented here should be considered as a first step towards the description of the flow structure and processes that drive the large pelagic system of the GMR. Since we did not have a reliable biomass time series to fit our simulations to observed data, we chose to work with assumptions and scenario explorations.

One of our fundamental assumptions based on different literature sources was that the primary productivity was decreased by about 50% during a ten-month El Niño period. Since the correctness of this assumption is difficult to prove, we evaluated (not shown here) how other combinations of length and magnitude of reduction in primary productivity (30–70%; 8–12 months) would affect the outcome of our simulations and found that the general tendencies of model outputs were quite insensitive to the different combinations. Another assumption was that the fishing ban reduced the impact of industrial fishery in the GMR by 90%, allowing 10% of clandestine fishery to still operate after 1998 (Altamirano and Aguiñaga, 2002; Reyes and Murillo 2007). According to Altamirano and Aguiñaga (2002), the operation of industrial fishery slowed gradually during the 1998 to mid-1999 period, with some boats illegally operating over the next years. It can be assumed that this gradual closure did not affect the final simulation much, however, since the El Niño effect was overriding the effect of the release in fishing pressure. Due to the lack of time series to be compared and fitted by our simulations, it was impossible to derive estimates of the vulnerability (v) parameter of Ecosim for the prey–predator relationships, which influence the simulated magnitude of biomass changes. Our use of the default value of $v=2$ for a situation of mixed control may thus have produced either too high or too low biomass changes. We think, however, that the general tendencies in biomass changes revealed by our simulations should still hold.

Our model simulations only captured trophic/prey–predator effects (including "predation" by the fishery) but other possible effects of the El Niño warming, such as enhancing reproductive activity of some species or reducing physiological fitness of others were not considered. The heavy rain fall during the El Niño event may have also impacted those groups that spend substantial time onshore to mate or breed such as *sea lions*, *turtles*, *penguins* and *cormorants*.

Conclusions

The GMR has, despite a 2–3 year system disruption caused by the 1997–1998 El Niño, undergone a substantial recovery process for large pelagic fish and sharks since the industrial fishery was banned 12 years ago. This may explain why large numbers of industrial fishing boats are constantly spotted at the borders of the GMR where, due to a spillover effect, catches seem to be higher than further away from the GMR (WildAid 2010). Our simulations suggest that it takes a no-industrial fishing period of 3–5 years for large pelagic fish and about a decade for large sharks before populations recover substantially. The very strong growth in dive tourism, which has been observed over the last years in the GMR, is a reflection of the healthy state of the system. The willingness to pay for a dive experience, which includes spotting hundreds of hammerhead sharks during a single dive as well as frequent encounters with whale sharks, is high and still increasing and has made the GMR a dive destination of immense value for the tourism industry.

Acknowledgements

We thank the Galápagos Conservation Trust (GCT) and Galápagos Conservancy (GC) for sponsoring this study

Appendices

Appendix 13.1 Literature sources used for the input parameters

No	*Group*	*Elements*	*Catches*	*Biomass in habitat area*	*P/B /year)*	*Q/B (year)*	*Ecotrophic efficiency*	*Diet*
1	Boobies, frigates and others	Frigate birds, boobies, terns, shearwaters, petrels	—	Population size: Gustavo Jiménez, pers. comm. (2009) and Individual weight: Tomkins and Milne 1991. *Pterodroma phaepygia*, around 20,000 in the GMR multiplied by 399 grams/indiviual = 7,980,000 g, 7.98 TM/138000 km^2 = 0.00005862 TM/Km2. Jiménez and Wiendfield 2002.	Olson and Watters 2003	Olson and Watters 2003		Castro and Phillips 1996.
2	Cormorants and penguins	*Phalacrocorax harrisi* and *Spheniscus mendiculus*	—	Estimated from Jiménez (2008) 2 kg/ adult individual. Sum of 0.000022 and 0.0003 estimated for penguins and cormorants				Castro and Phillips 1996; Vargas *et al.* 2006.
3	Sea turtles	Primary *Chelonia mydas*; Less considered, *Eretmochelys imbricata, Lepidochelys olivácea* and *Dermochelys coriacea*	—	Zarate and Dutton (2002) 90kg/adult females of mean size	Olson and Watters 2003	Olson and Watters 2003		Carrión *et al.* (unpublished).
4	Sea lions and seals	*Zalophus wollebaeki* and *Arctochepalus galagoensis*	—		Olson and Watters 2003	Olson and Watters 2003		Salazar 2005.
5	Dolphins	Common dolphins, Bottlenose dolphins, *Stenella* spp., pilot whales	—	Olson and Watters 2003	Olson and Watters 2003	Olson and Watters 2003		Pauly *et al.* 1998.
6	Sperm whales	Sperm whales and dwarf sperm whales	—	Olson and Watters 2003	Olson and Watters 2003	Olson and Watters 2003		Pauly *et al.* 1998.
7	Killer whales	*Orcinus orca*, *Pseudorca crassidens and* pilot whales	—	Olson and Watters 2003	Olson and Watters 2003	Olson and Watters 2003		Pauly *et al.* 1998.
8	Baleen whales	*Balaenoptera musculus*, *B. edeni* and *B. borealis*	—	Olson and Watters 2003	Olson and Watters 2003	Olson and Watters 2003		Pauly *et al.* 1998.

9	Large zooplankton feeders	*Manta birostris, Mobula munkiana, Rhincodon typus*	—					Notarbartolo-Di-Sciara 1998; Nelson and Eckert 2007; Ketchum *et al.* 2010.
10	Juvenile sharks	Juveniles of black tip, white tip, Galápagos and hammerhead sharks						
11	Benthopelagic sharks	Galápagos sharks (*Carcharhinus galapagensis*), tiger sharks (*Galeocerdo cuvier*), silver tip (*C. albimarginatus*) and black tip sharks (*C limbatus*)	Estimated from Castrejón and Moreno 2008; Murillo *et al.* 2004; and SPNG–FCD 2002		Olson and Watters 2003	Olson and Watters 2003		Papastamatiou *et al.* 2006.
12	Large pelagic sharks	Blue (*Prionace glauca*), threashers (*Alopias vulpinus, A. pelagicus*), mako (*Isurus oxirhincus, I. paucas*), oceanic sharks (*Carcharhinus longimanus*) and silky sharks (*C. falciformis*)	Estimated from Castrejón and Moreno (2008); Murillo *et al.* (2004); and SPNG–FCD 2002					Velasto 2005; Cedeño-Figueroa *et al.* 2007; Bocanegro 2007; Rendón-Macías *et al.* 2007
13	Hammerhead sharks	Primary *Sphyrna lewini*	Estimated from Castrejón and Moreno (2008); Murillo *et al.* (2004); and SPNG–FCD. 2002					Bolaño-Martínez and Galván-Magaña 2007; Castañeda-Suarez and Sandoval-Londoño 2007
14	Marlins	*Makaira* spp. and *Tetrapturus audax*			Olson and Watters 2003	Olson and Watters 2003		Abitía-Cardenas *et al.* 1999; Abitía-Cardenas *et al.* 2002; Bocanegro 2007
15	Swordfish	*Xiphias gladius*			Olson and Watters 2003	Olson and Watters,2003		

continued

Appendix 13.1 continued

No	*Group*	*Elements*	*Catches*	*Biomass in habitat area*	*P/B /year)*	*Q/B (year)*	*Ecotrophic efficiency*	*Diet*
16	Sailfish	*Istiophorus platypterus*			Olson and Watters 2003	Olson and Watters 2003		Rosas-Alayola 2002.
17	Wahoo	*Acathocybium solandri*	Estimated from Castrejón and Moreno (2008)		Olson and Watters 2003	Olson and Watters 2003		Bocanegro 2007
18	Dorado/ Dolphinfish	*Coryphaena hypurus*	Estimated from Castrejón and Moreno (2008); Murillo *et al.* (2004); and SPNG–FCD. 2002		Olson and Watters 2003	Olson and Watters 2003		Olson and Galvan-Magaña 2002
19	Tunas	*Thunnus albacares* and *T. obesus*	IATTC bulletins and technical repots from 1950 to 1998; Bustamante *et al.* 1999		Olson and Watters 2003	Olson and Watters 2003		Alverson 1963; Bocanegro 2007; Alatorre 2007
20	Benthic fish	Primary: Serranid spp. and Labridae spp.						
21	Small benthopelagic fishes	Haemulidae (*Anisostremus interruptus*, *Haemulon scudderii*, *Xenichthys agassizi*, *Xenocys jessiae*), mullets, Lujanidae spp., *Paranthias colonus, Caulolatilus affinis* and *C. princeps*, *Mulloidichthys dentatus*, Sparidae spp. and rays	Estimated from Castrejón and Moreno (2008); Murillo *et al.* (2004); and SPNG–FCD 2002					Olson and Watters 2003; Bocanegro 2007
22	Small pelagic fishes	Clupeidae, Nomeidae, Balistidae, Ostraciidae, Tetraodontidae, Diondontidae, Engraulidae, pelagic Mugillidae, Carangidae (*Trachinotus stilbe* and *Alectis ciliaris*), *Chanos chanos*, pelagic mullets, flying fishes (Exocoetidae spp.)	Estimated from Castrejón and Moreno (2008); Murillo *et al.* (2004); and, SPNG–FCD 2002					Olson and Watters 2003; Bocanegro 2007

23	Small pelagic predator	*Scomberomonus sierra, Auxis rochei, Katsuwomus pelamis, Euthyneus lineatus, Scomber japonicus, Sarda orientalis*, jacks (*C. lugubris, C. sexfasciatus, C. caninus*), *Elagatis bipinnulata, Seriola peruna, S. rivoliana. Sphyraena idiastes, Lepidocibyum flavobrunneum* (Gempylidae), juvenile tunas (*Thunnus alalunga, T. obesus* and *T albacares*) and juveniles of billfishes (Istiphorid and Xiphiidae spp.)	Estimated from Castrejón and Moreno (2008); Murillo *et al.* (2004); and, SPNG–FCD 2002				Alverson 1963; Bachok *et al.* 2004; Alatorre 2007; Bocanegro 2007
24	Mesopelagic fishes	Primary: Phosichthydae, Myctophidae					Based on Olson and Watters, 2003.
25	Macrobenthos	Crustaceans, sea cucumbers, sea stars, bivalves	—				
26	Cephalopods	Octopuses and squids	—		Tam *et al.* 2008	Tam *et al.* 2008	Based on Olson and Watters 2003.
27	Gelatinous plankton	Primary: Siphonophores, hidromedusa, scyphomedusa, tunicates and apendicularia	—				
28	Pelagic decapods	Penaeoidae, Caridae	—				
29	Mesozooplankton (copepods) (2000 μm)	Euphausids, Chaetognaths, Ostracods Copepods	—	Pennington *et al.* 2006; Tam *et al.* 2008			
30	Microzooplankton (<200 μm)	Flagellates, Ciliates, other	—	Pennington *et al.* 2006; Tam *et al.* 2008			
31	Macrophytes	Macrocystis spp. Sargassum spp. Ulva. spp.	—				
32	Dino- and silicoflagellates	Several species	—	Pennington *et al.* 2006; Tam *et al.* 2008			
33	Diatoms	Several species	—	Pennington *et al.* 2006; Tam *et al.* 2008			
34	Detritus		—				

Appendix 13.2 Diet matrix used for model

	Groups	*1*	*2*	*3*	*4*	*5*	*6*	*7*	*8*	*9*	*10*	*11*	*12*	*13*	*14*	*15*	*16*	*17*	*18*	*19*	*20*	*21*	*22*	*23*	*24*	*25*	*26*	*27*	*28*	*29*	*30*
1	Boobies, Fragates and others	0	0	0	0	0	0	0	0	0	0	0	0	0	0	0	0	0	0	0	0	0	0	0	0	0	0	0	0	0	0
2	Cormorants and Penguins	0	0	0	0	0	0	0	0	0	0	0	0	0	0	0	0	0	0	0	0	0	0	0	0	0	0	0	0	0	0
3	Sea turtles	0	0	0	0	0	0	0.1	0	0	0	0	0	0	0	0	0	0	0	0	0	0	0	0	0	0	0	0	0	0	0
4	Sea lions and seals	0	0	0	0	0	0.1	0.1	0	0	0	0	0	0	0	0	0	0	0	0	0	0	0	0	0	0	0	0	0	0	0
5	Dolphins	0	0	0	0	0	0	0.1	0	0	0	0	0	0	0	0	0	0	0	0	0	0	0	0	0	0	0	0	0	0	0
6	Sperm whales	0	0	0	0	0	0	0	0	0	0	0	0	0	0	0	0	0	0	0	0	0	0	0	0	0	0	0	0	0	0
7	Killer whales	0	0	0	0	0	0	0	0	0	0	0	0	0	0	0	0	0	0	0	0	0	0	0	0	0	0	0	0	0	0
8	Baleen whales	0	0	0	0	0	0	0	0	0	0	0	0	0	0	0	0	0	0	0	0	0	0	0	0	0	0	0	0	0	0
9	Mantas and whale sharks	0	0	0	0	0	0	0.1	0	0	0	0	0	0	0	0	0	0	0	0	0	0	0	0	0	0	0	0	0	0	0
10	Juvenile sharks	0	0	0	0	0	0	0.1	0	0	0	0.1	0	0	0	0	0	0	0	0	0	0	0	0	0	0	0	0	0	0	0
11	Benthopelagic sharks	0	0	0	0	0	0	0	0	0	0	0	0	0	0	0	0	0	0	0	0	0	0	0	0	0	0	0	0	0	0
12	Large pelagic sharks	0	0	0	0	0	0	0	0	0	0	0	0	0	0	0	0	0	0	0	0	0	0	0	0	0	0	0	0	0	0
13	Hammerhead sharks	0	0	0	0	0	0	0	0	0	0	0	0	0	0	0	0	0	0	0	0	0	0	0	0	0	0	0	0	0	0
14	Marlins	0	0	0	0	0	0	0.1	0	0	0	0	0	0	0	0	0	0	0	0	0	0	0	0	0	0	0	0	0	0	0
15	Swordfish	0	0	0	0	0	0	0	0	0	0	0	0	0	0	0	0	0	0	0	0	0	0	0	0	0	0	0	0	0	0
16	Sailfish	0	0	0	0	0	0	0.1	0	0	0	0	0.1	0.1	0	0	0	0	0	0	0	0	0	0	0	0	0	0	0	0	0
17	Wahoo	0	0	0	0	0	0	0.1	0	0	0	0	0	0	0	0	0	0	0	0	0	0	0	0	0	0	0	0	0	0	0
18	Dolphinfish	0	0	0	0	0	0	0.1	0	0	0	0	0	0	0	0	0	0	0	0	0	0	0	0	0	0	0	0	0	0	0
19	Thunnus spp.	0	0	0	0	0	0	0	0	0	0	0	0.3	0	0.1	0	0	0.1	0	0	0	0	0	0	0	0	0	0	0	0	0
20	Benthic fish	0	0.4	0	0.2	0	0	0.1	0	0	0.4	0.3	0	0	0.1	0	0	0.1	0	0	0	0.1	0	0	0	0	0	0	0	0	0
21	Jacks and others	0	0.3	0	0.1	0.2	0.2	0	0.1	0	0.2	0.1	0.1	0.1	0.1	0	0.1	0.1	0	0	0	0	0	0	0	0	0	0	0	0	0
22	Small pelagic fishes	0.4	0.3	0	0.3	0	0	0	0	0.1	0.1	0.1	0	0.2	0.3	0	0	0.2	0.5	0.2	0.1	0.3	0	0.4	0	0	0.2	0	0	0	0
23	Scombrids and others	0.1	0	0	0.1	0.1	0.1	0	0.1	0	0	0	0	0	0.3	0.3	0.3	0.3	0.1	0.2	0	0	0	0	0	0	0	0	0	0	0
24	Mesopelagic fish	0	0	0	0.1	0.1	0.1	0	0.1	0	0	0	0	0.1	0	0.1	0	0.1	0.1	0.1	0	0.1	0	0	0	0	0.2	0	0	0	0
25	Macrobenthos	0	0.2	0	0	0	0	0	0	0	0.2	0.1	0	0	0	0	0	0	0	0	0.7	0.1	0	0	0	0	0	0	0	0	0
26	Cephalopods	0	0	0	0.2	0.3	0.5	0	0.6	0	0	0.3	0.5	0.5	0.1	0.5	0.6	0.1	0.1	0.2	0	0.1	0	0.1	0	0	0	0	0	0	0
27	Gelatinous plankton	0.1	0	0.1	0	0	0	0	0	0.3	0	0	0	0	0	0	0	0	0	0.1	0	0.1	0	0.1	0	0	0.2	0	0	0	0
28	Pelagic decapods	0.4	0	0	0.1	0.3	0.1	0	0.2	0.3	0.1	0	0	0	0.1	0.1	0	0.3	0.1	0.3	0	0.3	0.1	0.4	0.8	0	0.5	0.2	0	0	0
29	Copepods	0	0	0	0	0	0	0	0	0.4	0	0	0	0	0	0	0	0	0	0	0	0.1	0.3	0	0.1	0	0	0.5	0.2	0	0
30	Microzooplankton	0	0	0	0	0	0	0	0	0	0	0	0	0	0	0	0	0	0	0	0	0	0	0	0	0	0	0	0.2	0.1	0.1
31	Benthic macroalgae	0	0	0.9	0	0	0	0	0	0	0	0	0	0	0	0	0	0	0	0	0.2	0	0	0	0	0.2	0	0	0	0	0
32	Dinoflagelates	0	0	0	0	0	0	0	0	0	0	0	0	0	0	0	0	0	0	0	0	0	0.3	0	0	0.3	0	0	0.2	0.4	0.3
33	Diatoms	0	0	0	0	0	0	0	0	0	0	0	0	0	0	0	0	0	0	0	0	0	0.3	0	0.1	0.4	0	0.3	0.4	0.5	0.3
	Detritus	0	0	0	0	0	0	0	0	0	0	0	0	0	0	0	0	0	0	0	0.1	0	0	0	0	0.1	0	0	0	0	0.4
	Import	0	0	0	0	0	0	0	0	0	0	0	0	0	0	0	0	0	0	0	0	0	0	0	0	0	0	0	0	0	0
	Sum	1	1	1	1	1	1	1	1	1	1	1	1	1	1	1	1	1	1	1	1	1	1	1	1	1	1	1	1	1	1

Appendix 13.3 Estimates of residence time of the pelagic top predators and stock increase predictions

Species	*Lifetime fraction spend in GMR*	*Rationale*	*Source*	*Stock increase (1998–2010)*
Benthopelagic sharks	0.7–0.8	11 from 12 tagged Galápagos Sharks remained within the limits of the GMR. Shark catches from illegal fishing around the limits of the GMR presented high indices of other species than Galápagos sharks; while illegal catches within the GMR are more represented by *C. galapagensis, C. limbatus* and *S. lewini*. While residency seems to be really high for the Galápagos shark (0,9), other shark species as *C. limbatus* use the GMR as nursery ground but seems to migrate to other parts of the pacific. Final value for the group: 0.8	Ketchum *et al.* 2009; Shilligner *et al.*, unpublished	37.3–41%
Large pelagic sharks	0.2–0.3	The observed border effect may imply an increase in population size of those species in the GMR due to some effectiveness in protection. Though their status of highly migratory raise level of uncertainty. Residence value therefore set low as for the Striped marlins.	Author's estimate	14.8–23%
Hammerhead sharks	0.5–0.6	Based on satellite tracking data and calculated from the amount of time sharks spent inside the GMR. It is not yet clear if hammerhead sharks breed within the GMR.	Ketchum *et al.* 2009	15.2–18%
Marlins	0.2–0.3	According to kernel analysis, *Tetrapturus audax* remains for about 50 percent of their time within the limits and around the border the GMR. So 30% residence time in the GMR seems realistic.	Domier 2006	6.3–9%
Swordfish	0.2–0.3	Estimated to be similar than for marlins		2–3%
Sailfish	0.2–0.3	Estimated to be similar than for marlins		2–3%
Wahoo	0.5–0.6	Jobstvogt (2010) reported catches all year around. Migration is still unclear, but presence of different size classes suggests the presence of all age groups in the GMR. In addition, the low importance of this species in industrial fishing fleets in the surroundings of the GMR in comparison to the artisanal fishery within the GMR also suggest that wahoo population is aggregated around the island shelve, as suggested by Jobstvogt, 2010; Vaske *et al.* 2006 and Uchiyama 2006.	Jobstvogt 2010; Vaske *et al.* 2006; Uchiyama 2006	12.8–15%

continued

Appendix 13.3 continued

Species	*Lifetime fraction spend in GMR*	*Rationale*	*Source*	*Stock increase (1998–2010)*
Dolphinfish	0.3–0.4	Strong seasonality in catches (peak in warm season) (Castrejón and Moreno, 2008). Behavior is considered similar to that of skipjack.	Castrejón and Moreno 2008	6–8%
Yellowfin tuna	0.5–0.6	According to Dagorn *et al.* (2007), yellowfin (YF) tuna has high residency around FADs in Hawaiian Waters. Cole (1980) reports reduced migrations of YF between nearshore and offshore areas, based on tagging studies in the Eastern Tropical Pacific by Fink and Bayliff (1970) and by Susuki (1978). Though YF tunas are known to migrate across the entire Pacific Ocean, it is believed that and important part of the population remains within the waters of the GMR, as shown by Fink and Bayliff (1979). Here, almost all recaptures were in the release areas or close by. Information of fisheries monitoring has shown several size classes of YF individuals caught in the GMR (Castrejón y Moreno, 2008) suggesting Galápagos as a nursery ground for this species. The elevated fishing effort for tuna and pelagic species in the GMR boundaries (WildAid, 2010) also support the theory that tunas are very representative in Galápagos waters after the closure of industrial fishing.	Dagorn *et al.* 2007; Klimley 2003; Cole 1980; Fink and Bayliff 1970; Susuki 1978; Castrejón y Moreno 2008; WildAid 2010	12.9–14.00%

References

Abitía-Cárdenas, L.A., A. Muhlia-Melo, V. Cruz-Escalona, and F. Galván-Magaña. 2002. Trophic dynamics and seasonal energetics of striped marlin Tetrapturus audax in the southern Gulf of California, Mexico, *Fisheries Research* 57(3):287–295.

AlaTorre, V.G. 2007. *Dieta de AAA y Barrilete en el oceano pacifico tropical*, Tesis previa la obtencion del título de Master en Ciencias, Instituto Politécnico Nacional, Centro interdisciplinario de Ciencias Marinas, La Paz, Baja California Sur.

Altamirano, M. and M. Aguiñaga. 2002. Control y respeto al marco jurídico (Capítulo 26), in E. Danulat and H.J. Edgar (ed.), *Reserva Marina de Galápagos: Línea Base de la Biodiversidad*, pp. 146–165 (Charles Darwin Foundation: Puerto Ayora, Galápagos, Ecuador).

Alverson, R.G. 1963. The food of yellowfin and skipjack tunas in the Eastern Tropical Pacific Ocean, *IATTC Bulletin* VII(5).

Avaria, S. and P. Muñoz. 1987. Effects of the 1982–83 El Niño on the marine phytoplankton of Northern Chile, *Journal of Geophysical Research*, 92 (C13):14369–14382.

Bachok, Z., M.I. Manson, and R.M. Noordin. 2004. Diet composition and food habits of demersal and pelagic marine fishes from Terenguaqno waters, east coast of Malaysia, NAGA, *WorldFish Center Quarterly* 27(3–4).

Bakun, A. and S.J. Weeks. 2008. The marine ecosystem off Peru: what are the secrets of its fishery productivity and what might the future hold?, *Progress in Oceanography* 79: 290–299.

Banks, S. 2002. Ambiente fisico, in E. Danulat and H.J. Edgar (ed.), *Reserva Marina de Galapagos: Linea base de Biodiversidad*, pp. 22–47 (Charles Darwin Foundation: Puerto Ayora, Galápagos, Ecuador).

Barber, R.T., and F.P. Chavez. 1983. Biological consequences of El Niño, *Science* 222:1203–1210.

Barber, R.T., and F.P. Chavez. 1986. Ocean variability in relation to living resources during the 1982–83 El Niño, *Nature* 319:279–285.

Bolaño-Martínez, N. and F. Galván-Magaña. 2007. Feeding habits of juvenile *Sphyrna zigaena* Linnaeus 1758 (Chondrichthyes:Sphyrnidae) in Santa Rosa of Salinas, Ecuador, in Martínez-Ortiz and Galván Magaña (ed.), *Sharks in Ecuador: Case studies* (EPESPO–PMRC: Manta, Ecuador).

Brush, M.J., J.W. Brawley, S.W. Nixon, and J.N. Kremer. 2002. Modeling phytoplankton production: Problems with the Eppley curve and an empirical alternative, *Marine Ecology Progress Series* 238:31–45.

Bustamante, R. 1999. *La pesca industrial del Atun y Galápagos - Elementos Descriptivos Básicos para Evaluación del Estado Actual y Significado de un Conflicto para la Conservación y el Manejo de la Reserva Marina de Galápagos. Documento preparado para la Ministra del Medio Ambiente Dra. Yolanda Kakabadse* (Charles Darwin Foundation: Puerto Ayora, Galápagos, Ecuador).

Castañeda-Suarez, J.D., and L.A. Sandoval-Londoño. 2007. Feeding habits of the scalloped hammerhead Sphyrna lewini at the Ecuadorian Pacific, in Martínez-Ortiz and Galván Magaña (ed.), *Sharks in Ecuador: Case studies* (EPESPO–PMRC: Manta, Ecuador).

Castrejón, M. 2008. *El sistema de co-manejo pesquero de la Reserva Marina de Galápagos: situación actual, retos y perspectivas de cambio* (Charles Darwin Foundation: Puerto Ayora, Galápagos, Ecuador).

Castrejón, M. and J. Moreno, 2008. Galapagos Marine Reserve, Ecuador, in D.J. Starkey and J.H. Nicholls (comp.), *Shifting Baselines: INCOFISH WP2 Data Pages*. www.hull.ac.uk/incofish.

Castro, I. and A. Phillips. 1996. *A guide to the birds of the Galapagos Islands* (A&C Black Publishers: London, UK).

Cedeño-Figueroa. L., C. Estupiñan-Montaño, and F. Galván-Magaña. 2007. Feeding habits of the silky shark Carcharhinus falciformis in the Ecuadorian Pacific, in Martínez-Ortiz and Galván Magaña (ed.), *Sharks in Ecuador: Case studies* (EPESPO–PMRC: Manta, Ecuador).

Chavez, F.P. 2005. Biological consequences of interannual to multidecadal variability, in A. Robinson, and K. Brink (ed.), *The Sea, vol. 13*, pp. 643–679 (Harvard University Press: Cambridge, MA).

Chavez, F.P. and R.C. Brusca. 1991. The Galapagos Islands and their relation to oceanographic processes in the tropical Pacific, in M. James (ed.), *Galapagos Marine Invertebrates*, pp. 9–33 (Plenum Press: New York, NY).

Chavez, F.P., P.G. Strutton, and M.J. McPhaden. 1998. Biological-physical coupling in the central equatorial Pacific during the onset of the 1997–98 El Niño, *Geophysical Research Letters* 25:3543–3546.

Christensen, V. (1996) Managing fisheries involving predator and prey species, *Review in Fish Biology and Fisheries* 6(1):1–26.

Christensen, V. and D. Pauly (ed.) 1993. Trophic Models of Aquatic Ecosystems, *ICLARM Conference Proceedings* 26.

Christenen, V. and C. Walters 2004. Trade off in ecosystem-scale optimization of fisheries management policies, *Bulletin of Marine Science* 74(3):549–562.

Christie, D.M., R.A. Duncan, A.R. McBirney, M.A. Richards, W.M. White, K.S. Harpp, and C.G. Fox. (1992) Drowned islands downstream from the Galapagos hot-spot imply extended speciation times, *Nature* 355:246–248.

Coello, S. 1989. Consideration on the management of the Galapagos bacalao fishery *Mycteroperca olfax* (Jenyns) (Pisces: Serranidae), *Revista del Pacífico Sur* Número especial:705–709.

Cole, J.S. 1980. Synopsis on Biological data on the yellowfin tuna, Thunnus albacares (Bonnaterre, 1978) in the pacific ocean, in W.H. Bayliff (ed.), Synopses of biological data on eight species of Scombrids. *InterAmerican Tropical Tuna Commission* Special Report No. 2.

Dagorn, L., K.M. Holland and D.G. Itano. 2007. Behavior of yellowfin (*Thunnus albacares*) and Bigeye (*T. obesus*) tuna in a network of fish aggregation devices (FADs), *Marine Biology* 151:595–606.

Domier, M. 2006. An analysis of pacific striped marlin (Tetrapturus audax) horizonal movement patterns using pop-up satellite archival tags, *Bulletin of Marine Science* 79(3):811–825.

Edgar, G.J., R.H. Bustamante, J.M. Fariña, J.M. Calvopiña, M. Martinez, and M.V. Total-Granda. 2004. Bias in evaluating the effects of marine protected areas: the importance of baseline data for the Galapagos Marine Reserve, *Environmental Conservation* 31:212.

Fink, B. and W.H. Bayliff. 1970. Migrations of yellowfin and Skipjack tuna in the Eastern Pacific Ocean as determined by tagging experiment 1952–1964, *InterAmerican Tropical Tuna Commission Bulletin* 15 (1).

Granda, D. 1995. *Estudio de la pesca de especies para el seco-salado en las islas Galápagos, periodo 1988–1990* (Estación Científica Charles Darwin: Santa Cruz, Galápagos, Ecuador).

Halpern, B.S. and R.R. Warner. 2002. Marine reserves have rapid and lasting effects, *Ecology Letters* 5:361–366.

Hearn, A. 2008. The rocky path to sustainable fisheries management and conservation in the Galapagos Marine Reserve, *Ocean & Coastal Management* 51:567.

IATTC, 1956. *Annual Report of the year 1955* (Inter-American Tropical Tuna Commission: La Jolla, California).

IATTC, 1960. *Annual Report of the year 1959* (Inter-American Tropical Tuna Commission: La Jolla, California).

IATTC, 1961. *Annual Report of the year 1960* (Inter-American Tropical Tuna Commission: La Jolla, California).

IATTC, 1963. *Annual Report of the year 1962* (Inter-American Tropical Tuna Commission: La Jolla, California).

Jiménez, R. 2008. *Aspectos biológicos de El Niño en el Océano Pacífico Ecuatorial. Universidad de Guayaquil*, Facultad de Ciencias Naturales, Centro de Biodiversidad CENBIO, Guayaquil, Ecuador.

Jobstvogt, N.A. 2010. *Fish stock assessment of top-predator wahoo, Acanthocybium solandri, in the Galapagos Islands*, Diploma Thesis, Department of Biology, Chemistry and Pharmacy, Freie Universitat, Berlin.

Ketchum, J.T., A.R. Hearn, G. Shillinger, E. Espinoza, C. Peñaherrera, and A.P. Klimley. 2009. Shark movement and the design of protected pelagic environments within and beyond the Galapagos Marine Reserve, *Proceedings of the Galapagos Science Symposium, Galapagos, Ecuador*, pp. 127–130. (20–24 July 2009).

Ketchum, J.T., F. Galván-Magaña, and A.P. Klimley. 2010. Segregating and foraging ecology of whale sharks, Rhincodon typus, in the Southwestern Gulf of California, *Sharks International, Cairns, Australia* (6–11 June 2010).

Klimley, A.P., S. Jorgensen, A. Muhlia-Melo, and S.C. Beavers. 2003. The occurrence of yellowfin tuna (Thunnus albacares) at Espiritu Santo Seamount in the Gulf of California, *Fisheries Bulletin* 101: 684–692.

Laurie, A. 1985.The effects of the 1982–83 El Niño on marine iguanas, in G. Robinson and E.M. del Pino (ed.), *El Niño in the Galápagos Islands: 1982–1983 event*, pp. 199–209 (Charles Darwin Foundation: Puerto Ayora, Galápagos, Ecuador).

Mitchell, A.H. and H.G. Reading. 1969. Continental margins, geosynclines, and ocean floor spreading, *The Journal of Geology* 77:629–646.

Murillo, J.C., H. Reyes, P. Zarate, S. Banks, and E. Danulat. 2004. *Plan piloto de pesca de altura con palangre* (Fundación Charles Darwin y Servicion Parque Nacional Galàpagos: Puerto Ayora, Galapagos, Ecuador).

Nelson, J.D. and S.A. Eckert. 2007. Foraging ecology of whale sharks (Rhincodon typus) within Bahía de Los Angeles, Baja California Norte, Mexico, *Fisheries Research* 84:47–64.

Nicolaides, F., J.C. Murillo, M.V. Toral, and G. Reck. 2002. *Bacalao*, in E. Danulat and G. Edgar (ed.), *Reserva Marina de Galápagos: Línea Base de la Biodiversidad*, pp. 146–165 (Fundación Charles Darwin y Servicio Parque Nacional Galápagos: Santa Cruz, Galápagos, Ecuador).

Notarbartolo-Di-Sciara. 1998. Natural history of Mobula in California Gulf, *Fishery Bulletin* 86(1):45–66.

Olson, R. and F. Galvan-Magaña. 2002. Food habits and consumption rates of common dolphinfish (Coryphaena hippurus) in the Eastern Pacific Ocean, *Fisheries Bulletin* 100(2):279–298.

Ochoa, N. and O. Gomez. 1987. Dinoflagellates as indicator of water masses during El Niño 1982–83, *Journal of Geophysical Research* 92(C13):14,355–14,367.

Olson, R. and G. Walters. 2003. A model of the pelagic ecosystem in the Eastern Tropical Pacific Ocean, *Inter-American Tropical Tuna Commission Bulletin* 22(3).

Papastamatiou, Y., B.M. Wetherbee, C.G. Lowe, and G.L. Crow. 2006. Distribution and diet of four species of carcharhinid sharks in the Hawaiian Isalnds: Evidence for resource partitioning and competitive exclusion, *Marine Ecology Progress Series* 320:239–251.

Pauly, D., A.W. Trites, E. Capuli, and V. Christensen. 1998. Diet composition and trophic levels of marine mammals, *ICES Journal of Marine Science* 55:467–481.

Pennington, J.T., K.L. Mahoney, V.S. Kuwahara, D.D. Kolber, R. Calienes, and F.P. Chavez. 2006. Primary production in the eastern tropical Pacific: A review, *Progress in Oceanography* 69:285–317.

Peñaherrera, C. 2007. *Spatial and seasonal variations in fin fish catch composition in the Galapagos Marine Reserve*, Bachelor Thesis in Biological Sciences, Catholic University of Ecuador. Quito, Ecuador.

Peñaherrera, C, and A. Hearn. 2008. Toward an Ecosystem-based approach to fisheries: a risk analysis, in *Galapagos Report 2007–2008* (Charles Darwin Foundation, Galapagos National Park and Galapagos National Institute: Puerto Ayora, Galápagos, Ecuador).

Piu, M. (1998) La Pesca Industrial en el Ecuador y su relación con Galápagos, *Informe Galápagos* 1997–1998: 20–24.

PNG. 2005. *Plan de Manejo del Parque Nacional Galápagos: Un pacto por la conservación y el desarrollo sustentable del archipiélago* (Parque Nacional Galápagos y Ministerio de Ambiente del Ecuador: Puerto Ayora, Ecuador).

Rendón-Macías, L., F. Pacheco-Triviño, and F. Galván-Magaña. 2007. Trophic habitats of the thresher sharks: Alopias pelagicus Nakamura, 1935 and Alopias superciliosus (Lowe, 1839), in Martínez-Ortiz and Galván Magaña (ed.), *Sharks in Ecuador: Case studies* (EPESPO–PMRC: Manta, Ecuador).

Reyes, H. and J.C. Murillo. 2007. *Esfuerzos para el control de la pesca ilícita*, Reporte Galapagos 2002–6 (Fundación Charles Darwin, Instituto Nacional Galápagos and Parque Nacional Galapagos: Santa Cruz, Galápagos, Ecuador).

Robinson, G. and E.M. del Pino (ed.). 1985. *El Niño en las islas Galápagos; El evento de 1982–1983* (Charles Darwin Foundation: Puerto Ayora, Galapagos, Ecuador).

Salazar, S.K. 2002. Lobo marino y lobo peletero, en E. Danulat and G.J. Edgar (ed.), *Reserva Marina de Galapagos: Línea base de Biodiversidad*, pp. 267–290 (Charles Darwin Foundation: Puerto Ayora, Galápagos, Ecuador).

Salazar, S.K. 2005. *Varicación espacial y temporal del espectro trófico del lobo marino de Galápago, INP-CICIMAR*, Tesis previa la obtención del Título de Maestro en Ciencias con Especialidad en Manejo de Recursos Marinos, Laz, Baja California Sur, Mexico.

Salazar, S. and R.H. Bustamante. 2003. Effects of the 1997–98 El Niño on population zise and dieto f the Galápagos sea lion (Zalophus wollebaeki), *Noticias de Galápagos* 62,40–45.

Sekharam, K.V. 1974. Estimates of the stocks of oil sardine and mackerel in the present fishing grounds of the west coast of India, *Indian Journal of Fisheries.* 21(1):177–182.

Schaeffer, B.A., J.M. Morrison, D. Kamykowski, G.C. Feldman, L. Xie, Y. Liu, W. Sweet, A. McCulloch, and S. Banks. 2008. Phytoplankton biomass distribution and identification of productive habitats within the Galapagos Marine Reserve by MODIS, a surface acquisition system, and in situ measurements, *Remote Sensing of Environment* 112:3044–3054.

Shimada, B.M. and M.B. Schaefer. 1956. *A study of changes in fishing effort, abundance and yield for yellowfin and skipjack tuna in the Eastern Tropical Pacific* 1(7) (IATTC: La Jolla, California).

Susuki, Z., P.K. Tomlinsion, and M. Honma. 1978. Population structure of Pacific yellowfin tuna, *InterAmerican Tropical Tuna Commission Bulletin* 15(5):273–441.

Tam, J., M.H. Taylor, V. Blaskovic, P. Espinoza, R.M. Ballón, E. Díaz, C. Wosnitza-Mendo, J. Argüelles, S. Purca, P. Ayón, L. Quipuzcoa, D. Gutiérrez, E. Goya, N. Ochoa, and M. Wolff. 2008. Trophic modeling of the Northern Humboldt Current Ecosystem, Part I: Comparing trophic linkages under La Niña and El Niño conditions, *Progress in Oceanography* 79:352–365.

Taylor, H.M. and M. Wolff. (2007). Trophic modeling of Estern Boundary Current Systems: a review and prospectus for solving the "Peruvian Puzzle", *Revista Peruana de Biología* 14(1):1–14.

Tomkins, R.J. and B.J. Milne. 1991. Differences among dark-rumped petrel populations within the Galapagos archipelago, *Notornis* 38:1–35.

Uchiyama, J. and C. Boggs. 2006. Length-weight relationships of dolphinfish, Coryphaena hipparus, and Wahoo, Acanthocybium solandri: seasonal effects of spawning and possible migration in the central North Pacific, *Marine Fisheries Review* 68:1–4.

Ulanowicz, R.E. and C.J. Puccia. 1990. Mixed trophic impacts in ecosystems, *Coenoses* 5:7–16.

Valle, C.A., F. Cruz, J.B. Cruz, G. Merlen, M.C. Coulter. 1987. The impact of the 1982–1983 El Niño southern oscillation on seabirds in the Galapagos Islands, Ecuador, *Journal of Geophysical Research* 92:14437–14443

Valle-Castillo, C.A. 1985 Alteración de las poblaciones del cormorant no volador, el pinguino y otras aves marinas en Galápagos por efecto de El Niño 1982–83 y su subsecuente recuperacion, in G. Robinson and E.M. del Pino (ed.), *El Niño in the Galápagos Islands: 1982 – 1983 event*, pp. 245–258 (Foundation Charles Darwin: Quito, Ecuador).

Vargas, H., C. Lougheed, and H. Snell. 2005. Population size and trends of the Galapagos penguin *Spheniscus mendiculus*, *Ibis* 147:367–374.

Vargas, H., S. Harrison, S. Rea, and D.W. Macdonald. 2006. Biological effects of El Niño on the Galapagos penguin, *Biological Conservation* 127:107–114.

Vaske, T., R.P. Lessa, M.F. Nóbrega, F.M.D. Amaral, and S.R.M. Silveira (ed.). *Arquipélago de São Pedro e São Paulo: Histórico e Recursos Naturais 1* (Livro Rápido: Olinda).

Velasto, P.M. 2005. *Hábitos alimenticios e isótopos de 13C y 15N del tiburón mako Isurus oxyrinchus (Rafinesque, 1810) en la costa occidental de Baja California Sur*, Tesis previa la obtencion del título de Master en Ciencias, Instituto Politécnico Nacional, Centro interdisciplinario de Ciencias Marinas, La Paz, Baja California Sur.

Walters, C., V. Christensen, and D. Pauly. 1997. Structuring dynamic models of exploited ecosystems from trophic mass-balance assessments, *Review in Fish Biology and Fisheries* 7:139–172.

Watkins, G. and F. Cruz. 2007. *Galapagos at Risk: A Socioeconomic Analysis of the Situation in the Archipelago* (Charles Darwin Foundation: Puerto Ayora, Province of Galapagos, Ecuador).

WildAid, 2010. *An Analysis of the Law Enforcement Chain in the Eastern Tropical Pacific Seascape*. WildAid Inc. EIN: 20-3644441.

Wolff, M., H.J. Hartmann, and V. Koch. (1996). A pilot trophic model for Golfo Dulce, a fjord-like tropical embayment, Costa Rica, *Revista De Biologia Tropical* 44(Suppl.3):215–231.

Wolff, M., J.B. Chavarria, V. Koch, and J.A. Vargas. 1998. A trophic flow model of the Golfo de Nicoya. Costa Rica, *Revista De Biologia Tropical* 46(Suppl.6):63–79.

Zárate, P. and P.H. Dutton. 2002. Tortuga verde, en E. Danulat y G.J. Edgar (ed.) *Reserva Marina de Galápagos: Línea base de la biodiversidad*, pp. 305–323. (Fundación Charles Darwin/Servicio Parque Nacional Galápagos: Santa Cruz, Galápagos, Ecuador).

14 Mediated Modeling

A useful tool for a collaborative and integrated assessment of the Galápagos?

Marjan van den Belt

Introduction

Consider the story of the Galápagos; the story is quite generic and applicable to other island nations, such as New Zealand. It goes as follows: since about 1970, the Galápagos Islands are visited by an increasing number of people. As more people visit the islands over time, for various reasons, non-native animal and plant species are being introduced. As people became aware of the rarity of these islands, even more visitors came. Visitors pay money to come and provide the basis for economic exchange. To accommodate the visitors more mainlanders are attracted to provide the services and earn a living. With every movement of people and goods, there is an increased risk for additional introduced species. These non-natives threaten the native species and alter the habitat and community composition. The very basis of the visitor attraction is changing. How to intervene and manage for the undesirable and unintended consequences? Culling non-natives? Limiting inhabitants? Limiting accommodation for visitors? Tourist taxes? Using visitors in a different manner? And so the story goes.

This story can be captured in computer-based software, which helps to both analyze and synthesize the story. Mediated modeling (MM) refers to the use of computer model building as a mediation tool (van den Belt 2004). Systems thinking (the use of causal diagrams) and system dynamics (quantitative representations of feedback loops and time lags to understand systems) provide the underlying modeling philosophy. This type of modeling aims to improve the understanding of changes in systems and their complex behavior rather than aiming for precise predictions. MM is geared toward scoping for and understanding of broad systemic drivers together *with* a group of stakeholders rather than *for* a group of stakeholders, often holding conflicting viewpoints. MM is a way to bring forward relevant information and scope for inter-linkages, share information among stakeholders and foster a dialogue for collaborative learning required for effective decision support. The dialogue is simultaneously interpreted by a mediated modeler and reflected back into the dialogue for all participants to reflect and comment on in real time. This increases transparency and often exposes the real issues, as well as information gaps and uncertainties. Even though MM or similar processes can be used on any complex topic, the integration of ecology, economics and social issues for sustainable development is often considered a normative objective in a MM process.

Is this approach suitable for the Galápagos? Moreover, could this approach provide a contribution to the valuation of ecosystem services?

"All models are wrong; some models are useful" is an often heard quote with regard to model building (often attributed to Box or Deming). What is useful about MM is that the practice of developing a model helps to structure information and changes over time. To a certain extent, everybody is a modeler. Computer-based modeling assists those who have the patience and inclination to engage with technology, to think in a more structured way, use more data and moreover, think in systems, assess uncertainties and examine trade-offs. Systems thinking includes feedback loops and time lags, features that are easily overlooked in often linear, fragmented decision-making. Assuming that the practice of model building is a useful way for individuals or expert modelers to increase their understanding of complex systems and build consensus, MM with a group can then facilitate collaborative learning and provide a framework for an effective, in-depth dialogue (Figure 14.1). People learn from making mistakes; model simulations allow a group to make many mistakes quickly and learn from them before decisions are made in the real world. The premise of this chapter is that modeling is useful as a group process. Modeling is storytelling and a model is by definition an abstract reflection of reality.

When to use MM?

The anticipated fit of when and how to use MM can be assessed by evaluating the timing and the degree of participation (Figure 14.1). A MM process can be

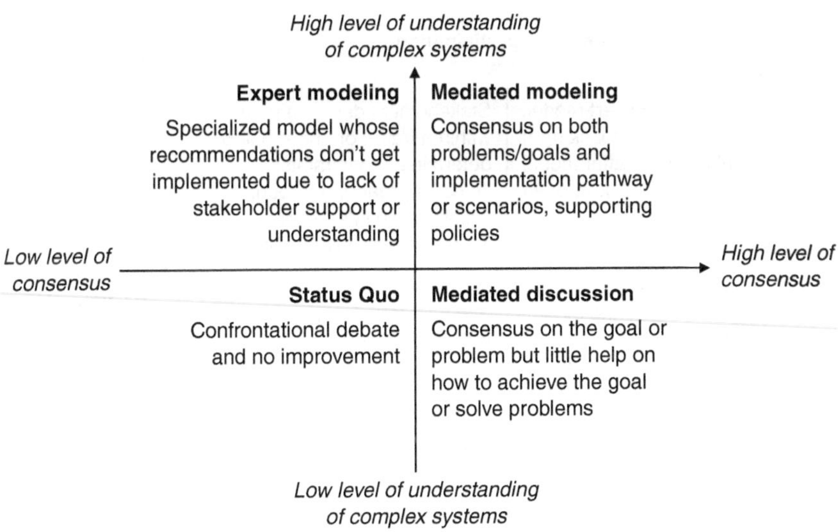

Figure 14.1 Understanding of systems versus consensus (source: van den Belt 2004).

used in a variety of situations, but it is ideally suited for early engagement with a high degree of participation. It is often suggested by those contemplating a MM process that "the data has to be gathered first, before engaging stakeholders in a model building process". However, MM is intended to scope for what stakeholders already know and to integrate this knowledge with data and information already available.

Stakeholder participation

Participants present during the construction of a Mediated Model determine how the model will look. Therefore, the identification, selection and contextual management of relevant stakeholders is crucial (Figure 14.2).

The goal is to find those participants who can make decisions when joint recommendations are developed; those with access to information and human resources; and those affected by decisions. Some higher level decision-makers will not prioritize a MM process, as it requires about 30–50 hours of meeting time. If high level decision-makers don't prioritize such a collaborative learning process (often for time management reasons), these gatekeepers can be kept informed and perhaps be presented with the final results. In Galápagos, as in most other places, the gatekeepers are most important and without their buy-in any collaborative process is at the risk of stagnation and reversion back to "politics as usual". In addition, many people may have an interest and/or relevant information to contribute. Unfortunately, there is a limit to how many stakeholders can directly participate. Hence, a form of interaction (web-based, meetings in public spaces or participants sharing a place) can be worked into the process to accommodate such a situation.

Figure 14.2 Timing versus degree of participation (source: van den Belt 2004).

Stakeholder Analysis (SA) is the process used to identify the key people/organizations that should participate in the MM exercise. SA is the basis for Stakeholder Management and helps us think about which 10–20 organizations or people need to be involved in the MM for it to be successful, and how to go about managing the process of recruiting people to be involved in a MM project. Figure 14.3 illustrates the type of high level–high interest stakeholders that could guide a stakeholder analysis.

A stakeholder is any organization or person that can affect or be affected by the key issue. A narrow perspective limits stakeholders to those who have legal and presumed stakes. A broad perspective pays attention to networks and wider community well-being. The narrow perspective of stakeholders dictates at a minimum inclusion of certain key stakeholders. Enough space should be left to include a broader perspective to ensure creativity. When of future implementation of solutions brought forward in a MM process is anticipated, it is important to branch out the stakeholder group and work with coalitions, shared participation or the option to observe workshops. A sociologist or network analyst could go to great lengths determining the correct participants. However, for practical purposes, the process outlined in Box 14.1 is often sufficient.

Box 14.1

1. Identification of stakeholders by principal host and/or consulting/research team as a starting point.
2. Agree on criteria of what makes a balanced, fair and productive stakeholder group.
3. Prepare material to request input on the evolving stakeholder list from external organizations.
4. Request input for stakeholder list from a wide variety of perspectives.
5. Check for self-referencing and make sure that the stakeholder participant group reaches beyond "business-as-usual".
6. Build a substantial database before selecting stakeholders.
7. Determine number of direct participants.
8. Identify the basic, non-negotiable direct stakeholder organizations.
9. Identify knowledgeable persons with authority to speak for these organizations or establish a clear line of delegation.
10. Identify the gaps of knowledge in terms of obvious subjects that can be expected to emerge during the dialogue.
11. Identify knowledge and the people with the capacity to think out-of-the-box.
12. Use a "spider chart" to check for balancing of intended criteria.

When stakeholders are invited, the following questions require an answer:

1. What kind of information will participants need?
2. What commitment do you need from participants?
3. What is the next step participants may expect?

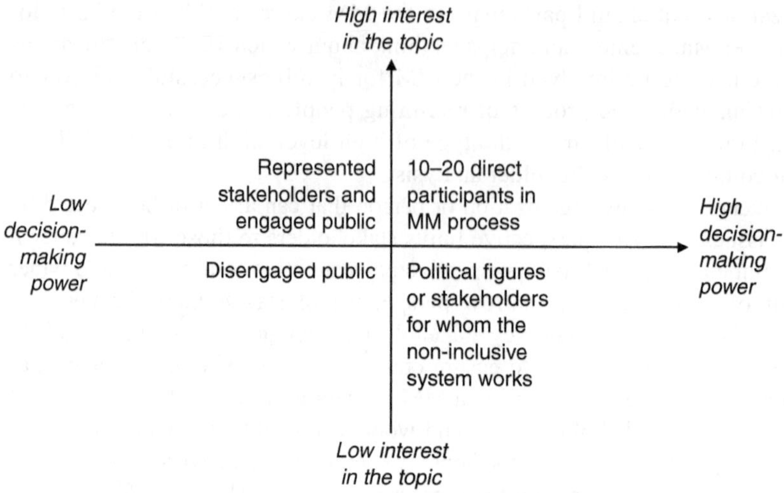

Figure 14.3 Stakeholder analysis and selection.

Number of stakeholders

Between 10 and 20 participants is an ideal number. The lower boundary is determined by the diversity of perspectives the participants bring to the process. The upper boundary is determined by the number of participants that can be effectively and satisfactorily facilitated. If the interest in a MM process is high during the SA and selection phase, a mechanism may be designed to observe the workshops and/or additional communication venues such as website or blog.

The software

An important aspect of a MM process is the quick feedback between facilitator/modeler and participant group, also referred to as "listening cycles" (Conklin 2006). The supporting software or even qualitative mapping method is of secondary importance. Several software packages are available. STELLA is one trademarked software package that can be used for MM processes (www.isee.com). STELLA seems to communicate well with groups that consider themselves non-modelers.

Generic series of workshops

The circumstances determine the duration of a MM process. The trade-offs between depth of the dialogue, the ability to gather relevant data and communicate the use of it to the participant group, and the ability of the group (often non-modelers) to simulate or use the resulting model for Adaptive Management purposes are factors to consider during the design of a MM process. Figure 14.4 illustrates a hypothetical MM process (adapted from Videira *et al.* 2011, in press).

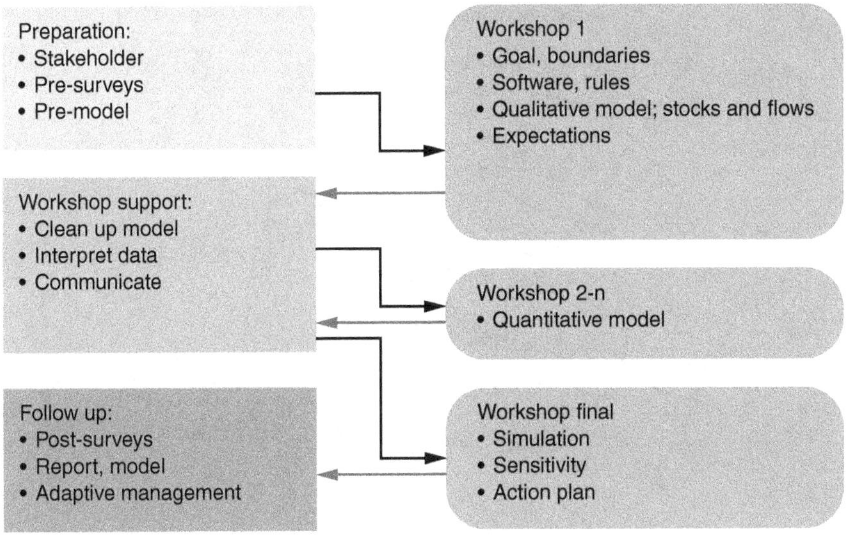

Figure 14.4 Example of flow in Mediated Modeling workshops (adapted from Videira *et al.*, in press 2011).

Integrated modeling for adaptive capacity building

MM is proposed for "scoping" purposes, i.e. to scope for the driving forces and inter-linkages within a system as determined by a relevant group of stakeholders. This form of modeling should be transparent to the stakeholders benefitting from the model building experience. There are good reasons to develop more detailed, data-intense models. Costanza and Ruth (1998) reasoned in favor of a progressive three-step modeling framework. They propose a sequence of model building from scoping models to more detailed "research" models and finally "management" models for frequent and accurate decision-making. The progression indicates an increase in precision while trading off communicability of the structure, parameters and data quality of a computer model. More recently, the three-step framework was presented in a spiraling model called the "Multiscale Integrated Modeling for Sustainable Adaptive Systems" (MIMSAS) (van den Belt, 2009). The MIMSAS framework emphasizes adaptive capacity among stakeholders and decision-makers in the design process of models as assessment tools, following the modeling process through implementation, monitoring and refining of an underlying vision (van den Belt 2009) (Figure 14.5).

Figure 14.5 conveys the elements of Adaptive Management – envisioning, assessment, planning, implementation and monitoring – on outward pointing axes, which represent an increasing level of detail (increased resolution in scope/content) and resolution in time (van den Belt, 2009). After a full Adaptive Management cycle, the scoping model is ideally revisited to evaluate the following

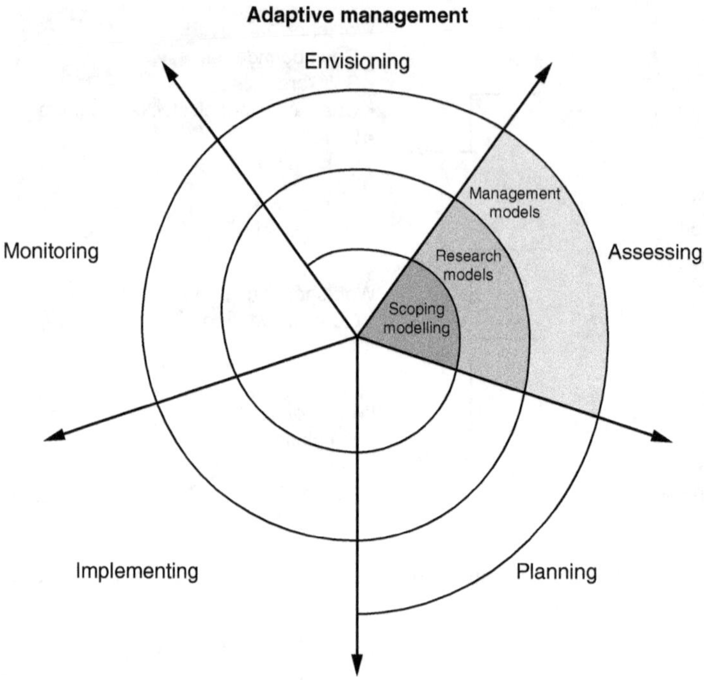

Figure 14.5 Multi-scale Integrated Modeling for Sustainable Adaptive Systems (MIMSAS) framework (source: van den Belt 2009).

questions. Were we right in our assessment through the modeling toolbox? Does the monitored data mean that we "only" change/narrow a few parameters? Or should the model structure be updated, because we missed major feedback loops or time lags? Can the results from research models be integrated in a meaningful way in the scoping model or is the scoping model obsolete?

Research models are developed to answer precise correct-based questions and may correct a particular linkage between two parameters in a scoping model. Research models can be used to verify the scoping models against the larger knowledge base that is available within the literature and other scientific databases. The requirements put on research models are to confirm model results against scholastic and scientific thought and to be validated against existing data for confidence estimates. The required conformation to the disciplines tends to make the research models more detailed and explicitly targeted with quality assured data requirements, and generally less transparent to those unfamiliar within the disciplines. Calibration of MM models with the outputs of Research Models may help to gain confidence in the scenario based outputs of MM models. This is important if the scoping models are to be communicated outside the scoping group.

Even though "scoping" models are useful in addressing (and often dissipating) a complex and potentially contentious situation, "revisiting" scoping models could in part be hampered by the fact that a mediated modeler is often hired on a consulting basis as a neutral party to facilitate an often contentious area of investigation, bringing together stakeholders that would otherwise be unlikely to put their minds together in a collaborative manner. In addition, public organizations often lack the capacity to pursue these tools, because incentives tend to reward short-term, centralized, segmented decisions with a competitive rather than collaborative underpinning (Boland and Fowler, 2000).

The next step up is management models; such models should be able to support regular management decisions and are often expensive to develop. For example, in the field of ecosystem services valuation the Multiscale Integrated Modeling of Ecosystem Services (MIMES) provides a promising framework for future development (Boumans and Costanza 2007a, b). MIMES aims to develop a repository of freely available modeling modules that can be accessed online and adapted to a need. MIMES use Simile software, which allows for some level of spatially explicit dynamic modeling of ecosystem services.

Telling the story of the Galápagos using STELLA

Let's revisit the story of the Galápagos from the introduction, which will now be told with the assistance of STELLA software. Figure 14.6 illustrates a model overview providing a framework to describe natural capital assets, such as native species, or liabilities, and non-native, introduced species. From the natural capital asset basis, which can be described with increasing detail, ecosystem services are derived. These services are often divided into provisioning services, such as food and water; regulating services, such as flood and disease control; cultural services, such as spiritual, recreational and cultural benefits; and supporting services, such as nutrient cycling, that maintain the conditions for life on Earth (Millennium Ecosystem Assessment 2005). For this simple example, recreation is highlighted as an ecosystem service and the assumption is made that tourism is attracted by species native or endemic to the Galápagos Islands. In addition, it is assumed that if/when the ratio of native over non-native species declines, the attractiveness of the Galápagos Islands for recreation may decline, be it with a time lag, even though the majority of contemporary tourists have only a minor interest in nature (Mark Gardner, personal communication).

This has economic implications. Statistics show the number of tourists has increased exponentially over recent decades. In addition, the number of inhabitants has also increased to support the growing tourist industry with associated added value to the GDP.

However, with every tourist and additional inhabitant, there is a biohazard risk of introduction of additional non-native species, often with detrimental consequences for native species.

Various policies have either been implemented or discussed over time. The important question remains how any of such policies or management initiatives improves the natural capital over time and how should such progress be monitored?

Figure 14.7 illustrates the model structure in STELLA using stocks, flows, auxiliary variables and information connectors, i.e. the four building blocks in STELLA.

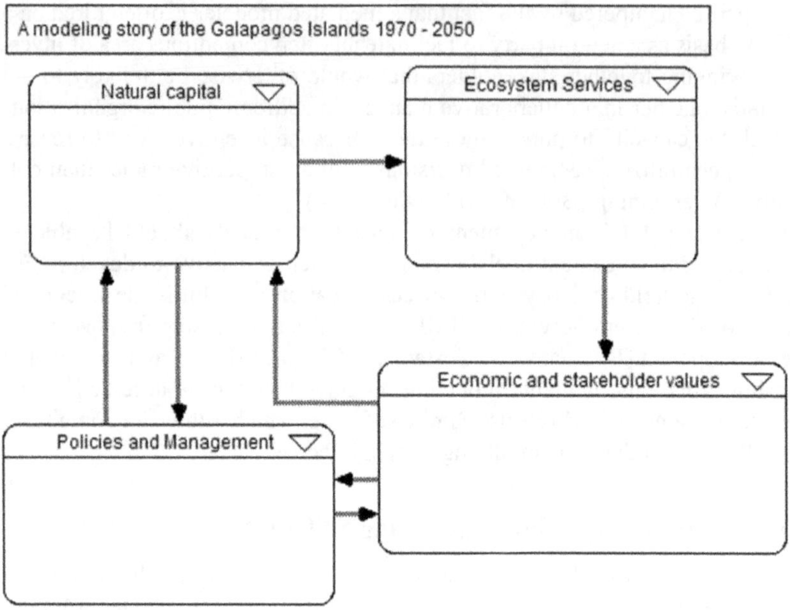

Figure 14.6 Galápagos model overview.

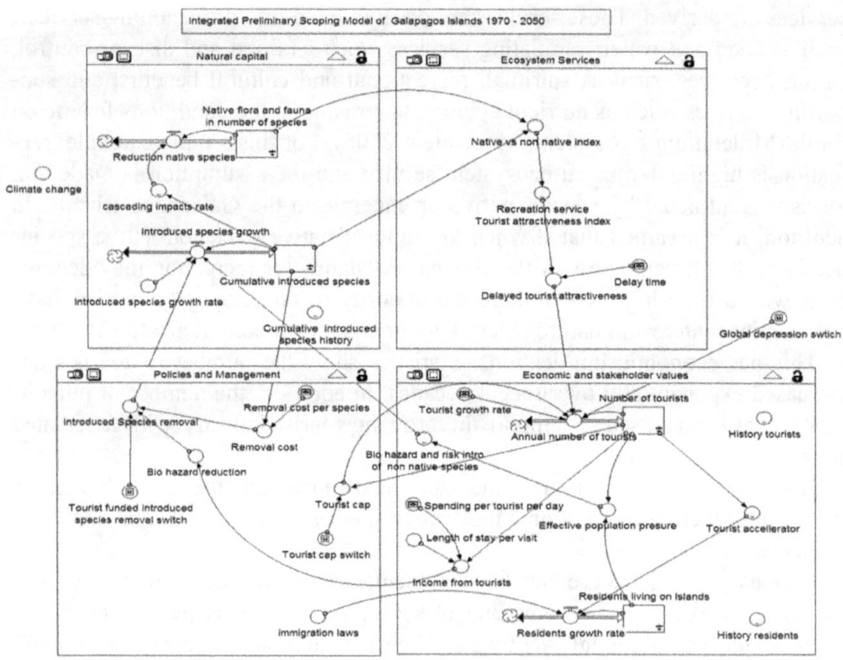

Figure 14.7 Model structure for Galápagos system using STELLA.

This model can be used to commence a dialogue among stakeholders and elicit their perceptions, while contrasting with available data. The user interface may show graphs of how relevant parameters have changed over time. For example, Figure 14.8 shows the history of cumulative non-native species introduced since 1970 (line 3); between 1995 and 2008, its exponential nature becomes apparent. The model (line 2) simulates a continuation of the historic trend. In addition, the number of native flora and fauna has declined steadily; again, the model (line 1) simulates a continuation of this trend.

Figure 14.9 illustrates the historic numbers of visitors to the Galápagos Islands, which have been increasing exponentially, as has the income from tourism. However, the model simulates a reduced income from tourism in the future under the assumption that the attractiveness for tourism may be reduced when there are fewer native species.

All the various policy- and management-related questions have been raised in various forums and dialogues. In themselves, these questions are not original. Some basic numbers and trends are available to support the dialogue. But have these questions and available data been integrated in a consistent manner before? An important question then is; who has the wisdom to examine the trade-offs and should be at the table to make a substantial difference on the future of these islands? Through my brief visit to Galápagos in 2009 to participate in the Galápagos Science Symposium, it became clear that there are many opinions and views on how to balance the unique and sensitive ecology, which is a crucial natural capital asset base, with a growing economy and its social and cultural associations. Perhaps systems thinking and stakeholder involved modeling can contribute to this ongoing and vibrant dialogue.

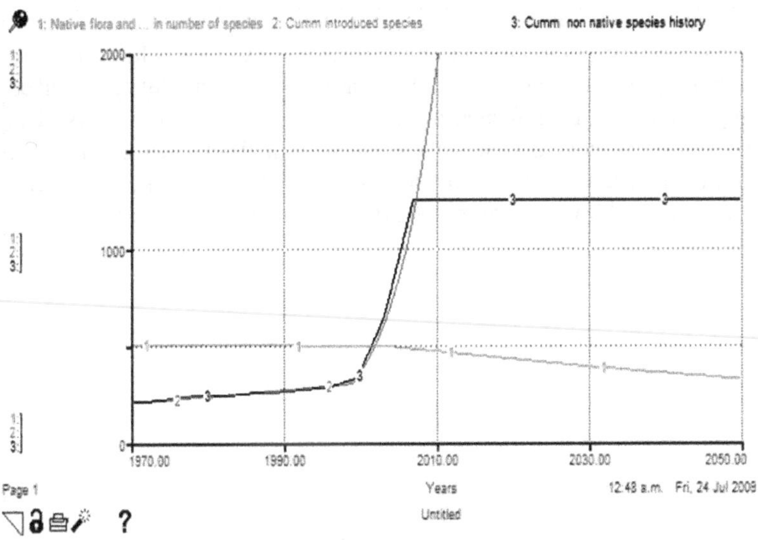

Figure 14.8 Native versus non-native species.

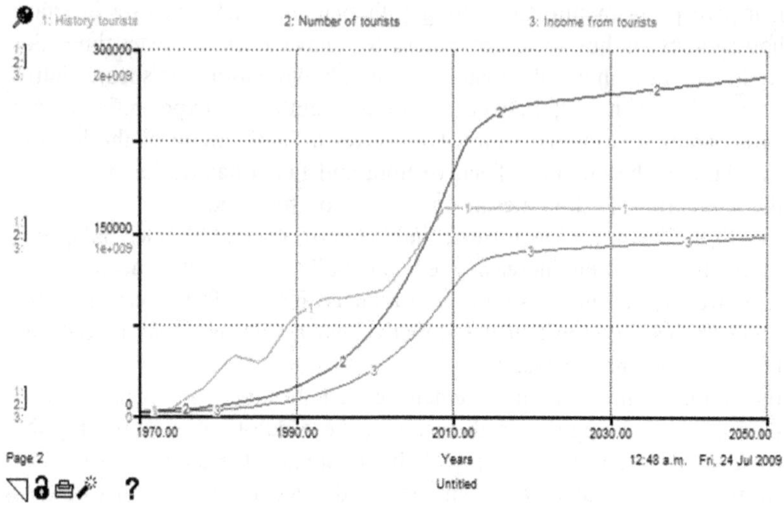

Figure 14.9 Tourism: history, numbers and income.

Conclusion

This chapter presents MM as a tool that can be used to pursue an integrated, evidence-based dialogue among stakeholders with divergent views. MM can be used for scoping purposes before embarking on or in conjunction with other modeling approaches or stakeholder negotiations. MM provides a process of scoping for relevant information as deemed by a group of participants (between 10 and 20), and aims to interrelate otherwise segmented information. As an example, a framework of ecosystem services is used and filled in with indicative (but not precise) parameters. Such a preliminary model can be used as a starting point to elicit information and opinions from stakeholders. The purpose of a MM process is that stakeholders learn from each other while building a model structure. Such a model can simulate what-if scenarios and can also be revisited in subsequent years as part of developing adaptive capacity.

References

Boland, T. and A. Fowler. 2000. A systems perspective of performance management in public sector organizations, *Int. J. Public Sector Management* 13:417–446.

Boumans, R. and R. Costanza. 2007a. The multiscale integrated Earth Systems model (MIMES): the dynamics, modeling and valuation of ecosystem services, in C. Bers, D. Petry, and C. Pahl-Wostl, C. (eds.). 2007. *Global Assessments: Bridging Scales and Linking to Policy, Report on the joint TIAS-GWSP workshop held at the University of Maryland University College, Adelphi, USA, 10–11 May 2007. GWSP Issues in Global Water System Research, No. 2* (GWSP IPO: Bonn, Germany). www.gwsp.org.

Boumans, R. and R. Costanza, 2007b. The Multiscale Integrated Model of the Earth Services (MIMES) The Dynamics, Modeling and Valuation of Ecosystem Services, *Proceeding of the 6th European conference on Ecological Modeling conference, ECEM 2007 Trieste Italy* (27–30 November 2007).

Conklin, J. 2006. *Dialogue Mapping: Building Shared Understanding of Wicked Problems* (John Wiley & Sons Ltd: Chichester, UK).

Costanza, R. and M. Ruth. 1998. Dynamic Systems Modeling for Scoping and Consensus Building, *Environmental Management* 22:183–195.

Millennium Ecosystem Assessment. 2005. *Ecosystems and Human Well-Being: Current State and Trends* (Island Press: Washington, DC).

Van den Belt, M. 2004. *Mediated Modeling: a System Dynamics Approach to Environmental Consensus Building* (Island Press: Washington, DC).

Van den Belt, M. 2009. Multiscale Integrated Modeling for Sustainable Adaptive Systems, *Conference Proceedings System Dynamics Society, Albuquerque, New Mexico* (26–31 July 2009).

Videira, N., M. van den Belt, P. Antunes, R. Santos, and R. Boumans. In press 2011. Integrated Modeling of Coastal and Estuarine Ecosystem Services, in M. van den Belt and R. Costanza (eds.), *Ecological Economics of Estuaries and Coasts, Treatise on Estuarine and Coastal Science, Volume 12* (Elsevier: Amsterdam, The Netherlands).

15 Part III summary

A systemic approach – modeling and restoration

Mark Gardener and Matthias Wolff

Part III looks at the reasons why research and modeling at the scale of the entire ecosystem (e.g. socio-ecosystem) is fundamental to understand complex system functioning and to help optimizing management for both biodiversity conservation and sustainable use of resources.

Rachel Atkinson and colleagues review eradication as a tool for invasive species management in Galápagos. They report on the history of species introductions in Galápagos and show that the rate of introductions steadily increased since the 1830s, rising most rapidly during the last 50 years. In 2008, the tally of introduced terrestrial species was 1,445 including 870 plants, 536 invertebrates, 30 vertebrates and ten diseases. Of these introduced species, many have invaded native ecosystems. Vertebrate invasions were the first to cause impact and alarm in the latter half of the twentieth century. These have been followed by plant and invertebrate invasions that now cover huge areas, particularly in the highland regions of the inhabited islands, and further invasions are expected in future. The authors encourage the reader to consider potentially positive and negative impacts of eradication programs to the whole ecosystem, not just iconic species. They consider four main criteria before deciding to attempt eradication: (1) strategic–operational; (2) biological; (3) economic; and (4) socio-political. They list the following important considerations: (1) an eradication operation should not be attempted if reintroduction cannot be prevented; (2) the rate of removal must exceed the rate of population increase; (3) species with limited distributions, that are easily detectable, with a short-lived dormant stage (e.g. a seed or egg bank), and that have a known control method for reproductive individuals, are prime candidates for eradication; (4) eradications, especially when carried out at the early stages of invasion, are cost-effective and theoretically neat solutions to prevent the future or current impact of invasive species. Additionally, eradications should not be started if there is insufficient funding to address unforeseen consequences of the operation on ecosystem dynamics. Another frequently overlooked requirement is the need for governmental and public support for all aspects of the project from the start in order to ensure that there are no barriers to the program from beginning to end. The tool of eradication is attractive to both donors and managers alike, as there is a measurable outcome and a definite endpoint to the project. However, there are limits to the use of eradication as a tool for conservation. The authors discuss these limits, analyzing 57 eradication projects of vertebrates, invertebrates and vascular plants from 1961 to present. Of these, 27 have been successful, 20 unsuccessful and ten are ongoing. The majority of successes were of large vertebrates, whereas most plant and invertebrate eradication attempts were unsuccessful. They found common trends in project successes and failures with operational, biological, economic and social criteria all contributing. They discuss the future of eradications and the alternatives in Galápagos.

Matthias Wolff and coworkers use a trophic modeling approach to integrate ecological and fisheries data for a holistic description of the Galápagos Marine Reserve (GMR) ecosystem and to evaluate the effect of the banning of industrial fishing in the GMR in 1998 and the coinciding El Niño event. For the construction of their baseline flow model they used data from the late 1990s when industrial fishery was still in place. Estimated pre-1998 catch volumes in the GMR were in the realms of average catches in other oceanic and shelf systems, hence, the model was considered to be realistic. Top order predators were the warm-blooded toothed whales, but large pelagic fish and cephalopods also played a prominent role. Simulations suggest that the GMR has undergone a substantial recovery process of large pelagic fish and sharks since industrial fishery was banned 12 years ago. According to the model simulations, most large pelagic fish would have – under normal environmental conditions – attained 10–20% stock increase after only two years after the fishery ban, concordant with literature findings showing that marine reserve closure is almost immediately effective in less than two years. Nevertheless, the El Niño event suppressed this rapid response for a further two to three years, suggesting that the bottom-up effect on the system of reduced primary productivity was stronger than the top-down effect from the release in fishing pressure. The first species predicted to surpass the pre- El Niño reference level was the yellowfin tuna, followed by wahoo, dolphin fish and sailfish. Owing to their slow population turnover rates, sharks followed later. Juvenile sharks are predicted to maintain reduced biomass throughout the time due to strong control by increased levels of top predators. Sea lions, cormorants, penguins and sea turtles needed the whole 12-year period to rebuild their populations. The authors emphasize that the disruption of the system by the El Niño impacted in the medium term (three to nine years), leading to higher biomasses of large pelagic fish predators than under the same fishery conditions without the El Niño impact. This suggests that, since predator biomass is reduced during the El Niño, prey populations find an "open loophole" to proliferate first and are then followed by their predators in a Lotka–Volterra fashion. It then takes several years for the system to normalize. Long-term monitoring data for marine mammals, birds and sea turtles confirmed the El Niño driven population reductions simulated by the model.

Marjan van den Belt presents mediated modeling (MM) as a computer-based tool that can facilitate the participation of diverse stakeholders in the identification and valuation of ecosystem services from a conservation and human perspective. Systems thinking (the use of causal diagrams) and system dynamics (quantitative representations of feedback loops and time lags to understand systems) provide the underlying modeling philosophy. MM is presented as a decision support tool that can feed into all phases of adaptive management: envisioning; assessment; planning; implementation; and monitoring. The discussion between the stakeholders involved is interpreted by a mediated modeler and reflected back into the dialogue for all participants in real time. The integration of ecology, economics and social issues for sustainable development is often considered a normative objective in a MM process. In her contribution, Marjan uses a first pass example of how MM – based on a model produced using the STELLA software – could work in Galápagos to demonstrate how this tool could promote stakeholder dialogue.

Part IV

Reconciliation of conservation with socio-economic development

16 The value of ecosystem services and biodiversity conservation

A challenge for the Galápagos

Robert Costanza

What are ecosystem services?

Ecosystem services are defined as "the benefits people obtain from ecosystems" (Costanza *et al.* 1997; Millennium Ecosystem Assessment 2005). These include provisioning services such as food and water; regulating services such as regulation of floods, drought and disease; supporting services such as soil formation and nutrient cycling; and cultural services such as recreational, scientific, spiritual and other nonmaterial benefits (Costanza *et al.* 1997; Daily 1997; de Groot *et al.* 2002).

This is an appropriately broad and an appropriately vague definition. It includes both the benefits people *perceive*, and those they do not. The conventional economic approach to "benefits" is far too narrow in this regard, and tends to limit benefits only to those that people both perceive and are "willing to pay" for in some real or contingent sense. However, the general population's information about the world, especially when it comes to ecosystem services, is extremely limited. We can expect many ecosystem services to go almost unnoticed by the vast majority of people, especially when they are public, non-excludable services that never enter the private, excludable market. Think of the storm regulation value of wetlands (Costanza *et al.* 2008). How can we expect the average citizen to understand the complex linkages between landscape patterns, precipitation patterns, wetlands and flood attenuation, when even the best landscape scientists find this an extremely challenging task? We need to remember the definition of ecosystem services (the benefits provided by ecosystems), and acknowledge that the degree to which the public perceives and understands them is a separate (and very important) question. Conventional economic valuation presumes that people have well-formed preferences and enough information about trade-offs that they can adequately judge their "willingness-to-pay". Since these assumptions do not hold for many ecosystem services we must: (1) inform people's preferences by showing the underlying dynamics of the ecosystems in question using models; (2) allow groups to discuss the issues and "construct" their preferences within a framework to inform the discussions; or (3) use other techniques that do not rely directly on preferences to estimate the contribution to human well-being of ecosystem services (i.e. to directly infer marginal contributions to well-being), for example through the use of computer models.

In addition, the benefits one receives from functioning ecosystems do not necessarily depend on one's ability to pay for them in monetary units. For example, indigenous populations with no money economy at all derive most of the essentials for life from ecosystem services but have zero ability to pay for them in monetary terms. To understand the value of these ecosystem services we need to understand the trade-offs involved, and these may be best expressed in units of time, energy, land or other units, not necessarily money, remembering that the local population may or may not understand or be able to quantify these trade-offs. Finally, if one can express the trade-offs (value) in one set of units (numerator) and can express the trade-offs between that numerator and another, then one can convert the trade-offs into the other numerator. For example, if we can express trade-offs in units of time and can estimate the time–money tradeoff, we can express the time units in monetary terms.

Intermediate v. final goods and services

A second issue is that ecosystem services are, by definition, not ends or goals, but means to the end or goal of sustainable human well-being. This does not imply that ecosystems are not also valuable for other reasons, but that *ecosystem services* are defined as the instrumental values of ecosystems as means to the end of human well-being. An important, but different, distinction some authors have made is one between intermediate services and final services (Boyd and Banzhaf 2007). It is certainly true that for the purposes of certain aggregation exercises adding intermediate and final services would be double counting; but that does not imply that intermediate services are not services. Think of the production of tires in an economy. Some tires are sold directly to consumers and are part of the final demand, while others are sold to car companies and are intermediate products, sold to consumers as parts of cars. The tires themselves are indistinguishable from each other, the only difference being who buys them. When calculating GDP (Gross Domestic Product, which is the aggregate of sales to final demand) it would not be appropriate to count both the tires sold to final demand and the tires sold to car companies, since those tires are already counted as parts of the cars sold to final demand. However, tires in both cases, whether intermediate or final products, are means to the end of human well-being and are not ends in themselves. Likewise, ecosystem goods and services, whether intermediate (or "supporting" in the Millennium Assessment typology) services or final services are all contributors to the end of human well-being. Also, ecosystem processes (or functions) and services are not mutually exclusive categories. Some processes or functions are also services; others are not. Some services are intermediate, some are final and some are partly both.

Classifying ecosystem services

There are several important and useful ways to classify and group ecosystem services. Here are just two by way of example: classification according to spatial characteristics and classification according to "excludability and rivalness" status. Table

16.1 groups the 17 ecosystem services listed in Costanza *et al.* (1997) into five categories according to their spatial characteristics. For example, services such as carbon sequestration (an intermediate input to climate regulation) is classified as "global: non-proximal", since the spatial location of carbon sequestration does not matter. The atmosphere is well mixed, and removing carbon dioxide (or other greenhouse gases) at any location is equivalent to removing it anywhere else. "Local proximal" services, on the other hand, are dependent on the spatial proximity of the ecosystem to the human beneficiaries. For example, "storm protection" requires that the ecosystem doing the protecting be proximal to the human settlements being protected. "Directional flow related" services are dependent on the flow from upstream to downstream as is the case for water supply and water regulation. And so on for the other categories listed in Table 16.1.

Another way to classify ecosystem services is according to their "excludability and rivalness" status. Table 16.2 arrays these two characteristics against each other in a matrix, which leads to four categories of goods and services. Goods and services are "excludable" to the degree that individuals can be excluded from benefiting from them. Most privately owned, marketed goods and services are relatively easily excludable. I can prevent others from eating the tomatoes I have grown, or the timber I have harvested or the fish I have caught unless they

Table 16.1 Ecosystem services classified according to spatial characteristics (from Costanza 2008)

1. Global Non-proximal (does not depend on proximity)
    - 1 and 2. Climate Regulations
    - Carbon sequestration (NEP)
    - Carbon storage
    - 17. Cultural/Existence value
2. Local Proximal (depends on proximity)
    - 3. Disturbance Regulation/Storm protection
    - 9. Waste Treatment
    - 10. Pollination
    - 11. Biological Control
    - 12. Habitat/Refugia
3. Directional Flow-related: flow from point of production to point of use
    - 4. Water regulation/flood protection
    - 5. Water supply
    - 6. Sediment regulation/Erosion control
    - 8. Nutrient regulation
4. In situ (point of use)
    - 7. Soil formation
    - 13. Food production/Non-timber forest products
    - 14. Raw materials
5. User movement related: flow of people to unique natural features
    - 15. Genetic resources
    - 16. Recreation potential
    - 17. Cultural/Aesthetic

pay me. However, it is difficult or impossible to exclude others from benefiting from many public goods, for instance a well-regulated climate, fish in the open ocean, or the aesthetic benefits of a forest. Goods and services are "rival" to the degree that one person's benefiting from them interferes with other people also benefiting from them. If I eat the tomato or the fish, you cannot also eat it; but if I benefit from a well-regulated climate, you can also do the same. Excludability is largely a function of supply (to what extent can producers exclude users) and is related to the cultural and institutional mechanisms available to enforce exclusion; while rivalness is a function of demand (how benefits depend on other users) and is more a characteristic of the good or service itself. Table 16.2 places ecosystem services into the four categories that this two by two matrix creates.

These two examples should be enough to indicate that there are many useful ways to classify ecosystem goods and services and our goal is not a single, consistent system, but rather an intelligent pluralism of typologies that will each be useful for different purposes.

Complex systems and ecosystem services

Ecosystems with embedded humans are complex, dynamic, adaptive systems with non-linear feedbacks, thresholds, hysteresis effects, etc. (Costanza *et al.* 1993). Ecosystem services are therefore not the product of a linear chain from production (means) to direct benefits by people (ends) with no feedbacks or any of the other complexities of the real world. All ecosystem services are, by definition, means to the end of human well-being. Ecosystem processes or functions can also be services (they are not mutually exclusive categories), and the same services can be both intermediate and final. The real world is complex and messy and our systems of classification and definition of ecosystem services should recognize that and work with it, not ignore it in a misguided attempt to impose unrealistic order and consistency.

We need to build models of these complex, interconnected systems that can help us better understand the dynamics and patterns of ecosystem services production and benefits. For example, the GUMBO (Global Unified Metamodel of the Biosphere) model (Boumans *et al.* 2002) and the more recent MIMES (Multiscale Integrated Models of Ecosystem Services) framework are attempts to do just that. MIMES is a framework to address the magnitude, dynamics and spatial

Table 16.2 Ecosystem services classified according to rivalness and excludability (from Costanza 2008)

	Excludable	*Non-excludable*
Rival	Market goods and services (most provisioning services)	Open access resources (some provisioning services)
Non-rival	Congestible services (some recreation services)	Public goods and services (most regulatory and cultural services)

patterns of ecosystem services at multiple scales (Figure 16.1). The MIMES framework explicitly addresses the linked dynamics of natural, human, built and social capital, and allows one to integrate site-specific information with regional and global surveys, Geographic Information Systems (GIS) and remote sensing data. MIMES is process-based, spatially explicit, dynamic, non-linear simulation model (including carbon, water, nitrogen, phosphorous, plants, consumers (including humans) and a range of ecosystem services) under various climate, economic and policy scenarios. MIMES is spatially scalable. Each "location" in MIMES includes the percentage of land surface in 11 biomes or ecosystem types: *Open Ocean*; *Coastal Ocean*; *Forests*; *Grasslands*; *Wetlands*; *Lakes and Rivers*; *Deserts*; *Tundra*; *Ice and rock*; *Croplands*; and *Urban*. The relative areas of each biome at each location change in response to urban and rural population growth, economic production, changes in temperature and precipitation and other variables. Among the biomes, there are exchanges of energy, carbon, nutrients, water and mineral matter. The model calculates the marginal product of ecosystem services in both an economic production and welfare function as estimates of the prices of each service. The number of "locations" or cells in MIMES is variable and can include either grid or polygon representations of multiple locations. For each of these applications, the basic MIMES structure remains the same, but the parameters must be recalibrated.

Conventional economic valuation presumes that people have well-formed preferences and enough information about trade-offs that they can adequately judge their "willingness-to-pay." These assumptions do not hold for many ecosystem services. Therefore, we must: (1) inform people's preferences (for example by showing them the underlying dynamics of the ecosystems in question using models like MIMES; (2) allow groups to discuss the issues and "construct" their preferences (again using the MIMES framework to inform the discussions); or (3) use

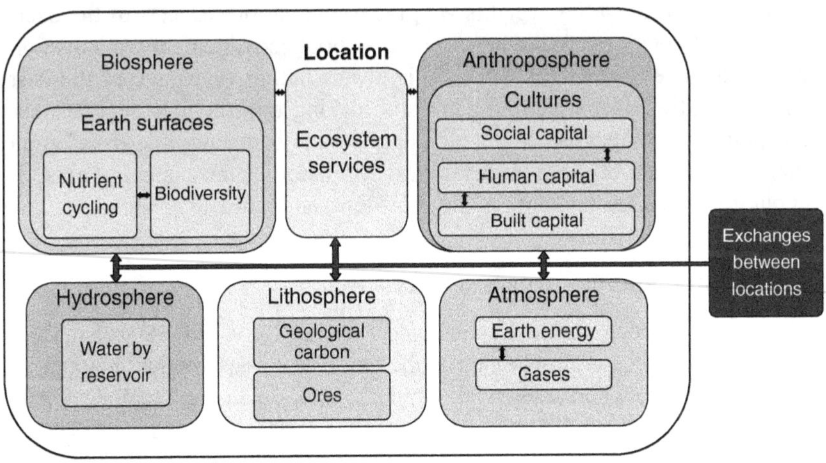

Figure 16.1 Basic structure of the MIMES (Multiscale Integrated Models of Ecosystem Services) framework.

other techniques that do not rely on preferences to estimate the contribution to human welfare of ecosystem services (i.e. using the MIMES to directly infer marginal contributions to welfare). We combine these three methods to develop new and more integrated methods to value ecosystem services.

Valuation of ecological systems and services

The issue of valuation is inseparable from the choices and decisions we have to make about ecological systems. Some argue that valuation of ecosystems is either impossible or unwise. For example, some argue that we cannot place a value on such "intangibles" as human life, environmental aesthetics or long-term ecological benefits. But, in fact, we do so every day. When we set construction standards for highways, bridges and the like, we value human life – acknowledged or not – because spending more money on construction would save lives. These are *statistical* lives, however, not particular lives and one should not confuse the two.

Another often-made argument is that we should protect ecosystems for purely moral or aesthetic reasons, and we do not need valuations of ecosystems for this purpose. However, there are equally compelling moral arguments that may be in direct conflict with the moral argument to protect ecosystems; for example, the moral argument that no one should go hungry. All we have done is to translate the valuation and decision problem into a new set of dimensions and a new language of discourse. Therefore, while ecosystem valuation is certainly difficult, one choice we do *not* have is whether or not to do it. Rather, the decisions we make, as a society, about ecosystems *imply* trade-offs and therefore valuations. We can choose to make these valuations explicit or not; we can undertake them using the best available ecological science and understanding or not; we can do them with an explicit acknowledgment of the huge uncertainties involved or not; but as long as we are forced to make choices, we are doing valuation. The valuations are simply the relative weights we give to the various aspects of the decision problem. Society can make better choices about ecosystems if the valuation issue is made as explicit as possible. This means taking advantage of the best information and models we can muster and making uncertainties about valuations explicit too. It also means developing new and better ways to make good decisions in the face of these uncertainties. Ultimately, it means being explicit about our goals as a society, both in the short-term and in the long-term.

Natural capital and ecosystem services

Sustainability has been variously construed (Pezzey 1989; WCED 1987; Costanza 1991); but one useful definition is the amount of consumption that can be sustained indefinitely without degrading capital stocks – including "natural capital" stocks (Pearce and Turner 1989; Costanza and Daly 1992). Since "capital" is traditionally defined as produced (manufactured) means of production, the term "natural capital" needs explanation. It is based on a more functional definition of capital as "a stock that yields a flow of valuable goods or services into the future". What is functionally important is the relation of a stock yielding a flow – whether the stock is manufactured or natural is in this view a distinction between kinds of capital and not a defining characteristic of capital itself. For example, a stock or population of trees or fish provides a flow or annual yield of new trees or fish, a flow that can be sustainable year after year. The sustainable flow is "natural income"; the stock that yields the sustainable flow is "natural capital". Natural capital may also provide services like recycling waste materials or water catchment and erosion control, which are also counted as natural income. Since the flow of services from ecosystems requires that they function as whole systems, the structure and diversity of the ecosystem is a critical component in natural capital.

To achieve sustainability, we must incorporate natural capital, and the ecosystem goods and services that it provides, into our economic and social accounting and our systems of social choice. In estimating these values, we must consider how much of our ecological life support systems we can afford to lose. To what extent can we substitute manufactured for natural capital, and how much of our natural capital is irreplaceable? For example, could we replace the radiation screening services of the ozone layer if it were destroyed? Because natural capital is not captured in existing markets, special methods must be used to estimate its value. These range from attempts to mimic market behavior using surveys and questionnaires to elicit the preferences of current resource users (i.e. willingness-to-pay (WTP) to methods based on energy analysis (EA) of flows in natural ecosystems (which do not depend on current human preferences at all) (Farber and Costanza 1987; Costanza *et al.* 1989; Costanza 2004). Because of the inherent difficulties and uncertainties in determining these values, we are better off with an intelligently pluralistic approach that acknowledges and utilizes these different, independent approaches.

The point that must be stressed is that the economic value of ecosystems is connected to their physical, chemical and biological role in the long-term, global system – whether the present generation of individuals fully recognizes that role or not. If it is accepted that each species, no matter how seemingly uninteresting or lacking in immediate utility, has a role in natural ecosystems (which *do* provide many direct benefits to humans), it is possible to shift the focus away from our imperfect short-term perceptions and toward the goal of developing more accurate values for long-term ecosystem services. Ultimately, this will involve the collaborative construction of dynamic, evolutionary models of linked ecological economic systems that adequately address long-term responses and uncertainties, like those mentioned above.

Uncertainty and ecosystem services

Valuation of ecosystem services and natural capital will always involve large uncertainties. How do we make good decisions in the face of this uncertainty? Current command and control systems of direct environmental regulation are not very efficient at managing environmental resources for sustainability, particularly in the face of uncertainty about long-term values and impacts. They are inherently reactive rather than proactive. They induce legal confrontation, obfuscation and government intrusion into business in a way that reduces efficiency. Rather than encouraging long-range technical and social innovation, they tend to suppress it. They do not mesh well with the market signals that firms and individuals use to make decisions and do not effectively translate long-term global goals into short-term local incentives.

We need to explore promising alternatives to our current command and control environmental management systems, and to modify existing government agencies and other institutions accordingly. The enormous uncertainty about local and transnational environmental impacts needs to be incorporated into decision-making. We also need to better understand the sociological, cultural and political criteria for acceptance or rejection of policy instruments.

For example, one policy instrument designed to incorporate uncertainty into the market system and to induce positive environmental technological innovation is the flexible environmental assurance bonding system (Costanza and Perrings 1990; Costanza and Cornwell 1992). In addition to direct charges for known environmental damages, a company would be required to post an assurance bond equal to the current best estimate of the largest potential future environmental damages; the money would be kept in interest-bearing escrow accounts. The bond (plus a portion of the interest) would be returned if the firm could show that the suspected damages had not occurred or would not occur. If they did, the bond would be used to rehabilitate or repair the environment and to compensate injured parties. Thus, the burden of proof would be shifted from the public to the resource-user and a strong economic incentive would be provided to research the true costs of environmentally innovative activities and to develop cost-effective pollution control technologies. This is a combination of the "polluter pays" principle with the "precautionary" principle to produce the "precautionary polluter pays principle" or 4P approach to environmental management under uncertainty (Costanza and Cornwell 1992).

Instead of being mesmerized into inaction by scientific uncertainty over our future, we should acknowledge uncertainty as a fundamental part of the system. We must develop better methods to model and value ecological goods and services, and devise policies to translate those values into appropriate incentives.

Biodiversity and ecosystem services

Biodiversity is the variability among living organisms from all sources. This includes diversity within species, between species and of ecosystems (Heywood, 1995). In the past 100 years biodiversity loss has been so dramatic that it has been recognized as a global change in its own right (Walker and Steffen 1996). This has raised numerous concerns, including the possibility that the functioning of the Earth's ecosystems might be threatened by biodiversity loss (Ehrlich and Ehrlich 1981; Schulze and Mooney 1993). If biodiversity has an influence on ecosystem functioning (in addition to any other roles it may play) then it will affect ecosystem goods and services and human welfare. Research on the relationship between biodiversity and ecosystem functioning is therefore of direct relevance to public policy, and this relationship has been the subject of considerable interest and controversy over the past decades (Kinzig and Pacala 2002)

The relationship between biodiversity and ecosystem functioning has historically been a central concern of ecologists. However, the direction and underlying mechanisms of the relationship have been a topic of ongoing controversy, which has been complicated by the many different types (i.e. species, genetic, community, landscape, functional) and measures (i.e. richness, evenness, Shannon–Weaver) of diversity. The discussion has also been complicated because in the public policy arena, the term biodiversity is often erroneously equated with the totality of life, rather than its variability. Obviously, the links between biodiversity and ecosystem functioning are complex, and it should come as no surprise that simple answers have not emerged.

Experimental studies of the relationship between biodiversity and ecosystem functioning in microcosms and field mesocosms (Naeem *et al.* 1994, 1996; Tilman *et al.* 1996) have indicated positive relationships between species richness and net primary production (NPP). Costanza *et al.* (2006) using global NPP estimates aggregated by country and data assembled by the World Resources Institute for biodiversity by country, estimated that vascular plant diversity accounted for approximately 50% of the variation in NPP. The general conclusion of positive links between diversity and ecosystem functioning is strengthened by these empirical results combined with earlier experimental results in micro- and mesocosms. Costanza *et al.* (2006) also linked these results to estimates of the economic value of ecosystem services (Costanza *et al.* 1997, 1998) to derive estimates of the value of the biodiversity contribution to these services. From this assessment they concluded that one-fifth to half of the estimated US$33 trillion/year value of global ecosystem services could be attributed to biodiversity. They also derived an equation linking plant diversity and the value of ecosystem services at the global scale. They estimated from this equation that an individual species of vascular plant contributes at minimum from US$10,000 to US$90,000 per year to global ecosystem services, or, using a 3% discount rate, a present value of US$300,000 to US$3,000,000. These values would be orders of magnitude larger for animal species and particularly for the charismatic fauna found on the Galápagos.

More recent studies have looked at the linkages between biodiversity conservation and ecosystem services values (ESV) by mapping both of these variables at the global scale and looking for areas of overlap or divergence. Turner *et al.* (2007) found that

> published global priority maps for biodiversity conservation harbor a disproportionate share of estimated terrestrial ESV. Overlap of biodiversity priorities and ESV varies among regions, and in areas that have high biodiversity priority but low ESV, specialized conservation approaches are necessary. Overall, however, our findings suggest opportunities for safeguarding both biodiversity and ecosystem services.

Naidoo *et al.* (2008), using different estimates of ESV and biodiversity found less spatial overlap, but concluded that, despite a general lack of spatial concordance between areas of high biodiversity and high ESV, "win-win" areas – regions important for both ecosystem services and biodiversity – could be usefully identified. In addition, strategies to deal with both areas of concordance and of lack of concordance need to be developed.

The Galápagos, ecosystem services and biodiversity

The Galápagos represent an area high in biodiversity conservation value, but of only moderate importance for several other more "production"-oriented ecosystem services. This is due to the unique endemic flora and fauna of the Galápagos, and its unique value as a laboratory for the scientific study of biodiversity and evolution. The largest values for the Galápagos are in the realm of "cultural" ecosystem services. Quantifying, modeling and valuing these unique features is an ongoing challenge. Hopefully some of the ideas presented in this, and in other chapters in this book, will be useful in meeting that challenge.

References

Boumans, R., R. Costanza, J. Farley, M.A. Wilson, R. Portela, J. Rotmans, F. Villa, and M. Grasso. 2002. Modeling the Dynamics of the Integrated Earth System and the Value of Global Ecosystem Services Using the GUMBO Model, *Ecological Economics* 41:529-560

Boyd, J. and S. Banzhaf. 2007. What are ecosystem services? The need for standardized environmental accounting units, *Ecological Economics* 63,616–626.

Costanza, R. (ed.). 1991. *Ecological Economics: The science and management of sustainability* (Columbia University Press: New York, NY).

Costanza, R. 2004. Value theory and energy, in C. Cleveland (ed.), *Encyclopedia of Energy. vol 6*, pp. 337–346 (Elsevier: Amsterdam, The Netherlands)

Costanza, R. 2008. Ecosystem Services: Multiple classification systems are needed, *Biological Conservation* 141:350-352.

Costanza, R. and L. Cornwell. 1992. The 4P approach to dealing with scientific uncertainty, *Environment* 34:12–20, 42.

Costanza, R. and H.E. Daly. 1992. Natural capital and sustainable development, *Conservation Biology* 6:37–46.

Costanza, R., R. d'Arge, R. de Groot, S. Farber, M. Grasso, B. Hannon, S. Naeem, K. Limburg, J. Paruelo, R.V. O'Neill, R. Raskin, P. Sutton, and M. van den Belt. 1997. The value of the world's ecosystem services and natural capital, *Nature* 387:253–260.

Costanza, R., R. d'Arge, R. de Groot, S. Farber, M. Grasso, B. Hannon, K. Limburg, S. Naeem, R.V. O'Neill, J. Paruelo, R.G. Raskin, P. Sutton, and M. van den Belt. 1998. The value of the world's ecosystem services: putting the issues in perspective, *Ecological Economics* 25:67–72

Costanza, R., S.C. Farber, and J. Maxwell. 1989. The Valuation and Management of Wetland Ecosystems, *Ecological Economics* 1:335–362

Costanza, R., B. Fisher, S. Liu, and T. Christopher. 2006. Biodiversity and ecosystem services: a multiscale empirical study of the contribution of species richness to net primary production, in P. Lebrun (ed.), *Biodiversité: État, enjeux et perspectives*, pp. 9–26 (De Boeck: Brussels, Belgium).

Costanza, R., O. Pérez-Maqueo, M.L. Martinez, P. Sutton, S.J. Anderson, and K. Mulder. 2008. The value of coastal wetlands for hurricane protection, *Ambio* 37:241–248.

Costanza, R. and C. Perrings. 1990. A flexible assurance bonding system for improved environmental management, *Ecological Economics* 2:57–76.

Costanza, R., L. Wainger, C. Folke, and K.-G. Mäler. 1993. Modeling complex ecological economic systems: toward an evolutionary, dynamic understanding of people and nature, *BioScience* 43:545–555.

Daily, G. (ed.). 1997. *Nature's Services: Societal Dependence on Natural Ecosystems* (Island Press: Washington, DC).

Ehrlich, P.R. and A.H.E.B. Ehrlich. 1981. *Extinction: The Causes and Consequences of the Disappearance of Species* (Ballantine Books: New York, NY).

Farber, S. and R. Costanza. 1987. The Economic Value of Wetlands Systems, *Journal of Environmental Management* 24:41–51.

Groot, R.S. de, M.A. Wilson, and R.M.J. Boumans. 2002. A typology for the classification, description and valuation of ecosystem functions, goods and services. *Ecological Economics*, 41(3):393–408.

Heywood, V.H. 1995. *Global Biodiversity Assessment*. (Cambridge University Press: Cambridge, UK).

Kinzig, A.P., S.W. Pacala, and D. Tilman (ed.). 2002. *Functional consequences of biodiversity: empirical progress and theoretical extensions* (Princeton University Press: Princeton NJ)

Millennium Ecosystem Assessment. 2005. (Island Press: Washington, DC).

Naeem, S., K. Hakansson, J.H. Lawton, M.J. Crawley, and L.J. Thompson. 1996. Biodiversity and plant productivity in a model assemblage of plant species, *Oikos* 76:259–264.

Naeem, S., L.J. Thompson, S.P. Lawler, J.H. Lawton, and R.M. Woodfin. 1994. Declining biodiversity can alter the performance of ecosystems, *Nature* 368:734–737.

Naidoo, R., A. Balmford, R. Costanza, B. Fisher, R.E. Green, B. Lehner, T.R. Malcom, and T.H. Rickets. 2008. Global mapping of ecosystem services and conservation priorities, *Proceedings of the National Academy of Sciences* 105:9495–9500

Pearce, D.W. and R.K. Turner. 1989. *Economics of natural resources and the environment* (Wheatsheaf: Brighton, UK).

Pezzey, J. 1989. *Economic analysis of sustainable growth and sustainable development. Environment department working paper No. 15* (The World Bank, Washington, DC).

Schulze, E.-D. and H.A. 1993. Mooney *Ecosystem Function of Biodiversity* (Springer: Berlin, Germany).

Tilman, D., D. Wedin, and J. Knops. 1996. Productivity and sustainability influenced by biodiversity in grassland ecosystems, *Nature* 379:718–720.

Turner, W.R., K. Brandon, T.M. Brooks, R. Costanza, G.A.B. da Fonseca, and R. Portela. 2007. Global conservation of biodiversity and ecosystem services, *BioScience* 57:868–873

Walker, B.H. and W.E. Steffen. 1996. *Global change and terrestrial ecosystems* (Cambridge University Press: Cambridge, UK).

World Council on Environment and Development (WCED). 1987. *Our Common Future: report of the world commission on environment and development* (Oxford University Press: Oxford, UK).

17 Nature and the world

A geohistory of Galápagos

Christophe Grenier

Introduction

The human history of Galápagos is short and relatively well-known (Bognoly and Espinoza 1904; Rose 1923; Naveda 1953; Hickman 1985; Silva 1992; Latorre 1999), but has seldom been analyzed in relation to the geography of the archipelago and its connections with the rest of the world (Grenier 2002, 2007). Geography studies human footprints on Earth, or rather how the environment is transformed and organized in space and by social action. Spaces are systems of relations between places, and they are social products, or the projections of societies on the planet (Brunet 1986). Geographic spaces have evolved throughout the course of human history, they have different scales and forms (areas – mostly political spaces, or networks – mostly economical spaces), and they are often appropriated as territories. They may also experience changes of geographical situation, that is, of location in relation to other spaces. The isolation or the connectivity of a particular space evolves as a result of human activity. The history of the evolution of geographic spaces is known as geohistory.

Ecology and geography share the importance given to location, scale, and time to explain the environment or the relations to the environment. As with most islands and archipelagos, isolation as a key factor of natural evolution depends on their geographic space, that is on the degree of human connectivity of such islands with the rest of the world (e.g. by transport networks). Though Galápagos is a worldwide icon of wilderness, the archipelago's ecology has been transformed by humans for two centuries. Most of the ecological impacts caused by human activity are related to the exploitation, by or for outsiders, of the archipelago's natural resources or strategic situation.

We cannot, therefore, consider the conservation of Galápagos without an understanding of the geohistorical process of the connection of these islands to the rest of the world. Galápagos natural resources and strategic situation are the products of the "World System"[1] history. They were invented and exploited according to the needs, technologies, representations, and interests of actors from Western Europe, the United States, mainland Ecuador, and Eastern Asia. That is why Galápagos geohistory is the linkage of island nature with the world.

Several recent publications by scientists and Galápagos National Park managers show that, in Galápagos, conservation thinking is impregnated by geographical notions never explicitly assumed. For instance, the main threat to Galápagos biodiversity is said to be species introduction (Bensted-Smith *et al.* 2006), which is a typical issue of spatial connectivity caused by human activity and the associated movement of goods. Another report explains that the main driver of economic growth in Galápagos is tourism, which stimulates the increase in flights and cargo ships from mainland Ecuador, thereby threatening the ecological isolation of the archipelago (Watkins and Cruz 2007). This again is the same question of spatial connectivity. Finally, Galápagos is qualified as a "social ecological system" (SPNG 2006; Gonzalez *et al.* 2008). The relations of this system of regional scale with the outside world are not well analyzed, though they explain many of the problems confronting island conservation. An assumption that spatial connectivity is a key issue in Galápagos conservation may help to define conservation policies that reduce accessibility and flows in a sustainable manner.

While none of the publications quoted above present a single map showing the relations between Galápagos and the rest of the world, the present geohistorical approach is based on six schematic maps. These spatial models illustrate how a large part of the current trend in the degradation of Galápagos nature is due to the progressive connection of this archipelago to the World System.

An isolated ecosystem at the margin of the world system

At least until the sixteenth century, Galápagos was a group of ecologically isolated oceanic islands that could qualify as a "semi-closed" ecosystem. It was nevertheless half open, since two main oceanic currents – the Humboldt or Chile–Peru Current, and the Panama–South Equatorial Current – and the trade winds, moving westward from mainland America to the archipelago, brought most of the "native" terrestrial flora and fauna to the islands, where they arrived gradually over many millennia. Once there, the oceanic barrier isolated the Galápagos natural settlers from their source populations in the Americas, allowing divergent evolutionary processes in certain island populations. This "geographic speciation" – by ecological isolation – explains the high level of endemism in oceanic islands like Galápagos, and the consequent extreme vulnerability of these locally adapted organisms to the broad and rapid opening of their island ecosystems (Figure 17.1).

The first humans to have landed in the Galápagos are said to be the pre-Columbian people of Manta–Huancavelica, who once inhabited the coast of present Manabí, in Ecuador. However, as they left no lasting footprint in the archipelago and did not impact its ecosystem, they should not be considered as geographical actors in Galápagos. We mention them, however, for this is still a matter of strong debate between the diplomatic historians of Ecuador (Villacres Moscoso 1985; Luna Tobar 1997) and those of Peru. Both sides claim that their own Amerindians were the first supposed discoverers of Galápagos, each country pretending thus to have pre-European historic rights of sovereignty on the archipelago.

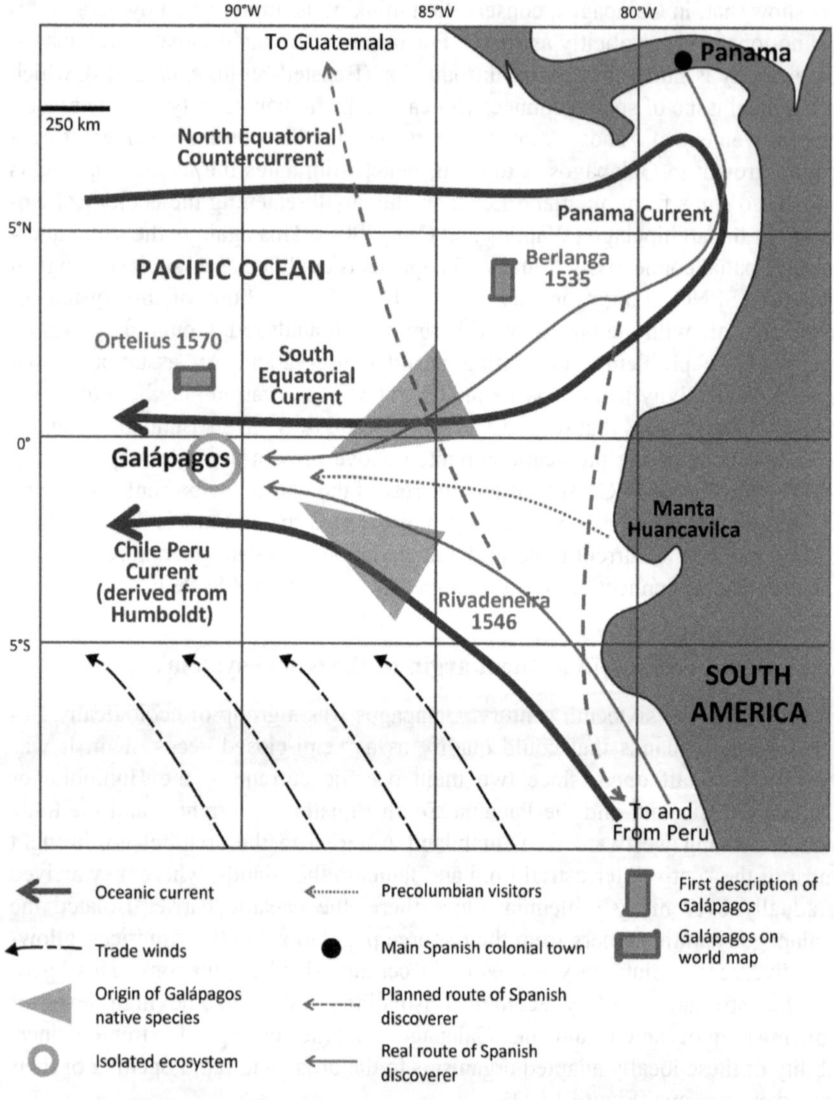

Figure 17.1 Galápagos in the sixteenth century: an isolated ecosystem at the margin of the World System.

The official discoverer of Galápagos is the Spanish Bishop Tomás de Berlanga, who is also credited with having introduced the banana to the Americas, yet only one hamlet in the highlands of Isabela remembers his name, which is quite ungrateful with respect to his huge contribution to Ecuador's present economy. Sailing from Panama to Peru in 1535, Berlanga was caught in the doldrums and drifted westward to the archipelago with the Panama Current. Eleven years later, en route to Guatemala from Peru, Diego de Rivadeneira, the second Spaniard to see the archipelago, also drifted westward, this time by the Humboldt Current. As with most of the native flora and fauna of Galápagos, these Spaniards reached the islands by floating passively, but unlike the plants and animals, they did not settle in the archipelago. Berlanga described the islands as lacking fresh water and being covered with stones. However, the Spaniards named the islands "Galápagos" in honor of the strange giant tortoises, whose carapaces reminded them of their horse saddles.

The sixteenth century saw the formation of the modern World System through the worldwide expansion of the Iberian Empires and the incorporation of the Americas into the "Old World" economy. One of the manifestations of these beginnings of globalization was the publication of maps of the world: The most famous was that drawn by the Flemish cartographer, Ortelius in 1570, on which the newly discovered archipelago is marked as Galápagos Islands.

Even if they were not settled and not really explored, Galápagos had made its entry at the margins of the World System since its very beginning, and under the name of one of its endemic animals. During the next centuries however, the Spaniards never used the islands (it was far more interesting to exploit the wealth and populations of the American mainland), which therefore became a no man's land.

An open space facing colonial South America

Once located on the world map, this no man's land no longer remained so, even though changes took some time (Figure 17.2). By the end of the seventeenth century, the World System was expanding, notably through the worldwide actions and activities of the states, merchants, and adventurers of England, France, and the United Provinces and at the expense of the Spanish and Portuguese empires.

In 1684, considering the Caribbean too heavily fortified by the Spaniards, some British buccaneers, led by the famous figures of Dampier and Davis, rounded South America and raided the Pacific Coast of the Spanish Empire, as Drake had done a century before. They inaugurated the "open space" period of Galápagos and its full integration into the World System. An open space refers to a region where no state authority can prevent foreign actors from entering and freely exploiting its resources: this situation describes Galápagos from the end of the seventeenth to the mid-twentieth century (Grenier 1994).

However, it was not yet the natural resources of Galápagos, but rather its strategic situation in regard to the routes of the Spanish galleons between El Callao (Peru) and Panama – a major shipping route in the World System of that time, which was of great interest to the British buccaneers. Thus, they wove their networks across the few oceanic islands of the Eastern Pacific, facing mainland America's wealth. The integration of Galápagos into the World System at that time may be illustrated by the three following facts. First, a British buccaneer, Ambrose Cowley, drew the first map of the archipelago, thus the individual islands were originally identified with English place names. This "*Islas Encantadas*"[2] period only lasted about 40 years, and ended with the opening of the

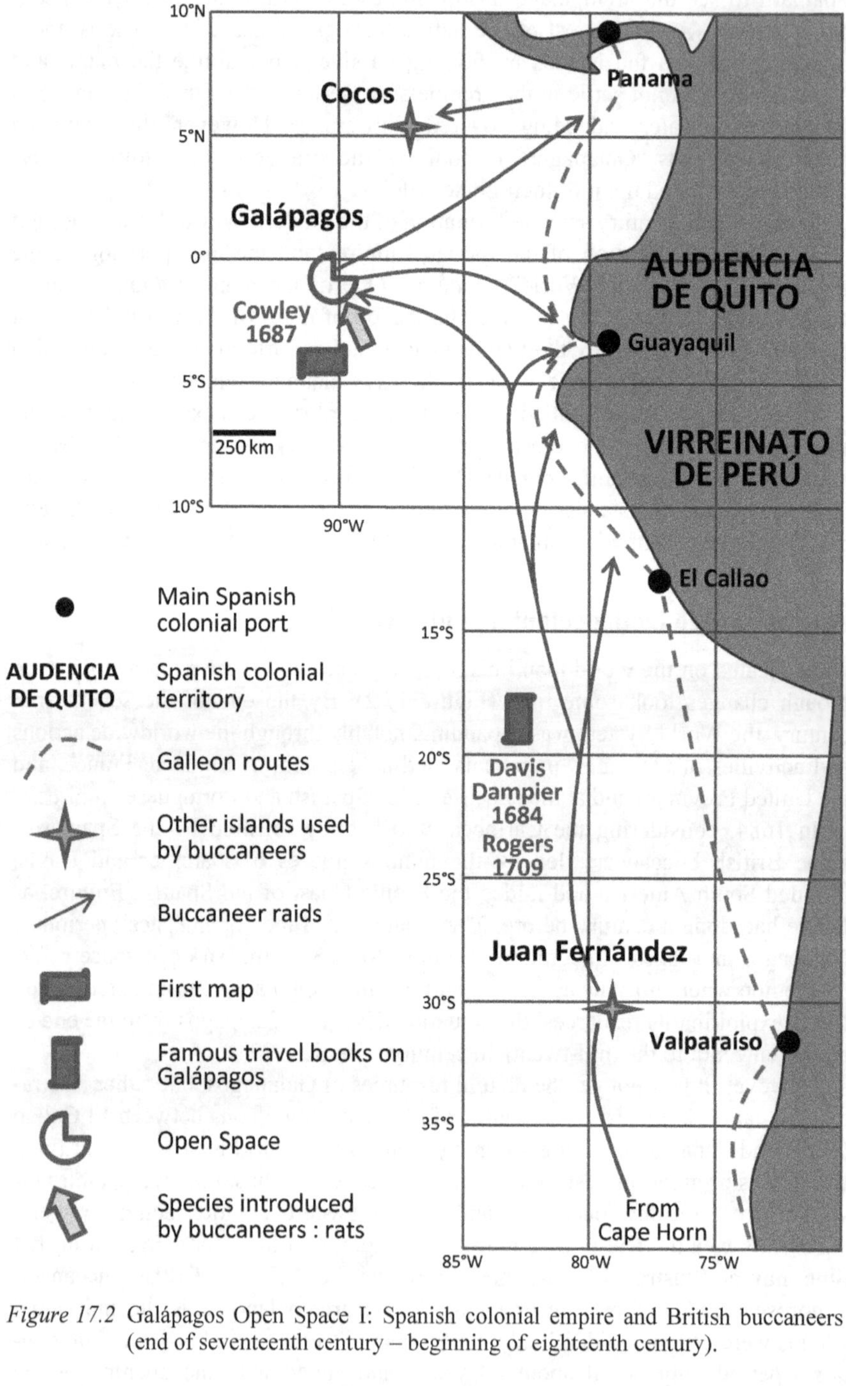

Figure 17.2 Galápagos Open Space I: Spanish colonial empire and British buccaneers (end of seventeenth century – beginning of eighteenth century).

Spanish empire in the Americas to British commerce. Second, an international treaty made Galápagos sink into oblivion during most of the eighteenth century. Finally, a British pirate vessel brought rats to Galápagos: the first ecological impact caused by human activity was the introduction of an invasive species.

Whaling hub and first human settlements

The human impact on nature, in Galápagos as elsewhere, was much more severe during the nineteenth century, with the huge expansion of the World System through the quest for raw materials by the industrializing north. During the first half of the nineteenth century, US whalers and the first Ecuadorian settlers took advantage of the archipelago's open space to plunder its natural resources (Figure 17.3). The English whaler James Colnett discovered the "Galápagos Grounds" at the end of the eighteenth century, but the British were expelled from the archipelago's waters after the Anglo-American War of 1812. During this campaign, Captain David Porter of the USS *Essex* released goats on James Island. Galápagos was henceforth the domain of Nantucket whalers (Herman Melville published *The Encantadas* on that topic in 1854), who caught tens of thousands of cetaceans and an estimated 100,000 giant tortoises to be converted into fresh food supplies for the lengthy whaling expeditions (Epler 1987). Galápagos was thus a major provisioning hub as the US whaling network expanded throughout the Pacific connecting these once-remote oceanic islands to the North American whale oil market.

During the same period, the Spanish Colonial Empire split into independent republics. This added a national scale of geographical action in Galápagos, which was annexed by Ecuador in 1832. Ecuador was a young and heavily indebted state without the means to properly colonize this distant oceanic territory. The task was assigned to the adventurer José de Villamil, who established a private colony on Charles Island, which he immediately renamed Floreana in honor of Ecuador's first president.

However, the Galápagos remained an open space freely used by foreign actors who gave an Anglo-Saxon toponymy to the islands (Woram 1989). In 1835, the HMS *Beagle* expedition led by Robert Fitzroy, sent to chart places of interest to the British Navy around South America, provided the best map of the archipelago, still in use a century later. In his travel journal, the first scientific description ever made of Galápagos, Charles Darwin (1845) briefly mentions the recent Ecuadorian settlement and documents some human impacts on the islands, such as the presence of feral cattle and the hunting of giant tortoises.

The situation of Galápagos in the world system: a shift to the North

Until the mid-nineteenth century, Galápagos connectivity to the World System had been established through oceanic networks that linked both the European and North American sides of the Atlantic to the archipelago, which was at that time reached from the south, around Cape Horn. During the next century, the

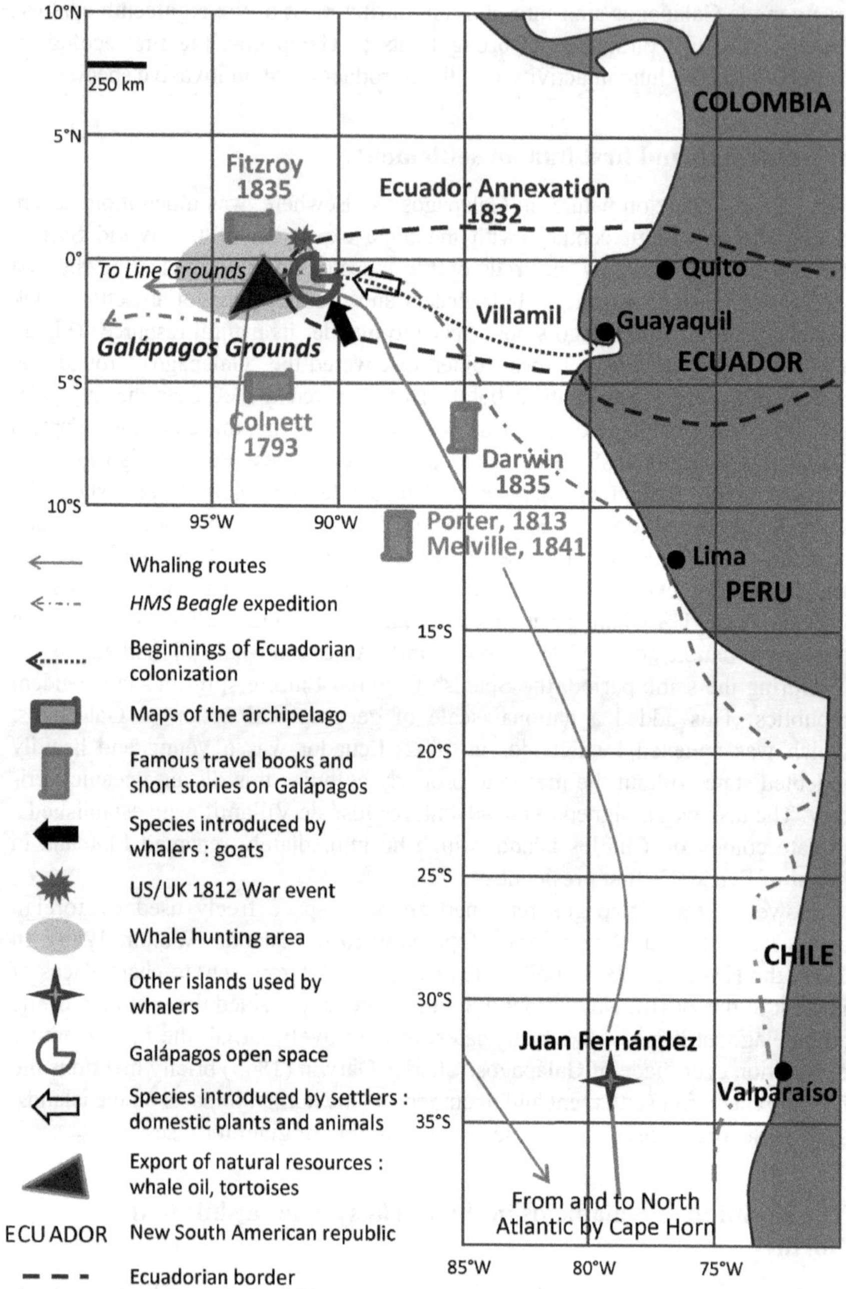

Figure 17.3 Galápagos Open Space II: whalers and first Ecuadorian colonization (1800–1850).

connectivity of Galápagos open space with mainland America increased significantly from Ecuador to California, and with the North Atlantic after 1914, due to the Panama Canal. Since then, the Galápagos became much closer to the Americas through various links created by different actors, who imported domestic plants, animals, and workers to the archipelago, and/or who exported its natural resources, as well as utilizing its strategic location. Indeed, the Galápagos group is the only archipelago located at a relatively short distance west of the Isthmus of Panama. Well in advance of the construction of the Panama Canal, this strategic location was coveted by the imperialist powers of the time, which were racing for oceanic island bases to complete their worldwide maritime networks. Although some Ecuadorian governments tried to sell the Galápagos to the United States, to the United Kingdom, or to France, every attempt failed owing to the mutual opposition of the imperialist states: better that Galápagos remain an open space under the sovereignty of distant Ecuador than controlled by a rival.

During the second half of the nineteenth century, the present United States west coast was incorporated into the federal territory. Henceforth, California became the Galápagos' closest "North". Some giant tortoise oil had been sold in the California boom towns during the Gold Rush, and Manuel Cobos, an Ecuadorian businessman who built his fortune on *orchilla,* a tinctorial lichen, in Baja California, started the definitive colonization of the Galápagos when he hired and provisioned a work crew to collect *orchilla* on the island of San Cristóbal. However, of much greater importance to Galápagos was California's involvement in the archipelago's science and fisheries issues (Figure 17.4).

The publication of *On the Origin of Species* made Galápagos famous in the scientific field, even if Darwin did not "discover" his theory of evolution in these islands (Sulloway 1987). However, it was an opponent to Darwin's theory, Louis Agassiz of Harvard, who launched the period of scientific expeditions in the archipelago by making a stop-over in the Galápagos en route to San Francisco in 1872. Since then, many Californian naturalist expeditions have visited the Galápagos, the most famous being that of the California Academy of Sciences, which spent about a year in the archipelago in 1905–1906. The naturalist expeditions from California collected huge amounts of specimens in the Galápagos (Larson 2001), among them giant tortoises for the San Diego Zoo. Furthermore, some California tycoons, such as Allan Hancock, financed their own expeditions to the archipelago in the 1930s, thus inaugurating the ambiguous relations between science and tourism in Galápagos. Last, but not least, San Diego's tuna fleets were at home in archipelago's waters between the World Wars.

Once the Panama Canal opened, the Galápagos became a stop-over in the North Atlantic–South Pacific maritime route, and the few navigators travelling to Polynesia who visited the islands contributed to the spread of the Galápagos image as a strange archipelago "out of time". Nothing compares, however, with the world fame brought to these islands by William Beebe's best seller, *Galápagos World's End.* Published in 1924 after a short expedition in the archipelago by the New York Zoological Society, the book was translated into many languages. In Norway as in Germany, Beebe's book convinced some people to

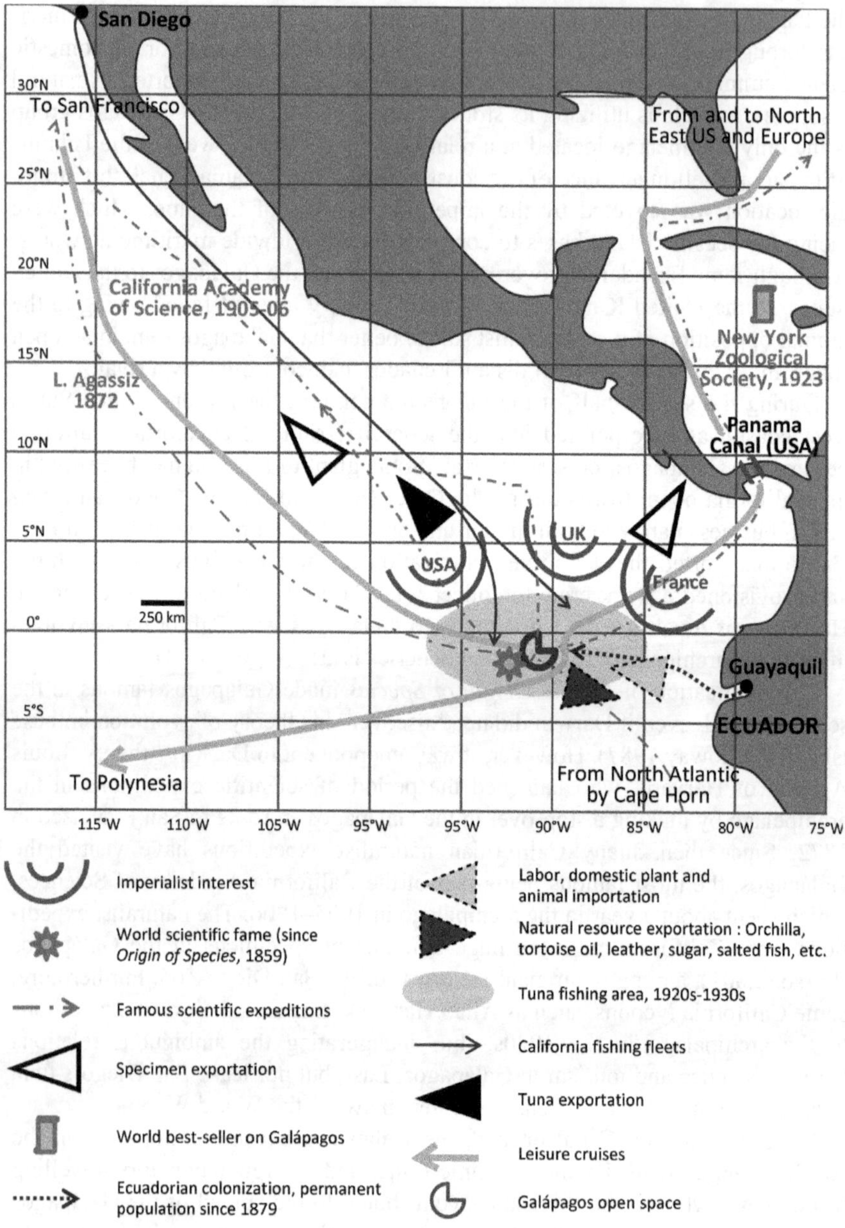

Figure 17.4 Galápagos Open Space III: connections with the North and further colonization (1850–1940).

abandon their countries to settle in a "Pacific Paradise": *Galápagos World's End* is directly responsible for the fourth (Norwegian) and fifth (German) colonizations of Floreana Island (Wittmer 1989).

Indeed, in spite of an initial failure, Ecuadorians tried twice more to settle in Floreana during the nineteenth century. However, other islands were more interesting for colonial enterprises, which looked for places with exportable natural resources. San Cristóbal was the first island to be populated permanently from 1879 onward, when Cobos founded *Hacienda El Progreso*. In 1897, the southern slope of the Sierra Negra volcano in Isabela was settled because of its huge populations of giant tortoises and the massive presence of feral cattle. Ecuadorian settlements were located in the highlands, but the *colonos* also had a small harbor to export raw or semi-processed natural resources to mainland Ecuador and beyond, including *orchilla*, tortoise oil, feral cattle leather, salt and dried fish, sugar cane, and so on. In 1892, Ecuador's government decided to rename the main Galápagos Islands as well as the whole archipelago according to the Columbus epic. Unable to control what remained an open space, Ecuador thus attempted to affirm its sovereignty at least through a Spanish toponymy; nevertheless, the Anglo-Saxons continued to use their own names and the "Archipelago of Colón" only exists on Ecuadorian maps.

This initial colonization, driven by entrepreneurs who harshly exploited both nature and labor, rendered the Galápagos repulsive to Ecuadorians until the last third of the twentieth century. Like Ecuador and other South American countries or regions in similar situations at the periphery of the World System, the Galápagos entered a cyclic boom-and-bust economy. The foreign or national actors exploiting the nature of Galápagos depended on the world market's fluctuating demand and on the technological progress that replaced natural resources with industrial products, such as whale and tortoise oils being replaced by petroleum, and *orchilla* by chemical coloring agents. As an open space with no public regulations, Galápagos was essentially a mining economy where the resources were exploited until they became too scarce to be commercially viable. This last characteristic extended to the numerous quests for huge collections of specimens for museums and public or private zoos. North American and European scientists and collectors rushed to grab the "last" giant tortoises, sometimes leading to the extinction of certain species that had become extremely vulnerable due to massive hauls by the whalers and settlers of the previous century (Thornton 1971).

By the 1930s, when the private colonies and the extraction of specimens by naturalist expeditions had ceased, the nature of Galápagos existed in a new state of contrast, but one that was equally threatening. On the one hand, the archipelago then had only one or two connections a year by cargo ships from mainland Ecuador, was inhabited by about 700 people who survived mostly through subsistence farming, and counted a relatively low number of introduced species (about 150). On the other hand, feral cattle, goats, and pigs, combined with agriculture, caused severe damage to the native vegetation of the highlands. Furthermore, native species such as the giant tortoises and fur seals had difficulty recovering from a century of exploitation.

The geographical opening: airport, national park, and tourism

From the 1940s, Galápagos entered a process of "geographical opening", which designates the deep ecological and social transformations of a region caused by its full integration to the globalized world, through numerous transport and communications networks and subsequent flows. In 1941, after a short war, Peru annexed about 80% of Ecuador's Amazonian territory, an open space almost uninhabited and with no state control. From then on, Ecuador's priority was to integrate Galápagos, its other open space, into its national territory, taking advantage of the fact that the international field of the World System was consolidating after World War II through multilateral organizations and treaties attempting to regulate the globalization process. Thus, the weak national sovereignty over the archipelago, symbolized by laws impossible to apply in such an open space, would be respected through international treaties on the three most important foreign interests in the Galápagos: a strategic location from which to guard the Panama Canal, its prodigious marine resources, and its singular nature.

In 1940–1941, the US government was looking for military bases to prevent a German or Japanese attack on the Panama Canal, and Galápagos was considered to be the best place for that purpose (Bryan 1941). After Pearl Harbor, the US Navy built air and naval facilities on Baltra Island within a few months, importing all materials and labor necessary from Panama and mainland Ecuador, but later incorporated local resources and labor that created an economic boom in Galápagos. From Baltra, the US Air Force patrols covered a triangle of Pacific Ocean for which the two other angles were the US bases of Salinas (Ecuador) and Fonseca (Nicaragua), thus protecting the western approaches to Panama (Anonymous 1947).

Once the war was over, the Baltra base was ceded to Ecuador, finally providing a modern transport infrastructure to enable a strengthened link between the archipelago and its mainland *Patria.* The presence of the US military base proved that the Galápagos Islands, even the more arid ones, could support a large population if adequately supplied from the continent. In other words, geographic opening with high energy inputs could colonize any environment. In this way, the US military base provided a preview of the current situation in Galápagos (Figure 17.5). Meanwhile, California's tuna fleets had resumed their plundering of Galápagos seas. In 1952, Ecuador joined Chile and Peru at the Santiago Conference, where these countries claimed their economic sovereignty over maritime areas as far as 200 miles off their coasts.

However, this was not sufficient for the real integration of Galápagos into Ecuadorian territory. According to a common geopolitical doctrine in South America concerning empty and/or open spaces at that time, the archipelago should be populated by more national citizens to be definitively saved from foreign interests. In 1956, after the semi-failure of the Santa Cruz highlands settlement campaign organized by the Ecuadorian colonization agency (IERAC), the government looked for ways of making Galápagos attractive to Ecuadorians, at a time when western biologists backed by powerful international conservation

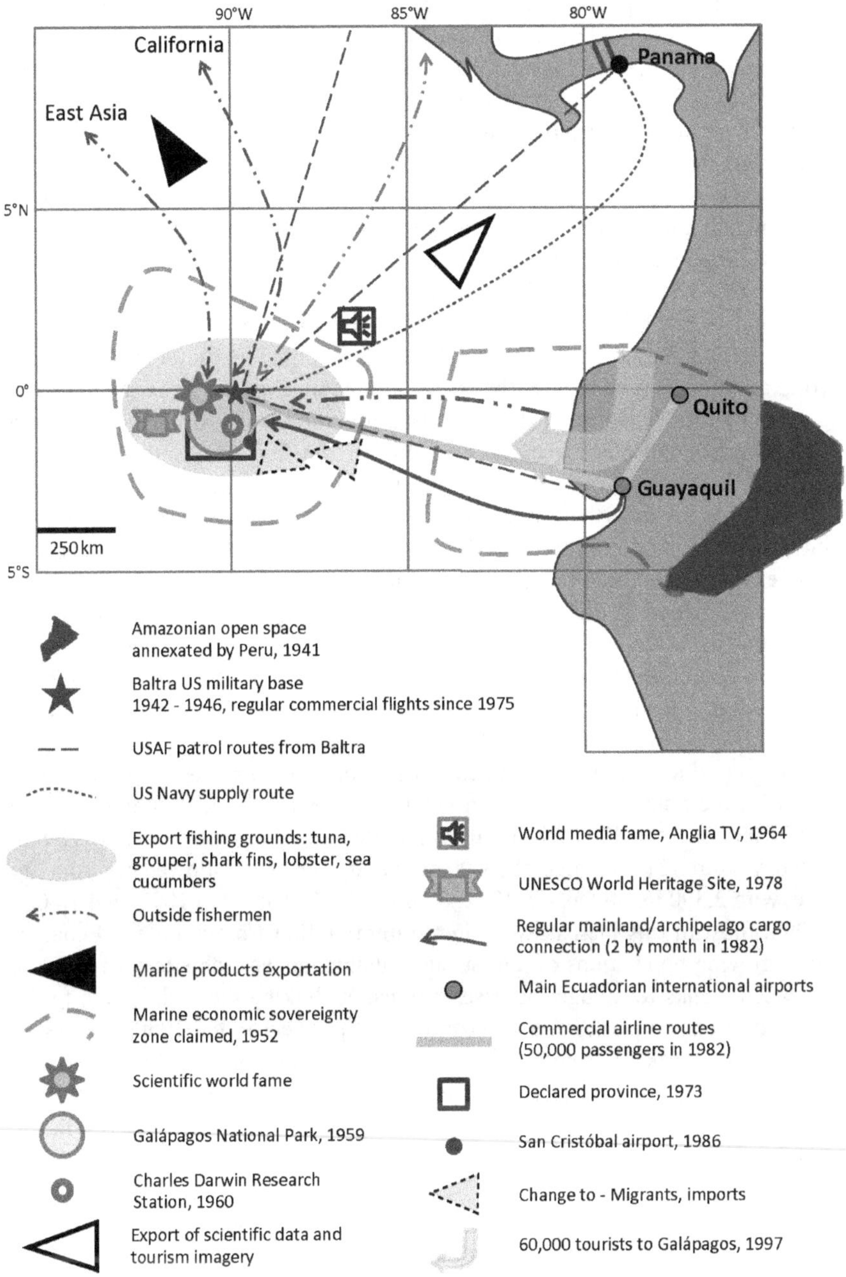

Figure 17.5 Integrating Galápagos Open Space to the Ecuadorian territory (1941–1997).

organizations wanted strict protection of the archipelago (Corley Smith 1990). These contradictory goals were nevertheless achieved in 1959 by the creation of the Galápagos National Park (GNP) on 97% of archipelago's surface. In accordance with the presidential decree that created the GNP, the latter was destined to become "a pole of international tourism" (Larrea 1990), an aim that may be interpreted as follows: from Quito, an international conservation project with powerful media advertising should start organized tourism in Galápagos, whose subsequent development would attract migrants from mainland Ecuador in order to consolidate a weak national sovereignty on this still-open space.

The Charles Darwin Foundation (CDF), an international scientific organization, was created in 1959 to advise Ecuador's government on Galápagos conservation and to establish a base for scientific research in the archipelago. The Charles Darwin Research Station (CDRS) was installed in 1960 close to Puerto Ayora, and inaugurated in 1964 in an event that launched a worldwide advertising campaign for Galápagos nature and its conservation, a message well received by the tourism industry. According to one of the first CDRS directors, "the Galápagos Islands enjoyed in those years an aura of almost mystical remoteness. They had few visitors; there was no tourism; nor was there any regular contact with the mainland by sea" (Perry 2000). During the 1960s, CDRS welcomed scientific expeditions, began the goat eradication and tortoise captive-breeding programs, and helped to design the tourism model. Tourism was supposed to support conservation by donations to CDF and entrance fees to the national park. This was apparently organized and limited by the GNP's first Management Plan of 1974. Consequently, Galápagos was one of the first four sites to be put on the UNESCO World Heritage list in 1978.

However, since the first organized cruises for "the happy few" at the end of the 1960s, the number of tourists in Galápagos never stopped climbing. There were 17,000 in 1980, 41,000 in 1990, and 65,000 in 1998, about two-thirds being foreign visitors. The archipelago's demographic growth followed the tourism curve, with 2,300 inhabitants in 1962, 6,700 in 1982, 10,000 in 1990, and 18,000 in 1998: most of this increase was due to immigration from mainland Ecuador. These growing populations of tourists and inhabitants were able to visit or settle Galápagos thanks to a huge increase in transport linking the archipelago to the mainland. From no planes and two cargo boats per year in the 1950s, there was one plane per week and one cargo ship per month in the mid-1970s (Castillo *et al.* 2005), and roughly two-weekly cargo ships and two or three daily flights by 1998 (a second airport was opened in San Cristóbal in 1986). As a result, the number of introduced species also boomed, from 166 plants species in 1970 to 437 in 1999 (Tye *et al.* 2008).

In the meantime, the oil boom of the 1970s allowed the Ecuadorian government to invest in the archipelago, which became a province with three municipalities in 1973, each ruling its own territory and covering 3% of the surface of Galápagos. The archipelago was endowed with a Public Institute for Development (INGALA) in 1979, which had theoretical control over everything but experienced mixed results and fluctuating power. The 1980s marked a shift in the Galápagos economy, with a sharp decline in agriculture – which had no external market – and a boom in tourism. This entailed the move of the local population from the highlands to the ports, mostly to Puerto Ayora. Since the 1960s, the archipelago's economic capital has been wide open to mainland Ecuador (through migrants, civil servants, and business people) and to the world (through scientists, tourists, and tourism investors), and the town experienced rapid growth. Invasive plants began to cover large parts of the Santa Cruz highlands as in the other inhabited islands, and Galápagos agriculture was exposed to competition from mainland products, some even imported from abroad.

The fisheries sector did better, since new resources were exploited for foreign markets. The 1990s witnessed a boom in sea cucumbers exported to East Asia. The archipelago's conservation authorities first tried to ban this activity because of its high ecological cost. However, the *galapagueño* fishermen, whose number had been increased by mainland migrants attracted by this bonanza, and who were backed by local politicians, protested vehemently against the conservation and tourism sectors, accused of being *afuereño* ("outsider") interests. The harm to the archipelago's "nature sanctuary" image caused by the fishermen's protests was perhaps greater than the concern for the damages caused to archipelago's marine ecosystems by their fishing activities, but the government finally authorized sea cucumber fishing under certain restrictions. Nevertheless, illegal fishing boats from the mainland continued to enter the Galápagos Marine Reserve (GMR) established in 1986, some of them catching sharks for fin export to the Asian market. The marine area of Galápagos was still an open space where the GNP Service and the Navy did not control marine movements.

At the end of the 1990s, the geographical opening of Galápagos was growing fast, and entailed an ecological and social "continentalization" of the inhabited islands of the archipelago: a process of reduction of the islands' singularities in both ecosystems and human communities by massive introduction and distribution of organisms and lifestyle habits from the mainland.

The continentalization of Galápagos

In 1998, Ecuador's Parliament issued a "Special Law" for Galápagos, which tried to reduce this continentalization process, notably by implementing migration control via permanent or temporary resident status for archipelago inhabitants and setting up a quarantine system between the islands and the continent (Figure 17.6). The Special Law also installed a participative management board with local stakeholders for the GMR, which was extended to 40 miles beyond the archipelago's baseline to cover a surface of 133,000 km^2. Only *Galapagueños* were allowed to fish in the GMR but, though apparently regulated, the sea cucumber fisheries collapsed some years later because of the "mining" of this activity. Furthermore, illegal shark fisheries and intrusions of foreign fishing boats into the GMR still go on, and new kinds of unlawful activities may flourish in the "open seas" surrounding Galápagos, another means to link the archipelago with mainland America.

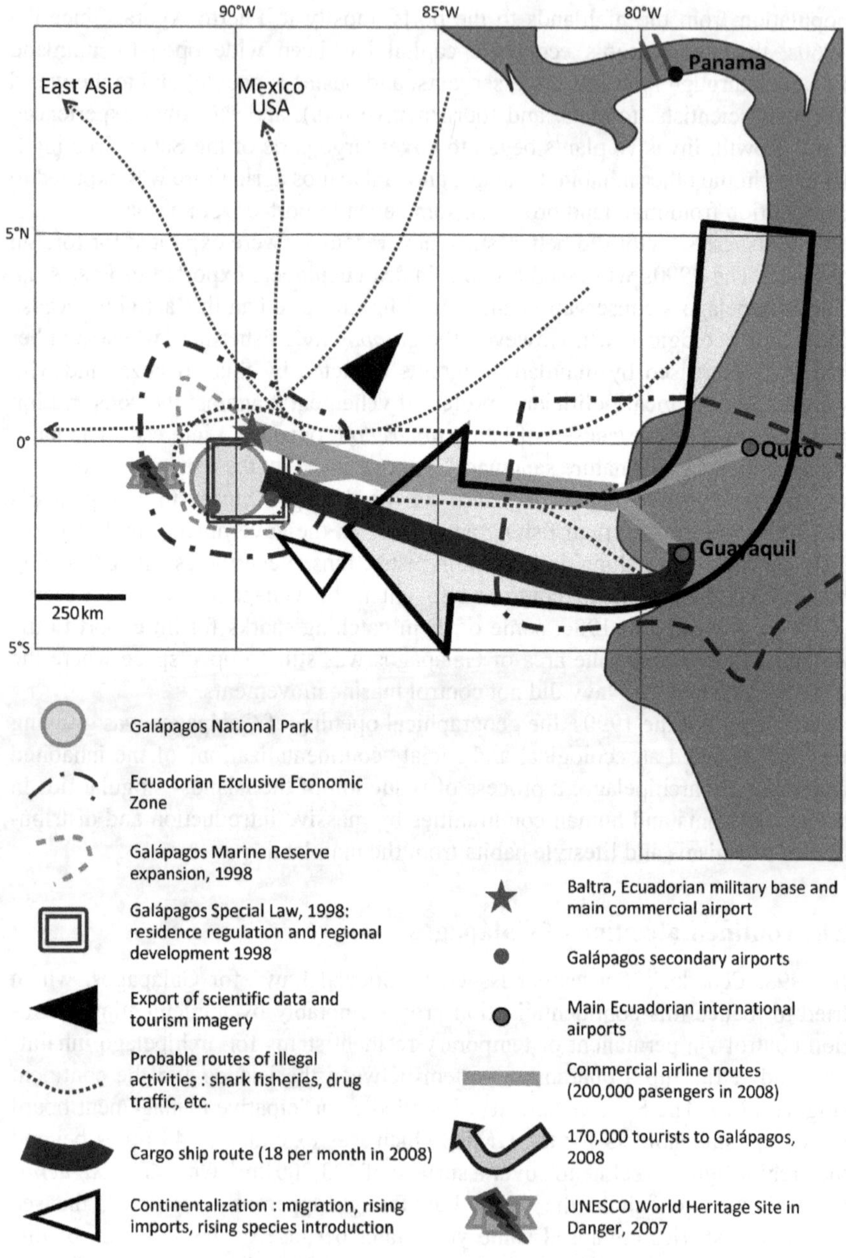

Figure 17.6 Galápagos Rapid Geographic Opening (1998 – present).

In terms of conservation, the principal weakness of the Special Law is that it did not limit tourism, which is by far the main driver of the continentalization process in Galápagos. Consequently, both tourism and population numbers continued to rise, reaching, in 2008, 173,000 visitors (166% increase since 1998) and about 30,000 inhabitants (40% increase since 1998). Indeed, another Special Law objective was to pacify social relations in the archipelago through the redistribution of part of the tourism income to the local institutions. Since 1998, almost half of the GNP entrance fee revenue is given to INGALA and to the municipalities of Galápagos, with the aim of promoting "sustainable development".

Instead of helping to build a kind of island autonomy, the Special Law, combined with tourism and migration growth, has consolidated the links with mainland Ecuador and beyond, for the development of Galápagos entails more imports of everything and an increasingly mobile island population. Thus, four to six jets land daily at the archipelago's two airports connected to Quito and Guayaquil (the third, in Isabela, has only local traffic), and the number of cargo ship rotations between the mainland and the archipelago may reach 18 per month. Not surprisingly, the number of organisms introduced from the mainland continued to rise sharply in the last decade. In 2007, 754 introduced plant species were known in Galápagos (Guézou *et al.* 2010). The rapid continentalization process of Galápagos is quite visible in the landscapes of the inhabited islands. Invasive mainland species cover major parts of the highlands, and the urban lifestyle that is replacing the *galapagueño* way of life is illustrated by the boom in cement constructions and by the growing use of motorized vehicles, most notably in Puerto Ayora.

In 2007, UNESCO placed the Galápagos on its list of World Heritage Sites in Danger, notably because of "inadequate implementation of the Special Law and lack of enforcement", "poor governance", "inadequate regional planning", "inadequate and ineffective quarantine measures", "illegal fishing", "high and unregulated illegal in-migration and resulting impacts of development on biodiversity", and "unsustainable tourism development". In 2009, UNESCO maintained the Galápagos "in danger" status but for political reasons removed the archipelago from that list in 2010, though no real progress has been made in the main issues quoted above.

Conclusion

Today, the continentalization process in Galápagos continues faster than ever. The archipelago is fully integrated with the World System at this stage of globalization, that is, the general geographical opening of every region on the planet that presents economic or strategic interests for transnational, international, or national actors. The consequences of this growing geographical opening of Galápagos are enormous, whether directly or indirectly. The archipelago is rapidly losing its singularity, not only from an ecological point of view, but also culturally. Both are linked. The main actors concerned – the Ecuadorian state, regional institutions, island inhabitants, local and foreign tourism enterprises, etc. – consider Galápagos to be like an ordinary region, ruled by the same economic "laws", seeking the same kind of "development", and wanting the same lifestyle as urban populations from other parts of the world. For these reasons, many of the archipelago's ecosystems are in danger.

A geohistorical approach to the human history of Galápagos demonstrates that people are the main drivers of the archipelago's recent natural history, by opening it to the outside world. Putting geographic space at the core of conservation policy may help to find solutions to reduce the Galápagos geographical opening in a sustainable manner for the island population. This implies a change in the tourism model in order to shift from quantity to quality by curving down the number of visitors and organizing a real ecotourism, to end government fuel subsidies and promote alternative energy sources, to ban further imports of motor vehicles and implement public transport, to control immigration, to provide better local education and training, to improve the quality and availability of locally produced food instead of importing most of the food supply, and so on.

These steps require a reduction in the number of flights and maritime links between mainland Ecuador and the archipelago, in order to decrease the number and volume of transport flows entering Galápagos from the rest of the world. Galápagos is now embedded in the World System and it is part of the globalized world: this does not necessarily imply that its geographical opening should continue, but that we are collectively responsible for creating and implementing conservation policies which may enable people to live differently in order to keep places like this one in a sound ecological state, for the enjoyment of inhabitants and visitors alike. Rather than be defined by its destructive links between "Nature and the World", Galápagos human history should be enabled to implement a sustainable way to live together with "Nature in the World".

Acknowledgements

Many thanks to Emmanuel Cléder (CDF) for reviewing the maps, and to Mary Witoshynsky (CDF) for reviewing the text.

Notes

1 A world system links different regions of the Earth by transport networks allowing regular flows, mostly economic but also human, cultural, biological, etc. The "Modern World System" (or "World System") is closely related to the global expansion of capitalism, which emerged in Western Europe during the fifteenth century and expanded since then to encompass the entire planet, thus producing a World Space (Braudel 1979; Wallerstein 1979; Dollfus 1990, 1994).

2 Or the Enchanted Isles, as the Spaniards called the Galápagos, because of the strong currents and thick fog that characterized these 'disappearing' islands. The British buccaneers also used and spread this appellation.

References

Anonymous. 1947. *Building the Navy Bases in World War II, vol. 2* (US Government Printing Office: Washington, DC).

Beebe, W. 1924. *Galápagos, World's End* (Putnam: New York, NY).

Bensted-Smith, R. (ed.). 2002. *A Biodiversity Vision for the Galapagos Islands* (Charles Darwin Foundation and WWF: Puerto Ayora, Galapagos).

Bognoly, J. and J.M. Espinoza. 1904. *Las Islas Encantadas o el Archipélago de Colón* (Imprenta del Comercio: Guayaquil).

Braudel, F. 1979. *Civilisation matérielle, économie et capitalisme, XVème-XVIIIème siècles, 3 vol.* (Armand Colin: Paris).

Brunet, R. 1986. L'espace, règles du jeu, in Auriac, F. and Brunet, R. (Ed.), *Espaces, jeuxet enjeux*, pp. 297–316 (Fayard: Paris).

Bryan, G.S. 1941. Geography and the Defense of the Caribbean and the Panama Canal, *Annals of the Association of American Geographers* 31(2):83–94.

Castillo B., C. Herrera, H. Jarrín, C. Ricaurte, R. Serrano, and S. Serrano. 2005. Desde las islas encantadas, in P. Ospina (ed.), *Historias de vida de colonos en Galápagos* (UNDP)

Corley Smith, G.T. 1990. A Brief History of the Charles Darwin Foundation for the Galápagos Islands, *Noticias de* Galápagos 49:1–36.

Darwin, C. 1985. *Voyage d'un naturaliste autour du monde* (La Découverte: Paris).

Dollfus, O. 1990. *Le Système Monde* (Hachette/Reclus: Paris).

Dollfus, O. 1994. *L'Espace Monde* (Economica: Paris).

Epler, B. 1987. Whalers, Whales and Tortoises, *Oceanus* 30(2): 86–92.

Gonzalez J., C. Montes, J. Rodriguez, and W. Tapia. 2008. Rethinking Galápagos as a complex Social Ecological System: Implications for conservation and management, *Ecology and Society* 13(2): www.ecologyandsociety.org/vol. 13/iss2/art13/.

Grenier, C. 1994. De l'espace marginal à l'espace pionnier frontalier: ouverture et attraction des Galápagos, tome XXIII, *L'Espace Géographique* 3: 250–262.

Grenier, C. 2002. Océaniques ou Américaines ? Analyse comparative du rattachement aux Amériques des Galápagos et de l'île de Pâques, *Mappemonde* 66:38–44.

Grenier, C. 2007. *Conservación contra Natura: Las islas Galápagos* (Institut Français d'Etudes Andines; Embajada de Francia en Ecuador; Institut de Recherche pour le Développement; Universidad Andina Simón Bolivar; Ediciones Abya-Yala).

Guézou A., M. Trueman, C. Buddenhagen, S. Chamorro, A.M. Guerrero, P. Pozo, and R. Atkinson. 2010. An Extensive Alien Plant Inventory from the Inhabited Areas of Galápagos, *PLoS ONE* 5(4):e10276. doi:10.1371/journal.pone.0010276.

Hickman, J. 1985. *The Enchanted Islands* (Anthony Nelson: Oswestry, UK).

Larrea, G. 1990. *Patrimonio Natural y Cultural Ecuatoriano* (Banco Central del Ecuador: Quito, Ecuador).

Larson, E. 2001. *Evolution's Workshop* (Basic Books: New York, NY).

Latorre, O. 1999. *El Hombre en las Islas Encantadas* (Fundacyt: Quito, Ecuador).

Luna Tobar, A. 1997. *Historia Política Internacional de las Islas Galápagos* (Abya-Yala: Quito, Ecuador).

Naveda, B. 1953. *Galápagos a la vista* (Casa de la Cultura Ecuatoriana: Quito, Ecuador).

Perry, R. 2000. *Island Days* (Minerva Press, London, UK).

Rose, R. 1923. Man and the Galápagos, in Beebe, W. (ed.), *Galápagos, World's End*, pp. 332–417 (Putnam: New York, NY).

Silva, P. 1992. *Las Islas Galápagos en la historia del Ecuador. Nueva Historia del Ecuador, vol. 12*, pp. 253–30 (Corporación Editora Nacional: Quito, Ecuador).

SPNG. 2006. *Plan de Manejo del Parque Nacional Galápagos* (Ministerio del Ambiente, Quito; SPNG, Agencia Española de Cooperación Internacional).

Sulloway, F. 1987. Darwin in the Galápagos: Three Myths, *Oceanus* 30(2)79–85.

Thornton, I. 1971. *Darwin's Islands* (The American Museum for Natural History/The Natural History Press: New York, NY).

Tye A., R. Atkinson, and V. Carrión. 2008. Increase in the number of introduced plant species in Galápagos, in *Galápagos Report 2006–2007*, pp. 133–135 (CDF, GNP and INGALA: Puerto Ayora, Galápagos).

Villacres Moscoso, J. 1985. *Las ambiciones internacionales para las islas Galápagos* (Casa de la Cultura: Guayaquil, Ecuador).

Wallerstein, I. 1979. *The Capitalist World Economy* (Cambridge University Press: Cambridge, UK).

Watkins, G. and F. Cruz. 2007. *Galápagos at Risk* (FCD, Galápagos Conservancy: Puerto Ayora, Galápagos).

Wittmer, M. 1989. *Floreana* (Anthony Nelson: Oswestry, UK).

Woram J. 1989. Galapagos Islands Names, *Noticias de Galápagos* 48:22–32.

18 Towards a self-sustained Galápagos?

Matthias Wolff and Mark Gardener

Context and the problem with the concept of carrying capacity

Since numbers of visitors and local residents have increased dramatically in Galápagos over the past decade (to about 175,000 and 30,000 respectively in the year 2009), as has the number of introduced species, the physical extension of urban areas, the pool of taxis and private cars, and the production of waste, more people believe that the carrying capacity (CC) of the archipelago has already been reached or may have even been surpassed. The present tourism model of continued growth and its indirect impacts may therefore soon lead to a substantial biodiversity loss, endangering the small populations of emblematic species of the Galápagos tourism, such as marine iguanas, penguins, finches, mockingbirds, and others. Under these conditions of ecosystem degradation, the industry of the present "nature tourism" may ultimately collapse and with it the dependent Galápagos society (see *Galápagos at risk* by Watkins and Cruz 2007).

So, are we already at a crossroad, which requires immediate action, or is all this talk of limited CC just an invention of the conservationists, who aim to protect nature at the expense of socio-economic development? According to Wikipedia the "carrying capacity of a biological species in an environment is the population size of the species that the environment can sustain indefinitely, given the food, habitat, water and other necessities available in the environment". Here the idea is expressed that nothing in nature can grow indefinitely and that everything is limited by the available resources (food, habitat area, shelter, oxygen, etc.). If the population surpasses its natural limits, members start to suffer from starvation or other limitations and the population shall eventually collapse to a size that can be carried by the environment. We think this definition is clear and does not need further discussion. However, do these limits also apply to our own species? As we shall see, things are quite confusing where *Homo sapiens* is concerned.

If we look up the term CC as used for systems that involve our species, we find numerous definitions divided into physical, economic, social, and biological–environmental realms, with few referring to the natural biological limits. The

United Nations World Tourism Organization (UNWTO 1997), for example, describes the CC for tourism as "the maximum number of people who may visit a tourist destination at the same time, without causing destruction of the physical, economic and socio-cultural environment and/or an unacceptable decrease in the quality of visitors' satisfaction". Mexa and Coccossis (2004) define CC as "a measure of the tolerance a site or building is open to tourist's activity and the limit beyond which an area may suffer from the adverse impact of tourism". Middleton and Hawkins Chamberlain (1997) describe it as "the level of human activity an area can accommodate without the area deteriorating, the resident community being adversely affected or the quality of visitors experience declining". What these definitions agree on is that CC is the point at which a destination or attraction starts experiencing adverse effects as a result of the number of visitors. What they avoid is specifying any quantitative ecological or ecosystem CC. According to Saveriades (2000), the term CC can even be described as a process rather than a number:

> Carrying capacity is not just a scientific concept or formula of obtaining a number beyond which development should cease, but a process where the eventual limits must be considered as guidance. Carrying capacity is not fixed. It develops with time and the growth of tourism and can be affected by management techniques and controls.

Using this definition, CC is very much a question of judgment by the interests of the stakeholders involved. We will also find that owing to the problems associated with the concept of CC, a related one called the "Limits of Acceptable Change" (McCool *et al.* 1998) was created, which attempts, through a several step procedure involving all relevant stakeholders, to determine how much resource or social impact is too much.

We may ask here why people have departed from the clear definition of CC as used by ecologists. An obvious explanation seems that most human communities do not directly depend on the local environment and its ecosystem services anymore. Furthermore, the ecological definition is in direct conflict with the market economy paradigm of endless growth and hence is difficult to reconcile. In our globalized world, anything may be moved to anywhere, if it is economically profitable. A tourist visiting an island may thus be supplied by products (food, water, etc.), of which almost nothing is produced locally, and even the wastes produced may be shipped away minimising the local ecological footprint. Under these conditions, the CC of a tourist site is not defined locally, since the outside world shoulder the burden of supply.

In this chapter, we want to explore whether a possible alternative to the current model of development exists that is more closely related to the biological definition of CC, and we ask whether Galápagos can produce sufficient food to support its human population (residents and tourists). To answer this question we analyze the potential and current trends in food production originating from the sea and the land, and discuss the cost and benefits of local foodstuffs compared to those imported from the continent. In addition, we reflect on other aspects related to the development of an island lifestyle for Galápagos.

So why not build skyscrapers in Galápagos like in other tourist locations and allow the local population and tourist sector to grow further?

The attraction of Galápagos to the naturalist visitors lies in the uniqueness of its flora and fauna, which is being substantially altered through the indirect impacts of growth. These indirect impacts are both physical (more landscape is being urbanized, more roads are being constructed) and ecological (more exotic species are invading the archipelago, some of which already transforming large parts of it (e.g. blackberry (Renteria *et al.* 2009) and guava), thereby substantially changing ecosystem structure and function. Increased flow of people and goods provide more vectors for the introduction of diseases for native wildlife and for humans (e.g. avian malaria in penguins, dengue in humans) (Parker *et al.* 2009; this book). Increased shipping also increases the risk of marine contamination (through oil spills or through offshore dumping of waste products) and of invasive marine species (on the hull and in ballast water). Air contamination through increased use of fossil fuels greatly increases the per capita carbon footprint of the archipelago (e.g. Puerto Ayora has the highest household energy consumption of any town in Ecuador). Waste production exceeds the archipelago's capacity for absorption or recycling, impacting directly on the natural ecosystem services (e.g. potable water). The level of urbanization in Puerto Ayora (the economic hub of the Galápagos) greatly resemble those of continental Ecuador, with a decrease in personal safety; increases in traffic, air pollution and noise levels; and the rapid degradation of landscapes in inhabited areas, mostly urban but also rural.

None of these problems are new (Watkins and Cruz 2007), but many people believe that there is a technological solution for each, which would allow further increases in the CC of the archipelago and thus further growth. Let us analyze this argument point by point. Can we reduce the introduction of invasive species including diseases? We may be able to reduce the relative rate of introductions (number of introduced species and number of visitors) through an improved quarantine system, but a further increase in visitor numbers and in imports to meet growth would easily outbalance this effect. The same argument holds for marine, terrestrial, and air pollution. We could reduce air pollution by mandating the use of renewable energy (wind, waves, sun, biofuels, etc.) but the cost would be enormous compared to the current highly subsidized fossil energy. To pass such costs on to the consumer would strongly be contested and the government does not have resources for even further subsidies. Can we reduce the impact of waste production on the environment? Yes, probably we can, by using improved technologies and by shipping large parts of the non-organic waste to the continent. This also has strong cost implications and would mean that waste treatment would increase the ecological footprint on the continent. Can we expect a technical solution to the impacts of urbanization? Yes, to some extent, if urbanization is done in previously disturbed areas and best practice is used in planning and in the use of local and renewable construction materials.

We can conclude that some consequences of development can, to a certain extent, be mitigated by technology, but the problem of a substantial ecosystem change, habitat degradation, and the introduction of species from outside will further increase if the current development model is continued. Moreover, technologies to mitigate the consequences of development are very expensive and would require strict policing by the authorities. These high costs and the necessary policing are currently not acceptable to either the community or politicians.

Sketch of an alternative development model: a vision towards sustainability

The present development model implies an increased growth of the tourism industry, a continued and possibly increasing dependence of the Galápagos archipelago on goods and services from continental Ecuador (Grenier 2009, this book). Thus, the archipelago's capacity to sustain human life will more and more be defined by inputs from outside. The question we try to answer is how many people (inhabitants and tourists) could be sustained by the archipelago's ecological services. Knowledge of this biological CC would allow us to derive a defined limit. To move in this direction the Galápagos stakeholders would need a vision of the archipelago in which self-sustainability is the central objective. The human population would mainly consume what is produced locally, use energy based on renewable resources, minimise consumption and recycles wastes.

The society would also start to diversify and to explore alternative economic activities, besides those that directly serve the tourism sector. Galápagos could become a world in itself of innovative and multidisciplinary science (natural and social), animal husbandry, forestry, artisanal manufacturing and ecologically sustainable agriculture and fishery, of aquaculture, of modern, green architecture, and many other economic activities. This would allow the development of a society with strong island values and commitment for their living habitat, which is Galápagos. For this to happen Galápagos needs both – further creation of a strong island identity but also to open up its society to attract innovative and skilled people who want to live a different life from the continental one.

This model would greatly attract visitors with a naturalist and artist's mindset and a particular interest in the uniqueness of this natural heritage. The tourist's willingness to pay for this unique experience will even be higher than under present conditions, positively affecting the Galápagos local economy. It is needless to say that such a model would be unique on our planet and would possibly also enhance the interest of aid /conservation organisations in helping to achieve these goals. To evaluate the feasibility of this alternative vision we looked at a small component: the fishery and the agricultural sector of Galápagos. We assembled available information on current productive potential of Galápagos and compared it to imported goods. Information was taken from unpublished government data, local reports, and published literature.

The seafood potential of Galápagos

The huge Marine Reserve of Galápagos (138,000 km^2) already satisfies the demand for fresh fish and invertebrates of Galápagos of about 24 t/month. This figure for the year 2006 given by Manabu (2007) only considers Santa Cruz Island, where about 60% of all catches of Galápagos are landed (Schuhbauer, personal communication). Since about 30% of fish products are exported to the continent (Manabu 2007), it is evident that catch volumes could sustain an even larger local and tourist population. Figure 18.1 summarizes the product chain of the fishery and shows that about 46% and 17% of the fish sold in Galápagos is consumed by tourists on board tourist vessels and in restaurants and hotels, respectively, suggesting a great potential for the marketing of local "value-added" seafood products. The figure does not consider the lobster catch, which has been around 30 t over the past years (2004–2009) (Reyes and Schuhbauer 2010). Of this catch, about half is being consumed locally, while the other half is exported to the continent. While these figures suggest a great potential for self-sustaining Galápagos with seafood, two of the main resources, spiny lobster and sea cucumber, have already shown alarming signs of over fishing (Hearn 2008; Schuhbauer *et al.* 2010). This is due to the fact that both products are marketed outside

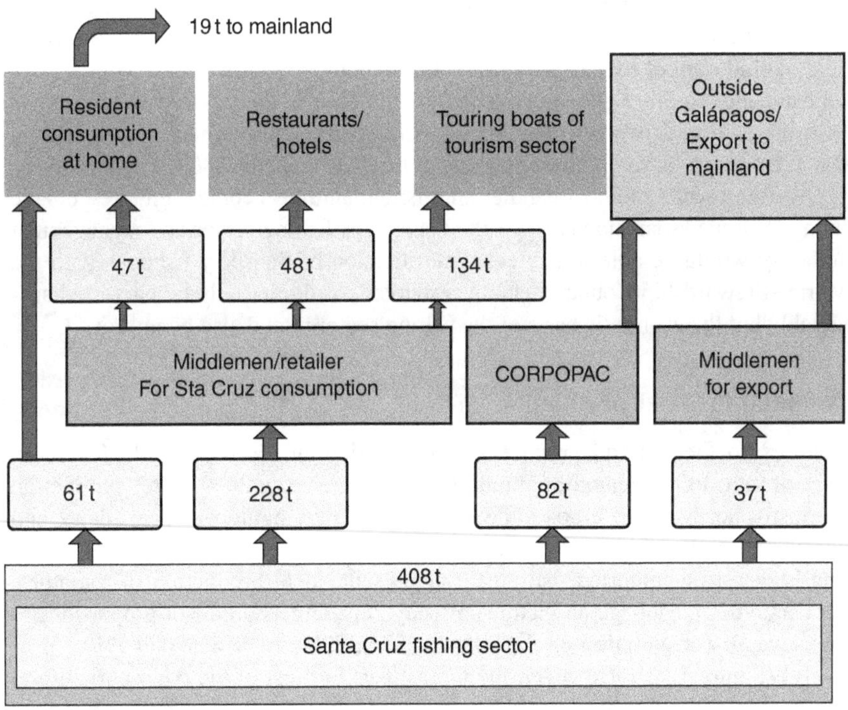

Figure 18.1 Flowchart of fin fish distribution and consumption structure in Santa Cruz Island (adapted from Manabu, 2007).

Galápagos and hence, the market is limitless. In case of the sea cucumber, the whole catch has been exported to an insatiable Asian market, whose demand cannot be sustained by the relatively small Galápagos sea cucumber population.

Recently fishermen have proposed to the management authority a new fishery that would supposedly help them to compensate for the economic loss from the failing sea cucumbers and lobsters fisheries. This fishery mainly targets yellowfin tuna (*Thunnus albacares*) and Barrilete (*Katsuwonus pelamis*) and consists of fishermen operating from small boats with handheld fishing poles that are baited with live fish. The catch is immediately transferred to- and frozen- to a large mother boat with refrigerated storage (120 t) capacity, which takes the catch to the continent, where it is commercialized to the international market. Since costs are very high due to the mother ship operation, catch volumes need to be substantial to make the fishery profitable. Since the global market demand is beyond what can be sustainably harvested from the Galápagos Marine Reserve, it is very probable that this fishery will have the same fate as that of the sea cucumbers. Hence, a fishery policy aiming only at sustaining the needs of the Galápagos consumers (residents and tourists) without export seems to be the way to go if catch volumes are to remain sustainable. Moreover, for a small capital investment, low running costs and relatively simple technology, a profitable living can be made. White fish retails in Galápagos for around \$5/kg and in continental Ecuador for \$4/kg. Once the cost of air transport (\$0.80), middle men (10%) and handing are added (\$0.50), the continental product is more expensive and not as fresh because it takes a minimum of two days to arrive. Capital outlay of less than \$10,000 buys a second hand, 8m fibre glass boat, outboard and diving compressor (which enables both line and underwater spear fishing). Looking at a fisherman's log for 2009, the average profit for a two-day fishing trip was around \$300. On this, three people (the owner, the boat handler and fisherman/diver) could earn a reasonable living by Ecuadorian standards. If the Galápagos fishing sector and management authority would be able to achieve a certification of their key fisheries with the Marine Stewardship Council, fishing resources would not only be harvested sustainably but the economic basis of the fishing sector would also be improved.

Potential for food production on land

Contrary to the seafood production, local agriculture provides only for about 10% of total food demand of about 500 t/month (Zapata 2009). This production is mostly horticultural crops although there is also significant beef, dairy and coffee production. Significant chicken, egg, and pork production also exists but this is based on imported fish-meal. At present, local production of tomatoes, peppers, yucca, cabbage and lettuce already contribute significant proportions to their overall consumption on the islands (57%, 22%, 12%, 8%, and 7% respectively) (Figure 18.2.). However, the largest part of most of the other agricultural products is still imported from the continent (Figure 18.2.) and import volumes are increasing with the local population and the number of tourists. The high increase in tomato production was possible due to the use of new greenhouse

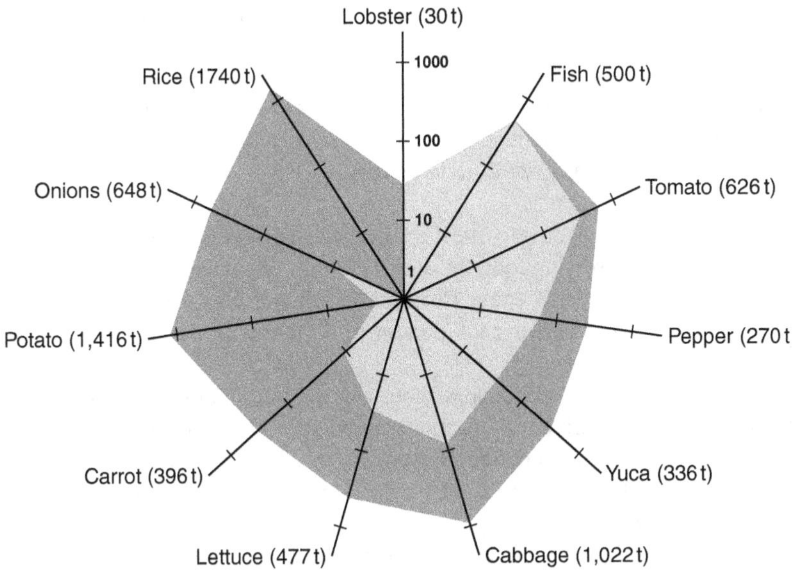

Figure 18.2. Main products consumed in Galápagos; numbers in parenthesis refer to estimated total annual consumption (assembled from Zapata 2009 and Manabu 2007); the light grey area refers to the contribution through local production, while the dark area to the total (values are logarithmic to allow for better visualization).

technology, which saves water and allows for year-round production, which under natural conditions is impossible since plantations easily get affected by fungi (*Alternaria solani, Phytophthora infestans*) and bacteria during wet periods of the year. In October 2009, 14 ha of greenhouses existed in Santa Cruz, 4.5 ha in San Cristóbal and 2 ha in Isabela islands (Zapata 2009). Tomatoes of the Cascajo area (Santa Cruz) are produced during the entire year and directly sold to tourist companies. The surplus product is sold at the local market on Saturdays and Tuesdays. Some producers only sell their tomatoes on these markets.

A number of serious limitations exist to increasing agricultural production. Agriculture is only possible in the humid highlands of the non-national park areas of Galápagos for reasons of sufficient rainfall and fertile soil (Figure 18.3). Open-air production is limited from June to November when rainfall is reliable, although light and warmth for photosynthesis during this time is limiting. Rainfall during the hot season (December to May) is highly variable and therefore unsuitable for agricultural production. The use of a greenhouse system, which optimizes water use (the greenhouse roof catches water, which is then stored in a reservoir, and drip irrigation and humid conditions reduce water use) and provides near optimal condition for year-round production, may greatly enhance the productivity. However, many open-air grown products such as oranges or pineapple will still have limited production periods as related to natural conditions and plant biology. The tourist market has a year-round demand for such products; hence, the short fall is presently made up by importation, which provides a more reliable supply.

A further, and possibly intractable, limitation to increased and sustainable agricultural production is economical. It is far cheaper to grow products in continental Ecuador and import them. Boat transport is subsidized. Below is a list of extra costs associated with agriculture in Galápagos.

1. Labor costs are high due to the fact that the agriculture sector needs to compete with the growing tourism sector that pays high salaries.
2. Labor generally needs to come from the continent, which includes paperwork and transport cost for each person to be hired. Daily rates can be as high as $30.
3. None of the activities can occur without a continual input to control weeds. Based on estimates given by farmers, weed management cost may range between $500 and $2,000 per ha per year.
4. Costs for products such as fertilizer, pesticides, fencing material are almost double than in the continent.
5. In times of drought brackish water needs to be trucked in from the lowlands at a cost of $10 per 4,000 l.

Given the cost of production compared to the value of the products, it is easy to see that the profit margin is low. Currently, most labor in the agricultural sector is still sourced from the family. If this cost were included, most products would be prohibitively expensive.

Possible solutions for making Galápagos products competitive

There are possible solutions to the problem of uncompetitive high prices for the local products of Galápagos. These include (1) price protection of Galápagos products in a way that all external costs for local products are included (including a "risk tax" for species invasions associated to imported products) and the price is fixed to a level where it is profitable to local producers (e.g. a producer currently receives $3.40 per kg of red meat and needs $6 per kg to be profitable). This implies a considerable tariff on imported products. Unfortunately, such a solution would be unpopular with the consumers, who are used to central government subsidies on transport and free market rhetoric. They expect to pay the continental price for everything. Another is (2) the direct subsidization of farmers for production or labor. This solution perpetuates a system where consumers do not pay real costs of products and requires permanent input from an external benevolent agency (usually the government). It is conceivable that some part of the entrance fee, tourist pay for visiting Galápagos, could be used for these subsidies.

The positive side of the local products is the low costs for transport and storage, and the fact that they are usually fresher than products imported from the continent.

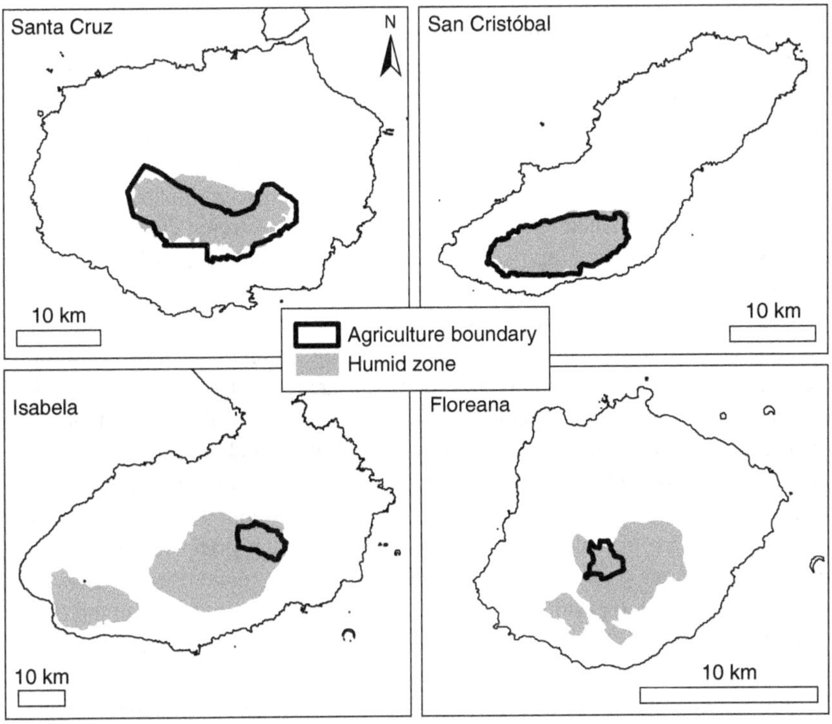

Figure 18.3 Potential areas for agricultural production in the four inhabited islands of the Galápagos. These are areas where the humid zone vegetation (grey area, which is a surrogate for sufficient rainfall) intersects the agricultural boundary. These areas potentially suitable for agriculture are: Santa Cruz (9,055 ha), San Cristóbal (7,741 ha), Isabela (5,178 ha) and Floreana (257 ha) respectively.

A recent project by the Galápagos Tourism Chamber (Piu 2009) aims to improve the productive sectors through technical assistance in the production of certified quality products. This adds value and optimizes product commercialization. Initiatives like these are promising and important steps towards a self-sustained Galápagos. Zapata (2009) believes that Galápagos has the potential for production to meet most of the present food demands for the local population of about 30,000 and the tourists, which account for another 4,000–5,000 consumers/day. However, this does not include staple bulk items such as rice, wheat products, and potatoes. He also suggests that the productive sector of Galápagos could greatly profit by value adding to the natural unprocessed food, such as: pickles, tomato sauce, dried food products, natural flowers, cultivation of the "Floreana" potato, canned products, medicinal plants, and fruit pulp.

We may also mention here the great potential for other artisanal local non-food products such as toys, handicrafts, or artwork made of renewable resources such as leafs, seeds, wood, sea shells, fish bones, and so on.

Conclusions and outlook

It may be argued that the alternative model outlined here is utopian, since the global opening and economic development of Galápagos over the past years (at rates of 9–10% per year) (Castrejón 2008) has already pushed the archipelago far beyond the point where it could be a biologically self-sustaining system. It is also often stated that the productive sector (fishery, agriculture, animal husbandry, forestry, and artisanal manufacturing) is rather insignificant in terms of its contribution to the Galápagos National Park (4%) (Castrejón 2008), and since only 3.3% of the archipelago's total area is colonized (26,356 ha) (Paredes 2009), the available land area for providing the ecosystem services for a population of the present size is far too small.

While we showed that there are important ecological and economic constraints for changing the present development model, our analysis identified measures that could help steer the development of Galápagos towards a higher level of self-sustainability within the limits of the biological CC of the archipelago. These measures aim to enhance the production and improve the quality and value of food products. However, until the question of profitability is addressed through either protecting the price of Galápagos products and/or through direct subsidization of farmers, this system will not be sustainable. Under these conditions of increased self-sustainability through shifting much of the foodstuff production from the continent to the archipelago, the risk of further species introductions and the dependency from the continent would be greatly reduced.

While a modernized, enhanced sustainable agriculture and a sustainable fishery for Galápagos are crucial to reach this goal, other complimentary measures should also be considered to improve the conservation status of the archipelago. These are: (1) reduction of access points to the archipelago, by sea and air to reduce probability of species invasions; (2) optimization of quarantine measures (applying phytosanitary practices in cruisers and freighters; ensuring ships meet basic conditions for cargo and food transportation; applying regulations to fumigate aircraft); (3) improving governance and capacity building among local residents on all levels by strengthening local institutions; (4) implementing the Integral Educational Reform; (5) building capacity for early detection and eradication of invasive species; and last, but not least, (6) fostering an island life style and reorienting the tourism to a small-scale, high quality and low impact ecotourism, which allows the maintenance of the singular conservation status of Galápagos.

References

Abitia-Cárdenas, L., D. Arizmendi-Rodríguez, G. Napoleón Gudiño, and F. Galván-Magaña. 1999. Feeding of blue marlin Makaira nigricans off Mazatlan, Sinaloa, Mexico, *Lat. Am. J. Aquat. Res.* 38(2):281–285.

Bocanegro, N. 2007. *Relaciones tróficas de los peces pelágicos asociados a la pesquería del atún en el Océano Pacífico oriental*, Tesis previa la obtención del título de Doctor en Ciencias, Instituto Politécnico Nacional, Centro interdisciplinario de Ciencias Marinas, La Paz, Baja California Sur.

Castrejón, M. 2008. *El sistema de co-manejo pesquero de la Reserva Marina de Galápagos: situación actual, retos y perspectivas de cambio* (Fundación Charles Darwin: Santa Cruz, Galápagos, Ecuador).

Grenier, C. 2009. Nature and the World: A geohistory of Galapagos, in M. Wolff and M. Gardener (ed.), *Proceedings of the 2009 Galapagos Science Symposium*, pp. 79–83 (Charles Darwin Foundation: Puerto Ayora, Galapagos, Ecuador).

Hearn, A. 2008. The rocky path to sustainable fisheries management and conservation in the Galapagos Marine Reserve, *Ocean & Coastal Management* 51:567–574.

McCool, S., F. Cole, and N. David. 1998. Proceedings – Limits of Acceptable Change and related planning processes: progress and future directions, *20–22 May 1997, Missoula, MT. Gen. Tech. Rep. INT-GTR-371* (U.S. Department of Agriculture, Forest Service, Rocky Mountain Research Station, USA: Ogden, UT).

Manabu, E. 2007. *Report of study of fisheries products distribution and consumption in Santa Cruz Island: The project of conservation of the Galapagos Marine Reserve in the Republic of Ecuador* (JICA: Puerto Ayora, Galapagos, Ecuador).

Mexa, A. and H. Coccossis, 2004. Tourism carrying capacity: a theoretical overview, in Coccossis and A. Mexa (ed.), *The Challenge of Tourism Carrying Capacity Assessment*, pp. 37–53 (Ashgate Publishing Limited: Hants, UK).

Middleton and Hawkins Chamberlain. 1997. Cited at www.biodiversity.ru/ coastlearn/ tourismeng/ introduction.html.

Paredes, M. 2009. Perspectivas de Galapagos, *Revista del Gobierno Provincial de Galapagos* 1:133.

Parker, P., S. Deem, and E. Miller. 2009. Pathogens and parasites of Galapagos birds: evolutionary studies and conservation, in M. Wolff and M. Gardener (ed.), *Proceedings of the 2009 Galapagos Science Symposium*, pp. 84–87 (Charles Darwin Foundation: Puerto Ayora, Galapagos, Ecuador).

Piu, M. 2009. Impulsando el desarrollo sostenible de los sectores productivos de Galapagos, Proyecto DSSPG-BID/FOMIN ATN/ME-9410-EC, *Perspectivas de Galápagos*, 1:59–61.

Renteria, J.L., R. Atkinson, M. Gardener, and M. Crawley. 2009. Towards an optimal management of the invasive *Rubus niveus* in the Galapagos islands, in M. Wolff and M. Gardener (ed.), *Proceedings of the 2009 Galapagos Science Symposium*, pp. 170–172 (Charles Darwin Foundation: Puerto Ayora, Galapagos, Ecuador).

Reyes, H. and A. Schuhbauer. 2010. *Informe tecnico preliminar de la pesqueria de langosta espinosa 2009* (Parque Nacional de Galápagos: Puerto Ayora, Galápagos, Ecuador).

Saveriades, A. 2000. Establishing the social tourism carrying capacity for the tourist resorts of the east coast of the Republic of Cyprus, *Tourism Management* 21:147–156.

Schuhbauer, A., Wolff, M. and M. Castrejón. 2010. Una estragegia revisada para el monitoreo y manejo del pepino de mar de Galapagos, *Informe de Galapagos* 2009–2010:76–82.

SPNG-FCD. 2002. *Informe del viaje experimental de pesca con palangre B/P Tohalli*, Internal report.

United Nations World Tourism Organisation (UNWTO). 1997. http://ec.europa.eu/ environmen /iczm/ pdf/ tcca material.pdf.

Watkins, G. and F. Cruz. 2007. *Galapagos at risk: A socioeconomic analysis of the situation in the archipelago* (Charles Darwin Foundation: Puerto Ayora, Galapagos, Ecuador).

Zapata, C. 2009. *Estudio de oferta y demanda deproductos agrícolas de Galápagos, Ecuador 2009, Proyecto ATN-ME-9410-EC CAPTURGAL* (Puerto Ayora Galapagos, Ecuador).

19 Part IV summary

Reconciliation of conservation with socio-economic development

Matthias Wolff and Mark Gardener

This last book chapter describes the theoretical framework related to the valuation of ecosystem services and biodiversity conservation, analyzes the Galápagos development history by looking at its geographical connectivity with the world and proposes an alternative production model for Galápagos, which defines its development capacity in terms of the archipelago's potential for providing ecosystem services to its population of local residents and tourists.

In his chapter, *Robert Costanza* clarifies concepts in ecological economics and shows that the assessment of the trade-offs among ecosystem services and between ecosystem services and other contributors to human well-being requires profound research with regard to the interconnections between humans and the rest of nature. He presents conceptual and empirical tools for making these connections and discusses the difficulties in valuing biodiversity and ecosystem services with reference to the Galápagos Islands. He insists that to achieve sustainability we must incorporate natural capital and the ecosystem's goods and services into our economic and social accounting and our systems of social choice. In estimating these values, we must consider how much of our ecological life support systems we can afford to lose. Costanza defines sustainability as the amount of consumption that can be sustained indefinitely without degrading "natural capital", here defined as "a stock that yields a flow of valuable goods or services into the future"; for example, a stock or population of trees or fish that can provide a flow or annual yield which is sustainable year after year. The sustainable flow is "natural income"; the stock that yields the sustainable flow is "natural capital". Natural capital may also provide services like recycling waste materials or water catchment and erosion control, which are also counted as natural income. Since the flow of services from ecosystems requires that they function as whole systems, the structure and diversity of the ecosystem is a critical component of natural capital. Costanza emphasizes that the Galápagos Islands represent a huge asset for humanity just like the Great Barrier Reef in Australia, both being producers of ecosystem services and having iconic natural features, and are large stores of unique biodiversity and a source of scientific knowledge about biodiversity and its role in the co-evolution of humans and the rest of nature. He sees the largest values for the Galápagos in the realm of "cultural" ecosystem services (i.e. conservation value) and only moderate importance for several other more "production"-oriented ecosystem services (but see the essay of Wolff and Gardener, who see great scope for a development towards a self-sustained Galápagos using its "production"-oriented ecosystem services in order to reduce the Galápagos dependency to the continent).

In his chapter "Nature and the World: A Geohistory of Galápagos", *Christophe Grenier* shows that the Galápagos archipelago is fully integrated into the World System geohistory and analyses the increasing connectivity of this once isolated oceanic archipelago with mainland America and beyond through a series of schematics. Globalization, that is the general geographical opening of every region on the planet that presents economic or strategic interests for transnational, international or national actors, is complete in Galápagos. He shows that the consequences of this growing geographical opening of Galápagos are enormous, whether direct or indirect. The archipelago is rapidly losing its singularity, not only from an ecological point of view but also culturally. The main actors concerned – the Ecuadorian state, regional institutions, island inhabitants, local and foreign tourism enterprises, etc. – consider Galápagos to be like any ordinary region, ruled by the same economic "laws", seeking the same kind of "development" and with Galapagueños wanting the same lifestyle as urban populations from other parts of the world. For these reasons, many of the archipelago's ecosystems are in danger.

His geohistorical approach to the human history of Galápagos demonstrates that people are the main drivers of the archipelago's recent natural history, by opening it to the outside world and a flood of introduced species. Putting geographic space at the core of conservation policy may help to find solutions to reduce the Galápagos geographical opening in a sustainable manner for the island population. This implies a change in the tourism model in order to shift from quantity to quality by reducing the number of visitors and organizing a real ecotourism; to stop fuel subsidies and promote alternative energy sources; banning further imports of motor vehicles and implementing public transport; controlling immigration; providing better local education and training; and improving the quality and availability of locally produced food instead of importing most of the food supply.

In the final chapter *Matthias Wolff* and *Mark Gardener* continue with the analysis of the present development of Galápagos and reflect on the problem of estimating the population and visitor carrying capacity of the Galápagos archipelago. It is argued that through the strongly growing tourism industry (9–10% economic growth per year), the process of habitat degradation, biodiversity loss and contamination is accelerated. While technological solutions for reducing the local ecological footprint (such as shipping waste away and improving quarantine systems) may slow this degradation process down, they will not stop it. An alternative model is proposed, which defines the development capacity (i.e. the number of people the archipelago may sustain) in terms of the archipelago's potential for providing ecosystem services to its population of local residents and tourists (food, waste recycling and renewable energy). This increases self-sustainability and reduces dependence on the continental and the global market.

The analysis reveals that sea food can easily meet the archipelago's demand, while agriculture will probably never meet total demand but can be greatly enhanced through the use of modern green technologies. According to their analysis, a great increase in the self-sustainability of Galápagos to meet human demands for foodstuff seems achievable, although present market conditions would need to be modified (more realistic pricing, removal of transport subsidies and/or direct subsidization of farmers) to make the Galápagos products competitive with those presently being imported from the mainland. While a modernized, enhanced sustainable agriculture and a sustainable fishery are crucial to reach this goal, the authors also mention important complementary measures to improve the conservation status of the archipelago. These are (1) reduction of access points to the archipelago by sea and air to reduce the probability of new biological invasions; (2) optimization of quarantine measures (applying phytosanitary practices in freighters, ensuring ships meet basic conditions for cargo and food transportation and applying regulations to fumigate aircraft); (3) building capacity for early detection and eradication of invasive species; (4) improving governance and capacity of local institutions, enhancing co-management and implementing the Integral Educational Reform; and (5) fostering an island life style and reorienting the tourism to a small-scale, high quality and low impact ecotourism, to allow the maintenance of the singular conservation status of Galápagos.

Index

Page numbers in *italics* denote tables.

www.ingramcontent.com/pod-product-compliance
Lightning Source LLC
LaVergne TN
LVHW011115300926
849160LV00008B/385
* 9 7 8 1 1 3 8 2 4 3 8 6 6 *